MW01096892

# THE COMPLETE BOOK OF GARLIC

# THE COMPLETE BOOK of
# GARLIC

## A Guide for Gardeners, Growers, and Serious Cooks

TED JORDAN MEREDITH

TIMBER PRESS
Portland ~::~ London

Published in 2008 by
TIMBER PRESS, INC.

The Haseltine Building, 133 S.W. Second Avenue, Suite 450
Portland, Oregon 97204-3527
www.timberpress.com

2 The Quadrant, 135 Salusbury Road
London NW6 6RJ
www.timberpress.co.uk

Printed in China

Library of Congress Cataloging-in-Publication Data

Meredith, Ted Jordan.
The complete book of garlic : a guide for gardeners, growers, and serious cooks / Ted Jordan Meredith.
p. cm.
Includes bibliographical references and index.
ISBN-13: 978-0-88192-883-9
1. Garlic.  I. Title.
SB351.G3M47 2008
635´.26--dc22          2007036403

A catalog record for this book is also available from the British Library.

# ❡ CONTENTS ❡

~: Part Two :~

# THE ESSENTIALS

# ❦ ACKNOWLEDGMENTS ❧

I LOOK UPON MY ROLE in horticultural writing not as that of an expert, for I am surely not that, but as that of a gatherer and assembler of information from those who have all manner of specialized knowledge or expertise. When the diversity of information is brought together, a larger, richer fabric emerges, and we see a connectedness and depth that were not readily apparent when the bits of information stood in isolation. I think this is so with everything, but especially so with garlic. It is my hope that this book will help us to see a bit more of that larger, richer fabric.

Both directly and indirectly, through written materials and personal communications, many people have contributed to this book. The bibliography reflects the written works of some of these individuals, but the help I received goes far beyond what is included in that listing.

In particular I want to acknowledge the technical reviews of my manuscript materials, which broadened and deepened my understanding of the garlic genome and greatly benefited the content of this book. Gayle Volk, plant physiologist at the National Center for Genetic Resources Preservation in Fort Collins, Colorado, generously and graciously gave her time responding to my inquiries and reviewing the manuscript sections relating to genetic diversity and taxonomy. The study "Genetic Diversity Among U.S. Garlic Clones

as Detected Using AFLP Methods," conducted by Dr. Volk and her colleagues Adam Henk and Christopher Richards, is a landmark for scientists and garlic enthusiasts alike. The study's findings and diagrams reveal garlic's genetic diversity and complex genetic relationships that were not readily apparent in previous studies using older molecular tools and simpler, hierarchical analytical models. I want to thank Dr. Volk for her review and for the suggestions she made regarding the modified genetic diagrams included in this book. My thanks also to Dr. Richards for responding to my inquiries and clarifying technical issues. His explanations greatly helped my interpretation of the findings and diagrams.

As I began my research, Richard Hannan, the now retired USDA research leader, supervisory horticulturist, and curator of the garlic germplasm at Pullman, Washington, was exceptionally helpful in pointing me toward important information resources and answering numerous questions. Dr. Hannan is not only a research scientist but also a plant explorer, garlic grower, and unabashed garlic enthusiast. When he started working on the garlic germplasm in 1983 the collection consisted of only 13 accessions. It now comprises well more than 200. Dr. Hannan was kind enough to interrupt his retirement vacation and fishing trip to review sections of my manuscript and offer insightful information and comments. Given a similar circumstance I am not sure I would have been so graciously generous with my time.

While it is essential that I acknowledge the reviews of manuscript sections by Volk, Richards, and Hannan, and the benefit that the added rigor brought to bear on this work, it is also essential to state that the final content and wording are mine alone and that I am solely responsible for all opinions and positions in this book, as well as for any errors that it may contain.

Others have also assisted me in this project. Philipp Simon, USDA research leader and professor of horticulture at the University of Wisconsin, Madison, was a principal researcher in an early landmark molecular study of garlic, as well as in subsequent molecular studies. These studies helped reveal the diversity and interrelationships of the species, correlate flower-related morphological traits, and identify fertile garlic clones. Dr. Simon was at the forefront in the early efforts to produce true seed from garlic, and he provided me with valuable information resources and answered my various inquiries regarding production of garlic seed. Maria Jenderek has also been of great help in providing me with publications and answering my inquiries regarding garlic seed production. Over a seven-year period Dr. Jenderek produced approximately 2 million garlic seeds from 64 seed-producing cultivars—a remarkable achievement.

Darrell Merrell and John Swenson organized a series of outstanding garlic symposiums, drawing worldwide experts to Tulsa, Oklahoma. The information and synergy from these seminars were invaluable. Mr. Swenson is responsible for introducing more than 400 garlic cultivars from around the world. His collecting trips to Central Asia, contacts with garlic germplasm curators, and generosity in sharing his garlic accessions and knowledge have greatly benefited us all. Mr. Sw-

enson understood the remarkable diversity of the species at a time when most of us had no clue that there was any distinction.

Thanks also to David Stern and Bob Dunkel, who founded and maintain the Garlic Seed Foundation, a clearinghouse for garlic information and a connecting hub for the garlic community. Barbara Hellier, Agricultural Research Service horticulturist and curator of the garlic germplasm in Pullman, assisted me in acquiring and evaluating a number of accessions in the collection. Tom Cloud of Filaree Farm in Okanogan, Washington, located accession records and helped me translate them into a file format readable by current software programs. Avram Drucker assisted me with information on garlic seed production and perspectives on numerous cultivars. Doug Urig was also a great help, though indirectly so, as editor and publisher of *Mostly Garlic* magazine, a substantive and enjoyable source of information. Sadly, Doug and the magazine are no longer with us.

My thanks also to virtually everyone I encountered in the community of garlic aficionados. From those at farmers' markets to those attending scientific symposiums, everyone in the community had something to share and an enthusiasm for sharing it.

I very much want to express my appreciation for my parents, Edward and Nelva Meredith. If it were not for their interest in fine food and distinctive cuisine during my formative years, I would likely not have involved myself in the culinary adventures that led me to discover and pursue garlic's rich diversity. At a time when Julia Child's recipes included canned mushrooms because fresh were rarely available, I remember my father excitedly arriving home with the first fresh mushrooms to make their way to our Montana town. I also remember helping my mother in the kitchen, including the first time I used fresh garlic in cooking, albeit in miniscule amounts by today's standards. Our use and enjoyment of garlic has grown considerably over the years. My mother's preparation of crushed raw garlic in olive oil over fresh corn on the cob remains a seasonal family favorite.

When my wife, Merrill, and I first met in Montana during the 1950s, neither of us had eaten fresh garlic. I was five years old and she was three. She proposed to me the first day we met. Nearly half a century later I inquired if the offer was still good. It was, and we married. The bonding we found as small children continues in adulthood and now includes a shared enjoyment for copious quantities of fresh garlic. Merrill is the principle weeder of our garlic beds. I am grateful not only for her lifelong support but also for her tolerance and forbearance, particularly when I fail to sufficiently process the grass and weed seed in our compost and weeding becomes something more akin to lawn removal. Of course, wanting to grow "just a bit more garlic," it does not help that I have made our garlic beds impossibly wide to tend and weed comfortably. I am grateful that I suffer only an occasional raised eyebrow for my misdeeds.

Exploring the world of garlic has been a wonderful and rewarding journey.

Thanks, everyone!

# PART ONE

# ALL ABOUT GARLIC

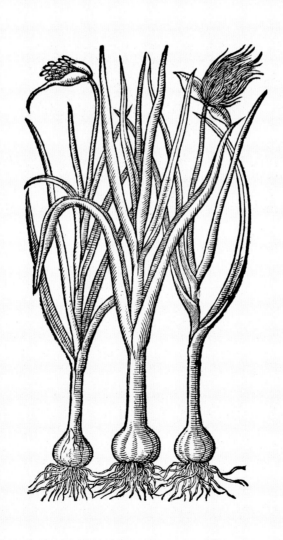

# ~ ONE ~

# Garlic, Economics, and Culture

SECOND ONLY to the bulbing onion, garlic is the most widely consumed allium. It is an important component in many of the world's cuisines. Because of its intense flavor, it is most often used as a flavoring condiment rather than as a bulk vegetable—the dedicated consumption of garlic by enthusiasts notwithstanding.

Worldwide, about 2 ½ million acres (about a million hectares) are dedicated to garlic production, yielding nearly 10 million tons of garlic each year. Although this amounts to only a tenth of the worldwide production of bulb onions, it is nonetheless an impressive sum given that bulb onions are commonly used as a bulk vegetable and not just as a flavoring component. When we think of garlic production, the image of fresh-market garlic comes to mind, but the prepared-food and dietary-supplement industries are large consumers of dried and processed garlic. In Western cultures the interest in and demand for garlic have increased along with the interest in diverse cuisines and less parochial culinary habits. The health benefits of garlic have also stimulated interest and consump-

tion. From 1970 to 2000 the area devoted to garlic production more than doubled.

Garlic can be successfully grown in a wide range of climates but is ideally suited to climates with some rainfall, sunny dry summers, and fairly moderate winters. In the United States, California readily meets these requirements, and that is where over 80% of all American commercial garlic is grown. Of that, more than 60% is grown for dehydration industries and use in processed food products. Most of the fresh-market garlic on grocery store shelves comes from California, although seasonally, garlic from other countries, notably China, can make a prominent appearance.

Asia produces most of the world's garlic crop. China alone accounts for two-thirds of the world's output, most of it coming from Shandong. South Korea and India are the next largest producers, each responsible for about 5% of the world's production, followed by the United States, which produces about 3% (Lucier and Lin 2000). The remaining countries in the Top 10 are Spain, Egypt, Turkey, Thailand, Brazil, and Pakistan. California

Garlic bulbs from four different horticultural groups. Clockwise from left, Silverskin, Porcelain, Artichoke, and Creole.

produces considerably greater yields than most other garlic-growing areas of the world due to the use of irrigation, mechanization, intense farming methods, and choice of high-yielding cultivars that are well suited to the growing climate of the state. The harvested weight per acre in California, for example, is more than five times greater than that in Thailand. California's high-yielding, mechanized bulk production of garlic cultivars with high-soluble solids is ideally suited to the needs of the food processing industry. It is, however, less ideally suited to the culinary needs of the chef and gourmet.

## ISN'T GARLIC JUST GARLIC?

Why bother growing garlic? Isn't all the fuss about different garlics just a fad, an affectation? Why not just buy the garlic offered at the grocery store? Or if you do grow your own garlic, why not just grow one kind? Isn't all garlic really the same, anyway? Isn't garlic just garlic?

Yes, garlic is just garlic, and apples are just apples—except that, as with apples, one finds major differences among the many cultivars of garlic. Apple varieties, for example, have a wide range of flavor characteristics and storage properties. There is a pronounced difference in taste between a Red Delicious and a Granny Smith—not to mention the differences in shape, texture, and color. Similarly, there are differences in taste and character between the garlic cultivars 'Spanish Roja' and 'Romanian Red', 'California Early' and 'Shvelisi', and so on. As with apples, some garlic cultivars are similar to others in taste and character, while others vary widely. The differences, especially if we enjoy good food, make a difference in our lives.

Garlic is not all the same. We think of garlic as all the same because we are primarily exposed to only one type of garlic in our grocery stores. If Red Delicious were the only apple we ever encountered, we would think that all apples were the same as well. What a surprise it would be, then, if we were to suddenly encounter a Granny Smith.

So just as there are different apples, tomatoes, carrots, onions, and peaches, there are different garlic cultivars. As consumer palates become more enlightened, and if the marketplace responds, we may one day have more choices in the grocery store, but for now nearly all grocery store garlic comes from the same horticultural group, Artichoke, and much of it is even the same cultivar.

In the United States some four companies produce nearly all of America's dehydrated garlic, and only a few large shippers account for the majority of fresh-market garlic (Lucier and Lin 2000). Grocery store garlic is not chosen by producers and marketers for culinary merit but for reasons of ease of growing, productivity, and storage. Flavor is not part of the choice, nor from a grower's or marketer's standpoint does it need to be. Customers might complain or go elsewhere if Red Delicious were the only apple available in a grocery store, but garlic is just garlic, so there are no other choices—or so most of us have come to understand.

The photographs of various garlic cultivars in this book give us a quick look at some of the overt differences among varieties, and chapter 7 explores in more technical detail the manifold genetic differences within the garlic genome. The type of garlic commonly sold in grocery stores has lost its ability to bolt and produce flowering parts. These are commonly called softneck garlics because they have no central flowering stalk. Garlics that produce a central flowering stalk are called hardnecks. Their woody flowering stalk runs through the center of the bulb and is quite evident in the cured bulb.

Bolting garlic cultivars are undesirable from the standpoint of commercial production. The flower stalk makes handling and processing more difficult, and if the flowering parts are not cut before harvest, the size of the bulb will be greatly reduced. From a commercial producer's standpoint, hardneck cultivars are more than a nuisance, they are simply bad choices—deficient cultivars that can thankfully be avoided.

However, those of us not involved in large-scale agribusiness might have a different perspective. Garlics that are capable of bolting and producing flowering structures embrace the greatest genetic diversity and greatest diversity in character. Hardneck cultivars include some of the world's finest-tasting garlics and have the greatest range of characteristics. They are closest to garlic's genetic roots, and some are the primordial ancestors of all garlics. We should not, however, dismiss softneck garlic cultivars out of hand. There is significant diversity and character among softneck garlic cultivars that rarely bolt, as well as among those that sometimes bolt but only under certain growing conditions. Once we understand that all garlic is not the same, we have the luxury of exploring its full range of diversity.

I have drawn parallels between garlics and apples. Are the differences in taste of various garlic cultivars as apparent as the differences in taste between a Red Delicious and a Granny Smith? I would say no. The differences in flavor are probably closer in degree to the differences one encounters in varieties of carrots, onions, beans, beets, corn, and the like. As with garlic, if we grow these vegetables ourselves, we are much more aware of the diverse flavors and choices among different varieties. We may have a few varieties of these vegetables from which to choose at the grocery store. We will have more choices at farmers' markets, and many more choices if we grow them ourselves. If you have ever

A bolting cultivar's coiling flower stalk.

grown some of the finest varieties of pole beans, you probably do not want to go back to commercial bush beans from the grocery store. Similarly, if you grow some of the finest Rocambole or Purple Stripe garlic cultivars you will not want to go back to grocery store garlic.

To return briefly to the apple: One might choose an apple based on personal taste preferences—say a tart, crisp Granny Smith over a sweet, more softly textured Red Delicious—but there are other reasons to choose one apple over another besides simply taste preference. For example, one might choose to grow or buy an apple that stores particularly well so that it can be enjoyed long into the season, or perhaps an early variety that can be eaten before the other varieties are ready for harvest. One might want an apple that holds up well when cooked in a pie or cobbler, or an apple that is best for eating fresh and crisp. Garlic offers a similar range of choices, but you won't find such a selection at the grocery store—at least not yet. For now, if you want a range of choices you need to buy garlic from farmers' markets, order it through the mail from specialty growers, or grow your own. Growing your own garlic and enjoying the differences of the many cultivars, both in the garden and on the table, is a large part of what this book is about.

Garlic is garlic—in all the richness of its variations.

Enjoy!

# TWO

# Natural History

**WHERE DID GARLIC** come from? To the extent that we think about it at all, many of us associate garlic with southern Italian cooking and, if pressed, might conclude that garlic originated in Italy or at least the Mediterranean. We would not be alone in this thinking: early taxonomists also considered garlic to be a Mediterranean species. In the mid 1700s Carl Linnaeus offered Sicily as garlic's place of origin, and in 1827, in a monograph on alliums, George Don affirmed Sicily as the origin of nonbolting (softneck) garlic and Greece or Crete as the origin of bolting (hardneck) garlic. Later in the 1800s, however, the prospect that garlic may have originated elsewhere began creeping into the literature.

## ORIGIN

In 1875 Eduard Regel reported seeing specimens from the Dzungaria Basin, a Central Asian area north of the Tien Shan in northwest China. Today that area is regarded as too desertlike to support wild garlic, giving rise to speculation that the climate may have been moister during earlier periods (Etoh and Simon 2002). Others, noting that Chinese scripts contain no reference to wild garlic, conclude that garlic was not part of China's natural flora. The Chinese name for garlic suggests that the term originated in western China, near Central Asia. If wild garlic was not native to China, it was certainly nearby.

In 1887 Regel indicated that the Central Asian areas near Tashkent and in Tajikistan were also garlic habitats. In 1886 Alphonse De Candolle concurred that garlic did not originate in the Mediterranean but in Central Asia, offering southwestern Siberia as the specific area of origin. During much of the 20th century, Central Asia was largely inaccessible to Western researchers. Active research continued within the Soviet Union, however, and Soviet researchers continued to confirm Central Asia as garlic's center of origin. By 1980 researchers had generally defined garlic's natural distribution as an area roughly delimited east to west by the Tien Shan in the east, which forms partial boundaries between China, southeastern Kazakhstan, and Kyrgyzstan, stretching westward in a long southerly arc through southern Uzbekistan to Tajikistan and the Pamir Mountains, continuing westward through northern Afghanistan and into northern Iran and Turkmenistan, where the Kopet-Dag roughly delimits its westward extension. In his landmark lay publication, *Growing Great Garlic*, Ron Engeland (1991) termed this region "the garlic crescent."

In 1986 Takeomi Etoh reported the discovery of a number of fertile garlic strains on the northwestern side of the Tien Shan in Central Asia and concluded that this was garlic's center of origin. Subsequent studies with biochemical and molecular markers that have identified the most primitive garlic strains have affirmed this conclusion: Central Asia is garlic's center of origin, and the area on the northwestern side of the Tien Shan is a likely point of origin.

In 1996 Brian Mathew extended the included area of garlic's natural distribution to encompass a region west and north of the Kopet-Dag, extending the arc of the garlic crescent into eastern Turkey. This expanded area now encompassed what Engeland had already called the extended garlic crescent.

Garlic may once have grown wild in a broad area from China and India to Egypt and Ukraine. Today wild garlic is found only in a much smaller area in Central Asia, centered in Kyrgyzstan, Tajikistan, Turkmenistan, and Uzbekistan (Simon 2002). In other parts of the world, various alliums growing in the wild are sometimes called wild garlic, but these other alliums are not true garlic. In North America, for example, the species *Allium vineale* is commonly called wild garlic.

Although allium researcher Philipp Simon (2002) reports encountering nonbolting softneck garlic in the wild in Central Asia, most garlic found in the wild is of the bolting or hardneck type. The ability to bolt and produce flowering structures is essential for sexual reproduction to maintain genetic diversity and the ability to adapt to changing conditions. The garlic found in Egyptian tombs was the bolting hardneck type. Many cultivated garlic strains, including the ubiquitous garlic found in grocery stores, are largely nonbolting softneck types that have lost their ability to form fully developed flowering structures, let alone produce seed from sexual reproduction. Some garlic cultivars have been asexually propagated for hundreds or perhaps even thousands of years, and in varying degrees have lost their ability to produce flowering structures and seed. We might speculate that garlic strains that bolted later, less frequently, or not at all may have been selected for replanting over strains that bolted quickly and vigorously. In general, strains that did not direct their energies to flower and seed production would likely have produced larger bulbs—no doubt a desired basis for preference and selection. The earliest writings did not reference distinctions between bolting and nonbolting types. Within the last thousand years, however, with the garlic cultivated in southern Europe, we begin to see references distinguishing between bolting and nonbolting garlic.

In addition to garlic, many other alliums, including onions and leeks, originated in the mountainous regions of Central Asia, a cultural crossroads that all but assured widespread distribution and cultivation. The genus *Allium* is comprised of more than 600 species. The area of greatest species diversity ranges from Turkey, Georgia, and northern Iran, east through the mountains of Central Asia, Turkmenistan, Uzbekistan, Afghanistan, Pakistan, Tajikistan, the Tien Shan of Kyrgyzstan and northeastern China, and into the mountains of Mongolia and southern Siberia.

We now have a good idea of garlic's geographic center of origin, but from what species did it evolve? What is garlic's immediate allium ancestry? We do not yet know, but this is a fruitful area of inquiry that may one day reveal more about the origins of this remarkable plant and its relationship with the equally remarkable genus *Allium*. At least one researcher has offered the hypothesis, based on morphological characteristics, that garlic may be derived from either *A. tuncelianum* or *A. macrochaetum* (Mathew 1996). These two species are closely allied, and both have a garlic smell when crushed. In Turkey *A. tuncelianum* is used as garlic. The flowering structures of *A. sativum* and *A. tuncelianum* share some common distinctive characteristics, including a flower stem that curls before anthesis; pale-colored, small, glabrous, narrow perianth segments; and glabrous filaments with exceptionally long lateral cusps. The area of natural distribution of these two species, however, is a counterargument to the hypothesis. *Allium macrochaetum* is distributed in parts of Iran, Iraq, Syria, and Turkey. *Allium tuncelianum* is distributed in Turkey. Although both species are within the range of garlic's area of natural distribution, they are at its western extension, and both are at nearly the opposite end of the distribution range from the Tien Shan, garlic's putative point of origin.

However, as with many things, particularly things involving nature, more complex considerations may be at play. Researchers have postulated an evolutionary progression for garlic plants, from plants that are fertile to plants that are sterile. The most primitive strains generate fertile flowers and are devoid of bulbils, the small garlic clove–like structures that are interspersed among the flowers in garlic inflorescences. Next in the evolutionary progression are flowering plants that have both flowers and bulbils in their inflorescences. And finally, last in the progression are plants that routinely form no flowers and rarely or never have a flower stalk.

Plants at the earliest evolutionary stage, those with inflorescences but no bulbils, have been found in eastern Turkey. Nearby, to the east and north in Georgia and the Caucasus, wild plants have been found that have both flowers and bulbils in their inflorescences, as well as plants that form no flower stalk. This has led Takeomi Etoh (1985) to conclude that the Caucasus is a secondary center of origin for garlic. A decade later Helga Maaß and Manfred Klaas (1995) conducted a study using molecular markers to evaluate several hundred strains of garlic from Central Asia and concluded that the most primitive strains with fertile flowers came from two areas: the easternmost part of Uzbekistan in the province of Andizhan in the Fergana Basin, and western and southern Georgia in the Caucasus. If not exact, the finding of the most primitive strains in the Fergana Basin is in general accord with the earlier discovery of a number of fertile garlic strains on the northwestern side of the Tien Shan, at the eastern end of the garlic crescent, and the conclusion that this Central Asian area is garlic's center of origin. How then does one explain that the opposite end of the extended garlic crescent, in western and southern Georgia, is also a source of some of the most primitive garlic strains? Other explanations may be plausible, but Maaß and Klaas suggested that the Georgian garlic may have been brought there from Central Asia. The connection between garlic and humankind is a very old one, and the transportation of garlic, whether seed or bulb, across ancient established migration and trade routes is a likely hypothesis.

This hypothesis of geographic origin does not seem to help the hypothesis that garlic could have derived from *Allium tuncelianum* or *A. macrochaetum*, species not found near the Tien Shan or Fergana Basin. These species are found at the opposite end of the extended garlic crescent, far from garlic's presumed geographic area of origin. A number of explanations could resolve the seeming inconsistency of the two hypotheses, however. For example, *A. tuncelianum* or *A. macrochaetum* may once have had a more extended range that included the eastern garlic crescent, or there may have been intermediate species in the phylogeny that are no longer in existence. If nothing else, *A. tuncelianum* and *A. macrochaetum* may at least provide clues to a more complex connection.

The dispersal, distribution, and adaptation of garlic around the world, and the role of humankind in its dispersal, is a story in itself, much of which long predates historical record. Since we are talking about highly transitory vegetative material rather than enduring objects, we are left with an inherently more speculative enterprise once we have exhausted the historical artifacts that remain. The distributed range of garlic today, and the adaptive characteristics of the distributed strains, reveals some of garlic's migratory story—if only obliquely.

## DISTRIBUTION

Garlic, onions, and other alliums are among humankind's earliest cultivated crops. Only seven of the more than 600 *Allium* species are cultivated commercially, but many are edible and local peoples still gather them for food. The alliums now in common cultivation are descendents of wild alliums. The onion, *A. cepa*, has been cultivated for some 5000 years or more. It does not exist as a wild species. Garlic, *A. sativum*, still exists in the wild, but it too has a long history of cultivation and an historical position of prominence among many world cultures.

The earliest record of garlic's role in human culture dates back nearly 6000 years. Highly ac-

curate clay artifacts representing garlic bulbs were found in a tomb at El Mahasna in Egypt. These clay representations have been dated to 3750 BC. Later accounts chronicle garlic consumption as an ongoing part of the common diet. Garlic was found in other Egyptian tombs, including the tomb of Tutankhamen, buried in 1352 BC. There, along with gold and lapis lazuli artifacts, were six dried garlic bulbs. A bundle of hardneck garlics with scapes, some 3500 years old, was found in a tomb of the 18th Egyptian dynasty. The Greek historian Herodotus, writing in the 5th century BC, recounted his visit to the Great Pyramid of Cheops (Khufu) at Giza, Egypt, and an inscription he saw describing the quantities of radishes, onions, and garlic consumed by the workers who built the pyramid. These findings suggest that garlic had a prominent role in the culture. There are many references to garlic in the ancient Sanskrit language and indications of dispersal to India by at least 5000 years ago, to Babylon by 4500 years ago, and to China by at least 2000 years ago, with some evidence indicating that garlic was cultivated in China as long as 4000 years ago. Garlic is also mentioned in the Bible and Qur'an.

If garlic achieved prominent recognition and wide geographic dispersion in established cultures at least 5000 or 6000 years ago, it could be presumed that garlic was valued and traded long before it achieved such a level of documented prominence. The Egyptian garlic artifact at El Mahasna is some 5750 years old, found at a location that is some 2500 air miles (4023 km) from garlic's center of origin. Such an early and prominent presence at a location so far from garlic's center of origin suggests that garlic was likely valued and traded for a good long time before its appearance in ancient Egypt. Just how long a time is a matter of speculation, but evidence suggests that trading and human dispersal of garlic may have occurred not long after the end of the last Ice Age.

In *Growing Great Garlic* (1991), Ron England's review of the historical accounts of garlic and evidence of the movement of humans in and through garlic's center of origin, leads him to postulate the likelihood that some 10,000 years ago seminomadic hunter-gatherers dispersed garlic throughout Central Asia's garlic crescent, extending the geographic range of dispersal over time. Garlic bulbs store for months, are concentrated in their effect, and weigh relatively little, further fostering their transport and dispersal among nomadic groups. Garlic was likely valued for many of the same reasons it is valued today, though in a modified context. It may have been used as an antibacterial preservative for food, as a pungent herb to mask the taste and aroma of spoiled meat, as medicine, and as food. Because of its uses and what would probably have been perceived as magical or transcendent properties, garlic was likely used and revered ritualistically as well.

We know that agriculture began more than 10,000 years ago, around the end of the last Ice Age, when humans began cultivating plants for food. The ability to generate food by remaining in a fixed location, and the corollary need to remain in a fixed location to produce the food, caused nomadic peoples to establish permanent living sites, and eventually villages, cities, and nation states. Nomadic culture and agriculture are not entirely exclusive of the other, however. Some peoples may be nomadic for part of the year but settled in an established location for the remainder of the year, and some civilizations continue to have nomadic groups within their populations, as well as non-nomadic groups interacting and trading with nomadic groups of other cultures.

One might well think that the collection and dissemination of wild garlic from Central Asia is simply an anthropological artifact, something that other people did a long time ago. However, on a 1989 collecting trip to Central Asia, in the countries now known as Turkmenistan, Uzbekistan, and Kazakhstan, Philipp Simon reported seeing nomadic herders moving sheep and goats through areas where there were populations of wild garlic. Over many millennia, nomadic peoples, as well as trade among established agricultural communities, helped spread food crops, including garlic, far beyond their area of origin. Garlic's center of origin, Central Asia, is along one of the major trade routes in the ancient world.

So then, we might well think that this is merely something that primitive peoples did and do—peoples other than ourselves. Yet we too are participants in this ancient ritual, driven now by what drove our ancestral antecedents: garlic, a plant that is both mundane in its everyday uses and mystical in its resonance with us. We today are ourselves participants in this anthropological artifact. Researchers and aficionados continue to make forays to Central Asia, collecting garlic in the wild, purchasing garlic from street vendors in the local markets, and transporting, planting, and sharing the garlic with others in places far from the garlic's origins. The anthropological and horticultural venture with garlic that began with our ancient ancestors many millennia ago continues with us in the present. When we plant, grow, eat, trade, and share garlic, we participate in this ancient thread, this ancient relationship between garlic and humankind. We apply science to our modern-day endeavors, but this is not at odds with our ancestors. Science, at least science well practiced, is simply part of contemporary ritual and reverence. We are the current participants in this anthropological and horticultural journey, the current temporal link in a long history of participation and discovery. We are not apart *from* this. We are a part *of* this.

Through trade, nomadic wandering, and military invasion, the valued and revered garlic plant quickly moved beyond its natural area of origin to other regions and climates. In the east, garlic migrated to western China (if it was not already there prior to human intervention) and on to modern-day Pakistan and India, southern China, south Asia, and Southeast Asia. In the Far East, garlic was introduced to Japan from Korea. In kinship with northern Europe, most of Japan seems to share a lack of enthusiasm for garlic. One might begin to suspect a connection, or lack thereof, with garlic and more northerly climates, but garlic is extensively cultivated and very prominent in Korean cuisine.

The Caucasus, a likely vital secondary center of origin for garlic, became a spring point for further northern, southern, and western distribution. Garlic made its way north and west around the Black Sea into Russia, Ukraine, and on into eastern Europe. The southern path of western dispersal brought garlic south of the Black Sea through Turkey and Greece and further into southeastern Europe and beyond. Ancient Greek and Roman writings make frequent mention of garlic. It already had a very early presence in Egypt, on Africa's northeastern corner, and likely made its way further west and south on the African continent. From Mediterranean Africa, garlic spread southward to Sub-Saharan Africa. It also made its way to the Americas from the Mediterranean courtesy of explorers, traders, and colonists, primarily from Spain, Portugal, and France. Most of the cultivars grown in Africa and the Americas are of Mediterranean origin. Broadly speaking, these cultivars are a step apart from the strains originating in Central Asia. They are generally more suited to warmer climates and possess little or no propensity to bolt. In more common vernacular, they are typically softneck cultivars.

Garlic has long been highly valued in the Mediterranean region, and thus has long been intensely cultivated. Over time the Mediterranean has established itself as an additional center of clonal diversity. Although garlic is quite hardy, cultivation is more problematic in far northern areas with severe winter cold, where garlic is less likely to be present in traditional cuisines. Although garlic is highly valued in southern Europe, it has been valued far less in Great Britain and northern Europe, though this is changing as the culinary world becomes less parochial and the health benefits of garlic become more widely known.

Garlic has been extensively cultivated and distributed via human commerce over many millennia. It is robust and enduring, highly prized for its culinary and medicinal properties, and readily transportable via its bulbs, all serving to assure garlic's wide distribution. During the course of its widespread distribution, garlic became adapted to a similarly wide range of climates, from the cold of Norway to the tropical heat of the equator. Much of garlic's diversity owes itself to sexual reproduction and considerable genetic heterogeneity arising within its relatively narrow center of origin in Central Asia. On the other hand, most of the garlic in existence reproduces almost exclusively by vegetative means. This is particularly the case for the nonbolting softneck cultivars that are prominent in warmer southern climates. These climates necessitate the greatest degree of adaptation from the plant, yet the greatest mechanism for adaptation lies in sexual reproduction and diversity—a feature largely foreign to warmer-climate cultivars, which rarely (if ever) reproduce sexually. Nonetheless, the garlic plant has demonstrated a capacity for considerable variation and adaptation within the constraints of vegetative reproduction.

# HABITAT

Alliums are widely distributed in the temperate zone of the Northern Hemisphere. They are uncommon in the tropics, usually inhabiting the cooler mountainous areas. *Allium schoenoprasum* (chive) is found as far north as the Arctic. With minor exception, it is the only allium indigenous to both North America and Eurasia. A few *Allium* species are found in grassland or woodland habitats, but this is not typical of the genus. Alliums generally compete poorly with other vegetation. Most are found in sunny, semiarid habitats in areas with low vegetation density. These are often rocky sites with sparse, scrubby vegetation.

Native to Central Asia, wild garlic is subject to harsh, hot, dry summers and severe winters. Although garlic can survive in dry climates with sunlight untempered by cloud cover, very dry desert climates are not sufficient to sustain the plant. In Central Asia it tends to occupy areas where the soil is a little less dry and where localized microclimates provide a bit more moisture and slightly more shelter from the heat of summer and cold of winter. Garlic's typical native habitat includes rocky valleys, riverbeds, streambeds, and gullies, sometimes situated so that the plant receives partial shading from the summer sun and some protection from radiational heat loss in the winter.

The tempered local microclimates, however, are far from lush. For example, on a collecting trip to the mountains of Uzbekistan, allium explorers found wild garlic growing on the side of a mountain in an intermittent streambed on a precipitous 45-degree slope. The area was virtually devoid of any other vegetation, and garlic collector and advocate John Swenson (1999a) reported that even with a collecting pick the team was unable to dig deep enough in the rocks to find the bulb. Un-doubtedly the bulb would have been quite small and quite unlike the large cultivated garlic bulbs grown in pampered conditions. Bulbils from the inflorescence are sometimes the only collectible planting stock. In its native Central Asian habitat garlic is of necessity a tenacious survivor, its life cycle shaped by survival strategies.

Over time garlic has been distributed to regions far from its center of origin, and to habitats that differ substantially from its Central Asian homeland. Through sexual breeding and adaptation, and through selection for vegetative propagation, garlic cultivars have gradually become adapted to a wider range of climates, notably climates with warmer winters and generally less extreme conditions than those of Central Asia. Garlic that has adapted to warmer climates requires less exposure to winter cold to produce a successful harvest. The period of cold is called vernalization and is a requirement for successful bulbing. Garlic cultivars from Central Asia, for example, require a more pronounced period of vernalization in order to form bulbs than the garlic cultivars commonly grown by the garlic industry in California. The need for at least some degree of vernalization remains, however. Garlic grown in climates with very warm winters or no winters at all will not develop normal-sized multicloved bulbs. In parts of North Africa, southern China, and south Asia, for example, garlic is grown for its leaves, not its bulbs, and garlic cultivars are selected for leaf production rather than bulb production.

## LIFE CYCLE AND GROWTH HABIT

Although it has been cultivated for thousands of years, sometimes in regions far different from its native habitat, garlic still demonstrates the fundamental growth habits of its ancestors, albeit sometimes in significantly modified form. In its Central Asian center of origin, wild garlic is subject to harsh, hot, dry summers and severe winters. Such inhospitable conditions require highly adapted survival strategies. Garlic grows rapidly during a brief favorable period, stores energy reserves in the garlic bulb, and then goes dormant until seasonal conditions are again favorable for growth. The cycle repeats year after year, decade after decade, century after century, millennium after millennium. Although garlic does not require human intervention, people have been participants and partners with this life cycle for thousands of years by gathering and cultivating the plant. It is a wonderful life cycle and survival strategy, not only because it works for the plant but also because it provides us with garlic's storage organ, the garlic bulb, which enriches our cuisine and benefits our health.

What is garlic's native life cycle? How do the fundamentals of garlic's survival strategy express themselves in the plants we cultivate, and how do cultivated plants differ in their growth habit from wild garlic?

In order to survive the heat, drought, and cold of its native Central Asian habitat, garlic has a relatively short aboveground growth period. This period generally begins in late winter or early spring, after the passing of severe winter cold, and continues through late spring and early summer. As the end of this growth period nears, garlic forms a bulb to store energy reserves. The aboveground growth dies, and the plant, now existing as a bulb, becomes

Aboveground growth emerging in early spring.

dormant just before conditions become impossibly hot and dry in later summer. After a period of summer dormancy, the decreasing temperatures and increasing moisture stimulate resumption of underground growth. After the severe cold of winter passes, garlic again initiates aboveground growth to take advantage of the brief period of favorable growing conditions.

Garlic must initiate aboveground growth very early to make the most of the short growing season, but in so doing may be exposed to periods of cold and freezing that would kill tender growth. To contend with these conditions, garlic has leaves that have evolved to withstand heavy frosts (though not deep freezing). Depending on the cultivar and growing region, aboveground growth

The new leaves continue their development.

The new leaves begin to assume their mature form.

may be initiated in the fall and persist throughout winter, though vigorous growth typically does not occur until spring.

The garlic bulb is the principal reproductive mechanism. It remains dormant in the ground until conditions for growth are favorable, begins growing roots, and then later initiates aboveground growth. High temperatures maintain dormancy, so the bulb does not begin growing again in the hot summer. As added insurance against inopportune growth, the bulb does not begin growing again until it has been exposed to a period of cold. If the temperatures are cooler, but still warmish, a longer period of vernalization is required to trigger growth. The decreasing requirements for cold exposure as the time in dormancy lengthens bal-

ances the need for certitude that growing conditions really are again favorable for growth with the need for the plant to again resume active growth at some point, since the bulb cannot remain dormant indefinitely. After a very lengthy period of time, growth resumes quickly, even with minimal exposure to cooling. In garlic's native habitat the cooling temperatures of fall fulfill the requirement for a period of cold, and the bulb resumes underground growth. Without the bulb's resumption of growth, the cold, moist soil might well cause the dormant bulb to rot. Although conditions for aboveground growth may not yet be suitable, the underground growth establishes the root system in preparation for a subsequent period of vigorous aboveground growth.

Unlike the onion, garlic has contractile roots that pull the plant deeper into the soil with each passing season. These roots are not particularly evident in cultivated garlic that is dug up each year, but in the wild the contractile roots play a role in ensuring the plant does not lift itself out of the soil, as one sees in onions. In this way the garlic plant is more deeply anchored and its environment more stable, with less radical fluctuation in heat, cold, and moisture.

After thousands of years of cultivation in a wide range of climates, garlic cultivars have adapted to various local conditions, including those that are much less severe than the conditions of their native habitat. Nevertheless, all cultivars respond with at least a modified form of the pattern just described. The vernalization requirements for commercial California garlic cultivars, for example, are relatively modest but still evident.

The habits of wild garlic are largely defined by the plant's response to the need for reproduction and perpetuation under harsh conditions. These defining tendencies carry over to cultivated garlic in varying degrees and help define cultural practices. Garlic is a tough survivor. In its native habitat wild garlic grows in dry, rocky, barren soils in a harsh, semiarid climate. It has little competition, since few other plants grow in such inhospitable conditions. The garlic plant's narrow leaves and relatively sparse foliage canopy are well suited for survival in its harsh native environment, but its foliage canopy is not designed to compete effectively with other plants, notably weeds, which are prevalent in more hospitable climates. Moreover, as a survival response, if garlic is shielded from sunlight by competing plants, it will form a bulb early and go dormant. The early bulbing facilitates survival, but the prematurely formed bulbs will be smaller than normal. What are the implications for cultivated garlic? If garlic is planted too densely or if weeds are allowed to proliferate and compete for sunlight, the garlic may bulb prematurely, reducing the average bulb size and decreasing overall yield (see also chapter 5). Since garlic competes poorly with fast-growing weeds, weed suppression and control is necessary unless one is somehow fortunate enough not to have tall weeds in the garlic bed. Garlic's legacy of survival imperatives makes our weeding chores all the more important if we are to have a good harvest of large bulbs.

If conditions are favorable garlic produces multicloved bulbs, each clove generating a new garlic plant in the following year's cycle. If conditions are unfavorable the garlic plant will form a single-cloved bulb. Even though unfavorable conditions may prevent a garlic plant from generating more plants, the iteration of a single-cloved bulb at least ensures the plant's own perpetuation and survival. Garlic's survival strategy works well both in the short term and long term. In very difficult growing conditions only single-cloved bulbs may be generated year after year until enough energy reserves and favorable conditions permit the formation of a multicloved bulb and reproductive expansion.

Wild garlic is not confined to a single, potentially vulnerable means of reproduction, but simultaneously takes advantage of several. We have been discussing the bulb. The bulbil and garlic seed are two additional mechanisms. Like the bulb, the bulbil offers another means of asexual reproduction. The bulbil is a part of the plant's flowering structure. Wild garlic and many cultivated garlic strains produce flowering structures and a flower stalk called a scape. These, again, are commonly called hardnecks. The scape supports the inflorescence, called an umbel. As is typical of alliums, the umbel constitutes garlic's flowering parts, with the numerous flowers connected at a common point and forming a globe shape. Within the umbel, numerous bulbils grow among the flowers, ranging in size from a grain of rice to a sugar pea. Depending on the cultivar, the umbel may contain several to more than a hundred bulbils. Bulbils are like miniature garlic cloves, and like cloves, they can be planted and eventually develop into bulbs. Because of their small size, one or more seasons may elapse before they are able to produce multicloved bulbs. When the garlic plant becomes dormant at the end of its season, the umbel withers, releasing the bulbils to the ground. Wild garlic is often found in intermittent streambeds. Seasonal rains can carry sediment to cover and "plant" the bulbils, or conversely may carry the bulbils downstream and plant them away from the mother plant, further distributing the garlic and helping preserve the plant from eradication, should untoward conditions devastate the original growing site.

Many cultivated garlics, including the major commercial cultivars grown in the United States, do not generate a flower stalk or any other visible flowering structures under typical conditions. Such softneck cultivars typically do not have the ability to reproduce via bulbils. However, under certain conditions softnecks may partially bolt and generate bulbils within the bulb or partway up the partially bolting stalk. Occasionally even softneck garlics may bolt and produce fully developed flowering structures and bulbils, though this is rare.

The production of flowering structures and bulbils requires energy. The price of generating bulbils, an additional reproductive and survival venue, is a decrease in the size of the main garlic bulb. This is particularly noticeable in wild garlic strains. It is an excellent survival strategy for wild garlic, but this habit is not necessarily desirable in cultivated garlic, where survival in harsh conditions is less of an issue than producing a large crop with large bulbs. For cultivated garlic the additional energies can be redirected to the bulb by removal

of the flowering structures at an opportune time. This is discussed in more detail in chapter 6.

Bulbs and bulbils are garlic's two asexual reproductive mechanisms. Garlic seed is a means of sexual reproduction. Although it is a rare occurrence unless plants are manipulated under controlled conditions, some strains of garlic are capable of producing new plants from seed. The capacity for sexual reproduction is largely confined to select strains of wild garlic and identical or closely related cultivars that have retained the ability to generate viable flowers and set seed.

We have noted that garlic cannot devote full and equal energy to all forms of reproduction, and that retaining the flowering structures may reduce the size of the bulb, especially for particular cultivars. This energy limitation also applies to bulbils and flowers for seed. If bulbils are present in the umbel, the plant directs its energy to the bulbils rather than to the production of seed, and the flowers wither and die without producing seed. Bulbils and flowers are packed tightly together within the umbel. For most cultivars bulbils must be removed before the garlic can set seed. The ancestors of today's garlic cultivars likely relied much more on sexual reproduction and seed. For most cultivars vegetative reproductive mechanisms, bulb and bulbil, now have precedence. The cultivars closest to the ancestral forms of garlic retain the greatest capacity for sexual reproduction from seed.

Although the role of flowering mechanisms appears to have diminished for wild garlic and seems all but absent in most softneck cultivars, ancestral triggering mechanisms remain. For example, before a clove can begin differentiation to generate a multicloved bulb, inflorescence initiation must occur to break the apical dominance of the plant and allow the formation of axillary buds. Even though nonbolting cultivars display no overt evidence of the formation of flowering structures, the early physiological processes of inflorescence initiation do occur and are essential. Without the inflorescence trigger, even the commercial softneck cultivars would fail to produce multicloved bulbs. Inflorescence initiation is inhibited by low moisture conditions, which apparently signal the plant that the marginal conditions may permit it only to reiterate itself and that survival should not be risked by directing critical energy to the formation of bulbils, seeds, or multicloved bulbs.

The harsh, inhospitable conditions of garlic's native habitat have shaped the plant's morphology, its survival strategies, and its responses to environmental conditions. Wild garlic is highly optimized for survival. The production of large bulbs when conditions permit is only one aspect of garlic's survival strategy, and in many respects it is a relatively minor one. Other survival strategies often take precedence. For example, wild garlic readily sacrifices bulb size in order to produce an umbel with numerous bulbils. Conversely, wild garlic does not sacrifice the production of numerous bulbils just to form a larger bulb. In general,

garlic readily sacrifices large bulb size to bolster other survival strategies. This is most evident in wild bolting garlic and in cultivars more closely related to wild garlic. However, even highly domesticated nonbolting cultivars display some of these tendencies when they respond to stress by partially bolting and producing bulbils. Although garlic has been in cultivation for many thousands of years, its fundamental survival strategies are still evident even in the most pampered cultivated plants.

To oversimplify a bit, for wild garlic, survival is the overriding imperative. For cultivated garlic, production of the largest bulbs is the overriding imperative. When we cultivate garlic we need to supply the conditions that foster large bulbs and, as a corollary, curtail competing survival responses from the plant. This is not particularly difficult and is largely just a part of normal cultural practices for most garlic growers. Nonetheless, knowing why something works helps focus attention and understanding, and helps us make accurate judgment calls for the plants we cultivate. Cultural methods are discussed in greater detail in chapter 6.

## ❦ THREE ❧

# Cuisine

**REGARD FOR GARLIC** in cuisine varies widely, from reverence to disdain, from casual abundance to timid inclusion and even steadfast exclusion. Mediterranean cultures and much of Asia use garlic in casual abundance. Great Britain and northern Europe have largely fallen into the category of disdain and timid use. Although the United States is a stewpot of cultures, what once passed for traditional American cuisine was largely dominated by the influences of Britain and northern Europe. This has changed a great deal as transportation, immigration, and information technologies continue to break down cultural barriers. The world is becoming less insular and less parochial in its cuisine. The rapidity of change has greatly accelerated in recent years, perhaps particularly so in the United States.

In their benchmark work on alliums, *Onions and Their Allies*, Henry Jones and Louis Mann (1963), in something of an apologetic defense of garlic, wrote, "Garlic is a condiment and is only rarely—and perhaps unwisely—used with a heavy hand." Well, I suppose that garlic is a condiment.

I also think of it as a vegetable that flavors other vegetables, and a heavy hand might be measured by an excess number of heads of garlic per person per serving. I might be exaggerating slightly here, but not by much.

My family and I did not always think this way. Somewhere around 1963, just about the time that Jones and Mann were writing their book, I remember helping my mother in the kitchen at our home in Montana. Always in the forefront of culinary daring, we were making a batch of homemade spaghetti sauce. To flavor the big vat of sauce, I put in not one but *three* cloves of garlic. Mother was aghast. I probably would have been aghast too had I thought about it, but I was too busy feeling outrageously daring. Fortunately, a miracle occurred: nobody died from the excessive garlic in the sauce. In fact the sauce was actually quite good. Nowadays I would never think of putting three cloves of garlic into a similar quantity of sauce—more like three heads or so. My mother's views on garlic have changed a bit as well. When fresh corn on the cob is in season, she mixes minced or crushed raw gar-

29

lic with salt and olive oil and drizzles it over freshly cooked corn.

A 1976 leaflet from the University of California (Sims et al.) states, "Garlic can easily be grown in home gardens. A few plants will supply the average family." Supply the average family for how long? A day? A week? Our cuisine is changing, and we are far richer for it. The increasing inclusion of garlic in our cuisine is a fine example of fortuitous change. Garlic brings not only the benefit of taste but also health.

Garlic was introduced into North America sometime in the 1700s. In 1919 the first estimates of garlic use showed a per capita consumption of less than 0.05 lbs. (0.02 kg), increasing to 0.12 lbs. (0.05 kg) by the 1920s. By the 1990s, per capita consumption had accelerated to about 2 lbs. (0.9 kg), a 115% increase over the 1980s (Lucier and Lin 2000). From 1947 to 1956, California, by far America's biggest producer of garlic, had an average of 2075 acres (840 hectares) of garlic in cultivation. By 1975 some 10,000 acres (4047 hectares) were dedicated to garlic production, and by 2001, 29,240 acres (11,833 hectares). The trend toward heartily incorporating garlic into our cuisine has gained even more momentum since that earlier era of culinary awakening. United States Department of Agriculture (USDA) economic research findings state that no other vegetable has had such strong, sustained growth.

Why did garlic take an early hold in some parts of the world and not others? Availability, of course, is one reason. Peoples near Central Asia, or along connecting trade routes, certainly had more opportunity to assimilate garlic into their culture. The general early adoption in southern rather than northern climates may also relate to an early awareness and dependency on garlic's medicinal properties. Among its therapeutic attributes, garlic has significant antibacterial and antifungal proper-

ties. In warmer southern climates it was likely employed in an overlapping role as a flavoring agent and as a food disinfectant and preservative. Given this scenario it is not hard to see how garlic would become thoroughly integrated in the cuisines and cultures of southern-climate peoples. It is also not hard to see how northerners, on first encounter, would be thoroughly frightened and appalled by such an unfamiliar and pungent presence. On the other hand, southern-climate peoples were likely frightened and appalled by the thought of fresh garden vegetables boiled for hours into a gray mass, as one might find in some northern culinary cultures. I know such a thought frightens and appalls me. Fortunately, many British, long the butt of culinary jokes, are now equally revolted by this style of cooking. In a relatively short time, and for many reasons, northern Occidental cuisines have improved dramatically. The widespread inclusion of garlic is both a cause and an effect. In America's heartland we may still suffer Jell-O salads with canned fruit cocktail and miniature marshmallows, but at least garlic is more likely to have a place at the table.

## COOKING, TASTE, AND HEALTH

It is not my intent to fill this section of the book with garlic recipes. A number of cookbooks are dedicated entirely to garlic, and countless recipes from the cuisines of the world include garlic. Instead I will draw upon our knowledge of garlic's taste chemistry and therapeutic constituents and apply that information in a culinary context.

Garlic's composition, chemistry, and enzymatic interactions determine how different preparation methods affect its taste and thus the taste of the culinary preparations that include it. These same preparation methods also define and determine the therapeutic effects of garlic. Understanding this nexus helps us better understand our culinary choices. Considerations of taste and health both help shape the methods we may choose to apply.

## Allicin, alliin, and alliinase

The chemistry of garlic is complex and dynamic. Some of these complexities are discussed in greater detail in chapter 9, but let us briefly touch upon three fundamental constituents and the role they play in taste and therapeutic effect. The sulfur compound allicin and its derivatives are substantially responsible for garlic's pungently complex flavor and aroma as well as for a substantial amount of its therapeutic benefit, yet a whole clove of garlic contains no allicin and has essentially no aroma. How can this be?

Allicin is only created when the enzyme alliinase interacts with the sulfur compound alliin. When alliinase and alliin are brought together, the creation of allicin occurs with great rapidity. Alliinase and alliin are held in isolation in separate cells of the garlic clove and are only brought together when the cell walls are compromised, such as occurs with crushing, chopping, slicing, and biting.

Try this. Smell a whole healthy clove of garlic, then smash it with the flat of a knife and smell again. The aroma instantly goes from nothing to intensely pungent. The creation of allicin happens that quickly.

## Preparation methods

Now that we have a basic understanding of garlic's taste chemistry, we can begin to see how the way garlic is prepared greatly affects its character. Bringing alliinase in contact with alliin not only produces allicin but also initiates a cascade of transformations that result in the creation of many more sulfur compounds that contribute to taste and therapeutic benefit. If garlic is cooked whole, no allicin is produced, and the flavor is not only milder but also simpler and very much different from garlic that has been chopped or crushed prior to cooking.

When I first started growing garlic and began to acquire some of the less common cultivars, I decided to have a garlic taste test. I sautéed whole cloves of a number of cultivars and carefully kept them identified and separate. I was disappointed in the bland flavor of each one and found very little difference between them. I did not realize at the time that their distinctive characteristics and flavors could only be realized if the cloves were chopped or crushed prior to cooking. Garlic that is baked or sautéed as whole cloves has a legitimate culinary role, but one should not expect the same flavors, complexity, or intensity of garlic that has been crushed or chopped.

Heat destroys allicin, but chopping or crushing garlic prior to heating allows the creation of numerous additional sulfur compounds, contributing to flavor as well as likely additional therapeutic benefit. As we will discuss in more detail in chapter 4, allicin and its secondary constituents are substantially responsible for garlic's therapeutic effects. If therapeutic benefit is the primary goal, garlic should be chopped or crushed and consumed raw. However, raw garlic need not be consumed in great quantities for therapeutic benefit: a clove per day is more than sufficient.

Garlic that has been chopped and sautéed still has significant therapeutic benefits, though not the full range of benefits as raw garlic. In any case, one should not feel constrained to eat only raw garlic for health purposes. For some culinary preparations raw garlic is the perfect match, while cooked garlic is preferable for other preparations.

## Crushed raw garlic

Most garlic aficionados, in the course of exploring their passion and affliction, will take a bite out of a clove of garlic or perhaps eat a whole clove at a time, being sure to chew it well so that the alliinase is thoroughly exposed to alliin to create allicin—and the cascade of related volatile sulfur compounds that follow. Eating raw garlic in this matter is certainly a bracing experience, particularly for the uninitiated. The intensity and heat can be startling and unpleasant. Some cultivars, such as many Silverskins, can be stingingly hot. Others, such as some Rocamboles, seem almost sweet in comparison—but only in comparison. Eating raw garlic by itself is usually not a culinary preference. However, raw garlic in combination with other food is an excellent choice in some preparations, adding a fragrant, vivid brightness not present in cooked garlic.

Although for raw consumption garlic can be chopped or minced, it is usually preferable to crush it. Crushing more fully combines alliinase with alliin to produce the maximum amount of allicin and other compounds. It also allows the garlic to be more thoroughly and evenly distributed with other food.

You can crush garlic by placing a peeled clove under the blade of a chef's knife, mashing it flat with a whack on the blade with the palm of your hand, and then mincing with the edge of the knife. This method works well, though I prefer a quality garlic press for the task if one is available. Some chefs crush the unpeeled clove and dispose of the skin afterward. I find this a bit messy and wasteful, but it is certainly an option. This method works better on some cultivars than others. If salt is part of the preparation it can be an ally in further crushing the garlic. Put the crushed garlic in a small bowl. Add salt and use the back of a spoon to crush the garlic by using the salt as miniature grinding particles. This method extracts the juices as well and quickly produces a garlic slurry.

When we incorporate crushed raw garlic into our cuisine we need to keep a few principles in mind. Acid and heat inactivate the enzyme alliinase, and heat destroys allicin. When garlic is crushed, alliinase interacts with alliin to form allicin. At room temperature the process is complete within 10 seconds. Although the process is extraordinarily rapid, it is not instantaneous.

If we are preparing a salad dressing for fresh greens, we should not press garlic directly into vinegar or citrus juice. Although much of the transformation of alliin into allicin would likely occur, it is better to ensure the transformation is complete before the alliinase is inactivated by the acid. Crush the garlic into a small bowl, then add the vinegar or citrus some 10 seconds or more later. If we are adding salt, pepper, or other herbs or spices, this would be a good point to add them, and if we desire, further crush the mixture into a slurry with the back of a spoon. Next, add the vinegar or citrus, mix together, and then add and mix the salad oil.

The same principles apply to other cuisines. For example, if we are making a classic Vietnamese or Thai dipping sauce or "salad dressing" with lime juice, *nam pla* (fish sauce), garlic, and sugar, we should crush the garlic first and wait at least 10 seconds before adding the lime juice.

Continental cuisine includes raw garlic in various preparations, such as tapenade, persillade, and gremolata. For the most part, however, classic Continental cuisine does not include raw garlic in sauces. When garlic is included in sauces it is typically minced and then sautéed until soft or straw-colored prior to adding liquids and other ingredients. This is a classic culinary approach and a basis for wonderful cuisine—but are there other possibilities?

The flavors of crushed raw garlic are hotter, more aggressive, more vivid, and more fragrant than garlic that has been chopped and sautéed. The allicin in crushed raw garlic is destroyed by heat, so putting crushed raw garlic into a bubbling hot sauce essentially cooks it and destroys the aromatics associated with raw garlic regardless of any culinary merit.

More frequently incorporating crushed raw garlic into our cuisine is certainly desirable from a therapeutic standpoint. From a purely culinary standpoint, could an expanded role for crushed raw garlic have merit as well?

In *The America's Test Kitchen Cookbook* put out by *Cook's Illustrated* magazine (2001), the editors explore different approaches to the classic dish spaghetti alla carbonara:

> At first we sautéed a few minced cloves in a little olive oil before adding it to the sauce, but this sautéed garlic lacked the fortitude to counterbalance the heavy weight of the eggs and cheese. Adding raw garlic to the mixture was just the trick. A brief exposure to the heat of the pasta allowed the garlic flavor to bloom and gave the dish a pleasing bite.

So what is happening here? The crushed raw garlic is warmed by the dish but not heated to the point of destroying the allicin and other aromatic volatiles. It is successfully incorporated into the sauce, where it plays a counterbalancing role to the other ingredients. In good cooking, and indeed in all great cuisines, ingredients are added to balance and counterbalance. Here the eggs and cheese give the dish a wonderful richness, but without the aro-matic bloom of the raw garlic the dish would be a bit heavy and dull.

This approach suggests a method for expanding the role of crushed raw garlic in our cuisine. Adding crushed raw garlic to a sauce or dish when it is warm but not hot preserves the allicin and other volatiles, retains their therapeutic benefits, and adds another flavor to our culinary toolset.

There are countless variations on this theme, but a basic cooking method in Continental cuisine calls for sautéing a meat; removing it from the pan; adding onions, garlic, or shallots; sautéing briefly; adding water, wine, or stock; scraping and stirring the *fond* from the pan into the stock; reducing and concentrating the mixture to create a sauce, sometimes including starch for thickening; and as the mixture is cooling, adding butter or aromatic olive oil for flavor and enrichment. After this last step is completed, and after the sauce has cooled from hot to warm, we can add another step if we so desire: we can fold in crushed raw garlic just prior to serving.

I sometimes employ sautéed garlic and other alliums for the rich foundation they contribute, and crushed raw garlic for the finish. Of course, this does not mean that one should always add crushed raw garlic. Sometimes a dish is best without it, and sometimes one's mood may call for one preparation over another. Just as one is not confined to only one herb or one spice, crushed raw garlic simply adds to our culinary choices.

As a finishing element, crushed raw garlic works well with red meats and rich sauces. It also works well with lighter meats and fish, usually augmented with lemon or other acids to lighten and brighten the effect. Crushed raw garlic can be added as a finishing element to other dishes as well. It may be sacrilege, but adding crushed raw garlic to such classics as, for example, beef bour-

Rocamboles are ideal for crushed raw garlic, but they store poorly. Many Creoles, such as this 'Pescadero Red', have a relatively sweet taste profile and store exceptionally well.

guignonne or Viennese goulash just prior to serving offers another culinary possibility. The dishes become something a bit different—but good.

An expanded role for crushed raw garlic is not confined to Continental cuisine but applies quite broadly. For example, crushed raw garlic works well with Thai curries. The flavors meld well. The additional heat is barely noticed and is counterbalanced by the dish's underlying sweetness, which is already employed to counterbalance the heat of the chilies.

In different ways sweetness and acidity help counterbalance the aggressive elements of raw garlic and emphasize its richness and fragrance. Cooked vegetables or greens, still warm, can be tossed with a mixture of crushed garlic, salt, balsamic vinegar, and olive oil—similar to a dressing for fresh greens but with less vinegar and more oil.

Experiment and explore.

Crushed raw garlic can be quite hot and aggressive. Consequently for raw garlic I usually prefer cultivars with a richer, sweeter, less hot profile, such as a Rocambole or Creole, or perhaps a Purple Stripe. I generally avoid hotter and more aggressively sulfurous cultivars such as Porcelains and Silverskins. For a dish such as a Thai curry, which again is already geared to counterbalance heat, the differences are less important. Other dishes are much more sensitive. For salad greens, for example, I always choose a sweeter garlic.

I am not advocating that we abandon the traditional methods used in classic cuisine or avoid cooked garlic in favor of raw garlic. Crushed raw garlic is simply an alternative that can add variety to our cuisine. Raw garlic has played a somewhat limited role in cuisine. Its therapeutic benefits are an incentive to explore an expanded role, and as we have seen, there is culinary merit to this pursuit.

## Sautéed garlic

Chopping or crushing garlic and then cooking it in oil is a basic preparation method throughout the world. The chopping or crushing generates the volatile, aromatic flavor, which is then tamed and deepened by the cooking. Although allicin is destroyed by cooking, many of the complex volatile sulfur compounds that were generated by the chopping or crushing (or their derivatives) remain. Whether one is preparing a sauce, stew, or stir-fry, chopping garlic and cooking it in oil is a fundamental step.

My favorite way to enjoy garlic is to chop it and sauté it in olive oil until it begins to turn straw-colored to light tan. Classically Mediterranean, garlic and olive oil are healthful and splendidly compatible from a culinary standpoint, creating a wonderful synthesis. Fine chopping or crushing releases the most flavor, but I sometimes leave a portion of the garlic in larger pieces in order to get a toothy bite. Cooking the garlic to a straw color both sweetens and deepens the flavor. Do not cook it to a deep brown, or worse yet, burn it, or it will taste acrid and unpleasant. The garlic should not steam, and lightly salting it helps bring out the flavor. This method brings out fine flavors from even the blandest cultivar and helps even the most sulfurous and aggressive cultivars taste rounded and nutty. With a Rocambole or Purple Stripe cultivar, the flavors are ambrosial. When I want to evaluate the taste of a new cultivar, this is one of my favorite ways to prepare it. Sautéed garlic is excellent with a good hard roll or crusty bread and makes a good side condiment on the dinner plate. It can be enjoyed by itself with bread or as a flavoring for other food such as grilled steak or sautéed fish fillet.

Cooking chopped garlic in oil can be readily adapted and extended. For example, after the garlic has sautéed briefly, you can add pole beans from the garden—or broccoli, zucchini, or greens such as chard, beet greens, spinach, and the like. How long the garlic should be sautéed before adding the vegetables depends on the heat of the pan and the length of time the vegetables will take to cook. The garlic should not steam and remain white or else the rich, nutty flavors will not develop. The idea is to end up with vegetables that are cooked but not overcooked, and garlic that has a light straw color. Regulating the heat of the pan and timing the addition of the vegetables are keys to success.

In another variation, after the garlic has turned straw-colored, add chopped arugula, or chopped basil, or a variety of other ingredients to suit your whim—perhaps a squeeze of fresh lemon—and then toss with pasta and finish with grated Romano or Parmesan. Or cook the garlic in peanut oil in a wok, add vegetables, then fish sauce or soy sauce, and toss and stir periodically until done. And so on. One quickly gets the hang of this technique after a time or two. It is applicable to many cuisines and well worth mastering.

## Roasted garlic

Roasted garlic has broad appeal. Its mild, sweet, somewhat caramelized taste is less intimidating to those with timid tongues. Because the garlic is not chopped or crushed prior to roasting, allicin and other volatiles are never produced, so the broad range of aromatic compounds and therapeutic benefits are not realized. This is not to say that roasted garlic is bad, however. It is certainly enjoyable, and the roasting adds to the range of ways that garlic can be enjoyed.

Roasted garlic is a tasty spread for crusty bread or toast and is even good in mashed potatoes. I confess, however, that the ubiquitous garlic mashed potatoes served in restaurants have ruined any affection I might have had for the dish. Garlic mashed potatoes may benefit a restaurant more than its customers, since it offers the opportunity for the restaurant to appear trendy and a bit daring while reaping the convenience and efficiency of maintaining the starchy glop on steam trays throughout the restaurant's operating hours. If the garlic is not adequately roasted prior to joining the potato mass, the flavors can be particularly sulfurous and unkind. No skill or effort is required on the part of the line cook other than ensuring that the mass falls from the scoop and onto the victim's plate. Roasted garlic deserves better.

There are various methods of roasting garlic. Here are a few. Remove the outer skins from a head of garlic and then slice off the top of the head so that the clove tips are exposed. Drizzle the exposed tips with oil, cover in foil, and roast at 350°F (175°C) for about an hour. As a variation, add about a tablespoon of water after the oil. In the last 15 minutes of cooking, uncover the garlic and baste with the juices. The heat and cooking time required will vary depending on the size of the heads and your preferences. Dry roasting individual cloves in a fry pan is another approach and yields garlic that is more toasty and toothy, less caramelized and pasty. Place unpeeled cloves in a skillet and toss and turn periodically for about 8 to 12 minutes until the skins have browned. Vary the time and browning according to the size of the cloves and your preference.

## Peeling, crushing, chopping, and mincing

Peeling garlic cloves can seem like an onerous chore, particularly if you like to use a lot of garlic in your cooking. Nonetheless, once you acquire a certain rhythm and efficiency the task becomes quick and automatic.

If a clove is relatively easy to peel, and if your fingers are fairly strong, simply pinch the clove between your finger and thumb, positioning either your finger or thumb along one edge of the clove. This causes the skin to buckle, crack, and pull away from the flesh. You can then use your thumbnail to pull away the root end or tip end of the clove and gain a purchase on the skin to begin separating it from the flesh.

A standard and more effective variation mentioned earlier in the chapter calls for placing a clove on a cutting board or similar surface, laying the flat of a chef's knife on top of the clove, and lightly whacking the knife with your fist or the palm of your hand. This buckles and cracks the clove skin and separates it from the flesh, making it easy to gain a purchase on the skin and peel it away. This is the method I most frequently use and recommend.

There are further variations on this basic method, from just tapping the flat of the blade to barely begin the separation, to giving the flat of the knife a good slam, flattening and thoroughly crushing the clove in the process. Crushing the clove immediately produces allicin and other volatile compounds, releasing the garlic's tumult of complex aromatic flavors. At this point the flesh can be stripped off the skin and further minced or crushed. The skin can be removed and discarded with varying degrees of effort depending on the particular cultivar, its age, and the degree to which the flesh and skin stick to one another. I prefer to buckle the skin and remove it before smashing, crushing, or mincing the flesh, since to my mind this is cleaner and less wasteful, and since it ultimately requires no more time. But it is a matter of personal preference.

In the marketplace one can find various tools and gimmicks for peeling garlic. I do not have much use for them. Once simple techniques are mastered there is little need to complicate the process under the guise of simplifying it.

On the other hand, I frequently use a garlic press if I want crushed garlic rather than minced garlic. One can also fully smash a clove with the flat of a chef's knife, and then quickly mince the smashed flesh with the knife's cutting edge. Professional chefs use both methods. It is a matter of personal preference, one's mood, and the tools that are handy. Garlic press manufacturers usually emphasize that no peeling is necessary. Although this may be true, some waste is inevitable, and there is often more mess. Artichoke cultivars, including standard supermarket garlic, suffer least if peeling is omitted. Many other cultivars have thicker skins and so require more hand strength and generate more waste and mess. I almost always peel garlic before crushing it.

Chopping and mincing are alternatives to crushing. Crushing ensures the maximum production of allicin and other volatiles, releasing all of the garlic's aromatic pungency. It also allows the garlic to be distributed thoroughly and evenly with other food. Crushed garlic is ideal for mixing with a dressing for fresh lettuce or other greens. It works well in other venues as well, but sometimes chopped or minced garlic is preferable. Cooked in oil until straw-colored or light tan, chopped or minced garlic takes on a wonderfully rich, sweet, nutty character. Chopped garlic is coarser than minced garlic and in larger bits. Mincing creates more of the aromatic sulfur compounds and is more flavorful in this regard, but a toothy bite of more coarsely chopped garlic is good as well.

Chop or mince garlic as you would other foods. No specialized technique is required. Use a good chef's knife, or Asian equivalent, for the purpose. An 8 in. (200 mm) chef's knife is a good all-around size for the kitchen, and with a bit of practice one can make quick work of slicing, chopping, and mincing. One sometimes sees a cook using a small knife for such chores—and indeed, with small cutlery they do become chores. Paring knives are for paring; chef's knives are for chopping and mincing (and many other tasks as well).

## Garlic presses

If you decide to use a garlic press, get a good one. A garlic press should be well made so that it can withstand extended use. The plunger should fit with little gap on the sides and fully extend into the chamber, so that the garlic does not escape up the sides but is thoroughly forced through the holes, leaving little wasteful residue at the bottom. The chamber should have many small holes so that the garlic is thoroughly crushed, but the press also needs to be compatible with your hand strength. More strength is required to force garlic through tiny holes, but better handle designs provide greater leverage and easier gripping. The press should also be easy to clean. Some form of plastic device with protuberances that match the holes in the chamber to push out the remaining residue usually fills this role. These seem like simple and obvious requirements, but it is surprising how many presses fall short in one way or another.

Avoid the kind of press with a cylindrical chamber and a plunger that is screwed downward, slowly forcing the cloves through a perforated bottom. This device is slow and cumbersome—and hopefully nobody actually keeps half-crushed garlic in the press waiting for tomorrow's dinner.

The Swiss-made, cast-aluminum Zyliss Susi is a longstanding classic. Mine is decades old and has withstood extensive use. The handle and plunger pivots are sturdily made from large-peened pins. On the downside, the chamber is on the small side, it requires a fair amount of hand strength, and the handle is a bit too short and angular for the best leverage and comfort. I also have a press of similar design that was manufactured in Taiwan. The handle is more comfortable, but the press is not as well made. The handle and plunger pivots are not peened pins and are less robust. The handle pivot on mine has worn, and the two halves of the press now slip apart. The press is still quite usable but is a bit of a nuisance.

Unfortunately for classicists, the Swiss-made Zyliss Susi is no longer produced. It has been replaced by two models that are manufactured in China. The Zyliss Susi 2 has a pinned hinge design for the handle, similar to the original. The plunger itself has protuberances that match the holes in the chamber, but they only penetrate partway and do not purge the residue. There is no separate cleaning device, and the press is very difficult to clean. It is either a poor design or a good design poorly executed. The second model is the Zyliss Jumbo. It has a handle and plunger pivot design similar to my Taiwanese model that eventually wore and failed, though the Zyliss Jumbo appears to be far more robust in design and construction. The chamber is large and easily handles multiple cloves. The handle design is comfortable and provides good leverage. The plastic cleaning device that comes with the press works well. On the negative side, the nonstick coating reportedly wears away in the dishwasher. However, since I do not wash my press in the dishwasher, this has not been a concern. The Zyliss Jumbo is currently my primary and favorite garlic press, though I cannot yet vouch for its longevity.

The increasing enthusiasm for garlic has resulted in many new garlic presses coming to market. Several models that I have seen look promising, though I have not yet tested them.

## Botulism

The title of this section could be "Storing garlic in oil," but "Botulism" gets quickly to the point. Having garlic preserved in oil on hand seems like a good idea, but in fact it is a very bad idea. Garlic is a low-acid vegetable. A clove of garlic has a pH range of 5.3 to 6.3 (Harris 1997). As with any low-acid vegetable, garlic is subject to botulism contamination if improperly preserved. It is certainly not unique in this regard. Other low-acid vegetables such as asparagus, green beans, beets, and corn are also vulnerable to contamination with botulism.

As it grows, the botulism bacterium, *Clostridium botulinum*, produces an extremely powerful toxin that causes the illness. Storing garlic in olive oil or any cooking oil is a seemingly logical preservation method, but it creates exactly the right conditions that support growth of the bacterium and production of the toxin. *Clostridium botulinum* thrives in moist, low-oxygen, low-acid conditions. The spores are resistant to heat. Room-temperature storage conditions increase the risk and rate of growth. In North America at least three botulism outbreaks have been attributed to garlic-and-oil mixtures. Cooking garlic does not necessarily eliminate the threat. Roasted garlic stored in oil, for example, is still subject to the same risk. Although storage at room temperature increases the risk of contamination, long-term refrigerator storage does not remove the threat.

Commercially prepared garlic-and-oil mixtures are subject to stringent protocols and must contain citric or phosphoric acid to increase acidity.

Do not attempt a similar process at home. There is no easy and reliable home method that can be performed with sufficient consistency and certitude to overcome the lethal risk.

A pH of 4.6 or lower does not support the growth of botulism, so storing garlic in vinegar is safe. On the other hand, you might not want to bother with acidified storage in any case. Storing whole cloves of garlic in vinegar destroys the alliinase and thus the possibility of producing allicin and related volatiles. Putting chopped or crushed garlic in vinegar allows temporary preservation of the volatile sulfur compounds, but the volatiles diminish at varying rates over time.

In short, storing garlic in oil is unsafe for the home gardener and cook, and commercial preparations often lack culinary merit. Garlic in oil, particularly olive oil, is an outstanding culinary marriage, but it is important to remember never to use oil as a storage medium for garlic (or, for that matter, for asparagus, green beans, beets, corn, or any other low-acid food).

## TASTING AND EVALUATING

Evaluating the success of a particular garlic cultivar is rather different from evaluating the success of most other garden crops. Every year I plant a number of varieties of tomatoes, consisting mostly of favorites that have performed well in the past, and a promising new variety or two. I plant the tomatoes in the spring, and by late summer I know how all of them have done. When winter comes and the seed catalogs are sent, I know which tomato seeds I want to buy and how many of each I want to plant.

Garlic is different. I plant garlic in the fall and harvest and cure it the following summer. By fall planting time, do I know which garlic cultivars have performed best and which ones I want to

emphasize? Not really. I know some information about the new cultivars, but not all that I need to know about them.

Garlic adapts to local growing conditions over a period of several years. Some growers have reported that the full adaptation process lasts up to eight years, but more typically one will see the most significant changes, if any, over the first several years. Sometimes there is little change, but other times, after a couple of years of small-sized heads, a cultivar may adapt sufficiently and begin to produce larger heads. Or not. A number of factors are at play in determining favored garlic cultivars. Taste, of course, is a major factor, as are storage longevity, ease of peeling, size of heads, size of cloves, tolerance for seasons that are wetter, drier, colder, or warmer than normal, and so forth. Some of these factors are not immediately apparent, and early guesses affect how soon we are able to choose our favorites and have enough planting stock to satisfy us.

Let me illustrate with my own experience. Rocambole cultivars are my favorite garlics. In my view the rich, complex, sweet taste of the best Rocamboles is unsurpassed. As an added benefit, their cloves peel easily. However, they need cold winters to grow well, and they have a short storage life. When I first started growing garlic I was exceptionally taken with the Rocambole cultivar 'Russian Red'. Ten months after planting, the harvested and cured garlic was finally ready to eat. It was superb. I also tasted 'Shvelisi', a Purple Stripe cultivar that I had grown. It was very good but not as good as the 'Russian Red', and the cloves were smaller and more difficult to peel. I was even less enthused with a third cultivar, 'Ajo Rojo'. In my cool growing climate the heads of this garlic were relatively small, and there were several layers of small, difficult-to-peel cloves. Although 'Shvelisi' and 'Ajo Rojo' were acceptable, far exceeding the quality of the garlic from the grocery store, why should I

'Shvelisi' cloves become easier to peel with time in storage.

bother growing them when 'Russian Red' was better? I planted small quantities of each nonetheless.

By January the 'Russian Red' was no longer in its prime. The cloves in the remaining heads were starting to wither, shrinking in their skins, and the cloves were developing a green shoot. The thick, loosely bound clove skins that make Rocamboles easy to peel also cause them to store less well. What about the 'Shvelisi'? By January the skins had loosened just enough so that peeling the cloves was easier, and the flavor had rounded and deepened. I discovered that it was an outstanding cultivar for mid storage season. It was an acceptable replacement for the 'Russian Red', even crushed and raw in a dressing for salad greens—a role, at least to my taste, that requires a richer, sweeter garlic. I

harvested other garlic cultivars as well, but for that time period in mid storage season, 'Shvelisi' suddenly became my favorite. And then the quandary. This was the garlic that I now most wanted to eat, but I had planted very little of it and would have a small harvest over the coming summer. Not only that, but I would need to save most of the harvest to expand my planting the following fall, and thus for two winters I would have less of this garlic to eat than I wanted, unless I bought more planting stock.

This, as we have seen, is quite different from evaluating which tomatoes to plant next year. The considerations and assessment are more involved, and the assessments play out over a much longer time interval. The decisions regarding what and

'Ajo Rojo', an excellent-tasting, long-storing cultivar.

how much to plant have a more long-term impact. Of course, I could have purchased more 'Shvelisi' planting stock, but instead I purchased other related cultivars to try.

And what of the 'Ajo Rojo', one of the more long-storing garlics? After the 'Shvelisi' began to wither, as had the 'Russian Red' before it, the 'Ajo Rojo' became my favorite garlic for eating in late spring and early summer. The inner clove layers were still small, but the tenacious clove skins were by then loose enough to peel fairly easily. The flavor was excellent, too, and the garlic could be used raw in salad dressings and a full range of other culinary preparations.

Are the largest heads and cloves the best? Large cloves are easier to peel, and one can prepare a larger quantity of garlic more quickly using larger cloves from larger bulbs. From this standpoint, the largest heads and cloves are the best. However, the very largest heads and cloves do not store as well as the smaller heads and cloves. Well-grown, healthy garlic, with heads and cloves that are only moderately large, taste and store much better than the giants that bring stars to one's eyes. The flavor of the larger bulbs is generally more diffuse and less intense. At the other end of the spectrum, the very smallest heads and cloves may not be ideal either. Not only are they more difficult to peel for a given amount of flesh, but their small size may also be an indicator that they were not well grown; their flavor, and particularly their storage properties, may be adversely affected. In many respects, an overall ideal may be moderately large heads that store well, have good flavor concentration, and offer reasonably large cloves that are not too burdensome to peel. Save your largest heads and cloves for the marketplace, which generally prefers them, and for planting stock.

## CONTROLLED TASTE TESTS

With so many garlic cultivars available, the desire to assess and objectify flavor is quite understandable, but this kind of evaluation is very difficult to do in an objective and repeatable manner. Taste is highly subjective, and the genetic makeup of tasters can also contribute to widely varying conclusions. Wine tasting offers an interesting parallel, and insight into the issues that confront the garlic taster. Wine tasting is most accurate when conducted by trained professionals and confined to assessment of objective criteria and the presence or absence of technical faults. Once wine tasting moves away from these narrow criteria, objectivity and repeatability are left behind. In fact, even within these narrow technical bounds, agreements on the merit of some compounds is a matter of debate among enologists and wine aficionados. And in any case, these limited, semiobjective criteria play only a small part in our appreciation and enjoyment of wine. Volumes have been written on the problems and pitfalls associated with wine tasting and evaluations, but we will touch only briefly on a few of the issues with parallels to garlic tasting.

How should garlic be tasted and evaluated: raw, crushed, sautéed, or baked? If sautéed, should the cloves be chopped? What about pickled cloves versus baked cloves? Garlic tastes dramatically different depending on how it is prepared.

To the limited extent that formal garlic taste tests are conducted, it is typically by biting and chewing a raw clove. Although devotees may routinely taste garlic this way, the sulfur compounds fiercely assault the palate, and one's ability to taste and evaluate subsequent samples is significantly diminished even if bread is consumed between cloves. Although wines seldom affect the palate in this manner, tasting a number of wines without food (as is typical to avoid the taste of the food from interfering with the evaluation of the wine) can also fatigue the palate. It is well known that some wines are ranked higher simply because they are lower in acidity or have some residual sugar that softens them and makes them more appealing to an exhausted, battered palate in this artificial context. One can see a similar syndrome in garlic tasting, but it is even more exaggerated given the intensity of the sulfur compounds.

On more than one occasion, for example, 'Inchelium Red' has won garlic taste tests. This cultivar, at least to my palate, is pleasant but rather bland. After one's palate has been assaulted by other garlic samples, however, 'Inchelium Red' may seem a soothing and welcome relief. Biting into a clove of 'Russian Red' releases not only the rich depth of the flavor but also quite a bit of heat (which also somewhat masks the underlying rich complexity). Does this mean that 'Inchelium Red' is a better garlic for eating raw? Perhaps I would think so if I were eating handfuls of raw cloves, but this is not usually how we enjoy garlic. Typically we enjoy garlic with food. I like crushed raw garlic in an oil and vinegar dressing. In this context the moderate heat of 'Russian Red' is not an issue, and its complex, rich taste shines through. Some may still prefer the milder 'Inchelium Red' in salad dressings—taste is largely subjective after all.

Even more so than with wine, garlic taste tests conducted under artificial conditions greatly distort the tasters' impressions of their subjects. Garlic is generally used to flavor and accompany other foods, and this is really how garlic needs to be evaluated. Does this mean that it is foolish to taste garlic by biting into a raw clove? I hope not, since I do so frequently. After a time, one can make connections between how a garlic tastes raw and how it might taste in other contexts. But it is still a major assault on the palate.

Food interacts with wine and affects our perception of it, so in the quest for a semblance of objectivity and repeatability, formal wine tastings are conducted without food, except perhaps a bite of bread or drink of water to refresh the palate. Of course, we normally enjoy wine with food, so this objectification introduces its own distortions, though not as severe as if we were to attempt something similar with garlic.

To evaluate the taste of various garlic cultivars, we need to taste them in the manner in which they would be consumed. This, of course, introduces major issues of consistency and repeatability. A single test would not be sufficient. For example, some garlic cultivars may be good roasted but not as good sautéed or raw. One can imagine an elaborate series of taste tests that might include a fixed weight of each cultivar crushed into a fixed amount of olive oil, or a test that would similarly objectify roasted garlics. One of my favorite ways to enjoy garlic, chopped and sautéed until straw-colored or light tan, would be somewhat more difficult to precisely repeat. Slight differences in the preparation can make a significant difference in taste. I can well see someone setting up an elaborate series of taste tests. Such an enterprise might be enjoyable, but it should be regarded in that context, rather than as a definitive way of tasting and evaluating garlic.

And at what stage of maturity would the garlic cultivars be evaluated? 'Spanish Roja' is among my favorite cultivars, but it cannot be successfully grown everywhere, and it matures and fades fairly

rapidly. 'Ajo Rojo' is difficult to peel when young and requires a fairly long time after harvest before its flavors fully develop, but it tastes its best long after 'Spanish Roja' is past its prime. If one attempted some sort of side-by-side taste test with these two, one or the other cultivar would not be in its prime.

There is really no meaningful way to evaluate the taste of garlic objectively. Although taste tests can be enjoyable and revealing, the best way to evaluate various garlic cultivars is to live with them. Grow them, store them, eat them in various ways, and discover your own preferences. You are likely to find that a number of different cultivars will suit your preferences at various times, depending on where they are grown, the climate conditions in the year they are grown, their storage properties and age, whether they are consumed raw or cooked via a variety of methods, and the recipes you use. Over time your own favorites will emerge. None of this really lends itself to ready objectification, but that is not our overriding concern. Enjoying garlic is what we are after, and living with it and knowing it over time is a splendid way to do just that.

## OTHER GARLIC FOODS

### Green garlic

Green garlic is garlic that is harvested after it has developed into multicloved bulbs but before the clove and bulb skins have dried. The term is often used inconsistently, however, and sometimes refers to garlic scallions. Consistent terminology would be helpful, but as long as it is clear what one is talking about, no great harm is done.

In its immature, uncured state, green garlic has a rather mild and modest character. As described in the next section, garlic scallions and garlic greens have meritorious roles in cuisine and as a specialty crop. I suppose a similar argument can be made for green garlic, but at this stage, parts of the plant are no longer tender, yet the intense, complex flavors of mature garlic have not fully developed. Even if the garlic is harvested in an immature state, sufficient space is still required for it to develop into the multicloved bulbs. Unless novelty is the goal, one might be better off waiting a bit and harvesting mature garlic, or planting small cloves or large bulbils closely together for garlic scallions. On the other hand, I have seen (and purchased) green garlic at farmers' markets, so apparently there is sufficient demand for it. For the farmer it may be valuable as another marketable early-season crop after a long winter.

## Garlic scallions

Before garlic grows to a height of more than 12 to 16 in. (30 to 40 cm) or so, it can be harvested in the manner of a green onion. Since it is similar in size and appearance to a green onion, it is sometimes called a garlic scallion. Although the taste is not the same, a garlic scallion can be used in many of the same ways as a green onion or small leek. Garlic scallions have a mild, pleasant flavor that is not overtly garlicky. After the roots have been trimmed away, garlic scallions can be chopped and added to a salad like green onions, although a bit of cooking seems to bring out the best flavor. Like leeks, the whole plants can be steamed or braised for 6 to 10 minutes. Steamed garlic scallions also make a visually attractive and tasty vegetable accompaniment for the dinner plate when drizzled with olive oil and sprinkled with salt. Roughly chopping garlic scallions generates the volatile flavor components that are absent when garlic scallions are cooked whole. Sautéing softens them a bit and intensifies their flavor. They are good by themselves, and they

work well in combination with other foods in vegetable or meat sautés or with a variety of Asian or Western noodle dishes. Although garlic scallions lack the complex, intense flavor of cured mature garlic, they are nonetheless a welcome addition to the culinary repertoire and extend the use of garlic in the kitchen.

Garlic scallions sometimes appear unintentionally from stray cloves or dropped bulbils that subsequently sprout and regrow. This unintentional nuisance is often the first way a garlic grower encounters garlic scallions—after removing them from the garlic bed, the gardener sets about thinking of a way to make use of them. As soon as the merit of this alternate crop is discovered, garlic scallions can be grown intentionally for the fresh market or simply for one's own enjoyment in late winter or early spring.

By definition, garlic scallions do not develop into multicloved bulbs. Cloves for garlic scallions can be planted much more densely, as one might plant green onions. A rather generous spacing of 1 in. by 1 in. (2.5 cm by 2.5 cm) yields nearly 150 plants in a small square-foot section of a garden, and garlic scallions can be planted even more densely, depending on growing conditions and the preferred size for the plant. After the spring harvest, the garden space is available for other plants.

When growing garlic bulbs, the largest cloves are selected for planting. The small cloves that are left over are ideal for garlic scallions. The large bulbils from Asiatic cultivars are also a good, free source of garlic scallion planting material, and will yield garlic scallions the spring after a fall planting. The rounds generated from smaller bulbils planted the previous year are also excellent planting stock for this purpose.

In northern and central China, garlic cloves are planted in July for a harvest of garlic scallions in November. In a variation on the theme, the Chinese also grow blanched garlic scallions. For blanched garlic scallions, the cloves are planted in furrows. When the plants reach a height of about ½ in. (1.25 cm) they are covered with soil to the top of the furrow to keep the leaves from turning green. The blanched garlic scallions are harvested when they are still small and before they are exposed to sunlight.

## Garlic greens

Garlic greens, the green tops of young garlic plants, are another variation on the theme of early-harvest green garlic. Many cultures, including those of such diffuse regions as east Asia, the Philippines, and Bulgaria, routinely harvest garlic greens. Garlic greens are available long before mature bulbs and can be harvested multiple times after periods of regrowth. In some tropical areas, garlic greens can be grown from imported planting stock, even though the heat and short days may not permit the formation of bulbs.

The garlic leaves, or greens, are not as tender as the leaves of green onions and need to be harvested long before the plant approaches maturity, particularly if they are to be consumed raw. The greens can be harvested when they are no more than 12 in. (30 cm) or so in height. As they reach greater lengths they become progressively less tender and may require a fine mince to be suitable uncooked. You can clip the greens to nearly ground level, then wait until they regrow and clip them again, repeating this until the plant has exhausted itself. As an alternative you can allow the last greens to remain and generate energy stores for the bulb, which will generate a harvest the following year. The harvest season for garlic greens can span several months, depending on growing conditions and one's preferences. These greens are an alternative to chopped green onions in salads. When finely minced they also make a good alternative to chives.

As with garlic scallions, you can use small cloves for your garlic greens planting stock. Although it is generally desirable to separate cloves prior to planting, entire intact heads can be planted or left in the ground for a harvest of greens. Bulbils are another alternative. Although any bulbil can suffice, bulbils from Asiatic and Rocambole cultivars are relatively large and make especially good planting stock for garlic greens. The smallest bulbils, notably those from Porcelain cultivars, will be much smaller and yield considerably less, though perhaps with the benefit of increased tenderness.

## Scapes

Garlic scapes are distinctive and visually appealing. They are essentially a mild garlic-flavored vegetable with a texture somewhat resembling asparagus. For some culinary preparations, the texture of the scapes is enhanced by parboiling for three to five minutes. This treatment tenderizes the scapes and gives them a quality more closely approximating asparagus.

Scapes are an added bonus for the home gardener, and they also have appeal in the nouveau cuisines of the restaurant trade. Removing the scapes from bolting garlic plants can increase the size of the harvested bulbs, particularly for some garlic cultivars, but the costs are labor-intensive. Harvesting the scapes for market can offset the costs and contribute additional income.

The scape first grows erect, then bends or coils as the cells elongate irregularly, at first on only one side of the scape. As the scape bends or coils, it also begins to lignify. It then unwinds and becomes erect. For culinary purposes the scape is ideally harvested when it initially emerges and before it has curled down. Harvesting the scape before its

This 'Killarney Red' scape has not uncurled, so it remains relatively tender. Harvesting scapes at this stage strikes a good balance between scape tenderness and the bulb's storage longevity.

initial curl will ensure that it is tender. Reportedly this is common practice in Italy, where local farmers and gardeners grow bolting garlic and harvest the scapes for the table. Delaying the harvest until the scape curls downward likely extends the storage abilities of the bulb, though at the expense of scape tenderness. Scapes harvested at this later stage can still be quite good if they have not become too woody. Unless you have a significant, established market for fresh scapes, it is best to treat them as an added bonus rather than as a focus of the harvest. If, as some growers do, you attempt to balance bulb size with storage longevity, you may choose to cut the scapes after the initial curl but before the scape has uncurled and extended upward. If so, this is the time you will harvest the scapes for your table or for the market.

Scapes are rather mildly flavored. The spathe's long, green, flat beak is the most flavorful part, but it is also rather tough. You may wish to either remove the green beak or mince it finely, depending on the culinary preparation. An array of steamed, partially curled scapes drizzled with olive oil and presented on a white plate is rather impressive, though the flavors are somewhat bland. On the other hand, a steamed whole clove of garlic is quite bland as well and certainly less visually appealing than an array of vivid green scapes. Sautéing the scapes brings out more of their flavor. Scapes are a welcome addition to stir-fried cuisine.

Grilling is one of my favorite ways to prepare garlic scapes. Lightly browning them brings out much more of the garlic flavor, and grilling accomplishes that task nicely. Various grilling approaches are effective. Most simply, garlic scapes can be lightly sprayed with oil, salted, and placed on the grill. I like to mix approximately one part balsamic vinegar with two to three parts olive oil, add salt to taste, and toss the scapes in the mixture before placing them on the grill. As the scapes cook they begin to lay flatter and can be turned with tongs.

When they have finished cooking, I put them back in their marinade and toss briefly. They are a splendid accompaniment to grilled salmon or other fish and to various grilled meats.

It is becoming more common to find scapes, both fresh and pickled, in Asian and other specialty markets, but be aware that these are often scapes from the so-called elephant garlic.

The scape harvest comes during the interval when my garlic supply from the previous season has dwindled and I am impatiently waiting to harvest and cure the new crop. This brings added enjoyment to the scapes, since they offer an early start on the harvest. Scapes are the first taste of the new crop's bounty and coincide nicely with spring and early summer's barbecuing season. Fresh scapes store quite well, lasting several weeks when kept in a plastic bag in the refrigerator.

## Bulbils

Bulbils are small storage leaves encased by a sheath. I cannot say that I have experimented a great deal with bulbils as food. For many cultivars, if the plant is allowed to mature to the point at which it produces mature bulbils, the bulb size may be considerably diminished. The sheath that encompasses the bulbil is also a bit tough, and the ratio of sheath to the bulbil's storage leaf is rather high. I have been more inclined to eat the scape at an earlier stage before bulbils are produced, or alternatively to harvest the larger bulbils and plant them for garlic scallions or garlic greens.

Some suggestions for eating bulbils include harvesting them at a slightly immature stage while their sheaths are still relatively tender and including them in cuisine as one might a miniature pearl onion. At the other extreme, one can fully dry the bulbils and crush them into a fine or coarse powder to sprinkle on food.

# PROCESSED GARLIC

Although heads of garlic are nearly universally available in grocery stores, most of the garlic harvest does not find its way to stores as a fresh-market crop, but rather as an ingredient in a processed food or on a spice rack as garlic powder or garlic salt. Although processing fresh garlic into other forms may have been practiced to some degree for millennia, only since the mid 20th century or so has processed garlic become a major feature in the culinary landscape. Processed garlic finds its way into all manner of foods, from the obvious, such as frozen lasagna, to the less obvious, such as pet food, chewing gum, and ice cream. Because of the heightened interest in the health benefits of garlic, it is also processed into capsules and tablets as a health supplement—though not always with the desired health benefits intact. Dehydrated garlic in various iterations is the main form of processed garlic, but there are others as well, such as garlic juices, oils, and oleoresins.

Setting aside for the moment the not so insignificant issue of the culinary and health merits of fresh-market garlic versus processed garlic, processed garlic offers the food and health supplement industries significant advantages. Processed foods constitute an ever-growing percentage of the food we consume. Food processors need a consistent supply of garlic that is independent of the yearly harvest schedule. They need less bulk in order to minimize handling and storage costs, and they need long storage without spoilage and deterioration. Fresh-market garlic does not meet these needs. Processed garlic does. For the consumer, processed garlic in its various forms offers convenience. Our demand for convenience foods drives the market.

Processing methods attempt to match characteristics with market interests, whether it is the flavor of roasted garlic, the light coloration of garlic powders and salts, or the absence of odor for products sold as health supplements. Not surprisingly, the needs of the garlic processing industry determine to a large degree how and what kind of garlic is grown. For example, because commercial producers of processed garlic strive for a light-colored product, cultivars with white flesh and skins are preferred over those with pale yellow flesh and darker skins. Cultivars with high solids and low moisture content are also preferred. Are these the best-tasting garlic cultivars for eating fresh? Most would say no, though the needs of the food processing industry drive and define large-scale commercial garlic growing.

Processed garlic does not have the taste of fresh garlic. All processing methods destroy or transform some of garlic's flavor precursors, and many prematurely destroy alliinase so that it becomes impossible to produce allicin and other compounds so essential to the taste, aroma, and health benefits of garlic. Since each processing method determines what volatiles can be produced and in what ratios, the flavor of the product becomes as dependent upon the processing method as it is upon the garlic itself.

## Peeled garlic

Peeled raw garlic cloves are now offered in the marketplace. This seems like a nice convenience, but let the buyer beware. The garlic may have been processed or stabilized by blanching, acidifying, or other processes that reduce or destroy its ability to produce allicin and related volatiles when chopped or crushed. You can determine for yourself the merit of prepared garlic. Put a clove of the commercially prepeeled garlic alongside a clove of fresh garlic that you have just peeled. Chop, mince, or crush both. The fresh garlic will have an intense bloom of fragrance. If the prepeeled clove does not have a similarly intense aroma, it is safe to assume that processing has reduced or destroyed the garlic's ability to generate allicin and related compounds.

## Dehydrated garlic

Dehydrated garlic is available in a range of forms relatively dependent on particle size, from powder to minced, granulated, chopped, and diced. It is a mainstay of processed foods, from frozen dinner entrees to lunch meats, sauces, and pet food.

Sun drying onions and other alliums has been practiced in the tropics for centuries, and onions were among the first vegetables used in dehydration experiments dating back to the 1700s. It was not until 1923, however, that a major onion and garlic dehydration program in California set the stage for subsequent commercial dehydration processing. By that time processed foods were becoming a bigger feature in the American culinary landscape. World War II spurred additional attention to commercial dehydration methods for food products that were lightweight, easily transported, and storable for long periods.

Dehydrated garlic finds its way into convenience health supplements as well as convenience foods. Claiming to supply the health benefits of garlic without the odor and inconvenience of the fresh product, some supplement makers have turned to odor-reduced dehydrated garlic. Supplement manufacturers produce "odorless" garlic by eliminating the alliinase interaction. This is accomplished in a variety of ways, including exposing the garlic to fumaric acid, physically separating alliinase from the garlic, and freeze-drying a mixture of garlic and cyclodextrin. Other supplement makers preserve alliinase and the potential for producing allicin but fail to provide a delivery mechanism that protects the alliinase from destructive stomach acids. Supplements are therapeutically effective in varying degrees. See chapter 4 for a discussion of the merits and pitfalls of these products.

On a commercial scale, dehydration processing may begin with rollers that break the bulbs apart. Next the roots, stems, skins, and other extraneous matter are vacuumed away. The cloves are surface-sterilized with flame or alkali and then washed, sliced, and dried in stages. The clove skins are vacuumed from the dried, sliced cloves, and the clove slices are ground and sieved. According to Henry Jones and Louis Mann (1963) it takes between 3.2 and 4.5 lbs. of garlic bulbs from the field to produce a pound of garlic powder and between 2.2 and 2.6 lbs. of sliced fresh garlic to yield a pound of garlic powder.

Hot air drying is considered the most economical dehydration method. Temperatures are kept below 140°F (60°C) to prevent discoloration, darkening, and other undesirable effects. Sulfur dioxide can be used to reduce discoloration, but it also reduces pungency. Untreated dehydration exhaust emissions from garlic processing plants are rich with stinky disulfides. Such emissions may violate air pollution regulations, and sprays and scrubbers in various forms are employed to reduce the offense.

The drying process itself does not eliminate bacterial contamination. While most bacteria is benign, the presence of coliform bacteria must be severely limited, and no salmonella is acceptable. Prevention of bacterial contamination in processed garlic may include treatment with ethylene oxide, hydrogen peroxide, brining, and irradiation. The degree of exposure to these treatments is a balancing act between the need to eliminate bacterial contamination and the need to preserve desired flavors.

## Garlic powder

Garlic powder and garlic salt are seemingly ubiquitous in American kitchens, except perhaps in the kitchens of two rather different groups: those who hate any kind of garlic flavor, and devotees of garlic who would not think of sullying their pantries with such products. Manufacturers produce garlic powder by finely grinding dehydrated garlic. Calcium stearate is sometimes added to prevent clumping. Garlic powder has a pronounced and familiar garlic character, but it does not have the same taste as fresh garlic. During processing, some sulfur compounds are produced that are not present in fresh garlic. Garlic powder is sometimes described as having a boiled character. Nonetheless, it is closer in composition to fresh garlic than any other form of processed garlic.

Most commercial garlic powders are produced by cutting peeled garlic cloves into smaller pieces, oven drying at 122°F to 140°F (50°C to 60°C), and pulverizing the pieces into a powder. At up to 140°F there is no loss of active components; above this temperature, degradation begins to occur. As a result of moisture removal, good-quality garlic powder is approximately 2 ½ times more concentrated than fresh garlic. Cutting the cloves helps speed drying, but it also causes alliinase to come into contact with alliin and other cysteine sulfoxides to produce allicin and other thiosulfinates. This interaction is undesirable at this stage as these are soon transformed into other sulfur compounds, reducing alliin and subsequent allicin potential when the garlic powder is consumed. Ironically, the more alliin that is lost during the cutting, the stronger the garlic powder will smell as a result of the volatile sulfur compounds that are produced.

The quality of garlic powder varies widely. A few garlic powders are produced by spray-drying cloves that have been homogenized. These powders have no remaining alliin and no potential for producing allicin. In general, garlic powders produced for the spice market have a lower potential allicin yield than powders produced for the medicinal market.

How do you get the aromatic and therapeutically beneficial allicin from garlic powder? When the garlic powder is moistened, alliinase is brought into contact with alliin, yielding allicin. This, of course, presupposes that the garlic powder is produced in a way that preserves both alliin and alliinase. Garlic powder is quite stable over time. After five years of storage at room temperature, allicin yield is reduced by only 10%. Low moisture is important, however. Moisture content should not exceed 7% and ideally should be maintained in the range of 4% to 6%.

## Garlic salt

Garlic salt is typically comprised of up to 81% salt, approximately 18% to 19% white garlic powder, and 1% to 2% calcium stearate to prevent clumping. A tablespoon of garlic salt is said to approximately equate to a clove of garlic. However, were I to use garlic salt for sautéed vegetables in the same quantities that I use fresh garlic (one tablespoon of garlic salt per clove of garlic) I would rapidly use up my daily sodium allowance for the next several lifetimes.

Flavor is another matter. The boiled garlic flavor that characterizes garlic powder characterizes garlic salt as well, since the garlic flavoring in garlic salt is garlic powder. Garlic salt plays familiar traditional culinary roles: it is often sprinkled on meats that are to be roasted or used as an ingredient in the flour mixture for fried chicken. One might consider instead rubbing the meat with a clove of garlic before roasting, or rubbing the chicken with garlic prior to flouring—not quite as convenient, perhaps, though not particularly inconvenient either.

## Pickled garlic

Pickling garlic with vinegar is very popular in some cultures. It is, for example, a common method of preparation in parts of China and Russia. Pickled garlic can be stored for a long time. Unfortunately, pickling also destroys much of the flavor and potential therapeutic benefits of garlic.

Pickling lowers the pH and irreversibly inactivates alliinase. If you chop pickled garlic, there will be no alliinase to interact with alliin to produce allicin. Pickling also reduces garlic's flavor precursors (Fenwick and Hanley 1990). In one study, after 10 days, garlic cloves stored in a weak acetic acid solution had a 70% reduction in allicin yield when the cloves were crushed. At 60 days, no allicin was produced. Flavor intensity decreased at a similar rate. In another study the concentration of sulfur compounds remaining in the garlic cloves was equivalent to the concentration in the vinegar after 60 days. This may be viewed as either good or bad, depending on whether one is interested in pickled garlic or garlic-flavored vinegar—though without the creation of allicin, neither product has the taste of fresh chopped garlic. In vinegar the sulfur compounds reach an equilibrium, so if a few cloves are pickled in a large volume of vinegar, the concentration of sulfur compounds in the cloves will be reduced accordingly.

## Oils

Fresh garlic contains very few oil-soluble compounds. How then does one explain the "garlic oil" we see in stores or the concentrated product used in industry? Some sources state that garlic oil is *extracted* by steam distillation of freshly chopped or ground garlic, but it is more accurate to say that garlic oil is *produced* by steam distillation of freshly chopped or ground garlic. Steam distillation converts allicin and other thiosulfinates to oil-soluble allyl sulfides. The resultant oil is reddish brown and mostly comprised of diallyl disulfide with a small portion of allyl propyl disulfide. It is so intense that it is seldom used on its own but is commonly diluted in vegetable oil or encapsulated. Some sources state that by weight, garlic oil is roughly 200 times as strong as dehydrated garlic powder and roughly 900 times as strong as fresh garlic. As we have seen, however, what is being compared is not really the same as fresh garlic, so there is no genuine equivalence.

## Solid flavorings

Garlic oils and oleoresins are too concentrated and inconvenient in form for many food products or consumer uses. One will not find vials of garlic oil in kitchen spice racks, for example. Garlic oils and oleoresins are blended with other materials to create various forms of solid flavorings. Salt, sugar, and dextrose are common vehicles in these concoctions. One does not want to find a solid lump of the mixture in one's shaker bottle, so manufacturers may add calcium stearate to prevent clumping. Coating the particles with a film of polymer, a process called microencapsulation, is another way to prevent clumping, and it carries the added benefit of protecting the mixture from oxidation and chemical changes from exposure to light. For garlic products, the polymers are typically based on modified starches or gum arabic. These products typically have about two to four times the flavor strength of dehydrated garlic powder.

Although garlic flavorings are most often dry products, other forms have found their way to the marketplace. Garlic pastes, for example, may include a variety of ingredients such as garlic powder, garlic juice, garlic oil, salt, dextrose, glycerin, acids, and other seasonings.

## Pectins

Dried garlic skins contain an abundance of pectins, a type of carbohydrate that readily absorbs water. Pectins have a range of commercial uses. In Egypt, garlic skins are a commercial source for pectins.

# ❦ FOUR ❧

# Therapeutic Benefits

FOR MILLENNIA, garlic has been among humankind's most revered herbal medicines. If there is such a thing as ancestral memory, garlic surely resonates with us. Even those of us who are primarily interested in garlic from a culinary standpoint cannot help but be impressed by studies affirming its therapeutic benefits. From culinary, cultural, and therapeutic points of view, garlic is indeed a compelling plant.

Many food products are subject to periodic health fads. In the case of garlic the fad has lasted thousands of years. The latest resurgence of interest in garlic's therapeutic benefits has the added weight of scientific research, with both fresh garlic and garlic supplements riding the wave. As we shall see, however, garlic supplements do not always provide the full range of benefit offered by fresh garlic.

Alliums in general are associated with beneficial therapeutic effects. Among the alliums, garlic surpasses the onion in the breadth and depth of benefit. Garlic has long been recommended as a treatment for wounds, foul ulcers, pneumonia, bronchitis, dyspepsia, and gastrointestinal dis-

orders. Garlic oil has been used as a strong antiseptic and as a vermifuge to expel roundworms. Reported effects include insecticidal, antibacterial, antifungal, antitumoral, hypoglycemic, fibrinolytic, antiatherosclerotic, antithrombotic, and hypolipidemic (Augusti 1990).

Garlic has played multiple roles throughout its lengthy historical association with humankind. It is food, flavoring agent, disease preventative, health preserver, and health restorer. The roles are often intermingled, most particularly in the traditional cuisines of various ethnic groups, from the European meat stews of the Middle Ages to the Indian and Middle Eastern dish *kofta*, to Italian salamis and German sausages. In these cuisines, garlic simultaneously flavors the dish, helps prevent spoilage, and contributes to the health of the consumer.

The use of garlic as a therapeutic agent is woven through history. An ancient Egyptian medicinal manual describes 22 drug formulations containing garlic, and garlic bulbs have been found in a number of Egyptian tombs. A Babylonian cuneiform tablet from 3000 BC includes a prescription for a tonic containing a substantial amount of garlic. Babylonian physicians used garlic as a successful treatment for intestinal worms. They also concluded that diseases were caused by harmful "tiny worms" that the eye could not see, and prescribed garlic as a treatment. For the day, this was an exceptionally insightful interpretation of garlic's antibiotic properties.

Throughout history, garlic has often been recommended as a treatment for intestinal worms and hemorrhoids, among other things. Sanskrit medical textbooks known as Ayurveda (Science of Life) date from about 500 AD, though their content is likely much older. These textbooks describe garlic as a remedy for many things, including skin diseases, dyspepsia, anorexia, abdominal diseases, rheumatism, and hemorrhoids. In the 1st century AD, Pedanius Dioscurides Anazarbeus, a Roman physician who came from Greece, recommended garlic as a stomachic and diuretic, and as a treatment for hemorrhoids and intestinal worms.

During the Great Plague of London in 1665, garlic reportedly protected many people from infection. Both earlier and later accounts of epidemics also associate protection with the consumption of garlic. According to various accounts, during a plague in Marseilles in 1721, four criminals were released from prison to collect and bury the dead. Although not expected to live long, the four apparently remained healthy, sustained by a mixture of crushed garlic and vinegar or cheap wine, a concoction that came to be called *vinaigre des quatre voleurs* (vinegar of the four thieves). In another variation of the account, the four thieves were robbing the sick and the dead. When caught by the authorities they explained that they were protected from the plague by this mixture.

In the 1800s Louis Pasteur was the first to describe the antibacterial effect of garlic juices. In the 1900s the renown German physician Albert Schweitzer treated amoebic dysentery in Africa using only garlic. By the 1990s there were some 1200 scientific research publications on garlic's therapeutic effects. Garlic supplements ranked as high as number two in herbal supplement sales dollars, and number one as the most widely used herbal supplement, with Americans consuming an average of 361 million lbs. (164 million kg) of garlic annually.

The garlic health fad of the last 6000 years or so continues unabated. Modern scientific studies affirm and elucidate what has been known by many cultures for thousands of years: garlic is a powerful and complex natural drug that offers a broad spectrum of highly beneficial therapeutic effects. Let us now look in more detail at what these studies show about the therapeutic constituents in garlic.

## VITAMINS AND MINERALS

Broadly speaking, garlic contains about the same nutrient levels as tuber vegetables such as potatoes. Even if consumed in relatively large quantities, garlic would not be a major contributor to one's daily requirements for vitamins and minerals. In general, the vitamin and mineral content of garlic is not a major reason for its health benefits.

Some popular literature describes selenium and germanium as important elements in garlic's therapeutic benefits. However, the amount of germanium in garlic is negligible, and while garlic does have a relatively high concentration of selenium, a large clove has only approximately 1.6% of the U.S. Recommended Dietary Allowance. One could make better headway in selenium intake by consuming a good portion of cauliflower or spinach, both of which contain similar concentrations. Interestingly, however, if garlic is grown in special selenium-enriched soils, a large clove can yield about four times the recommended daily intake of selenium. The concentration of sulfur compounds in garlic makes substantial selenium uptake possible, and available in a form that best benefits its antioxidant effect.

## ALLICIN AND OTHER CONSTITUENTS

Alliums, particularly garlic, have a distinctive alliaceous odor that is largely the result of organic sulfur compounds. Sulfur compounds are well-known antibacterial agents, and garlic in particular has long been known for its antibacterial properties. It was not until 1944, however, that Chester J. Cavallito and his colleagues identified the antibacterial principle in crushed garlic as an oxygenated sulfur compound they called allicin. Curiously, additional research showed that allicin was not present in garlic that had not been crushed. Within a few years researchers isolated the precursor of allicin, which they called alliin. Alliin has no known antibiotic activity of its own. Antibiotic capability is created when alliin is converted to allicin by the enzyme alliinase.

Garlic's numerous therapeutic benefits are most closely associated with allicin. The specific mechanisms of its pharmacology are not well understood, except as an external or intestinal antibiotic. Once allicin enters the bloodstream it is immediately converted into other substances, making it all the more difficult to fully and precisely assess the mechanisms at work. It is a seeming irony that a substance declared so important is rapidly converted to other substances. This is hardly a rarity, however. Vitamin A, vitamin B6, and linoleic acid, for example, must undergo conversions for pharmacological effect (Koch 1996a).

Cooking destroys allicin, so garlic must be consumed raw in order to assimilate allicin and its derivative compounds. Stomach acids also destroy alliinase, which is needed to produce allicin, so allicin cannot be created in the stomach under normal circumstances. Allicin can be created and assimilated in the intestine, however—a method employed in some garlic supplements with varying success.

What about those of us who enjoy eating cooked garlic? Since cooking destroys allicin, are there any therapeutic benefits to eating cooked garlic? Cooked garlic still contains numerous sulfur compounds and derivatives besides allicin that are associated with a range of therapeutic benefits, including reduction of blood pressure, anticancer effects, and immune system effects. Researchers Hans Reuter, Heinrich Koch, and Larry Lawson (1996) offer this summary of garlic's therapeutic role: "It is certain that the natural drug 'garlic' is not a monosubstance product, but rather a complex mixture of active ingredients which probably act synergistically to produce a clinical effect." Even though heat destroys allicin, chopping, crushing, or slicing garlic prior to cooking unleashes a string of reactions and transformations and ensures the presence of the greatest number of volatile compounds. Baking and boiling whole cloves produces by far the fewest volatile compounds, since keeping cloves whole prevents alliinase from coming into contact with alliin and other precursors, and since heat also destroys alliinase.

The effects and benefits of all of garlic's volatile compounds are not well understood, but if indeed garlic is a "natural drug" comprised of numerous active ingredients acting synergistically to produce therapeutic effects, then if one intends to cook garlic, one can see the likely benefit of generating the most volatiles by crushing, chopping, or slicing garlic prior to cooking. Baked whole cloves are likely to have the least therapeutic effect. For that matter, baked whole cloves have the least pungent and least complex flavor, though many enjoy the mildness of baked whole garlic cloves for just that reason.

# ANTIBIOTIC EFFECTS

Many studies have confirmed that garlic is an effective antibiotic on bacteria, fungi, protozoa, and viruses, and that garlic extract can suppress the growth of bacteria that are resistant to commonly used antibiotics. Garlic's antibiotic activity is primarily due to allicin. Crushed raw garlic is a powerful antibiotic, whereas whole boiled cloves, which have no allicin, have no antibiotic activity. Tests show that when the thiosulfinates, including allicin, are removed from garlic extracts, antibacterial and antifungal effects are eliminated. The effect of allicin is remarkably powerful. Even at dilutions as high as 1:125,000, allicin can completely inhibit some types of bacteria. Ajoene, a compound derived from the bonding of three allicin molecules, is present in steam-distilled garlic oil and other oil macerates, also has very strong antibacterial properties (Reuter et al. 1996).

Garlic helps protect against many, but not all, harmful bacteria. For example, in some food preparations garlic can help reduce the growth of salmonella, but it is not effective against some types of botulism, an anaerobic bacterium, and can itself be a vehicle for food-borne botulism. (See "Botulism" in chapter 3 for more details.) In a study with pathogenic aerobic and anaerobic bacteria, garlic had no effect on the anaerobic bacteria but was effective against the aerobic bacteria. The study also showed that garlic acted synergistically with antibiotics, so that both together were more effective against pathogenic bacteria than just one alone. Other studies show that garlic inhibits pathogenic intestinal bacteria that are responsible for diarrhea, but normal beneficial intestinal flora are less affected. Garlic is effective against the difficult pathogens of the typhus-paratyphus-enteritis group and has proven to enhance the effectiveness of antibiotics in the treatment of tuberculosis.

Garlic kills pathogenic protozoa. Physicians in the former Soviet Union used garlic for successful treatment of giardiasis, an intestinal infection caused by the protozoan *Giardia lamblia*. Israeli researchers tested allicin against *Entamoeba histolytica*, the source of amoebic dysentery and potentially the most pathogenic protozoan infecting the human gastrointestinal tract. Even at extremely low concentrations allicin destroyed the laboratory cultures. Diallyl trisulfide, a secondary constituent of allicin, is also effective at killing pathogenic protozoa. Ajoene, another secondary constituent of allicin, inhibits the proliferation of *Trypanosoma cruzi*, the protozoan responsible for Chagas' disease, a potentially fatal illness affecting the nervous system and heart.

Garlic is also effective against pathogenic fungi and yeasts. In a study of the effectiveness of aqueous garlic extract against a series of fungi and yeasts originating from patients with infectious vaginitus, including *Candida*, *Cryptococcus*, *Rhodotorula*, *Torulopsis*, and *Trichosporon*, the fungi and yeasts were all inhibited or killed by a weak solution of the extract diluted to 1:1024. Another study used aqueous garlic extract against dermatophytes, fungi that cause parasitic skin infections. The study included various species of *Microsporum*, *Trichophyton*, and *Epidermophyton*. Prior to treatment, guinea pigs and rabbits were infected with the fungi. Treatment with the garlic extract resulted in complete healing within 14 days. Other similar studies yielded similar results. In China aqueous garlic extract and preparations containing diallyl trisulfide, a secondary constituent of allicin, have been used to successfully treat patients with life-threatening cryptococcal meningitis.

Garlic's activity against pathogenic viruses is not as well documented as its other antibiotic activity. Garlic is not an antiviral panacea, but evidence does show that it is effective against some viruses, including certain types of influenza. In poorer countries garlic is often used in place of vaccine for preventative measures. Prior to the availability of vaccines, garlic was successfully used prophylactically against polio. Garlic has also proven effective against some types of herpes virus and against viral pneumonia. Allicin and the secondary constituents of allicin, such as ajoene, appear to be the effective agents. More study is needed to assess what types of viruses can be affected by garlic.

## CARDIOVASCULAR HEALTH

Garlic may reduce serum cholesterol in some instances, but the evidence is inconclusive. In the Jain community in India, individuals within the same families have widely varying eating habits with respect to onions and garlic. Some abstain from both, while others consume from 1.76 to 2.8 oz. (50 to 80 g) of onions and 0.25 to 0.35 oz. (7 to 10 g) of garlic every day. A study of the two groups showed that those who consumed onions and garlic had significantly lower serum levels of cholesterol and triglycerides, as well as lower body fats. In another study, onion juice alone was not able to prevent atherosclerosis in rabbits, but garlic juice had a significant ameliorating effect.

Some clinical studies indicate that garlic has a cholesterol-lowering effect, while other studies show no correlation. Most of the studies that have shown no correlation were conducted with garlic supplements that had little or no ability to produce usable allicin (Reuter et al. 1996). However, a well-designed clinical study using both garlic supplements and fresh garlic, and participants with moderate levels of cholesterol, showed no reduction in LDL cholesterol (Gardner et al. 2007). The results of the study did not rule out the possibility that higher doses of garlic or inclusion of participants with more elevated cholesterol levels might yield a different result, but it did not show the anticipated cholesterol-lowering effect.

Garlic has been used to treat elevated blood pressure since at least the early part of the 20th century. Numerous clinical studies have affirmed its therapeutic effect in reducing both systolic and diastolic blood pressure. Although allicin is associated with most of garlic's therapeutic benefits, it does not appear to have a role in blood pressure reduction. Several compounds and mechanisms appear to be at play, resulting in a relaxant effect on vascular smooth muscle and dilation of the blood vessels. Studies also show that garlic has significant antiarrhythmic effects in both ventricular and supraventricular arrhythmias. Numerous studies show that garlic inhibits platelet aggregation and is an effective antithrombotic in the human body. Allicin and its derivative ajoene appear to be primarily responsible for the antithrombotic effects.

Garlic inhibits the formation of free radicals, supports the body's radical scavenger mechanisms, and protects LDL ("bad") cholesterol against oxidation by free radicals (Reuter et al. 1996). The antioxidant effects are another aspect of garlic's overall protective benefit for the cardiovascular system. In vitro studies have demonstrated garlic's effectiveness in the scavenging of free radicals. The radicals present in cigarette smoke, for example, are reduced by garlic. Allicin and allicin-derived allyl sulfides appear to be the primary source of garlic's antioxidant activity. Both metabolize in the blood and liver to allyl mercaptan, a strong antioxidant.

## HYPOGLYCEMIC EFFECTS

Garlic lowers elevated blood glucose. Although it is not a substitute treatment for diabetes, it nonetheless can be beneficial in reducing elevated blood sugar and reducing insulin requirements, particularly for those with slight or threshold diabetic conditions. Tolbutamide is an orally administered antidiabetic drug. In comparative tests of 0.1 g/kg of tolbutamide and 0.1 mg/kg of allicin, tolbutamide reduced blood glucose levels by 24.1% and increased insulin activity by 26%. Allicin reduced blood glucose levels by 15.4% and increased insulin activity by 18%. In another study, the juice of 25 g of garlic, the equivalent of about six "average" cloves of garlic, had approximately the same effect as a standard dosage of 0.25 mg/kg of tolbutamide. Allicin is an effective hypoglycemic agent in garlic. Onions are also an effective hypoglycemic, but onions contain no allicin, so other sulfur compounds in garlic may be in play as well. Garlic increases the insulin level in the blood and the glycogen level in the liver. Garlic's hypoglycemic effects may be attributable to the enhanced release of insulin (Reuter et al. 1996).

## ANTICANCER EFFECTS

Studies show that garlic can reduce the risk of various forms of cancer, including gastrointestinal cancers (Reuter et al. 1996). Cooked garlic as well as raw garlic may be effective. Garlic is most closely associated with reduction in the risk of stomach cancer. In one notable epidemiological study, populations in two small regions in China were compared. The incidence of stomach cancer for one region where the average person consumed 0.7 oz. (20 g) of fresh garlic a day was only 8% of the rate in the other region where the consumption of garlic was less than 0.04 oz. (1 g) per day. In a large American study (Steinmetz et al. 1994) the consumption of 127 foods, including 44 fruits and vegetables, was assessed for a group of more than 40,000 women. In that study, garlic was the only food to show a statistically significant reduction in the risk of colon cancer. Those who consumed one or more servings of fresh or powdered garlic per week had a 35% lower risk of colon cancer and a 50% lower risk of distal colon cancer. Garlic has also been shown to decrease the incidence of tumors in a variety of laboratory animals. Its anticancer effects appear to be attributable to both allicin and allicin-derived compounds as well as to undetermined compounds unrelated to allicin (Reuter et al. 1996).

## IMMUNE SYSTEM

In vitro, animal, and human studies increasingly show that garlic enhances the body's immune system. Natural killer (NK) cells are a type of leukocyte, or white blood cell, that combat infection and disease. Several studies show that garlic increases NK cell activity. In a study of AIDS patients, for example, ingestion of garlic approximately doubled NK cell activity. Garlic also increases the production of interleukins, key elements in the body's immune system response. Allicin, as well as unidentified compounds other than allicin, are responsible for garlic's enhancements to the immune system. The immune system has several types of cells, and it appears that different compounds in garlic may be beneficial to different cell types (Reuter et al. 1996).

## OTHER EFFECTS

Garlic has a seemingly endless range of therapeutic effects, the full extent of which is not yet known. Some effects have only recently been discovered. Others are rooted in folk medicine and are not fully delineated in the context of modern science. The following are a few examples of other therapeutic benefits.

Thiamine, also known as vitamin B1, is critical for neurological health, and a deficiency can be particularly problematic for the elderly. Ongoing consumption of garlic, which facilitates the absorption of this vitamin, may help maintain neurological health, particularly for older individuals.

Some of the earliest medicinal uses for garlic were as protection from intestinal parasites. For this purpose, garlic enemas were often prescribed. On its own, garlic is not a dependable vermifuge, but it can have a beneficial effect and can augment other treatments. It can also play a preventative role. Methods include enemas and ingestion. Garlic has some effect against roundworms and hookworms and their eggs. Garlic powder and garlic oil in dog food have proven effective in eliminating filaria from the bloodstream. Allicin and its secondary constituents are likely the primary antiparasitic agents in garlic (Reuter et al. 1996).

Garlic reduces or eliminates many of the effects of chronic nicotine poisoning.

Allicin combines with thiamine to produce allithiamine, an effective antidote for cyanide poisoning. On its own, thiamine has no antidotal effect. Garlic has a protective effect against poisoning from heavy metals, such as mercury and cadmium. It reduces the toxic effects of arsenic poisoning and is a beneficial antidote to lead poisoning, reducing the lead content in liver and muscle tissues and decreasing the symptoms.

Garlic extracts have been effective in controlling liver disease and damage caused by acute hepatitis. Studies show that garlic can help protect the liver by neutralizing liver toxicants, activating enzymes that control detoxification. It appears that several compounds in garlic may play a role.

Garlic has been used in the treatment of various respiratory diseases, including chronic asthma and whooping cough.

In addition to formal studies that support therapeutic benefits, one may find oneself serendipitously discovering or validating an effect of garlic. For example, garlic can be affective in certain insecticidal applications. Diallyl disulfide, a major compound from garlic, is toxic to mosquito larvae. Allium researcher Fred Crowe (1995b) stumbled upon the effect first hand. During one growing season, white rot became pervasive in a field of garlic, and the crop was declared a total loss. For several reasons, including prevention of further increase in the disease, the contaminated field was continuously flooded between June and November. Crowe waded through the field weekly, collecting soil samples and monitoring garlic and pathogen survival. During that time period a slight garlic odor was present, suggesting that diallyl disulfide was being given off by the decaying garlic plants. Although many insects and other invertebrates were abundantly present, no mosquitoes were present in the garlic field or surrounding fields.

## THERAPEUTIC DOSAGE

Garlic's therapeutic effects are primarily due to the sulfur compound allicin, which, again, is not created until garlic is sliced, chopped, or crushed. Since allicin is destroyed by heat, garlic eaten for allicin's therapeutic effect should be raw. Other beneficial sulfur compounds do remain after cooking and offer their own therapeutic effect, but within a much narrower range and scope than allicin and its derivatives.

Raw garlic should generally be consumed with other food to avoid stomach distress. This is usually not an issue, since crushed raw garlic readily augments many cuisines. In the event that raw garlic is not a part of the day's food menu, it can still be conveniently ingested with a glass of milk, a spoon or two of yogurt, some peanut butter on a cracker, or the like.

A daily allicin dosage of 3.6 to 5.4 mg is sufficient to realize a significant therapeutic benefit. This roughly corresponds to 0.01 to 0.03 oz. (0.3 to 0.9 g) of properly processed garlic powder, or more to the point, 0.02 to 0.06 oz. (0.6 to 1.7 g) of fresh garlic (Pentz and Siegers 1996). German Commission E approves a dosage of 0.14 oz. (4 g) of fresh garlic per day. An "average" garlic clove weighs about 0.11 to 0.18 oz. (3 to 5 g), so the adage "A clove a day keeps the doctor away" is a good rule of thumb.

Of course, always consult your doctor before taking anything, including garlic, for therapeutic effect. Unless specifically prescribed by your doctor, garlic is not a substitute for prescription medications or clinical treatment.

Most people can consume relatively large quantities of cooked garlic without any notable side effects besides increased flatulence. However, if you are inclined to consume large quantities of raw garlic, seek concurrence from your doctor. Among other things, raw garlic is antithrombotic. If you are taking anticoagulant medication, raw garlic (and various other vegetables and fruits, for that matter) can create a serious imbalance and health risk.

## SIDE EFFECTS AND TOXICITY

For any substance as widely reaching and powerful as garlic and its constituents, it would be more than surprising if there were no potential side effects. Garlic breath is probably the most common and obvious. The strength and nature of garlic breath change over time. Allyl mercaptan is the primary sulfur compound in breath after fresh garlic is consumed, generally dissipating after an hour. Allyl mercaptan can also have a more enduring, though usually not very prominent, effect; after allicin and other sulfur compounds have been metabolized to allyl mercaptan in the bloodstream, allyl mercaptan is transported to the lungs and one's breath. Allyl methyl sulfide, diallyl disulfide, and diallyl sulfide decrease over several hours. Two terpenes, *d*-limonene and *p*-cymene, initially have a modest presence but increase rapidly after one to four hours.

Halitosis can be caused by gum disease, intestinal parasitic infections, and the like, but is mainly caused by food particles remaining in the mouth and interacting with aerobic and anaerobic bacteria. Mechanically removing residual food particles, including garlic, from one's mouth will ensure that bacteria-caused halitosis will not compromise and sully one's good garlic breath. Garlic breath is distinctive but not inherently offensive, being most noticeable to persons in garlic-impoverished subcultures and others who do not consume garlic. It is more prominent at something approximating intimate distance, another reason for choosing a compatible partner wisely. I do not know where the saying originated, but John Swenson, an icon in the world of garlic who is responsible for the introduction of more than 400 garlic cultivars into the United States, offers this advice: "If your friends are bothered by your garlic breath, get new friends."

Eating garlic, particularly in large quantities, can cause flatulence and indigestion. Cooked garlic can generally be consumed in rather large quantities without other deleterious effects. However, some restraint should be exercised in the consumption of raw garlic. In clinical studies, persons have consumed up to 0.5 oz. (14 g) of raw garlic per day, about three to five average cloves, with no reported side effects. Persons in Cangshan County of China's Shandong Province have a greatly decreased incidence of stomach cancer, but their consumption of an average of 0.7 oz. (20 g) of raw garlic per day, the equivalent of about four to five average cloves, is regarded by some as near the upper limit for raw garlic consumption (Koch 1996c). One clove of raw garlic per day is sufficient for therapeutic benefit. Raw garlic consumption can be increased as desired and as long as one's doctor concurs.

Raw garlic should be consumed with other food to avoid gastrointestinal distress. When ingested on an empty stomach it can irritate the mucous membrane and cause heartburn and stomach pain. Allicin and other thiosulfinates are believed to be the cause of the distress. Consuming large quantities of raw garlic can also cause diarrhea.

Although topical application of garlic can offer therapeutic benefit for burns and various skin disorders, it can also be an irritant that causes skin burn and dermatitis, particularly in young children. Although it is rare, some people are allergic to garlic and develop eczema after extensively handling.

Warfarin, an anticoagulant, has a very narrow therapeutic range. Because it interacts with other foods, including garlic, its dosage must be carefully monitored. As with other foods that interact with warfarin, raw garlic should be ingested with caution and only if one has the concurrence of one's doctor.

It should again be stressed that although garlic offers numerous therapeutic benefits, it is not a substitute for clinical medication or medical treatment. Do not self-medicate. Always seek your doctor's advice before taking anything, including garlic, for therapeutic effect.

## GARLIC SUPPLEMENTS VERSUS FRESH GARLIC

Properly processed garlic powder contains alliin and alliinase. Such powder does have the ability to produce allicin when hydrated. This can effectively take place in the kitchen or in one's mouth. However, if garlic powder is ingested in pill form, the pill must be encapsulated so that the coating dissolves in the intestine and not in the stomach. Unless one dramatically increases stomach pH by consuming a large, high-protein meal, such as a big steak dinner, the highly acidic environment of the stomach will immediately and irreversibly inactivate alliinase, and there will be no production of allicin. In order to preserve the ability to produce allicin, garlic tablets must have an effective enteric coating. A simple gelatin capsule will not withstand stomach acids.

A study (Lawson 1996) evaluating the effective allicin yield of 28 commercially available garlic tablets showed high variability. Seven of the 28 yielded no detectable allicin. Claims by the manufacturers regarding enteric coatings and allicin yield were not always accurate. Some tablets were very effective, others only minimally or moderately. Without standardized testing and labeling requirements, the reliability of over-the-counter tablet supplements generating and delivering allicin is something of a gamble.

Odor-reduced preparations can achieve results in a variety of ways, including methods that may still permit the creation and assimilation of allicin. However, truly odorless preparations almost assuredly prevent allicin creation or assimilation. Even if a supplement is effective in delaying allicin assimilation until allicin is released in the intestine, allyl mercaptan is still formed in the bloodstream and transported to the lungs and to one's breath. Allyl mercaptan is very odorous and is the primary sulfur compound in breath after fresh garlic is consumed. However, unless intestinally released garlic supplements are taken in large quantities, garlic breath from allicin assimilated in the intestine is at a level that is usually not noticeable.

Aged garlic extract has been particularly popular in Japan. The processes used in creation of the extract eliminate all of the thiosulfinates, including allicin. A relatively few sulfur compounds remain, constituting only a tenth of the total sulfur compounds found in fresh or cooked garlic. Although cooked garlic does not contain allicin, the far greater quantity of sulfur compounds in cooked garlic is likely to have substantially greater therapeutic benefit than the relatively modest amounts in aged garlic extract.

Garlic supplements vary widely in therapeutic benefit. Properly constructed supplements have adequate levels of alliin and alliinase and are encapsulated so that the alliin and alliinase combine in the intestine to produce allicin. Theoretically such supplements could produce a similar range and strength of therapeutic benefits as raw fresh garlic. However, without standardized testing, labeling criteria, and regulatory oversight, the true effectiveness of any given supplement is largely unknown. Eating raw, fresh garlic is cheaper and tastier, and its effects are more certain.

# ADDITIONAL READING

This book only lightly touches the topic of garlic's therapeutic effects. Many other books and informational resources cover the topic in greater scope and detail. A word of caution, however: Many studies and a number of books and informational materials have been funded by garlic supplement manufacturers. Some of these publications offer heavily biased coverage that emphasizes the merit of the manufacturer's product or method while minimizing, dismissing, or ignoring altogether the deficiencies of the supplement relative to fresh garlic or more effective supplements. Garlic supplements can be therapeutically effective, but on the matter of garlic supplements versus fresh garlic, let both buyer and reader beware.

For the general reader, *Garlic: Nature's Original Remedy* by Stephen Fulder and John Blackwood (2000) is easily accessible and contains generally accurate and unbiased information. Although out of print, *Garlic: The Science and Therapeutic Application of* Allium sativum *L. and Related Species*, edited by Heinrich Koch and Larry Lawson (1996), is a benchmark work on the topic. It includes an exhaustive review of the world's known scientific literature, covering the composition, chemistry, and therapeutic effects of garlic and its constituents. More than 2000 references are cited and summarized. Some of it is highly technical and would be difficult reading for nonscientists, but it makes an exhaustively thorough and unassailable case for garlic's wide-ranging therapeutic benefits. Much of the information on the therapeutic benefits of garlic in this book was drawn from this classic work.

# ❧ FIVE ❧

# Structure and Function

ALLIUM SATIVUM, true garlic, shares many common structural elements with the rest of the genus *Allium*. Nearly all alliums are herbaceous perennials. A few form thickened rhizomes. Most form bulbs that vary in prominence among the species. All alliums have foliage leaves that attach to an underground stem, though they may have long sheaths that form what looks like an aboveground stem from which the leaf blades appear to emanate. Inflorescence (flower cluster) stems have no leaves except those that form part of the inflorescence itself in the form of bracts. The perianth consists of six petal-like segments, and there are six anther-bearing stamens. The inflorescence is an umbel, with the individual flower stalks arising from a common point. In the bud stage, a single spathe (bract) surrounds the umbel. As with many taxonomic differentiations, complete distinction may only be evident in covert structures or at the molecular level, but the characteristics above are generally sufficiently defining for the gardener. A few related genera may share these characteristics, but they are uncommon, or unknown in cultivation, and consist of only a few species (Jones and Mann 1963). Some plants other than alliums have an alliaceous smell. Conversely, not all alliums have a strong alliaceous smell and taste. Nonetheless, the pronounced alliaceous smell and taste are generally characteristic of the genus, and in field identification of alliums, crushing a portion of a plant to release its odor is a common first step in assessing identity.

The seven *Allium* species that are commonly cultivated for food are quite distinctive from each other, without intergrading forms. They are *A. ampeloprasum*, which includes leek, kurrat, and elephant garlic; *A. cepa*, which includes the common onion as well as the potato or multiplier onion, shallot, and ever-ready onion; *A. chinense*, rakkyo, which is commonly pickled in Japan; *A. fistulosum*, which includes the Japanese bunching or Welsh onion; *A. sativum*, garlic; *A. schoenoprasum*, the widely distributed chive; and *A. tuberosum*, garlic chive. Some of these species have different groups

leaf                    scape

garlic
*Allium sativum*

elephant garlic
*Allium ampeloprasum*

common onion
*Allium cepa*

Japanese bunching onion
*Allium fistulosum*

chive
*Allium schoenoprasum*

garlic chive
*Allium tuberosum*

rakkyo
*Allium chinense*

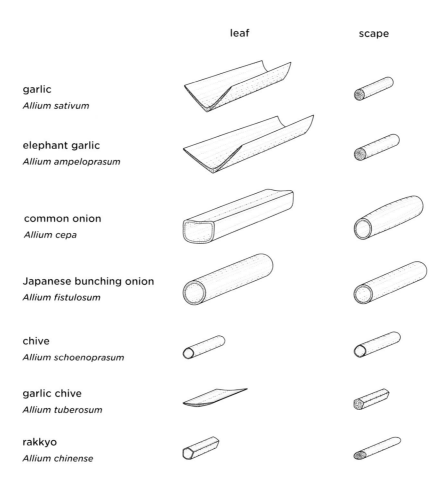

Figure 1. Leaf and scape cross sections of common food alliums. Sizes are not to scale.

of plants that differ considerably from those in other groups, such as leek and elephant garlic, but they all share the common species characteristics.

*Allium cepa, A. fistulosum,* and *A. schoenoprasum* have both hollow foliage leaf blades and hollow scapes (inflorescence stems). *Allium chinense* has hollow foliage leaf blades but a solid scape. *Allium tuberosum* has a solid scape and solid foliage leaves that are very shallowly U-shaped in cross section. *Allium sativum* and *A. ampeloprasum* both have solid scapes and solid foliage leaves that are V-shaped in cross section. In general appearance, elephant garlic, which belongs to *A. ampeloprasum,* resembles true garlic, *A. sativum.* (The morphological differences between elephant garlic and true garlic are described in chapter 10 under "Other Garliclike Alliums.") Now that we have an overview of the genus, let us examine the structural elements and their function in more detail and explore some of the features unique to garlic.

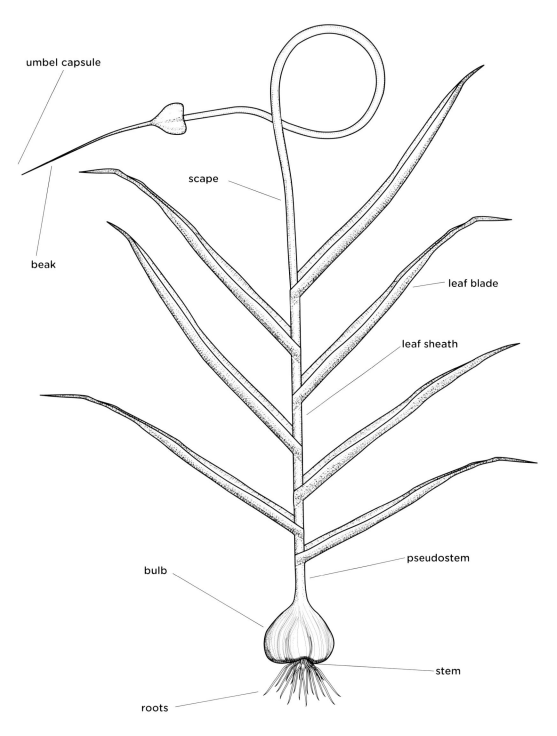

umbel capsule

beak

scape

leaf blade

leaf sheath

pseudostem

bulb

stem

roots

Figure 2. The parts of a garlic plant.

(above) The base of the bulb on the left shows the old roots connected to the flat underground stem. The cloves are initiating new roots, which are bursting through the bulb skins. On the right, new roots emerge from a clove's basal plate—the new stem for a new garlic plant.

(left) A garlic plant's pseudostem.

On the left, the broad leaves of a vigorous Porcelain plant. On the right, the narrow leaves of a Purple Stripe plant.

## VEGETATIVE STRUCTURES

### Stem

The stems of all alliums, including garlic, are underground structures. The stem is the flat plate at the base of the bulb. Both roots and leaves initiate from the stem. As new roots and leaves form, the stem expands radially to accommodate the new growth. The stem of a mature bulb eventually dies, but living basal plates remain on each clove to carry on future growth, forming a new stem for the new plant.

### Pseudostem

What appears to be an aboveground stem is actually the tightly wrapped, overlapping, long, sheathing bases of the leaves. This structure has the look of a stem and is sometimes called the pseudostem. The thick "stalk" of the leek is perhaps the most exaggerated and familiar illustration of the pseudostem, though the structure is very prominent in garlic as well.

### Leaves

Garlic leaves are sessile—they have no stalk. What we typically think of as a garlic leaf is actually the blade part of a foliage leaf. All garlic leaves originate underground, emerging from the shoot apex of the plant's underground stem. The shoot apex is at the top center of the stem plate. The sprout leaf initiates first and is the first leaf to penetrate the soil. The sprout leaf is bladeless and makes way for the bladed leaves that follow. Except for the sprout leaf, each leaf consists of a sheath and a blade.

The leaf sheaths encircle the shoot apex. As the garlic grows, the sheaths form a tube comprised of tightly wrapped sheaths through which new leaves emerge. This tube, projecting above ground, has the look of a stem. It is not a true stem, however, but a pseudostem comprised of leaf sheaths. Each new leaf grows through the center of the pseudostem and emerges higher on the plant, its own sheath contributing to the structure of the pseudostem and extending the pseudostem's height. At the juncture of the blade and the sheath is a small opening where the newest leaf emerges. The leaf blades are arrayed in two ranks, 180° apart, on alternating sides of the pseudostem. Garlic leaf blades are long, solid, and longitudinally folded. In cross section they form a V shape. Of the common food alliums, only *Allium ampeloprasum*, which includes leek and elephant garlic, has a leaf shape similar to garlic.

The number of leaves and their length and width varies among horticultural groups and among cultivars. Growing conditions also play a role. In a series of trials, cultivars grown in a warmer growing region produced more leaves than the same cultivars grown in a cooler region. The leaves of plants grown in the warmer region were also wider and longer.

As discussed in chapter 2, because garlic leaves are narrow and the plant's foliage canopy is relatively sparse, garlic does not compete well with fast-growing leafy weeds. A garlic plant typically has fewer than a dozen leaves, so the loss of even one leaf rep-

resents a significant reduction in the plant's foliage canopy and photosynthetic engine. The impact of losing just a single leaf was demonstrated in a study by John Zandstra and Robert Squire (2000). The study simulated the effect of accidental leaf removal when scapes are removed by mechanical means. For the study, leaves were selectively removed relatively late in the season at the time of scape removal. Removal of only one leaf decreased average bulb size by 13% and overall yield by 17.5%. Removal of additional leaves caused similar corresponding decreases in bulb size and yield. Loss of photosynthetic function by even a single leaf blade as a result of removal, death, or shading significantly impacts the plant's productivity.

## Roots

Like the root systems of most alliums, garlic roots are relatively thick, with little ramification, and generally lack root hairs. The roots are mostly adventitious and arise from all sides of the garlic bulb's flat underground stem. Some of the roots may grow nearly horizontally for a time before turning downward. In botanical literature it is often stated that the garlic root system, like the root systems of all alliums, is neither deep nor extensive. While this may be true in a relative sense, such a statement can be misleading. For example, in one field study, mature garlic plants had between 40 and 60 roots each, which extended up to 18 in. (45 cm) from the bulb and grew to a depth of up to 30 in. (75 cm). Most of the roots are in the top 24 in. (60 cm) of soil. In my own garden the spread and depth are less than cited here, but nonetheless

The roots from a garlic bulb left in the ground. The cloves are generating their own root systems from their basal plates and are beginning to sprout.

the root system can extend considerably beyond the width of the bulb. If plant spacing is too compressed, the plant may suffer in vigor if it encounters too much competition with the root systems of adjacent plants. In theory one might choose to space the plants 36 in. (90 cm) apart in all directions to avoid any competition from other plants. In practice, however, the plants retain vigor when planted considerably more densely.

Garlic roots are rather inefficient and poorly adapted for nutrient uptake, particularly when it comes to nutrients such as phosphate that are present in low concentrations in the soil and do not transfer readily from plant to soil. The roots are also poorly equipped for micronutrient uptake. How does the garlic plant get away with such a problematic root system in such adverse native growing conditions? Allium roots, including those of garlic, are readily colonized by mycorrhizal fungi. These fungi have a symbiotic relationship with garlic. Their mycelia increase the absorption area of the root system and enhance its ability to take up nutrients, particularly in difficult soils where nutrients are scarce. The mycelia compensate for the lack of extensive ramification and root hairs in garlic's root system. The root systems of wild alliums, including garlic, likely have evolved as they did because of the presence of these beneficial mycorrhizal fungi. The cooperating fungi turn an otherwise inadequate root system into one that is efficient and well matched to environmental conditions.

The stems of most bulbing plants grow upward and after several years would ease the plant out of the soil if it were not for contractile roots pulling the plant downward. Contractile roots in alliums are active or absent in varying degrees. They are generally inactive in the common onion, *Allium cepa*, but are active and effective in leek and garlic. Since cultivated garlic is dug up each year, the activity of the contractile roots is not particularly evident. In the wild, however, contractile roots play a significant role in long-term survival, particularly in the harsh conditions of garlic's native environment.

The optimal temperature for root emergence and development is likely partially dependent on the cultivar, but in one study the optimal temperature for root emergence from dormant cloves was 59°F (15°C). Rooting was significantly delayed at temperatures higher than 68°F (20°C) and lower than 50°F (10°C). If conditions were optimal, root emergence began in only a few days. The study showed that after emergence, roots elongated more rapidly at increasingly higher temperatures within a range of 32°F (0°C) to 77°F (25°C). Within a temperature range of 59°F to 68°F, new roots emerged in increasing numbers. They emerged in lower numbers at temperatures higher or lower than that range. For the development of the root system as a whole, including the development of new roots and the elongation of existing roots, 68°F proved to be the optimal temperature.

## Bulb

Many food alliums are harvested as fresh shoots for immediate consumption or short-term storage. These include green onions, leeks, chives, and garlic chives. Other food alliums are harvested for their bulbs, which can be stored and consumed over a longer period. Bulbing alliums are the most economically important as a food source—and arguably the most important from a culinary standpoint, particularly if one is a devotee of garlic. The bulbing alliums commercially harvested as food crops include onions, shallots, rakkyo, and garlic.

Allium bulbs are designed for long storage, though this can mean anything from a month or so to more than a year. Bulbs are a survival strategy arising from the need for the plant to become

(above) A bulb of 'Machashi'.

(right) The cloves removed from this bulb reveal the abscission layers on the bulb's stem plate.

(below) On the left, a small garlic bulb with differentiated cloves. On the right, an undifferentiated bulb, called a round. This round is unusually large. Most rounds are roughly the size of a clove or smaller.

(top photo) On the left, the exposed cloves of the Silverskin cultivar 'Silver White'. On the right, the Artichoke cultivar 'California Early'.

dormant when conditions are unfavorable for sustained growth. They are storage organs that sustain the plant's growth potential and store energy reserves necessary for subsequent resumption of active growth.

Many allium bulbs are formed from swollen leaf sheaths. This characteristic trait is expressed differently in different species. In rakkyo, *Allium chinense*, the swollen leaf sheaths are formed exclusively at the base of the leaf blades. In the common onion, *A. cepa*, the outer swollen leaf sheaths are formed at the base of the leaf blades, but the inner swollen sheaths are formed from bladeless storage leaves called bulb scales. Garlic bulbs are formed in another way. A garlic bulb is comprised exclusively of bladeless storage leaves, the bulb scales, more

commonly called cloves. The sheaths encasing garlic cloves do not themselves swell, but instead dry to form a papery or hardened encasement for the clove. Of the common food alliums, the garlic bulb is the most complex.

When a garlic plant is mature and fully ripened, the leaves, stem, and roots all die. Only the bulb remains to carry on the plant into the next season of growth. The cloves are isolated from the dying or deceased portion of the plant by an abscission layer. The dead leaves and stem remain to form the bulb's protective surround. What we colloquially call garlic skin or bulb wrappers are the dried protective leaf sheaths that remain. Because the garlic bulb is comprised of a number of easily separated cloves, garlic readily lends itself to vegetative propagation. This is fortunate, since seed propagation with all known cultivars is either impossible or requires special measures.

Garlic grown from small cloves or from bulbils may only have the capacity to develop into a bulb consisting of a single clove, called a round. Its name accurately describes its shape. Unlike a clove from a multicloved bulb, the round itself is also encased by leaf sheaths, offering additional protection from damage or desiccation, and the prospect of longer storage.

## Clove

A garlic clove is a complex structure that contains nascent elements of a mature bulb. Most garlic is vegetatively propagated by separating the cloves in the bulb and then individually planting the cloves. At maturity, in a normal growth cycle, a planted clove will develop into a multicloved bulb with cloves similar in size to the single clove that was planted. Broadly speaking, the cloves in the bulb of a bolting garlic cultivar tend to be similar in size, while the cloves in the bulb of a nonbolting cultivar may vary widely in size. Often, though not always, the innermost cloves are the smallest.

The clove is comprised of several different kinds of leaves or leaf primordia, though none are particularly what we think of as leaves. A tough, papery, sometimes hardened protective leaf forms the clove skin that protects the clove from damage, disease, and desiccation. The swollen storage leaf comprises the bulk of the clove and contains 30% to 40% dry matter (Brewster 1994). A sprout leaf and several foliage leaf primordia are at the heart of the clove. The foliage leaf primordia have nascent, though clearly defined leaf blades. The protective leaf, storage leaf, and sprout leaf have only vestigial leaf blades. During storage, additional foliage leaf primordia become differentiated. When the clove

sprouts, the sprout leaf elongates and emerges from a pore at the tip of the storage leaf. Next, the first of the foliage leaves elongates and emerges from the storage leaf's pore, adjacent to the sprout leaf. During the development of a clove, the protective leaf forms first, sheathing and protecting the soft tissues of the storage leaf.

Let us examine the formation of a clove in more detail. First, lateral bud primordia are formed in the axils of the foliage leaves. Typically this occurs in the youngest foliage leaves, though unfavorable conditions may cause the lateral bud primordia to initiate in the axils of older foliage leaves, creating "rough" bulbs. (The conditions that cause the formation of rough bulbs are discussed in more detail under "Bulb Formation" later in this chapter.) Each of the bud primordia in the axils of the foliage leaves then form between two and six growing points, each developing into a lateral bud, which will later develop into a clove. Temperature and increasing day length are the primary triggers for development of the clove. Although the exact triggering criteria for clove development varies among garlic strains, Hideaki Takagi (1990) indicates that when air temperatures reach approximately 50°F (10°C), the growing points begin to form leaf initials. As air temperatures continue to rise, the lateral buds successively initiate leaves. Under normal conditions development and growth of the cloves occurs rapidly and vigorously.

The first and second leaves of each lateral bud develop uniquely. The first leaf eventually becomes what we call the skin, the thick, dry protective wrapper surrounding the clove. The second leaf eventually becomes the main storage leaf—the preponderance of what we consider the flesh of the clove. When the second leaf, the storage leaf, begins to thicken and swell, the first leaf, the wrapper, stops thickening but continues to grow to enclose the second leaf. The warming and longer

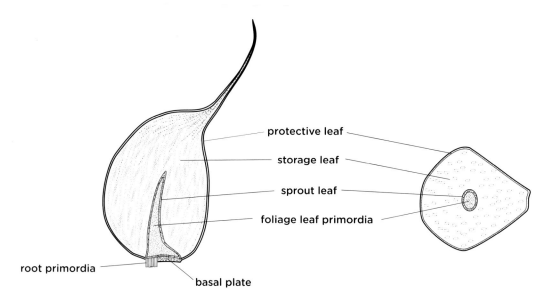

Figure 3. Anatomy of a clove—longitudinal and latitudinal cross sections.

days of spring cause the second leaf to swell rapidly, forming the bulk of the clove's flesh. The first leaf stops growing about two weeks before all of the plant's foliage leaves have senesced, and begins to develop into the dry protective wrapper that we see surrounding each clove when we break open a head of garlic. In some garlic strains the second leaf also develops into a dry protective wrapper, leaving the third leaf to form the main storage leaf. For most strains, however, the second leaf forms the main storage leaf, and the third leaf remains mostly undeveloped until the clove sprouts. Additional leaves are initiated but become dormant and well enclosed within the storage leaf until the clove sprouts.

Unusual conditions may alter the role of the clove leaves. If provided with sufficient cold and 24-hour light exposure, garlic may form a storage leaf from the first leaf initial on the lateral bud, thus forming a clove with no protective skin. Conversely, if plants are exposed to low temperatures followed by short days during bulb formation, several foliage leaves may be generated on a lateral bud, causing the storage leaf to form from the third leaf or sometimes even a subsequent leaf, thus creating several protective wrappers surrounding the storage leaf.

If a temperate-climate cultivar is exposed to neither low temperatures nor long days, the leaf primordia may develop only into foliage leaves and the plant may form neither the flowering structures nor the storage leaves (Takagi 1990). This is why some cold-climate garlic cultivars, without the benefit of special treatment, will either fail to form a bulb at all or else will form a small, weak bulb.

According to Hideaki Takagi (1990), bolting and nonbolting strains differ slightly in how the cloves and bulb are formed. He describes two variations, although one might readily conclude that there are more. For the Japanese bolting strains that Takagi examined, the lateral bud primordia are typically initiated in the axils of two, or some-

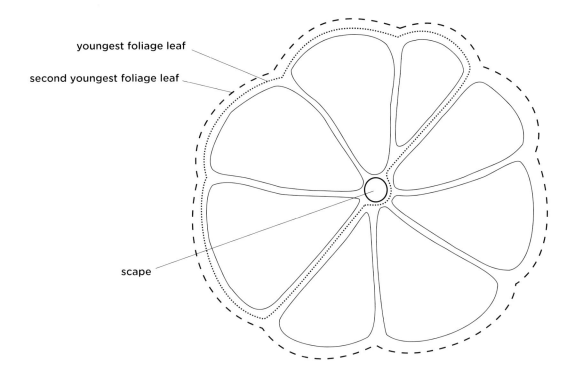

youngest foliage leaf

second youngest foliage leaf

scape

Figure 4. In this cross section of a Purple Stripe bulb, cloves are formed in the axils of the two youngest foliage leaves. The second youngest foliage leaf encircles the entire bulb and constitutes the innermost complete bulb wrapper.

times three, foliage leaves. Citing his observation of a nonbolting strain that he calls "California," Takagi observes that the lateral bud primordia formed in the axils of the youngest six to eight foliage leaves, rather than in the youngest two to three foliage leaves as had been observed in the bolting strains. In the same article, Takagi later offers that nonbolting strains form cloves in the axils of the youngest five or more foliage leaves, and he describes a third category of "incomplete bolting" strains, which form cloves in the axils of the youngest three or more foliage leaves. It should be noted that some of the nonbolting strains that Takagi describes do routinely bolt under certain growing conditions. Nonetheless, the clove formation characteristics

that Takagi describes still apply. Figure 5 shows a Silverskin cultivar with a scape, indicating that the plant has bolted. Under some growing conditions Silverskins almost always bolt, while under other growing conditions they almost never do.

From a practical standpoint, what does this all look like? As depicted in figure 4, strongly bolting cultivars, such as those from the Purple Stripe, Rocambole, and Porcelain groups, typically have cloves arrayed in a single layer. As you peel away the wrapper (dried foliage leaves) from the bulb, you come to a point where approximately half of the cloves are exposed. The remaining portion, on the opposing side of the bulb, will still be sheathed by a single foliage leaf. The cloves that are exposed

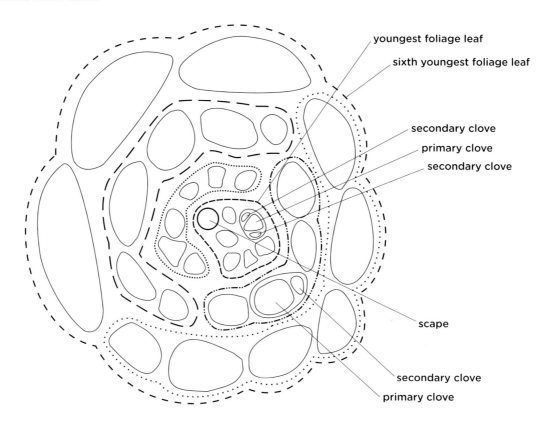

youngest foliage leaf

sixth youngest foliage leaf

secondary clove

primary clove

secondary clove

scape

secondary clove

primary clove

Figure 5. In this cross section of a Silverskin bulb, cloves are formed in the axils of the six youngest foliage leaves. The sixth youngest foliage leaf encircles the entire bulb and constitutes the innermost complete bulb wrapper. Two cloves have generated axillary buds that have formed smaller secondary cloves.

were formed in the axil of the foliage leaf that you last removed. The cloves on the other side of the bulb remain sheathed by the other foliage leaf that formed cloves in its axil. These illustrate the formation of cloves in two leaf axils, typical of a strongly bolting cultivar. If, on the other hand, you remove the wrapper of a Silverskin cultivar, as depicted in figure 5, you will see cloves arrayed in multiple layers, each layer separately encased in its own wrapper. Each wrapper is a foliage leaf and the cloves within were generated from that leaf's axil.

We have discussed how bud primordia form in the axil of a foliage leaf and lateral bud primordia form additional cloves within the same leaf axil.

Although for most cultivars, a lateral bud forms only one clove, lateral buds in some cultivars can form two or more cloves. When this occurs, secondary buds form in the axils of some of the first leaves of the primary lateral buds, forming their own storage leaves (cloves). This creates clusters of small cloves (figure 5). Some garlic strains rarely, if ever, produce secondary cloves, while other strains produce numerous clusters of small secondary cloves. Secondary cloves are produced in varying degrees among the many garlic strains and are part of a strain's distinguishing characteristics. Some Silverskin cultivars have this propensity, producing numerous tiny cloves within the inner clove layers.

The scapes on these two 'Kitab' plants were previously severed. Secondary leaves and scapes are emerging from lateral buds in the leaf axil.

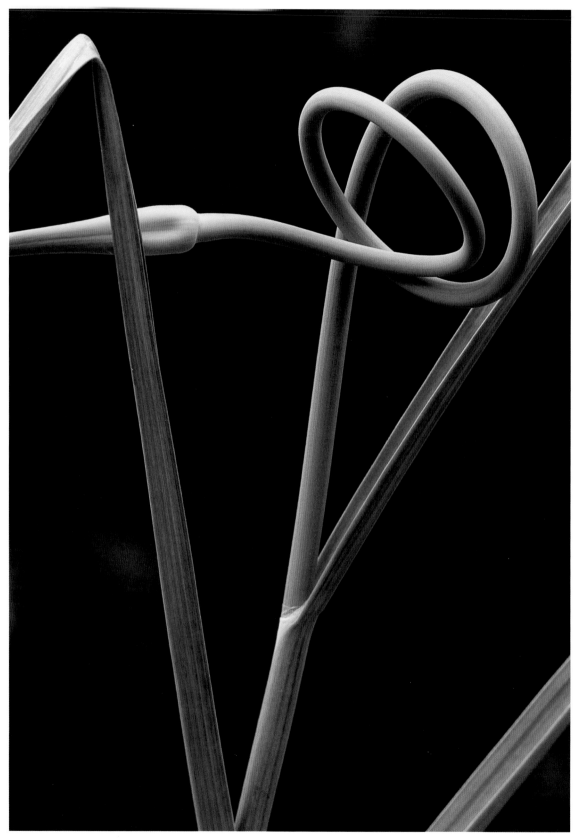

A Purple Stripe cultivar's dramatically coiled scape.

1. A scape of the Rocambole cultivar 'Killarney Red' emerges from the top of the pseudostem.

2. The scape begins its curl downward.

3. The scape coils.

4. As the scape uncoils, the lower, more lignified portion straightens and becomes erect. The spathe continues to change color from yellowish to white.

5. The uncoiling and straightening is nearing completion, and the characteristic white coloration and lumpy shape of a maturing Rocambole umbel capsule are evident.

The leaves on these Porcelain cultivars have withered, but the scapes have hoisted the umbels some 7 ft. (2.1 m) above the ground.

Lateral buds do not normally produce leaf blades at the time of clove formation. However, if growing conditions such as short days and heavy nitrogen application inhibit normal clove development for one or more months starting a few weeks before lateral bud formation, the lateral buds may produce leaf blades that extend from the leaf axils of the plant's foliage leaves. In extreme cases the lateral bud may even form its own small cloves and may bolt, acting like a plant within a plant (Takagi 1990). Some cultivars have a greater propensity for this behavior.

# REPRODUCTIVE STRUCTURES

As first mentioned in chapter 1, garlic cultivars that have lost their ability to bolt and produce flowering structures are commonly called softnecks by garlic enthusiasts. The name describes the absence of a woody stalk. Garlic cultivars that bolt are called hardnecks because of the presence of a solid scape that rises through the center of the bulb, forming the bulb's hard neck. Bolting garlic is also commonly called topset garlic or topsetting garlic, referring to the inflorescence, which contains bulbils as well as flowers. Most commercial garlic cultivars are of the nonbolting softneck type. Under certain conditions, some of these softneck cultivars may partially bolt and generate incomplete or vestigial reproductive structures, typically the formation of bulbils in the pseudostem. Some garlic cultivars always bolt unless prohibited by unusual growing conditions. Others routinely bolt but only under certain conditions.

Since the only garlic cultivars that we routinely encounter are the commercial nonbolting type, the existence of garlic's reproductive structures may be somewhat of a surprise, but there are many more unique bolting cultivars than there are nonbolting cultivars. Bolting cultivars include a wide range of garlic types that are collectively much more genetically diverse than nonbolting cultivars. Fully developed flowering structures are common in wild garlic. The garlics in the Purple Stripe group are the most primal ancestral strains. They are strongly bolting and have fully developed reproductive structures. Some of these strains have retained the ability to produce true seed, though human intervention and special procedures are generally required for success.

## Scape

The scape is the flower stalk. It is an apical extension of the underground stem, the flat plate at the base of the bulb. The scapes of common food alliums may be hollow or solid and are round, oblong, or flat-sided. Garlic scapes are always smooth, round, and solid throughout their entire length. The scape has no leaves except for a spathe. Informally, garlic growers sometimes collectively refer to the flower stalk and umbel capsule as the scape.

Although nonbolting softneck cultivars do not typically produce scapes, they may occasionally do so under certain conditions. Partial bolting may also occur in some typically nonbolting softneck cultivars. When this occurs, the plant generates a shortened scape and an inflorescence or partial inflorescence and bulbils within the bulb, or outside of the bulb but within the pseudostem. The partially bolting scape never extends beyond the pseudostem. Strongly bolting cultivars routinely produce fully formed flowering structures and fully extended scapes, exserted well beyond the pseudostem.

Scapes grow erect, bend or coil, and then unbend or uncoil and grow erect and taller. The coiling is caused by irregular elongation of the cells, which first occurs on only one side of the scape. As the scape starts to coil it also begins to lignify. As mentioned in chapter 3, if scapes are to be used for eating, they are best when harvested before coiling begins, although they are still good to eat after they coil downward. As scapes continue to coil and uncoil, they become increasingly lignified and less desirable for the table.

The degree of bending or coiling varies among horticultural groups. Rocambole scapes, for example, sometimes complete as many as three tight curls before straightening and becoming erect. Asiatic scapes bend downward but do not coil, subse-

The Porcelain cultivar 'Blazer'. The scapes and long-beaked spathes are evocative of the heads and beaks of graceful long-necked birds.

The spathe on the cultivar 'Blanak' has split, revealing the inflorescence and bulbils.

A small red spider nestles at the base of an umbel capsule.

An umbel capsule of the Asiatic cultivar 'Pyongyang', showing the characteristic broad, hollowed base of the beak.

An umbel capsule of the Porcelain cultivar 'Music'. Its beak has begun to wither, and the spathe will soon split to reveal the umbel's flowers and bulbils.

An umbel of the Porcelain cultivar 'Polish Hardneck', densely packed with flowers and bulbils.

quently becoming only semierect. Porcelain scapes are thick and sturdy, first forming a pronounced coil and then becoming steadfastly erect, sometimes reaching a height of up to 7 ft. (2.1 m) or so.

## Spathe

The spathe is the leaf, or bract, that encases the umbel during growth. When ripe, the spathe usually splits on one side, revealing the inflorescence and bulbils. After splitting, it gradually drops away from the umbel but remains attached to its base. The spathe has a long beak. As the scapes curl and uncurl, the long-beaked spathes can be a dramatic sight. The shape and coloration of the spathe are distinguishing characteristics among horticultural groups. Porcelain cultivars, for example, have yellowish white spathes with relatively long beaks. Rocambole cultivars have short beaks and spathes that turn from yellowish white to white near maturity.

## Umbel capsule

"Umbel capsule" is an informal term that refers to the immature umbel sheathed by the spathe. The shape and coloration of the umbel capsule are distinctive and distinguishing characteristics among

Two umbels of the Marbled Purple Stripe cultivar 'Siberian'. Bulbils have been removed from the umbel on the right, more clearly showing the individual flowers on their pedicels.

garlic groups and cultivars. The Turban group, for example, takes its name from the shape of the umbel capsule, which is evocative of a turban. Asiatic cultivars are readily identified by a distinctive umbel capsule that extends into a broad and hollow portion of the base of the beak area.

## Umbel

The inflorescence of garlic and of all alliums is the umbel. It is comprised of small individual flowers on their own flower stalks, called pedicels, which arise from a common point. The pedicels of some species vary in length, creating a flat-topped flower cluster. Garlic pedicels are similar in length and form a globe. Except for new genetic crossings, bulbils are also always present in garlic inflorescences.

Garlic flowers.

(above) The yellow anthers; style; knobbed, slightly broadened stigma; and swollen, three-chambered ovary of 'Killarney Red' are visible in this close-up.

(left) Flowers from the Asiatic cultivar 'Asian Tempest'. Asiatics are not known seed producers. Yellow anthers are usually, but not always, associated with infertility.

The continuing presence of bulbils has caused the flowers to wither on this plant of the Porcelain cultivar 'Romanian Red'.

This plant of the Artichoke cultivar 'Kettle River Giant' has partially bolted, and the bulbils have burst through the pseudostem.

## Flowers

Garlic flowers are smaller than those of the onion. Bulbils are generally heavily interspersed among the flowers, sometimes dominating the umbel. Some alliums have a relatively fixed number of flowers. *Allium schoenoprasum* (chive), for example, has approximately 30 flowers per umbel. For the garlic cultivars that are capable of generating inflorescences, the number of flowers per umbel varies widely, from some half dozen to several hundred. The number of flowers varies among horticultural groups as well. Asiatics have only a few, while Porcelains may have hundreds. Cultivars with fewer flowers typically have fewer but larger bulbils.

Each flower has six petals. Flower color may be white, off-white, pink, and purple. Other alliums may have flowers that are blue or yellow.

When mature, the opposing petals of most garlic flowers form a 45° angle, though flowers of some plants produced from true seed may have petals that are nearly closed. All allium flowers have six perianth segments (sepals and petals) arranged in two whorls of three, and six stamens, also arranged in two whorls of three. Each garlic ovary has a style with a knobbed stigma that is blunted at the top and only slightly broadened. The anther is positioned dorsally. The ovaries have three chambers. Each ovary chamber contains two ovules, thus a maximum of six seeds per flower is possible.

Purple anthers are strongly associated with garlic fertility and the ability to produce true seed. The association is not absolute, however. Not all garlic cultivars with purple anthers can produce

This plant of the Rocambole cultivar 'Russian Red' is exhibiting an occasional behavior pattern. A bulbil shoot initiates from the umbel and generates a bulbil of its own. Most of the bulbils were removed from the umbel, perhaps encouraging this response.

true seed, and a few cultivars with yellow anthers are also able to produce true seed. Garlic that has been grown from seed may have lilac or light gray anthers.

The anthers of garlic flowers release their pollen two to four days before the stigma of the same flower is receptive. Once receptive, the stigma remains so for one to two days (Simon and Jenderek 2003). In a garlic inflorescence, anthesis occurs over a period of 5 to 20 days, so there is potentially an extended period when individual flowers are able to provide viable pollen to other receptive flowers in the inflorescence.

The garlic plant preferentially directs its energy to the bulbils rather than the flowers. As the bulbils develop, the flowers typically wither before

anthesis can occur. Removing the bulbils permits the flowers to achieve anthesis in some instances, a technique that is artificially employed in the production of true garlic seed. See "Garlic from Seed" in chapter 6 for more information.

## Bulbils

Bulbils look like tiny cloves or bulbs. They are found in many lilies and many alliums. Except for new genetic crossings, bulbils are always present in garlic umbels. They compete with the flowers for the plant's energies, causing the flowers to wither much more quickly. Bulbils are sometimes present in nominally nonbolting softneck cultivars that have partially bolted. Depending on the degree of

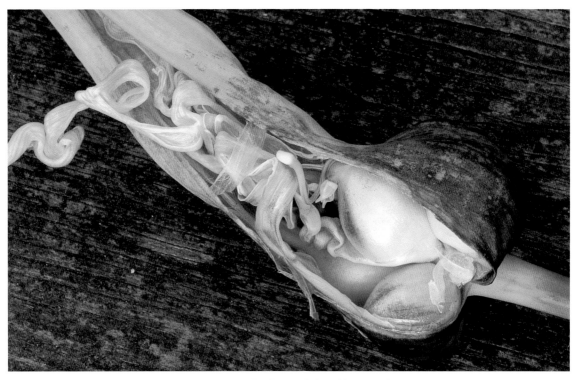

The elongated bulbil sheath leaves in the umbel capsule of the Asiatic cultivar 'Wonha'.

A 'Wonha' bulbil, showing its prominently elongated sheath leaf.

A bulbil's size, color, and shape are indicative of a cultivar's horticultural group. From left to right, these bulbils are from 'Russian Redstreak', an Asiatic; 'Spanish Roja', a Rocambole; and 'Romanian Red', a Porcelain.

bolting, the bulbils may appear within the bulb, outside of the bulb encased in the plant's pseud-ostem, or sometimes bursting through it.

Bulbils are somewhat unusual structures. They are essentially compressed lateral shoots comprised of a short shoot and two fleshy storage leaves encapsulated by a sheath (Hahn 1996a). Occasionally, shoots initiate even when still connected to the umbel. The sheath leaf may also extensively elongate. The sheath elongation is quite pronounced in some cultivars, particularly among some in the Asiatic group, where the shooting sheath tip may extend and coil for many inches within the hollow beak of the umbel.

Bulbil size and shape vary among horticultural groups and cultivars, ranging from something close to a grain of rice to a small marble. Coloration also varies from white to tan, brown, pink, red, reddish purple, and deep dark purple. In some cultivars,

such as those from the Asiatic group, the bulbils dominate the umbel to the near exclusion of the flowers. In other cultivars, such as Purple Stripes, the flowers and bulbils are equally numerous. Cultivars in the Porcelain group may have hundreds of tiny bulbils. At the other end of the spectrum, Asiatic cultivars may have as few as two to four huge bulbils per umbel.

Bulbils are asexual propagules. They can be planted in the ground like garlic cloves and will eventually grow into a fully differentiated bulb, though this may require several seasons of growth. The bulbils of some cultivars, such as Asiatics, are very large and are capable of producing a fully differentiated garlic bulb in one season if conditions are amenable. Most bulbils are smaller and require two or more years of growth before generating a fully differentiated multicloved bulb. The first year or so of growth typically yields an undifferentiated round. The bulbils from the Porcelain group are particularly tiny and may require three or more seasons of growth to produce a fully differentiated bulb.

## Seed

In the vernacular of garlic growers, cloves for planting are sometimes called seed, but this is a misnomer. For the sake of precision, except when otherwise specified, in this book the word "seed" always refers to true seed from sexual reproduction, not garlic cloves for planting.

Until the 1980s, garlic, *Allium sativum*, was generally thought to have lost its ability to produce seed through sexual reproduction. In 1875 Eduard Regel described the unique flowering characteristics of wild garlic, declaring a new species, *A. longicuspis*, and raising the prospect that wild garlic might still be capable of producing true seed. Molecular evidence now shows that all garlic, including the garlic that Regel described, belongs to the same species. Nonetheless, some garlic strains, notably some associated with the Purple Stripe group, have retained the ability to produce seed, though special procedures are generally required to make this possible.

As early as the 1950s, research groups within the former Soviet Union reported limited success in producing a few seeds from garlic strains originating in Central Asia (Simon 2000). Applying controlled methodologies, groups conducting subsequent experiments in Japan, Germany, and the United States have produced viable garlic seed, and it is now feasible for researchers and commercial enterprises to produce seed in quantities sufficient for plant breeding, experimentation, and the development of new virus-free cultivars. See "Garlic from Seed" in chapter 6 for more information.

All allium seeds have a thick black coat. Garlic seeds look like onion seeds but are approximately half the size. They have a dormancy period that can be shortened by exposure to cold. This appears to be an adaptive response to garlic's native origins. If seeds were to sprout just prior to the onset of a Central Asian winter, their chances of survival would be greatly reduced.

In some experiments, seed from garlic that had previously only been propagated vegetatively yielded a high ratio of nonviable, undersized seeds, and low germination rates ranging from 10% to 35%. Some seeds did not germinate until a full year after planting. Subsequent generations of seeds from plants that were produced from seed yielded many more seeds per plant, and seeds were larger and germinated more reliably, sometimes achieving up to 100% germination success.

## FLOWER INDUCTION AND BULB FORMATION

In this section we will examine the conditions that cause the bulb and reproductive structures to begin forming, and the conditions that cause the differentiation of the bulb into cloves. Grouping the development of the vegetative storage organ (bulb formation) with initiation of the reproductive structures (flower induction) may seem a bit odd, but the two processes are closely related and interdependent.

The relationship is complex. Bulbing is dependent upon flower induction, but the development of the bulbs and the development of the flowering structures competitively limit each other. Environmental conditions, the timing of exposure to these conditions, and the characteristics of the individual garlic cultivars are also major factors in the development of the flowering structures and bulbs.

Nonbolting softneck cultivars, especially those originating from warmer climates nearer the equator, have no overt flowering structures. Seemingly, they would be uninfluenced by flower induction, yet studies show that some preliminary elements of flower induction still likely take place.

For garlic cultivars that bolt, flower induction must begin before storage-leaf (clove) differentiation occurs in order to generate normal bulbs with multiple cloves. Why is this? Inflorescence initiation breaks the apical dominance of the plant and permits the formation of axillary buds, which are then able to differentiate storage leaves and form cloves (Brewster 1994). Inflorescence initiation begins with the differentiation of the spathe. Although nonbolting cultivars do not produce an inflorescence, they are still dependent on the occurrence of axillary branching before storage-leaf differentiation can take place. Even though nonbolting cultivars do not display overt evidence of inflorescence formation, Hideaki Takagi (1990) suggests that the early physiological processes involved in inflorescence initiation may nonetheless occur, thus breaking the plant's apical dominance and permitting the formation of axillary buds.

If garlic is planted in the fall in accord with typical cultural practices, inflorescence initiation will begin in early spring, just shortly before the storage leaves begin to differentiate. In other words, beneath the ground, development of the flowering structures typically begins in the spring, just before the cloves and bulb begin to form. This sequence is critical. If the order of these processes is reversed, and storage-leaf initiation begins prior to inflorescence initiation, the plant produces an undifferentiated bulb—a bulb comprised of a single clove.

The specific response varies among cultivars, but high temperatures and long photoperiods immediately following planting foster such a sequence

reversal. These conditions promote rapid storage-leaf differentiation before axillary branching of the foliage leaves can occur, precluding lateral buds that would otherwise develop into individual cloves.

Planting garlic in the fall exposes the plants to shorter days and generally decreasing temperatures, making the undesirable formation of single-cloved bulbs unlikely. If garlic is planted in the spring, however, these considerations become more critical. One can also see the implications when attempting to grow a cultivar adapted to a northern temperate climate in a warmer growing region nearer the equator. If the days are still relatively long and temperatures relatively warm in the fall, development of a normal multicloved bulb may be at risk. Studies also show that dry conditions in the spring can inhibit inflorescence formation, causing the development of single-cloved bulbs.

Now that we have a basic understanding of the interrelationship of flower induction and bulb formation, let us examine each process in more detail.

## Flower induction

For the common table onion, exposure to low temperatures initiates bolting and the formation of the flowering structures. The bolting triggers for garlic are much more complex. In their benchmark work, *Onions and Their Allies*, Henry Jones and Louis Mann (1963) tentatively surmise that although a period of low temperatures seem to be essential for garlic bulb formation, exposure to low temperatures does not seem to be a factor in the initiation of bolting. The authors' more focused experience with California's nonbolting or less frequently bolting commercial cultivars in somewhat more southerly, warmer growing conditions may have led them in this direction. They further conclude that "the fact that garlic plants are not readily induced to bolt by exposing the growing plants to cool winter temperatures accounts for the wide range of autumn planting dates that can be used for this crop." They also say, however, that the factors controlling bolting in garlic are not well understood.

Coming from a different experiential base, and writing years later with the benefit of additional data, Hideaki Takagi (1990) notes that garlic grows vegetatively after autumn planting, and neither lateral buds nor inflorescence is normally formed until spring. He notes that the cultivars that bolt in Japan do so when mean air temperatures reach approximately 46°F (8°C). Lateral buds begin to develop in the spring, after air temperatures reach approximately 50°F (10°C). In other words, neither bulb development nor bolting normally occurs in the fall, regardless of the temperatures, but temperature triggers for both bolting and bulb development come into play in the spring. For the cultivars in Takagi's test, inflorescence initiation begins at a slightly cooler temperature than bulb development.

In order for bolting to occur, garlic requires a period of vernalization. This is generally achieved by fall planting and exposure to cold during the winter, but it can also be achieved artificially. Cultivars vary in the degree of cold required. In a study of Japanese cultivars, the upper vernalization temperature limit for successful inflorescence induction ranged from 60°F (16°C) for some cultivars down to 50°F (10°C) for one cultivar. In general, exposure to temperatures of 36°F to 40°F (2°C to 4°C) proved optimal for inducing bulbing, but flower induction was optimal at the slightly lower temperature range of 28°F to 36°F (−2°C to 2°C). Takagi's study showed that the upper temperature limit for inflorescence formation tends to increase as the photoperiod decreases, and conversely tends to decrease as the photoperiod increases. Garlic that is grown at low temperatures after cold induction is more likely to form inflorescences even if other factors are not favorable to inflorescence formation. Inflorescence formation, however, will develop at a slower rate over a longer period. Short photoperiods after cold induction increase the likelihood that garlic will bolt. Short photoperiods and low temperatures after cold induction promote the formation of larger and more vigorous flowering structures. A longer photoperiod after cold induction accelerates inflorescence formation, but in such a scenario bulbing is even more strongly accelerated, preventing inflorescence expression in some cultivars. Garlic grown in low light conditions after inflorescence induction is less likely to form inflorescences. However, cool growing temperatures counteract this tendency. In one study, when plants were grown at 41°F (5°C) they all flowered, even though they were grown in total darkness.

In another study, garlic cloves were pretreated with a period of cold and then subjected to a variety of conditions after planting. Those that were grown in low-moisture conditions for two weeks had inhibited inflorescence formation and yielded single-cloved bulbs. This means that low moisture during a critical period in the spring can result in single-cloved rather than normal multicloved bulbs. Inflorescence formation does not occur during storage, regardless of the storage temperature or duration. This may reflect the need for external moisture, which would not be available until after the cloves have been planted.

Some garlic cultivars that rarely bolt and generate inflorescences in southerly growing regions may readily do so in more northerly regions. When some typically nonbolting cultivars were grown in Wisconsin (Etoh and Simon 2002), they began to bolt after several years of cultivation, suggesting that garlic adapts to local conditions over a period of years. This adaptation to local conditions has also been noted by garlic growers in other ways, such as production of larger bulbs after several seasons. The Wisconsin results also showed that a lengthier period of moderate cold tends to induce flowering more than a shorter period of more severe cold.

These various results suggest that vernalization, growing temperatures, and photoperiods play a significant role in the different regional experiences in growing some garlic cultivars. Some cultivars grow well in both northerly and southerly climates but bolt readily only in northern growing regions and only rarely in more southerly regions. Other cultivars may show a significant degree of malleability in their expression when grown under different conditions.

## Bulb formation

Garlic shares some of the same bulbing triggers with the common table onion. For both, increasing day length stimulates bulbing, and a high temperature accelerates bulb formation and plant maturity. As with the bolting triggers, however, the bulbing triggers for garlic are much more complex. Bulb formation and development are interrelated with inflorescence induction and development, and are also dependent upon either the dormant clove or the subsequent young plant having a period of vernalization. Without vernalization, garlic bulbing may not occur.

In many garlic-growing regions, established planting practices that are adapted to local environmental conditions and locally grown cultivars may automatically meet the needs of a garlic plant. Sometimes specialized treatments are routine practice. In Israel, for example, garlic for planting is stored at local ambient temperatures but is given a precooling treatment of 58°F (14°C) for two weeks. This practice works well with the local cultivars and ensures that the garlic will bulb. The same practice might not work as well with other cultivars or different climatic conditions.

If one grows local garlic cultivars in accord with established local practices, the factors that trigger bulbing may require little or no thought. However, the specific factors that trigger bulbing become more important when working with a variety of garlic cultivars, or when growing garlic in regions with climates that are more toward garlic's margins or limitations—or when necessity dictates planting garlic outside of the normal planting period. A more complete understanding of garlic bulbing triggers can make a difference in successful growing.

Let us then explore further the various factors that cause garlic to form a bulb. Bulb formation depends on a number of interrelated conditions. To quickly summarize: Bulbing may be stimulated by a prior period of exposure to cold temperatures, by warming temperatures, increasing day length, a lower ratio of red to far-red light, planting date, and the phylogenetic propensities of a particular garlic cultivar.

Garlic's wide-ranging distribution has resulted in cultivars adapted to a variety of conditions with a range of responses to different bulbing stimuli. For example, cultivars with origins nearer the equator, where day length varies less throughout the year, may be less sensitive to day length ratio as a stimulus for bulbing and may have diminished dependency on a period of cold. Cultivars from colder climates further from the equator may be more dependent on a period of winter cold and may be more sensitive to changes in day length and high temperatures during bulb development.

In temperate climates away from the equator, fall-planted garlic cloves naturally undergo a period of cold. This satisfies the need for vernalization. Garlic stored at warm temperatures without a period of cold may fail to bulb. For example, if garlic is stored at 68°F (20°C) or above and then planted during the warm temperatures of late spring, it may fail to bulb, simply continuing its vegetative growth until the onset of winter. Although high-temperature storage can prevent bulbing, the effect can be reversed by a period of cool storage—either in or out of the ground. For example, if garlic for spring planting has been stored in a warm environment, it can be exposed to cold prior to planting so that successful bulbing can occur.

In addition to requiring a cold period for successful bulbing, garlic cultivars originating in temperate climates away from the equator may also have day length requirements. If these cultivars are not exposed to lengthening photoperiods in the spring, bulbing may be delayed even if they were exposed to an appropriate period of cold during the winter. For some cultivars, bulbing may not occur at all.

The need for a period of cold exposure and the need for long photoperiods in the spring vary considerably among garlic cultivars. Some cultivars will form bulbs without either condition, while other cultivars require both conditions in order to bulb. Most cultivars fall somewhere in between these two extremes and will simply exhibit delayed bulbing if either condition is less than ideal. For most cultivars a beneficial exaggeration of one condition can compensate for a deficiency in the other. For example, a longer period of cold lessens the need for longer photoperiods prior to bulbing (Takagi 1990).

Recognizing a cultivar's requirements for exposure to a period of cold and longer spring photoperiods helps us understand what we may encounter if we try to grow the cultivar under conditions that are different from its origins—and what we might do to compensate for the differences. For example, if we want to grow a northern-climate bolting cultivar in a southern part of the United States where winters are generally warm, we know that we can expect delayed bulbing at best, and perhaps none at all with some cultivars. We know that an artificial period of cold treatment prior to planting will greatly help the bulbing prospects for most northern-climate cultivars grown in hot southern climates. The somewhat shorter late-spring photoperiods in the southern United States could delay bulbing and impact bulb development, though this would be far less of a factor than if we were attempting our efforts closer to the equator.

It may seem tempting to simply keep garlic at cold temperatures until one is ready to plant or eat it, but such a regimen is not advisable. Garlic stored at cold temperatures for an extended period tends to form cloves in the older leaf axils, increasing the prospect of rough bulbs. Cloves that are generated in this manner may form their own green top growth, appearing as lateral shoots from the pseudostem. As the bulb matures and some of the outer bulb sheaths are lost, the cloves that were formed in the older axils may become exposed. In more extreme cases an apical clove can form—a single clove bulb generated at the shoot apex. Field trials have also shown that other conditions may contribute to the production of rough bulbs, including early planting, heavy fertilization, and other situations that foster heightened vigor of individual plants. Water stress during the initiation of bulb formation can also cause rough bulbs.

The temperature during vernalization, the length of the vernalization period, and the time of planting can have a bearing on bulb size as well as bulb formation. Although spring planting is generally not recommended, it may sometimes be warranted. In one garlic cold-storage study (Mann and Minges 1958), bulbs of the commercial cultivar 'California Late' were stored at 32°F (0°C), 41°F (5°C), 50°F (10°C), 59°F (15°C), and 68°F (20°C) for a period of nine months and then planted in northern California on 29 April. Warm field temperatures and long day lengths prompted rapid bulb formation from the planting stock that had been stored at 32°F and 41°F. However, the plants were relatively small when bulbing began, and the resulting bulbs were also quite small. The planting stock that had been stored at 59°F and 68°F failed to form bulbs. The planting stock that had been stored at 50°F performed the best, forming the largest bulbs. These results should not be taken as a general prescription for optimal storage temperatures—spring planting is generally not recommended, storage duration at these temperatures was lengthy, and other cultivars would not necessarily respond the same way, whether in the same growing environment or in more northern or more southern environments where the impact of day length would differ. The experiment does illustrate how storage temperature and response to day length can have a major impact on the growth and bulbing of the garlic plant and the quality and size of the bulbs.

In a study using two temperate-climate garlic cultivars from Japan, Hideaki Takagi (1990) found that for a 30-day cold-storage treatment, a temperature range of 36°F to 40°F (2°C to 4°C) was optimal for bulb formation when the cultivars were grown at temperatures of 68°F (20°C) or greater. The cultivars differed in their optimal cold-storage temperature, however. One cultivar performed optimally at 36°F and the other at 40°F. For the latter cultivar, the results remained near optimal at 43°F (6°C), but the percentage of plants that bulbed dropped off dramatically for the other cultivar. Both cultivars failed to bulb at a storage temperature of 59°F (15°C). We see that if storage temperatures are not sufficiently cold,

many cultivars fail to form bulbs, but storage temperatures that are too cold also affect garlic's ability to form bulbs. In the same study, cloves that were stored at 32°F (0°C) showed a significant decrease in bulbing in one cultivar and near failure in the other cultivar. At 28°F (−2°C) and lower, neither cultivar formed bulbs.

Keep in mind that these studies (Mann and Minges 1958, Takagi 1990) attempted to assess the cold exposure necessary for bulb formation. This does not imply that one somehow needs to place garlic in cold storage prior to planting. While this may be beneficial or even necessary in some circumstances, such as when attempting to grow certain northern bolting cultivars in very warm southerly climates, for the most part simply planting garlic in the fall subjects it to the appropriate cold period and lengthening spring photoperiods.

Cultivars indigenous to tropical climates are far less sensitive to the length of the photoperiod or to cold treatment. In one assessment of garlic planted in India, a cultivar was planted in October and harvested some four months later—a very abbreviated growing season by temperate-climate standards. Cultivars that are more tropical may form bulbs without exposure to either a period of cold or long photoperiods. It is interesting to note, however, that studies show that some cultivars from Thailand and Hong Kong bulb more quickly after exposure to longer photoperiods. Thus it appears that even tropical cultivars respond to cooler temperatures and longer days, albeit in a more nuanced fashion than temperate-climate cultivars. Growing garlic in the tropics is challenging even with well-chosen cultivars. In Indonesia, for example, garlic in the lowlands generally yields small bulbs and a meager harvest, so garlic is considered primarily a highlands crop. In Bangladesh, experiments with artificial cold treatments and growth retardants have proven beneficial.

Temperature and day length after planting affect bulbing. We have seen how high temperatures and long days immediately following planting foster rapid storage-leaf differentiation and may cause clove formation to occur prior to axillary branching, resulting in single-clove bulbs. If, prior to planting, the cloves are stored for a prolonged period of time at temperatures cool enough to promote bulbing induction—say, for example, 36°F to 40°F (2°C to 4°C)—the effect is exaggerated. Cool temperatures and short day length immediately following planting encourage axillary branching prior to bulb development and development of normal multicloved bulbs. After axillary branching occurs, increasing temperatures and day length foster storage-leaf differentiation and the development of normal bulbs with multiple cloves (Brewster 1994). These responses illustrate why the practice of fall planting typically meets the plant's developmental needs. The cooler temperatures and shorter day length of fall encourage normal axillary branching prior to bulb development. In the spring, increasing temperatures and day length promote storage-leaf differentiation and the development of multicloved bulbs.

Competition for light rather than for water and nutrients tends to promote bulbing. Thus, competition among the underground structures of garlic or other plants is not a factor in bulbing, but competition among the aboveground foliage canopies of nearby plants is a factor. Specifically, the ratio of light in the red to far-red wavelength is a determinant in bulbing. A lower ratio of red to far-red light stimulates bulbing. When and how does this is occur? Competing foliage canopies reduce the general penetration of light but also change the balance of the light. The green foliage of competing plants absorbs more red light than far-red light, thus reducing the ratio of red to

far-red light. In other words, when the foliage of weeds or of other garlic plants creates shade, the ratio of red to far-red light decreases, promoting the onset of bulbing. This is likely an adaptive survival habit acquired in response to the presence of vigorous weedy competitors. Competition for light promotes bulbing, which allows the garlic plant to enter a period of dormancy until the next growing season when the competition from other plants may be reduced or eliminated. Although this may be a beneficial adaptive behavior, it is generally at odds with the behavior sought by the garlic grower. An early harvest is usually not an overriding factor for most growers, but achieving maximum bulb size and greatest yield are major concerns. Competition from weeds or from garlic that is planted too densely can cause premature bulbing and a reduction in average bulb size and overall yield.

Once bulbing has begun, what is the preferred temperature for bulb growth? Although the ideal is dependent on the individual cultivar and the context of other conditions, one study showed that the preferred temperature fell within the range of 63°F to 78°F (17°C to 26°C). Bulb development slowed below 63°F (17°C) and became exceptionally slow at about 48°F (9°C). Above 82°F (28°C) bulb development was also inhibited.

In a study of one temperate-climate cultivar, Hideaki Takagi (1990) found that garlic plants subjected to high growing temperatures and water stress have a reduced ability to form bulbs. In extreme conditions the plants may completely fail to form bulbs. A longer vernalization period lessens the effect. Likewise, if, after exposure to high temperatures and water stress, garlic plants are again exposed to a period of cold, the plants regain their ability to form bulbs. Watering the plants well during exposure to high heat considerably lessens any negative effects. Even at moderate temperatures, water stress negatively affects bulb growth. At 68°F (20°C), water stress somewhat reverses the previous period of cold treatment and impacts bulb growth. In general, water stress delays clove formation and causes the cloves to be formed in older foliage leaves, contributing to rough bulbs.

Garlic grown in hot southern climates may be subject to early-season heat waves, sometimes in conjunction with drying winds. These conditions can burn the plant's leaves, reducing its ability to produce large bulbs, and can also cause early bolting, further reducing the size of the bulbs.

As we have seen, the garlic plant reacts to harsh and unfavorable conditions by hurrying its growth cycle. This adaptive behavior is an effective survival strategy but is not necessarily helpful to the grower seeking the largest possible bulbs. For the best crop and largest bulbs, it is necessary to avoid conditions that trigger survival responses. Fortunately, this is not difficult. Garlic is highly responsive to favorable conditions, and normal cultural practices will serve the garlic grower well.

# ~ SIX ~

# Cultivation

**MOST ALLIUMS** are propagated from seed, but shallot (*Allium cepa*), rakkyo (*A. chinense*), and garlic (*A. sativum*) are often planted from the bulbing portion of the plant. Some garlic cultivars have the ability to produce viable seed, but usually only with special procedures and under highly controlled conditions. Except for experimental or specialized purposes, garlic is always propagated from garlic cloves.

Unless the winters are exceptionally severe, garlic cloves are usually planted in the fall for harvest the following summer. The clove begins developing a root system before any aboveground growth is visible. Depending on the climate and cultivar, aboveground growth may not be visible until spring. The plant grows rapidly from early spring into summer. Tightly wrapped overlapping leaf sheaths form a stemlike structure supporting narrow leaf blades that are arrayed on alternating sides of the plant. As harvest draws closer, bolting cultivars send up a scape topped by the developing umbel. The scape first grows straight, then bends or curls, and then straightens again. For some cul-

tivars the bending is modest, as is the straightening that follows. For other cultivars the activity is dramatic, the scape forming multiple tight curls, then uncurling and becoming rigidly straight. Nonbolting cultivars may reach a height of several feet. The top of the scape on some bolting cultivars may reach as high as 7 ft. (2.1 m).

The presence of the scape reduces the potential size of the bulb in most cultivars, so it is usually cut before it develops fully. As harvest nears, the garlic leaves begin to senesce, starting with the oldest at the base of the plant. Except in the case of certain large-scale commercial harvesting regimens, garlic is harvested while some of the leaves are still green. The garlic is then dried, trimmed, and cleaned. A portion of the crop is reserved for planting the following year.

In its area of origin, garlic survives in a harsh environment, enduring extremes in heat, cold, and drought. When we cultivate garlic, it is not our goal to mimic native conditions. Such a strategy would yield tiny bulbs and complicate cultivation. Although garlic can survive in harsh environments, it responds very favorably to optimal conditions, yielding large, healthy bulbs and fat cloves. Good cultivation practices include amending the soil, providing ample water, and purging competing weeds. Wild garlic remains in the ground year after year, continuing as a single bulb and plant, or as the smaller plants it may become if conditions are sufficiently favorable for the garlic bulb to divide into cloves. Cultivated garlic is dug from the ground every year. A portion of the crop is sold or consumed, and a portion is returned to the ground a few months later to produce the following year's crop. If all goes well, each clove planted will yield a bulb of multiple cloves at next year's harvest—some nine months away.

Left on its own, garlic will grow in a way that best ensures its survival. Bulbs and cloves will generally become increasingly numerous but much smaller, as the bulb divides into cloves, which then grow as separate plants and perhaps divide again into individual cloves, yielding more and more tiny plants. In long-abandoned farm gardens, one sometimes encounters garlic that is scarcely recognizable as such—tiny plants growing densely together, looking more like grass than garlic. Bolting garlics also generate plants from bulbils. Depending on the conditions, the bulbils may be scattered at varying distances and may also create additional densely spaced, tiny plants. Abandoned garlic can be cultivated and tended again to produce a viable crop, but recovery may take several seasons. Still, bringing back an heirloom cultivar that carries its history in its genetic memory can be a satisfying venture.

Garlic needs good sunlight throughout its aboveground growing period, particularly from early spring through harvest. Ideally it should be planted in open areas with no shading during the day. The small-scale grower may not have access to growing space that is totally shade free, but garlic can still grow well as long as there is substantial sun exposure. In many respects good growing conditions for garlic are very similar to those for most other garden plants: ample water, ample sunlight, and well-draining but moisture-retaining soil with ample organic matter. However, garlic differs from most garden plants in the length of time it requires to produce a crop: about nine months from planting to harvest.

## SOIL

In its native environment garlic grows in poor, rocky soils. It survives but does not thrive, at least in the sense of producing a big crop of large, fat bulbs. For a good crop, good soil is important. A loose, well-draining soil rich in organic matter with a neutral to slightly acidic pH is ideal.

Light sandy soils with little organic matter do not offer or foster beneficial micronutrients and microorganisms. They do not retain moisture well but rapidly dry out, potentially diminishing yield and causing irregular growth and misshapen bulbs. Heavy clay soils, on the other hand, make planting and harvesting difficult. They are slow to warm and can delay growth and harvest. They readily become compacted, suffocating roots and impairing growth and bulb development. Clinging clay soils are also a hindrance at harvest time and make bulb cleaning more difficult. Although garlic will grow in light sandy soils or heavy clay soils, a more balanced soil better meets the needs of the plant and ensures a larger, healthier crop. Organic matter helps retain moisture, prevents root suffocation, provides micronutrients, and fosters microorganisms beneficial to the plant. A soil that is rich in organic matter benefits plant growth and health.

Good soil also offers added protection in extreme growing conditions, when heat, cold, drought, or water saturation may otherwise be a threat. Some cultivars are more particular about soils than others. Artichoke cultivars, for example, are more tolerant than Rocamboles. In sum, though garlic is more tenacious in poorer soils than most other garden plants, it does best in good soil.

The soil should generally be worked to a depth of approximately 18 in. (45 cm). Clay soils benefit from deeper cultivation to avoid soil compaction. Good soil drainage is especially important if your growing site is subject to heavy rains, particularly if the rains come during the cold winter months.

How do you prepare the soil? If you are growing garlic in a small garden area, you can simply take over a portion of an existing garden bed. If you are preparing a new plot, work in ample compost to boost organic matter. The standard household compost of grass clippings, vegetable trimmings and peelings, and leaves from deciduous trees works well as a soil amendment. If compost is unavailable, coarsely textured composted steer manure or other manures from a local vendor will help build tilth and contribute nitrogen and other nutrients. Sand can be added to heavy clay soil, lime to acidic soil, and so forth, as needed.

If you are field planting, the practicalities call for a different preparatory regimen. If there is hardpan, deep subsoiling may be required to break it up, aerate the soil, and provide good drainage. New ground will need plowing and disking, but that is just the beginning. The soils on most new ground will need to be built up and amended for one to several years before planting. This is accomplished by multiple cycles of planting, mowing, and tilling cover crops. Once the new beds are prepared, establish a crop rotation regimen. There are many variations.

To reduce the likelihood that allium pathogens or pests will build up in the soil, garlic should be rotated with non-allium crops such as sweet corn, cucurbits (for example, squash, cucumber, pumpkin, and melons), and crucifers (for example, cabbage and broccoli). The frequency of crop rotation depends on a variety of factors, including the availability of land and the threat or presence of specific diseases or pests.

Ideally one might plant garlic in the same field or bed only once every half dozen years or so. For most of us, however, such a regimen is impractical. Planting garlic in the same bed every other year may be sufficient to avoid a buildup of diseases or pests in many growing regions, though once every three years would be preferable. Growing regions with conditions that make garlic more susceptible to diseases and pests necessitate a more rigorous and extended crop rotation regimen. Conversely, if growing conditions do not foster threatening diseases or pests, a less rigorous regimen will be feasible. If you are growing garlic on a small scale, you can more readily focus greater attention on measures that mitigate the pest and disease threat, allowing you to use the same beds more often. For example, plant debris left in the soil is a major vector for the spread of diseases and pests. Meticulously removing all debris and stray cloves at harvest will reduce the threat of spreading an infestation to next year's crop. If diseases take hold in the soil, extended crop rotation intervals may be necessary, depending on the disease causing the infection. Measures that mitigate risk are discussed in more detail in chapter 8.

My garlic affliction compels me to grow numerous garlic cultivars, and research preparations for this book exaggerated my garlic-growing propensities even more. Because I have so little available land, I seldom rotate garlic with other crops.

So far I have been fortunate, but I run the risk of losing my good fortune as well as a considerable amount of garlic—and perhaps the use of the beds themselves for a period of years. When feasible, crop rotation is always recommended.

Soil amendment, crop rotation, and mulching can all be part of an integrated regimen. Richard Smith (1999) of the Garlicsmiths in Washington State offers one example. The Smiths employ a yearly crop rotation and assign odd and even numbers to their garlic beds. To illustrate, in the fall of a given year, the even-numbered beds are planted with garlic, and the odd-numbered beds are either planted with a mix of ryegrass and hairy vetch or in spring are planted with annual alfalfa. When the garlic is harvested in July, the even-numbered beds are planted with buckwheat, which is tilled into the soil four to six weeks later. The beds are then planted with a mix of ryegrass and hairy vetch or with buckwheat. The buckwheat winter-kills and is followed by a spring planting of annual alfalfa. The cover crops in the odd-numbered beds are allowed to grow through summer. In September the hay from the cover crops is mowed and windrowed to one side of the bed, and the stubble is tilled into the soil. In October these beds are planted with garlic, and the hay that had been windrowed to the side is pulled back over the beds of garlic as a protective mulch. After harvest the following summer, the mulch is tilled into the soil, and the regimen begins again.

Fred and Laura Bacon (1999), who grow garlic and other vegetable crops at their organic farm in Vermont, employ a six-year rotation for their planting beds. For the first two years the beds are planted with green manure and cover crops to condition and enrich the soil. Garlic is planted in the third year, and other vegetables are planted in the following three years. The cover crops have multiple purposes: suppressing weeds; adding nitrogen, micronutrients, and organic matter to the soil;

and reducing erosion. The Bacons plant oats and field peas in the spring for nitrogen and weed suppression, followed in the summer by buckwheat or Japanese millet (which is mowed periodically), and then annual ryegrass in the fall in the beds where garlic will not be planted.

There are probably as many variations on this theme as there are garlic growers, but the idea is to incorporate crop rotation, soil amendment, and mulching into an integrated system that benefits the soil and the garlic crop with each passing year. Some cover crops can be a useful part of the regimen even for the small-scale gardener, though compost and organic fertilizers will likely have a larger role.

What are the effects of soil differences on garlic flavor? The flavor effects are not well documented, but experiments with onions have shown that plants grown in a medium with low sulfate concentrations may not produce all of the numerous sulfur-based flavor precursors that give onions their complex pungent character. However, sandy soils with low sulfur content are beneficial to producers of mild sweet onions, the Vidalia District of Georgia being a case in point. The information on onions suggests that light soils with minimal sulfate content might also yield garlic with less pungent character—not especially desirable unless one is trying to tame the character of some particularly strong Silverskin cultivars or the like.

## FERTILIZER

Unlike many other crops, garlic is not a heavy nitrogen feeder. Nonetheless, nitrogen is the fertilizer amendment most likely to be needed and beneficial. Nitrogen deficiency symptoms include a general yellowing of the plant, poor vigor, and small bulbs. Some cultivars may be more responsive to nitrogen than others. Virus-free plants generally respond more to heavier nitrogen applications. For most purposes an application of a moderate amount of nitrogen will foster healthy plants and reasonably large bulbs. Heavy fertilizing may produce even larger bulbs, but this may not be desirable. An exceptionally large bulb does not have the flavor concentration or storage longevity of a somewhat smaller bulb, and the garlic plant may be taxed to its limits in the process.

Heavy nitrogen stimulates the growth of foliage leaves but inhibits and delays bulb formation. This can cause cloves to form in the older leaf axils, increasing the prospect of rough bulbs and exposed cloves when the outer bulb sheaths are lost at maturity. Conversely, a shortage of nitrogen promotes early bulb formation, potentially producing bulbs that are smaller than desired from a less vigorous plant. When nitrogen is applied in the proper measure it helps stave off diseases by making the plant more vigorous and robust. Excessive fertilizer, however, can diminish disease resistance. Tests have also shown that applying excessive nitrogen as harvest approaches contributes to premature sprouting in stored bulbs. With fertilizer, as with most things, balance is the key.

We think of fertilizer as increasing yields, but late-season fertilizing can actually decrease yields. In New York, for example, trials have shown that fertilizing after May reduces crop yield. Side dressing with fertilizer as opposed to broadcast fertilizing avoids fertilizing weeds as well as garlic, but care must be exercised when banding fertilizer above or very close to the cloves. Tests have shown that concentrated dissolved fertilizer salts have a toxic effect on the clove, and yields may be reduced, not increased, if fertilizer is concentrated too closely to the clove.

Let us look more specifically at fertilizer requirements and different approaches to meeting them. Unless the soil is already rich in nitrogen, Henry Jones and Louis Mann (1963) recommend 60 to 80 lbs. of actual nitrogen per square acre (67

to 89 kg per hectare), which can be accomplished by adding 300 to 400 lbs. of ammonium sulfate per acre (336 to 447 kg per hectare). At least half should be applied at planting, with the remainder added in early spring either as a side dressing or in the irrigation water. For sandy or exceptionally heavy soils, supplemental phosphorus may be needed. Symptoms of phosphorus deficiency include dark green to purple leaves and stunted growth. Phosphorus should be applied near planting time for best results, either in bands a few inches below the plant rows or in bands just to the side of the plant rows. If both nitrogen and phosphate are needed, Jones and Mann recommend ammonium phosphate. One symptom of potassium deficiency is older leaves with scorched margins. However, garlic rarely exhibits either phosphorous or potassium deficiencies, and special applications are seldom needed. When phosphorus or potassium supplements are required, they should be added to the soil prior to planting.

A wide range of fertilizing regimens can be effective. Local growing conditions help dictate what works best. Northern New Mexico grower Cassim Dunn (1999) sprinkles manure over his garlic beds for leaching into the soil by the melting winter snow. Such a regimen is effective in Dunn's environment but would not be practical for areas that experience heavy winter moisture, which would leach the nutrients from the root system. A Garlic Seed Foundation publication (Kline 1990) suggests 35 to 60 lbs. of nitrogen per acre (40 to 67 kg per hectare) prior to planting, and one or two side dressings of 20 lbs. (9 kg) each in the spring. A baseline for commercial growers in Washington State calls for three applications of 50 lbs. (23 kg) per acre each: at planting time in the fall, in the spring when garlic begins active growth, and in early to mid June. However, this baseline is not ideal for growers of gourmet garlics. The relatively high levels of nitrogen and the late spring application may stress the plants, delay bulbing, and yield bulbs with diminished flavor and storage longevity.

A University of Minnesota publication (Rosen et al. 2007) recommends avoiding nitrogen applications after the first week in May to avoid delayed bulbing. The publication ties nitrogen recommendations to the percentage of organic material in the soil and prior planting with nitrogen-fixing cover crops. An application of 120 lbs. (54 kg) of nitrogen per acre is recommended for soils with low organic matter (less than 3.1%), 80 lbs. (36 kg) for highly organic soil (4.6% to 19%), and 50 lbs. (23 kg) for soil with more than 19% organic matter. Recommended nitrogen amounts are further reduced if the ground was previously planted with a nitrogen-fixing crop. The recommended rate of reduction per acre is 70 lbs. (32 kg) for alfalfa, 40 lbs. (18 kg) for clover, and 20 lbs. (9 kg) for soybeans or peas. This illustrates how organic soils dramatically reduce the need for supplemental nitrogen. Organic soils and rotation with nitrogen-fixing crops can eliminate the need for supplemental nitrogen applications.

In keeping with this approach, Fred and Laura Bacon (1999) grow cover crops to add nitrogen and other nutrients to the soil. However, in early spring, cold soil temperatures impede garlic's ability to assimilate nitrogen just when it is beginning its vigorous growth. To compensate, the Bacons begin a regimen of foliar feeding with fish emulsion every two weeks for a six-week period. To avoid burning the leaves, they spray after a rain during the cooler part of the day. Some growers employ a similar regimen and also include kelp in the foliar spray as a source of beneficial plant hormones and micronutrients.

In areas subject to heavy rainfall, fertilizer can be rapidly leached from the soil. Although most growers generally prefer organic fertilizer, liquid fertilizer and other quick-release fertilizers can be more precise in timing availability to the plant. On the other hand, mild slow-release fertilizers are not as subject to rapid decimation from leaching as the more concentrated quick-release fertilizers. Because I grow garlic in a region subject to heavy rains in fall and winter, in the past I used liquid fertilizers in the spring, with reasonably good results. I have changed regimens, however, and now work only two fertilizer amendments—compost and composted steer manure—into the soil in the fall prior to planting. With slow-release organic fertilizers there is inherently less control in timing of the uptake. However, this may not be a significant issue unless heavy fertilizer applications are employed—something that garlic does not need, in any case. So far the results have been positive. The plants respond well to moderate amounts of fertilizer that is available on an ongoing basis, as opposed to the fits and starts of quick-release fertilizers. Although I grow garlic on a very small scale, I have also begun experimenting with cover crops as a source of organic matter and slow-release nitrogen. On a larger scale, a regimen of crop rotation and nitrogen-fixing cover crops can be a highly effective approach.

We have been focusing on fertilizer requirements in this section, but as we have seen, fertilizer must be understood in the context of soil. Fertilizer is after all simply one aspect of good soil. Loamy soil that is high in organic matter and that has good drainage, good moisture retention, and a balanced pH is more important than any number of bags of fertilizer. One should strive for idealized soil conditions, only adding moderate amounts of fertilizer as necessary to foster plant vigor and achieve a balance of flavor concentration, yield, and storage longevity.

# WATER

Most of the world's garlic crop is irrigated. Although garlic grows in very harsh, dry climates in its native habitat, the best yields are obtained when the plants are grown in soils that are never allowed to completely dry out from the initial planting to the onset of maturity. Water requirements for garlic are generally intuitive. There must be ample water for the healthy growth of the plant and development of the bulb, but not so much that the soil becomes saturated and the bulb sits in heavy muck. If the soil is dry at the time of planting, water or irrigate immediately so that the root system has enough moisture to begin its growth. If garlic does not begin growing soon after planting, the cloves will be more at risk of deterioration and disease.

In general, throughout garlic's primary growth period, provide it with about the same ample amount of water that you would provide for other garden vegetables. Although garlic is considered a shallow-rooted plant, with most of its roots in the upper 2 ft. (0.6 m) of soil, it is important to ensure that the soil is moist to the depth of the roots. If the soil is only moist near the surface of the soil, the plant can be starved for water. The nature of the soil plays a role in shaping an appropriate watering regimen. Sandy soils with little water retention, for example, will require more frequent watering. Drought stress delays bulb formation and may cause rough bulbs. For more information on rough bulbs, refer to "Bulb Formation" in chapter 5.

As harvest time approaches, it is helpful for the soil to begin to dry down. In some growing climates excess rain can be a problem, particularly just prior to harvest. At the other end of the spectrum, hot and dry conditions during garlic's vegetative period necessitate watering. Protracted periods of very hot temperatures, particularly in combination with

Water droplets on the leaf of the Creole cultivar 'Morado de Pedronera'.

low moisture, can cause accelerated maturity and decreased bulb size. For these more extreme growing conditions, particularly on a large scale, drip irrigation lines run down the rows and covered with mulch may be most effective, the drip irrigation and mulch working together to conserve moisture and suppress weeds. The quality of the irrigation water is also important. Studies in Argentina show that saline water significantly reduces yields.

Allowing the soil to dry as harvest approaches facilitates the plant's maturation and the transition from vegetative growth to storage bulb. For more details, refer to the "Harvest" section of this chapter.

## WEEDS

Garlic has slender leaves and a minimal leaf canopy. This serves the plant well in harsh climates with sparse vegetation, but the plant needs to have essentially all of its minimal leaf surface to generate the best growth. Since garlic does not have a profusion of foliage, nor the capacity to generate supplemental or replacement leaves, it is all the more important to protect the leaves from damage and to eliminate shading. Low-growing weeds with shallow root systems near the soil surface are not a particular concern, but weeds become a problem when deep root systems compete with the garlic and when the weeds are tall enough to shade the garlic leaves. Since the lowermost leaves of the garlic plant are nearly on the ground, weeds do not need to be very tall before they begin having a negative effect.

Garlic's upright and minimal foliage canopy is largely ineffective in shading out weeds. Conversely, weeds can readily shade out garlic leaves, reducing the vigor of the garlic plant. Shading can also cause premature bulbing and senescence, which exacerbates the negative effect. Weed shading is a problem for young garlic plants, but removal of weeds at earlier stages may still allow garlic plants to develop and generate a nearly normal crop. Weed shading nearer the time when normal bulbing would begin is a greater problem. Shading at this time can cause the garlic plant to bulb prematurely, before the plant and leaf canopy are of sufficient size to produce a normally large bulb.

Since garlic is in the ground for some nine months, there is ample time for various weeds to take hold and cause problems. For a gardener growing just a plot or two of garlic, eradicating weeds is relatively easy, but for a garlic farmer, field-sized weeds in a large area of cultivated land can present an ongoing concern, requiring multiple returns to the field and potentially extensive hand labor.

Because garlic is relatively shallow-rooted, avoid deep cultivation to eradicate weeds. If the garlic roots are inadvertently pruned, plant growth slows and yields diminish. On a larger scale, farm machinery can take care of the weeds between the rows, but removal of weeds within the rows still requires hand hoeing. Herbicides can be judiciously employed, but for a variety of reasons most growers prefer to take care of weeding with machinery or hand hoeing.

## MULCH

Mulch can provide a variety of benefits, including temperature moderation, moisture retention, weed suppression, and soil amendment in subsequent years. For one or more of the above reasons, most growers find some sort of mulching beneficial. Depending on one's needs, resources, and inclinations, a layer of 2 to 6 in. (5 to 15 cm) or more of mulch can be added after planting. The mulch can consist of a wide variety of organic matter, such as straw, hay, sugarcane leaves, lawn clippings mixed with leaves, and the like. The mulch should not be too heavy or dense but should have some fluff to trap insulating air. Wood chips will deplete nitrogen and should only be part of a mulching regimen when provision is made for compensating nitrogen additions. Avoid mulch laden with weed seed, or you may be encouraging one or more seasons of heavy weeding labor. Mulches vary in quality. Good hay mulch will have few weed seeds, but some growers find that straw mulch more reliably has fewer weed seeds. Reportedly, rice straw may reliably have even fewer weed seeds, though rice straw is less widely available.

Strong winds can blow mulch away. In areas that routinely experience strong winter winds, some growers water mulch after placement so that it freezes in place. Putting chicken wire over mulch is another way to keep it from blowing away; it also discourages foraging deer and other venturesome animals.

For larger operations, mulching can be partially mechanized. At Seed Savers Exchange Heritage Farm, oat straw mulch is distributed with a bale-chopping machine towed behind a tractor. The chopper shoots the straw some 30 ft. (9 m) over the beds, at which point the final spreading is accomplished by hand.

In regions with cold winter climates, temperature fluctuations can cause the ground to heave, disrupting the plants and damaging their root systems. This freezing, thawing, and ground heaving is often more of a threat than the cold itself. Mulch can help prevent or reduce it.

Mulch is typically added after planting and removed in the spring, but different regimens are appropriate depending on the need. Mulch can be left on in the spring to help retain moisture, suppress weeds, and eventually provide organic matter to the soil. In regions with a propensity for spring freezing, mulch can continue to provide protection from the cold. As an incidental observation from a garlic study in Minnesota, some bulbs from one plot were malformed from freeze damage when the plot was subjected to an unexpected low of 5°F (−15°C) after mulch removal. The mulch had not been removed from another plot, and a similar cold temperature exposure caused no damage.

There are trade-offs to using mulch. Mulch helps keep the soil warm in the winter, but it can also delay soil warming in the spring. It may be essential in cold climates, but it can also foster botrytis molds. If the garlic pseudostem is wet at soil level and botrytis takes hold, it can potentially cause significant damage to the crop. In wet climates a layer of mulch can also harbor slugs, snails, and insects that can cause damage. If the mulch is too thick when the garlic begins to grow,

the sturdy but short sprout leaf may penetrate the mulch with ease, but the leaves that follow may not be able to push through. For sandy soils, mulch can be particularly beneficial, helping to retain moisture and tempering the effects of temperature and moisture fluctuation. While we generally think of temperature moderation as winter cold protection, growers in hot climates also use mulch to protect the soil from excess heat, which can contribute to moisture loss from the soil, premature maturation, and small bulbs.

Most garlic growers find that a layer of mulch is helpful, at least during a portion of the growing season, though mulching is not always necessary. In a cool, moist, maritime climate, for example, there is no need for temperature moderation, and mulching can increase the risk of molds and other infections, as well as harbor slugs and other undesirable vermin. Mulching in such a climate will also delay soil warming in the spring and early summer, which in turn may reduce the size of the bulbs and delay harvest. Although weed suppression is a good reason to mulch, hand cultivation may be no more labor-intensive than applying and removing mulch, unless the weeds are particularly rampant. In climates with cold though not severe winters, mulching may not be necessary for winter protection since garlic is quite hardy and can tolerate some frost even if aboveground growth does occur during winter. Having cited these exceptions, we can still say that although mulch may not be essential or desirable in all circumstances, a mulching regimen tailored to local growing conditions will be beneficial for most growers.

## WHEN TO PLANT

Unless the climate is so severe that a garlic plant would not survive the winter, garlic should generally be planted in the fall. As a starting rule of thumb, plant garlic three to five weeks before the soil begins to freeze. This gives the garlic clove time to establish a root system, but not so much time that aboveground growth is exposed to the winter cold. Garlic is quite hardy, and its leaves can tolerate temperatures as low as 20°F (7°C) or so without damage. Below approximately 10°F (12°C), significant plant damage may occur. Wind, low humidity, and lengthier exposure to cold negatively affect the plant's tolerance to low temperatures.

If the winter climate is severe, plant the hardiest cultivars and mulch well. Many bolting hardneck cultivars are more winter hardy than the nonbolting softneck cultivars. Mulching garlic beds to protect the plants from winter cold may be essential in some growing areas, but if the arrival of winter is marked by high winds, mulch may blow away unless a practical means is available for keeping it in place. If the winter cold is simply too severe for garlic to reliably survive, spring planting may be the best option. In parts of Ontario, hardy garlic cultivars are planted in the fall. In parts of northern China, however, the winter cold is too harsh for even the hardiest cultivars, and the garlic is planted in the spring. In most parts of North America, including many very cold areas, fall is still the preferred planting time.

Ideally garlic should be planted so that the root system is well established prior to winter freezing, but so that no aboveground growth occurs until spring. The vagaries of nature and the differences between seasons ensure that the ideal will not always be achieved. So, what are the implications if it is not? One year David Stern (1999), New York garlic grower and cofounder of the Garlic Seed Foundation, began planting garlic one week after harvest and continued planting until December. The garlic that was planted early showed up to about 3/4 in. (2 cm) of tip burn, but by 1 May the burning had disappeared. According to Stern the

harvest was generally good, except for the plants that were planted prior to 1 September, which had 12 in. (30 cm) of top growth exposed during winter and were beginning to form a third leaf. Garlic is very hardy and can readily withstand frost. Low temperatures are not the sole concern, however. Dehydration of the aboveground growth is a key factor. Freezing temperatures in conjunction with low humidity and strong winds are the greatest threat. Stern recalls talking with one grower from the Midwest whose garlic plants, with 6 in. (15 cm) of top growth showing, had been exposed to a temperature of −40°F (−40°C) and 35 mph (56 kph) winds, with no snow cover and no mulch. This combination of conditions wiped out his garlic crop. Although garlic is exceptionally hardy, it does have limits.

If there is aboveground growth during the winter, animals in search of winter forage, such as deer, elk, and moose, may eat it even if they have to dig through mulch to reach it. The garlic plants will regenerate their leaves in the spring, and they generally recover, but the situation is hardly ideal.

The commercial garlic industry in California is predicated on garlic cultivars and cultivation practices that are highly specialized and tightly focused. In the hot desert valleys of Southern California, garlic is planted between September and November for early harvesting in May and June. In the cooler regions of Salinas and Gilroy, it is planted from January to March for harvest in the fall. Such highly focused cultural practices notwithstanding, studies using successional planting dates in temperate growing climates show that garlic yields are better when planting takes place in the fall rather than in midwinter or spring. Such experiences are widespread. In Kalyani, West Bengal, India, for example, garlic planted in November produced higher yields than garlic planted in December. In a Bangladesh study, garlic planted in late October produced higher yields than garlic planted in November or December.

For most North American temperate-climate environments, October is a good baseline for planting garlic as long as neither frozen ground nor high heat are issues. Optimal planting dates may be earlier or later depending on local conditions. In very cold climates, garlic may need to be planted as early as the beginning of September. Climates with moderate winters can wait through November. Southern climates with warm winters can delay planting until December, or even January or February for some cultivars, and still produce healthy bulbs.

Although southern climates with warm winters offer more flexibility with respect to planting time, it is still preferable to plant the garlic in October or November (Anderson 1999)—or earlier, as long as temperatures are declining. If garlic is not at risk from winter cold, why not wait to plant until late fall? Garlic requires a period of exposure to cold for the plant to bulb normally. For some cultivars this period of vernalization is minimal. For others, typically those that bolt, the requirement is much more pronounced and lengthy. A lengthier time at moderately cool temperatures can substitute for a briefer time at colder temperatures. Depending on the relative coolness of fall, earlier fall planting may be closer to optimal for some cultivars in more temperate- or warm-climate growing regions. Although temperatures may not be exceptionally cool, the longer exposure to moderately cool temperatures may make the difference in normal bulbing and bulb development in some cultivars. Oklahoma garlic grower Darrell Merrell (2000a) normally planted garlic in October and November, but one year planted 'Inchelium Red' on 21 August for a television demonstration. The August-planted garlic produced larger bulbs than the same cultivar planted later in the fall.

In general, garlic planted in the spring may not develop into normal multicloved bulbs, and the bulbs that are successful are generally smaller than fall-planted bulbs. However, although fall-planted bulbs are usually preferable, carefully managed spring-planted garlic can yield an acceptable crop. Keeping garlic in a condition suitable for spring planting can be a challenge; refer to "Induced Vernalization" later in this chapter for details.

We have discussed how some cultivars need a period of cold more than others. Rocambole cultivars, for example, yield very poorly without a definite period of vernalization and tend to perform poorly in warmer southern climates. Artichoke cultivars, on the other hand, are generally less dependent on a pronounced period of cold for normal development. For areas with cold winters, fall planting provides the needed period of vernalization during winter. Without vernalization, bulbs may not form at all or may be small or poorly formed. For very warm climates, storing garlic in the refrigerator several weeks before planting can help ensure better bulb formation. The need for this will vary among cultivars. Regardless of climate, if garlic must be planted in the spring, exposing the cloves to a period of cold will accelerate growth and ensure better bulb formation.

Studies show that subjecting garlic to temperatures of 39°F to 41°F (4°C to 5°C) for a period of three weeks causes the cloves to rapidly break dormancy and begin shoot elongation. Such tightly controlled temperatures are not necessary, however. Keeping the garlic in a temperature range of 40°F to 50°F (4°C to 10°C) for a period of 15 to 45 days works well for most cultivars. In natural conditions, vernalization simply occurs in the ground.

Although many factors related to planting time and the success of garlic growth and bulbing are at play, fine timing is seldom that critical. For most growers, most cultivars, and most growing regions, a basic planting rule of thumb is sufficient for a good garlic crop: plant in the fall before the ground freezes. Attention to other factors is helpful in problematic growing regions with cultivars that are more particular about their requirements.

## PLANT SPACING AND YIELD

Relative to other plants of similar size, garlic is not deeply rooted, though its root system is somewhat spreading. Because the root system extends beyond the width of the bulb, it is not sufficient to simply allow enough space for the expected diameter of the bulbs. In considering plant spacing, one must also ensure that the root systems are not in competition to the extent that bulb size and growth are diminished, particularly if large bulbs are desired. The effect of shading on nearby plants is also a factor in successful growth. When I first started growing garlic, I did not take these factors into consideration, and some nine months later I was rewarded with a harvest of numerous tiny bulbs. The need to peel large numbers of tiny cloves for a meal afforded me the opportunity to develop excellent clove-peeling skills, but I did not repeat my mistake the following year.

Although I did not measure the yield by weight in my inadvertent experiment with dense plant spacing, it is likely that my beds actually produced greater total yield by weight. The downside, of course, is that the tiny bulbs and cloves were barely usable. On the other hand, commercial growers producing garlic for processing rather than the fresh market are far less concerned with the size of the individual plants than they are with yield by weight. Studies have shown that total yield generally increases as planting density increases throughout a range of approximately 1.5 plants to 10 plants per square ft. (17 plants to 100 plants per square m), though the optimal yield may be lower than the upper limit cited depending on the cultivar and growing conditions. However, even when maximum yield is the goal without regard to bulb size, the economic trade-offs are not insignificant when it comes to the number of plants that require planting, tending, and harvesting, and the amount of planting stock that must be saved from the harvest for planting at increased densities. The size of the cloves used for planting stock also makes a difference in the planting density that will give the highest yield. In one study, cloves that weighed 0.32 oz. (9 g) achieved the optimal yields at a planting density as low as half that of cloves that weighed 0.11 to 0.18 oz. (3 to 5 g). This calculation fits well for garlic grown for processing. Garlic is planted very densely for highest yield, which yields smaller bulbs and cloves, a portion of which are again planted (necessarily) densely for highest yield. The calculation also fits well for growers of fresh-market garlic, who plant the largest cloves possible, at lower densities, to achieve a balance of large heads and relatively high yields.

In one experiment garlic was planted in rows 16 in. (40 cm) apart and spacing was varied from 2 to 7 in. (5 to 17.5 cm). In another variation, garlic was planted 4 in. (10 cm) apart within the row, and rows were varied in spacing from 8 to 20 in. (20 to 50 cm). In both experiments, as spacing was increased, the size of the bulbs also increased—the closer the spacing, the more dramatic the difference. This suggests that when it comes to spacing there is a nonlinear sweet spot where the trade-off between yield and bulb size is optimal. So, where is the sweet spot? There really is no single sweet spot. The particular garlic cultivar, growing conditions, and local market expectations for bulb size are all factors in determining plant spacing, but it is important to know that bulb size will increase markedly at first, as spacing is increased from the most dense, and will then show decreasing benefit in bulb size as spacing is increased further.

Similar, though not identical, results were achieved in a trial that was conducted in a far northern climate with a bolting cultivar from the Porcelain group. In Ontario the cultivar 'Music' had typically been planted at a commonly recommended density of 26 in. (65 cm) between rows and 4 in. (10 cm) between plant centers within the rows. To determine if this common spacing practice was optimal, John Zandstra and Robert Squire (2000) conducted a trial that manipulated row and plant spacing to assess the effect on yield. With respect to spacing between rows, significant increases in yield occurred when spacing was reduced from 26 in. to 18 in. (45 cm), from 18 in. to 10 in. (25 cm), and finally from 10 in. to 6 in. (15 cm). A significant reduction in bulb weight only occurred when row spacing was reduced from 10 in. to 6 in. When in-row spacing was reduced from 4 in. to 2 in. (5 cm), yields increased by 74%, though the average bulb weight decreased by 15%. When in-row spacing was increased to 6 in. the average bulb size did not increase, but yields were reduced by 32%.

Although the study was limited in time and scope, it suggests that plant spacing that is more compressed than the existing norm may be optimal, perhaps something more closely approximating 10 in. (25 cm) between rows and 4 in. (10 cm) within the rows for garlic that is intended for the table or the fresh market. The study did not directly assess the simultaneous reduction of in-row spacing and the spacing between the rows, so an in-row spacing of 6 in. (15 cm) rather than 4 in. may be a safer beginning point. David Stern (2002) cites similar findings from experiments at his farm in New York State. Garlic grown on a 4 by 4 in. grid yielded unsalable 1 in. (2.5 cm) bulbs. Stern achieves 2 to

2 ½ in. (5 to 6.25 cm) bulbs by planting at a spacing of 10 in. between rows and 5 in. (12.5 cm) within the row.

Different cultivars in different growing environments will vary somewhat in response, but the experiments all show a nonlinear benefit in greater bulb size, with the greatest benefit occurring as spacing increases from the most dense. Optimal spacing achieves a balance between maximum yield by weight and satisfactory bulb size for the market or table. Both the spacing between the rows and the spacing within each row can be manipulated to achieve a sweet spot for your garlic cultivars, growing conditions, and market or table expectations. Once you have established a successful baseline for plant spacing, you can experiment with alternate spacings to optimize the harvest. Other factors will also influence decisions on plant spacing, including accommodations to farm machinery and cultivation practices.

## BED CONFIGURATION AND SPACING

Garlic can simply be planted in a row or two in a garden plot along with onions, greens, or whatever other vegetables one is growing, as long as taller plants do not inappropriately shade shorter plants. Some garlic cultivars can reach a height of 7 ft. (2.1 m), if one includes bolting cultivars with scapes that have been allowed to fully elongate. The garlic enthusiast or small-scale grower will more likely want a dedicated garlic bed or series of beds. A planting bed should permit reaching halfway across its width from either side. In this way, one has ready access to all of the bed without treading through it or straining to reach the center. For those growing garlic on a larger scale, row and bed spacing will be partly dictated by the particular machinery to be used, so that wheel tracks fall between rows and beds, and other such considerations.

Garlic is often planted in raised beds. This is a good general methodology, though not always essential. Garlic grown in heavy soils in cool, wet climates benefits the most from raised beds. However, in areas with severe winters, garlic is more vulnerable to cold damage in raised beds. In dry climates with little rainfall, less moisture may be available to the plant in a raised bed. If the soil texture is hard or otherwise tends to repel water, moisture may simply run off the raised bed, away from the garlic roots. The particular circumstances will dictate whether or not a raised bed is preferable.

Another type of raised bed system can be employed to protect against rodents. Garlic proponent and author Chester Aaron (2002) grows garlic in an area with a rampant gopher population. He uses redwood planting boxes that are 12 in. (30 cm) high, 4 ft. (1.2 m) wide, and 10 ft. (3 m) long. The bottoms have a chicken-wire screen to prevent gopher incursion, and the sides are just tall enough to prevent the rodents from climbing into them, though occasionally Aaron has lost a box of garlic to more venturesome or athletic gophers. As with any system, there are compromises: The redwood boxes lend themselves less well to soil and crop rotation, thus increasing the risk of soil contamination and disease. The current cost of redwood is very high, and quality has declined, so Aaron is experimenting with other materials. Also, the garlic roots extend through the wire mesh to the soil below and are "trimmed" by the gophers. Nonetheless, Aaron has had good success with this method for some two decades, and its appeal remains. More recently he has tried stacking his boxes on top of each other to create a 24 in. (60 cm) raised bed. With substantially increased depth for gopher-free root growth, his garlic plants are more robust and produce larger bulbs.

Row planting in a field is typically a large-scale commercial farming approach. It requires greater spacing between rows for tractor wheels and equipment but also allows for closer spacing within the rows. Row spacing is largely determined by the spacing needs of the equipment. Planting beds, rather than field rows, are the norm for smaller-scale specialty garlic growers with no or minimal farm machinery. The rows in planting beds will generally be closer together than field rows, but the planting distance of the cloves within the rows will generally be greater. Planting beds are also common for larger-scale farming operations for garlic produced for the fresh market. In this context the field is comprised of a series of garlic beds that may be many hundreds of feet in length. If tractors or other mechanized equipment are used to cultivate the garlic beds, the width of the beds and the spacing between beds need to accommodate the equipment.

Given these parameters, one might expect perhaps one or two recommendations to suit a particular set of requirements. However, the number of different spacing regimens seems to nearly equal the number of successful garlic growers. Both row spacing and plant spacing within the row can be manipulated to give the garlic plant the space it needs. The following are some baseline suggestions, starting points that will yield good crops. These parameters can and should be adjusted to best optimize plant spacing for your climate, growing conditions, machinery, garlic cultivars, and cultivation practices. Remember also that every garlic cultivar adapts itself to the conditions in which it is grown. If your growing conditions vary significantly from those where the planting stock was obtained, your best yields will usually come after several harvest seasons.

The width of a planting bed should be no greater than what would comfortably allow you to reach its center. The bed can be any length permitted by available space and desire. Garlic can be planted in rows either running along the length of the bed or across its width. Since I grow small quantities of many different cultivars, I plant my garlic in short rows across the width of the bed. As a baseline I plant the cloves in rows 10 in. (25 cm) apart with an in-row spacing of 6 in. (15 cm). My garlic beds are wider than they should be, seven to eight cloves across at the 6 in. spacing, and my wife and I suffer accordingly as we stretch to reach the center. With a 6 in. in-row spacing, planting six cloves across would result in a more reasonable bed width. I live in a relatively cool, northerly, marine climate with modest sunlight intensity and partial shade during parts of the day. If you are growing garlic in a more southerly climate, where the sun is more intense and directly overhead so that plants are entirely unshaded during the day, you may find that a tighter row and plant spacing will yield optimal results.

If you grow garlic on a larger scale, and particularly if you use machinery, your rows should be oriented lengthwise in the bed. Again, there are many spacing scenarios, some dependent upon the farm machinery in use. Texas garlic grower Bob Anderson (1999) plants raised beds 6 in. (15 cm) high and approximately 22 in. (55 cm) wide. He plants four rows in the bed. Within the rows the cloves are planted 6 in. apart. The beds are 5 ft. (1.5 m) apart from center to center. Montana grower Richard Wrench (1998) plants in beds that are 3 ft. (0.9 m) wide and separated by walkways that are 3 ft. wide. The rows are 6 in. apart. Within each row the cloves are planted every 7 in. (17.5 cm). Looking at it from another perspective, Wrench estimates that each garlic plant needs a minimum of 42 square in. (271 square cm) to grow properly, with a minimum of 5 to 6 in. (12.5 to 15 cm) between cloves. Inland Washington State grower

Richard Smith (1999) grows garlic in beds 4 ft. (1.2 m) wide and 200 to 350 ft. (60 to 107 m) long. Each bed has four rows of garlic spaced 12 in. (30 cm) apart. Within each row the cloves are planted 6 in. apart. Smith reports that closer spacing reduces the yield of large bulbs, particularly for the taller bolting garlic cultivars. Long-time New Mexico grower and author Stanley Crawford (1999) and his wife, Rosemary, plant rows 24 in. (60 cm) apart, with cloves spaced 5 to 6 in. apart within the rows. Fred and Laura Bacon (1999) plant their garlic in beds 2 ½ ft. (0.8 m) wide with an 18 in. (45 cm) walkway between each bed. At the Seed Savers Exchange Heritage Farm the garlic beds are planted with an 8 in. (20 cm) row spacing. Within the rows the plants are spaced 12 in. apart in a staggered pattern that reduces competition with plants in adjacent rows (Barthel 2002). The University of Minnesota Extension Service (Rosen et al. 2007) recommends double row beds 30 in. (75 cm) apart on center and 6 in. spacing within the row and between rows for a good balance of high yield and bulb size. They caution that the practice of planting 4- to 5-row beds on 3 to 4 ft. (0.9 to 1.2 m) centers with 6 in. spacing may cause too much competition for light and nutrients for the plants in the middle of the bed, which may result in smaller bulbs.

As you develop your own spacing, keep in mind this very important point: spacing considerations are for people as well as plants. You must have easy access for weeding, watering, mulching, harvesting, and general maintenance. You will want to be able to reach into the center of the bed, and there must be room between beds for work that involves tools or equipment. If you are hauling in bales of straw for mulch, how will you get it where you need it? If you are hoeing weeds or bending over to pick something up, is there enough space for you and your tools? I have little space for lots of garlic, so

I always push spacing to the limit. As I engage in contortive gymnastics to reach the center of the bed, I sometimes wish I had pushed the limits a bit less far. Some of my beds are on a slope, and as I stretch to reach the center from the uphill side, I envision myself tumbling head over tail feathers into the bed and smashing the plants not to mention myself. It has not happened yet, but I am sure it will. You (and I) have been warned.

## PLANNING

When it comes to planning and planting, I seem to modify my own ritual slightly each fall. If you are only planting a few cloves of one or two cultivars, little organization or planning is needed. At the other end of the spectrum, a large-scale commercial grower will need extensive farm crop management planning and cost analysis. The avid garlic enthusiast and small-scale commercial grower fit somewhere in between. I currently plant more than 70 cultivars into five beds of up to 176 cloves each, but even when I was only planting four cultivars in one small bed, some planning was in order.

Depending on whether space or garlic is at a premium, you should decide either how much garlic to plant within a fixed space or how much space to prepare for a fixed amount of garlic. My five beds define a fixed amount of space. Because I plant many different cultivars but relatively few cloves of any given cultivar, I plant each cultivar in short rows across the bed. This necessitates a carefully laid-out grid system.

I first measure the dimensions of the garlic beds to determine the number of rows and the number of cloves in each row. Next I list all of the garlic cultivars that I intend to plant. I allocate most cultivars at least one row. For those that are the least favored for whatever reason, I allocate only partial

Planning, measuring, and plotting a small garden bed for many different cultivars. Growing fewer cultivars would improve efficiency but would also limit the garlic aficionado's opportunity for exploration and discovery.

rows. In some instances I plant only two cloves, the second one solely as insurance in case the first one rots or otherwise meets its demise.

After allocating the minimum numbers for each cultivar, I count the number of rows left over and begin allocating them to favored cultivars. When the allocations are complete, I decide which beds will be planted with which cultivar and begin penciling in the relative locations in a listing of rows for each bed. Alternately, for a more graphical representation, I have also made a rough sketch of the bed and penciled in the locations of the cultivars. The locations can have a bearing on the harvest. For example, planting a short Rocambole cultivar in a center row, surrounded by tall Porcelain cultivars, is not the best idea and is likely to result in a harvest of small Rocambole bulbs. Generally I plant the Porcelain cultivars together in adjacent rows and where they are less likely to shade small or weaker cultivars. Except when it comes to height considerations, it does not matter a great deal which garlic is planted next to another, as long as the bed spacing provides the needed room to grow.

If you grow a number of different garlic cultivars, extensive labeling and attentive handling are essential. Garlic requires numerous operations from the initial plotting of the beds to planting, maintaining, harvesting, curing, and storing. If you are working with a number of cultivars it can be very easy to get confused or lose track of identity along the way. Always label the rows, and always have a separate map on computer or paper that shows where each cultivar is planted. Keep extra copies or backups of these records. Have a firm rule of thumb that you never move garlic without having some sort of label associated with it. If family members, friends, or employees help with the garlic, make certain they understand the importance of this rigor. If at any point you end up with garlic of uncertain identity, do not guess what it may be. Use it as generic stock. You have a responsibility to yourself, your customers, and to our garlic germplasm to ensure the integrity of its identity.

If you want to evaluate the yield of your harvest, you will need to weigh your planting stock. Weigh each cultivar separately, as some cultivars are more sensitive to the size of the clove planted relative to the size of the resulting bulb. Some cultivars, such as those from the Porcelain group, have large but very few cloves, requiring a higher percentage of the harvest for planting stock—and

thus limiting the effective yield for eating or selling. If you are evaluating other factors, such as different fertilizer regimens, scape removal, plant spacing, and the like, you will want to keep separate measurements for these factors as well.

## SELECTING PLANTING STOCK

Except for specialized purposes virtually all garlic is grown from cloves. If all goes well a garlic clove planted in the fall yields a garlic bulb the following summer. In selecting planting stock, avoid the garlic from supermarkets. It may have been irradiated or treated with growth inhibitors to delay sprouting. It may also have been stored under conditions that make it far from ideal as planting stock. Moreover, the specialty garlic cultivars that are the focus of this book are almost never found in supermarkets.

Ideally you should obtain your planting stock from a nearby grower or from a grower located at approximately the same longitude. The closer you are to the source of your planting stock, the less adapting your garlic will need to do to perform its best. That said, this ideal should not be an overriding concern. For the cultivars that interest you, there may not be a nearby grower. For a variety of reasons you may end up buying some or all of your planting stock from a distant location or much different latitude. This is not a major problem. It just means that some cultivars may require a bit longer to fully adapt and achieve their growth potential in your area. For some cultivars you may notice very little change in subsequent seasons. For other cultivars the adaptation may be more dramatic. Your garlic may continue to adapt and improve for three to five years or more, depending on the cultivar. The most significant improvements, however, will likely occur in the first few years. Ultimately, the best planting stock will be your own.

The quality of the planting stock is paramount. You do not want stock that is contaminated with disease. The proliferation of interest in specialty garlic cultivars, the emergence of many new specialty growers, and the expansion of informal networks for exchanging and trading cultivars have been a great boon to garlic enthusiasts. Unfortunately, these things also increase the risk of highly damaging allium diseases being inadvertently spread widely and rapidly. Although I have not yet encountered such a problem, the risk is there. New planting stock should be examined carefully before introducing it into your garlic beds. For that matter, you should carefully examine your own planting stock from the previous season's harvest before planting it for the new season.

Examine the heads and cloves for signs of mold. You may occasionally encounter individual bulbs with mold infection. Although this may not present a major long-term threat to your garlic beds, you should exclude infected bulbs from planting stock and isolate them from healthy bulbs. For bolting hardneck garlic, the central scape should be free of mold, both at the cut end and along its length at the center of the clove cluster. The base of the cloves should also be free of mold. Usually this is not a major problem, and you can quickly check as you select the cloves for planting. If any part of a garlic head has evidence of mold or other contamination or abnormality, avoid using any cloves in the head for planting stock. For more detailed information on the more serious threats to your garlic and garlic beds, refer to chapter 8.

Avoid any cloves that show nicks or bruising. Cloves should be firm, not soft, and the clove skins should adhere tightly to the clove with no evidence of withering or shrinkage. Select only the best-looking cloves from the healthiest, most robust bulbs. In general the largest cloves generate the tallest and heaviest plants, and more importantly, the largest heads at harvest. Clove size is especially important for many bolting cultivars. Usually the largest heads will have the largest cloves, but this is not always true. Sometimes the cloves in the larger heads will have divided into more numerous but smaller cloves. Examine the larger heads and select those with the largest cloves. Usually you can readily determine this by examining the whole head, but this will be more obvious in some garlic cultivars than others. The largest heads and cloves will dry out more quickly and will not store as long as smaller bulbs and cloves. This actually works out quite well. Plant the very largest garlic and save the slightly smaller ones for sale or for the table. The shape of the clove can vary, particularly with multilayered nonbolting cultivars that have inner cloves that differ substantially in shape from the outer cloves. Tests show that for cloves of equal weight, the clove's shape or position on the base plate of the bulb has no effect on growth or productivity.

Some cultivars, primarily certain Rocamboles, have a relatively high frequency of "double" cloves, meaning that the larger cloves are effectively two cloves fused together and contained within a single clove skin. If planted, these "doubles" will produce two bulbs that become flattened as they grow together. Although these oddly shaped bulbs are of minor consequence to the home gardener, they are of greater concern to the market gardener who will find them more difficult to sell. Cultivars with a propensity for doubles call for additional care and attention when selecting planting stock.

Sometimes planting stock for warm winter climates is intentionally subjected to a controlled period of cold to artificially vernalize the cloves. (The reasons for this are described in chapter 5 under "Flower Induction and Bulb Formation.") Unless you are intentionally vernalizing your planting stock, avoid planting stock that has been stored in a refrigerator or at temperatures below 50°F (10°C).

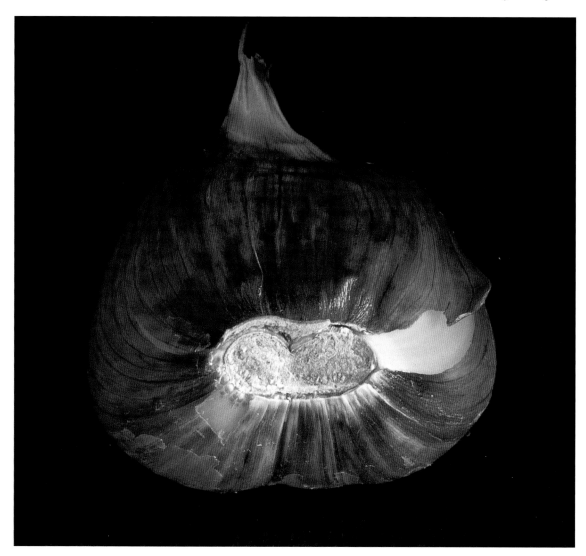

It is clear from looking at the basal plate on this large clove of the Rocambole cultivar 'Ontario Giant' that the clove has two divisions. A seam is also showing at the bottom. These are indications that this is a double clove. If planted, it will yield two flattened bulbs growing tightly together.

The garlic may fail to develop normally, producing small or misshapen bulbs.

Depending on the amount of planting stock you have on hand, you may want to break apart several heads to choose the largest cloves among them. Keep in mind that once a head is broken apart its storage life will be reduced. Any mechanical damage that may occur creates a vector for infection, which may not be overcome by growth in the ground if planting is delayed. Ideally you should not break heads of garlic apart until a day or two before planting. Keeping the garlic heads whole protects them from deterioration. However, garlic is normally planted within a few months of harvest and should generally be in excellent condition at that stage. Even if you break apart the garlic heads several days or more in advance, it is unlikely that you will see significant deterioration. One Israeli study found that large-cloved bulbs could be broken apart as far as a month in advance. As standard practice, however, you should separate your garlic closer to the time you will plant it. When a small cultural practice such as this is combined with many other small practices, the overall effect is multiplied, ultimately making the difference between a good garlic crop and an outstanding garlic crop.

Separating the cloves from heads of garlic for planting is sometimes called clove "popping" or "cracking." If you are field planting a large quantity of garlic, technique and practice are the biggest factors as thumbs begin to wear out and precious planting time is consumed. You will develop your own style and technique, but a few tips may be in order. Bolting cultivars usually have a more straightforward bulb structure, with the cloves arrayed in a single layer around the central scape. Most also have two natural halves, corresponding to the two leaf axils in which the cloves are formed. You can break the bulb skins by running your thumb around the scape just above the clove tips. At this point you can rock or twist the scape, and the bulb will yield along the natural fault line of the two halves. With the two halves apart, the cloves can easily be separated from the bulb. If you simply try to pop the first clove from a whole bulb by side or top pressure, you may be successful most of the time, but you risk damaging the clove. Nonbolting cultivars generally have multiple clove layers. You can slough off the outer bulb skins with your thumb until the outer cloves are exposed. After you have finished popping that layer of cloves, you will come to another inner layer of cloves encased in a bulb wrapper. Again, you can use your thumb to slough off the wrapper, exposing the cloves. The

process is repeated until all of the cloves have been popped. Silverskin cultivars in particular may have many clove layers and many tiny inner cloves.

How important is that funny little crusty part at the bottom of the clove? It is exceptionally important. This flat crusty plate is actually the plant's true stem. Both roots and leaves initiate from it. Garlic cloves usually pop handily and healthily from the bulb without inordinate attention to the clove's base plate, or stem, but the importance of the stem should not be forgotten, and damage to it must be steadfastly avoided. Cloves with a tiny or damaged stem are likely to have impeded growth, and damage is an entry point for infection. The health and size of the clove stem are usually not concerns that require attention, but if the stem is aberrant, plant vigor will be affected.

When you break apart bulbs to separate the cloves, some of the clove skins may separate from the clove flesh, leaving breaks in the skin or whole sides exposed, or even separating altogether from the clove. This is particularly true for Rocambole cultivars with their thick but loosely attached skins. While this phenomenon may not be ideal, it is not necessarily a cause for great concern. As an experiment one fall I completely removed the clove skins from a row of 'Russian Red', a Rocambole cultivar. In the other rows of 'Russian Red', I planted cloves with their skins intact. The cloves without skins grew completely normally, and there was no evidence of any difference with the cloves that had skins intact. It should be noted, however, that the clove skins do provide protection from mechanical damage, so cloves with exposed flesh will need to be handled with more caution. Although skins rapidly deteriorate in the ground, they may provide a temporary barrier from infection or dehydration. These caveats aside, it is not necessary to exclude exposed cloves from planting stock as long as they are handled with care and planted quickly.

## PLANTING THE CLOVES

Having discussed spacing and planning, we will now translate these mental and paper plans into holes in the ground and garlic cloves in the holes: it is time to plant. The next steps depend on the scale of your enterprise and your own habits and circumstances. Since I am a small-scale home garlic gardener (or perhaps large-scale in the context of home garlic gardens), I take my paper plan and begin to lay out a grid with a measuring tape or yardstick, and then I make planting holes at appropriate intervals with a dibble stick. I poke the first planting hole in each row in accordance with the spacing that I have decided. If the bed has been prepared properly, I do not need to dig a planting hole. If the soil has not been worked and is compacted, a narrow trowel can be used to dig a planting hole and loosen the soil below the clove. Properly worked soil, however, is certainly preferable.

After I have dibbled the first planting hole in each row, I then dibble the planting holes for the first row of cloves. This forms the x and y axes and becomes the template for the rest of the rows. If my calculations on the number of rows are not correct, I adjust the spacing slightly, or if necessary change the number of rows in the bed, adjusting my allocations and modifying the map of the bed. At this point I simply fill in the grid with the remaining planting holes, occasionally stepping back to eyeball the bed from front and side to make sure the rows are not wandering or converging. Before planting the cloves, I use the map for each bed to make labels for all of the rows. At this point all of the holes are prepared and all of the rows labeled, and it is a matter of planting the cloves.

Such detailed methodology is necessitated by numerous cultivars planted in short rows across the garlic bed. Most people grow far fewer cultivars, or larger numbers of each cultivar. If this is the case, it is more logical to plant the garlic in long rows along the length of the bed. It is still necessary to plan and mark the beds, but the process is far less elaborate. A planting jig offers greater efficiency and precision than a dibble stick. A jig can also be used for planting short rows, but it particularly makes sense for garlic planted in long rows. Many variations are possible, but a simple jig can consist of a handle and wooden dowels attached to one or more two-by-fours at the appropriate plant and row spacing. With a single press into the soil, the jig creates planting holes at a uniform spacing and depth. Single- or multiple-row designs are possible.

Various methods can be employed for larger operations. Some growers make custom machinery that can be pushed or dragged down the rows, creating planting holes at the appropriate intervals and depth as the device's spiked wheels turn. Another method involves creating furrows at the appropriate row spacing, and then, after the cloves are placed in the furrows at the appropriate intervals, dragging a small cultipacker down the row with a tractor to cover and firm the beds. Yet another strategy calls for using a cultivator on a tractor to mark the rows with shallow furrows, then using the wheel of a wheel hoe, or the like, modified with dibbles mounted at the desired spacing around the wheel. Running the dibble wheel down each furrow marks the row and prepares it for planting. Numerous variations on this theme are possible, depending on one's inclination and ingenuity.

Even on a relatively small scale, assembly line procedures speed the planting task. For example, one can pop the cloves the night before planting and put them in labeled sacks. If the cloves are ready, the rows labeled, and the holes dibbled, the final planting process can proceed quite quickly.

Plant cloves with the stem down and the pointed tip upward. This is easily accomplished if hand planting a small number of garlic cloves but more problematic if planting a large crop where there may be less control over the process, or where the need for mechanization arises. While planting cloves horizontally may not be ideal, tests have shown that it can be done without a decrease in yield. Planting cloves upside down, however, with the stems uppermost, reduces the yield of the crop. Apart from planting upright, most growers do not otherwise concern themselves with orientation of the clove along its axis. Interestingly, however, one study showed that if cloves were oriented such that their backs were along the row, 82% of the leaves were oriented along the row, facilitating cultivation between the rows.

Planting depth varies depending on the degree of winter cold. In California's Central Valley the cloves may be covered by only ½ in. (1.25 cm) of soil. In areas that experience severe winter cold, cloves may need to be covered with up to 4 in. (10 cm) of soil with an added covering of mulch. The range of planting depth need not vary that greatly between hot and cold growing regions. In Texas, Bob Anderson (1999) plants most cultivars 2 in. (5 cm) deep, 3 in. (7.5 cm) deep for the larger cultivars. In Montana, Richard Wrench (1998) covers the cloves with about 2 to 3 in. (5 to 7.5 cm) of soil, supplementing with an 8 in. (20 cm) mulch of wheat or barley straw. If the cloves are planted more deeply, with more than 4 in. of soil cover, germination may be irregular and bulbs may be smaller, particularly if the soil is poor and compacted. One need not be too precise, however. Garlic is not exceedingly fussy in this regard.

## BULBILS AND ROUNDS

Bulbils can offer an economical way to increase your planting stock, though you must leave some scapes on your garlic plants to harvest the bulbils from them. The bulbils from some garlic cultivars, such as those from the Asiatic and Rocambole groups, are fewer in number but quite large. You can plant them at the same time you plant the cloves, though the spacing can be much tighter. I have had some bulbils generate a fully differentiated bulb in the first year, although this is not necessarily desirable, as the bulb and cloves are quite small and are not the best planting stock. More typically the bulbil will generate a round (described in chapter 5 under "Bulb").

Ideally in the first year the round will be roughly the size of a clove you would select for planting stock, though the shape will be round in accord with its name. The following year the round should produce a good-sized, fully differentiated bulb. Rounds make excellent planting stock. Tests have shown that they are more productive and winter hardy than normal cloves. For cultivars with large bulbils, two years are required to get good-sized garlic bulbs from bulbils, but the planting stock is essentially free, and cultivating the bulbils allows you to significantly increase your production over a two-year period.

Many Asiatic cultivars have exceptionally large bulbils that are sometimes capable of producing a reasonably sized, fully differentiated, multicloved bulb in only one year. Other garlic cultivars, such as those from the Porcelain group, produce numerous tiny bulbils about the size of a grain of rice. These typically require three years or more to produce good-sized garlic bulbs, the first years typically yielding rounds of increasing size. Other garlic cultivars, such as those from the Purple

Bulbils from the Porcelain cultivar 'Romanian Red' are very small and require several years of growth before yielding good-sized garlic bulbs. Large Asiatic bulbils can produce differentiated bulbs in the first year of growth.

Stripe group, produce bulbils sized between the two extremes.

Prior to planting, bulbils should be stored as you would store other garlic planting stock. They respond to storage temperatures in the same way as garlic cloves. Keeping bulbils in the refrigerator, for example, can cause premature sprouting and

subsequent early bulbing and maturity, resulting in lower yields.

Generally, you should plant bulbils separate from other garlic, and separate from where you are growing or have recently grown other bulbils. Bulbils are small and elusive, and some are inevitably left in the ground at harvest, creating confusion if other garlic plants are subsequently planted in the same area. If space permits, this is another reason why you may want to rotate garlic beds on a yearly basis. In some climates, planting the bulbils in containers is another alternative for keeping them separated.

## SCAPE REMOVAL

The impact of scape retention varies among the horticultural groups. Evidence shows that for the cultivars of certain groups, leaving the scapes on until harvest usually reduces the size of the bulb. Porcelains and Purple Stripes are among the groups most greatly affected. For Rocamboles the effect is less but still significant, and the effect on Asiatics and Turbans is usually modest to negligible. As a general rule of thumb, the cultivars that produce the tallest, thickest scapes and largest umbels are the most affected by scape retention. A Porcelain plant with a mature scape is towering and statuesque, but its bulb is substantially smaller.

Should we immediately remove scapes to make sure we will achieve the largest bulbs? Scape removal is labor-intensive, particularly if you are dealing with a large number of plants. Cutting scapes also accelerates the plant's maturation and appears to reduce the storage longevity of the bulbs. Deciding if and when to cut the scapes is a matter of some debate. For cultivars that are heavily impacted by scape retention, most growers try an intermediate approach, removing the scapes so that bulb size is not severely reduced, but delaying removal so that storage longevity is not unduly compromised. As a good starting point when working with plants that are greatly affected by scape retention, try removing the scapes when they begin to uncurl. From there, experiment with removing scapes at different times until you deter-

The scapes of the Rocambole cultivar 'Carpathian' are an attractive display in the garden, but if the largest bulbs are desired, these scapes are overdue for removal.

mine the best balance for your growing conditions and cultivars. As a starting point for Asiatic and Turban cultivars, try leaving the scapes uncut on most of your plants. You may well find that their scapes can be retained with negligible effect on bulb size.

When you remove scapes, cut them with shears or a sharp knife just above the last leaf. This should be done on a dry, preferably sunny day so that the cut will rapidly seal and dry, minimizing the risk of infection and disease. Alternately, if scapes are removed relatively early in their cycle they can be snapped off by hand. Scapes are good to eat. (See "Scapes" in chapter 3.) For eating purposes, the most tender, youngest scapes are the best, but compromises are needed here as well, so that your bulbs have the most overall benefit from scape removal and you still have scapes that are good to eat. The quality of the bulbs, of course, will be the overriding concern.

Let us look at some examples and experiments with scape removal or retention. Growing conditions are a mitigating factor that may reduce the effect of scape retention. Richard Wrench (1998) conducted an informal trial manipulating nutrient levels and scape removal. With high nutrient levels, there was no difference in yield whether or not the scape was removed. With average nutrient levels, yield did increase when the scape was removed within three days after uncurling and becoming fully vertical. When the scape was removed prior to uncurling, however, no change in yield was observed. Since high nutrient levels increase yields generally, and appear to prevent the reduction of crop yield when scapes are allowed to remain, some growers may simply choose to fertilize heavily and forego scape removal. However, both heavy fertilization and scape removal may decrease storage longevity, so there are trade-offs to consider in formulating one's garlic-growing strategy. There is also evidence that heavy fertilization may not always be a material factor in mitigating decreased yields when scapes are not removed. Ample availability of water may more typically be the overriding factor in the effect of scape removal or retention on yield.

In controlled trials at two different growing sites in Minnesota, yields of a Rocambole cultivar increased when the scapes were removed at curling (Rosen and Tong 2001). The correlations with other factors were notable. Water and nutrient stress are key factors in the effect that scape removal has on yields. The site with highly fertile soil with high water-holding capacity showed a

yield increase of 5% when scapes were removed at curling. The site with low-fertility soil with low water-holding capacity had a yield increase of 15% when scapes were removed at curling. Soil nutrient amendments at this second site had an insignificant effect on yield. While this was not in accord with the results the researchers expected, it appears that the lower water-holding capacity of the soil, rather than nutrient deficiency, was the overriding factor. Except for soils with significant nutrient deficiencies, water and the water-holding ability of the soil appear to be greater factors in determining yield. The benefit of scape removal is most notable when the plant is under water or nutrient stress. Yield differences between scape removal and scape retention are significantly mitigated when water and nutrients are ample.

Carl Rosen and Cindy Tong (2001) found no statistically significant difference in storage quality resulting from scape removal. However, differences at storage temperatures of 63°F to 70°F (17°C to 21°C) may suggest that further study is warranted. Other studies and experiments point toward greater storage longevity when scape removal is delayed or not practiced. Ron Engeland (1991) describes several experiments overcoming short storage problems with the Rocambole cultivar 'Spanish Roja'. In one experiment he harvested, cured, and stored one bed of garlic with scapes intact. In the other beds the scapes were removed as usual. By October the bulbs from the plants with no scapes were dehydrating. The plants that still had scapes stored well throughout the winter.

Some growers believe that any scape removal should be done well before harvest time and that removing scapes just prior to harvest should be avoided, as it disrupts the plant's hydraulic system, causing slight shrinkage of the bulb and correspondingly decreased storage life. Other growers report that removal just prior to harvest has no deleterious effect. I have not observed any such effect in my own garlic garden. Of course, removing the scape just before harvest gives the plant little time to rechannel its energies to the bulb to increase its size.

Since scape removal is a labor-intensive practice, particularly for larger-scale growers, mechanizing the process may be desirable. Mowing the scapes is one approach, but inevitably some leaf material is removed as well, and the top leaves of the plant are the youngest and most vigorous. Keep in mind the study conducted by John Zandstra and Robert Squire (2000) in which the removal of only one leaf at the time of scape removal reduced bulb size by 13% and overall yield by 17.5%. When you remove scapes, take care not to injure the leaves.

Removing scapes costs time and sometimes money. It may or may not be economically justifiable when conducted on a larger scale. On the one hand, it generates additional overhead to coordinate workers and resources for the task. On the other hand, scape removal offers the prospect of increased yields, and the scapes themselves can be sold at market. Selling fresh-market scapes prior to the season's bulb harvest offers an additional and earlier source of income from garlic.

There is no universal agreement among garlic growers on the effects, importance, or timing of scape removal. The information in this section should give you a starting baseline. From there you can determine for yourself the best practices for your cultivars and growing conditions.

## CONTAINER GROWING

We do not often think of growing garlic in containers, but it is certainly an option. Although container growing is not as ideal as growing garlic in the ground, it can nonetheless be quite successful, and it offers those with limited space a way to grow garlic.

Garlic is portable. Its "seed" keeps relatively well. Unlike the actual seeds from most vegetables, garlic cloves are the food itself. For millennia, people have been carrying garlic around on their travels and migrations, and the traveling garlic has been both food and seed, depending on whim or need. In our own migrations the same principal often works well. However, our travels and migrations are not always arranged conveniently. Sometimes they occur when our prized garlic cultivars still need to be in the ground and cannot be harvested for transport. So, what then? If we know that we might be migrating while the garlic is still in the ground, we can plant garlic in containers for transport. We may need to leave behind most of our crop, but we can at least preserve the seed from our garlic library. In this scenario, instead of planting garlic in a planter box or the like, the garlic is planted in standard plastic nursery containers.

In general the regimen for container-grown garlic is similar to garlic grown in the ground. It should be planted in the fall and harvested the following summer. When growing garlic in nursery containers, keep in mind that it needs to be protected from hard freezing in cold climates. This can be accomplished in a variety of ways, including placing the containers in an out building that will protect them from a hard freeze but still allow for a period of vernalization, clustering the containers tightly together, burying them in the ground and covering them with mulch, or setting the clustered containers in a protected area and piling up mulch around the sides as well as on top of the containers. The specific regimen will depend on individual circumstances and the severity of the winters in a given growing area. The idea is to have the same conditions in the container as you would have in the ground. I have found that one-gallon containers work reasonably well, particularly if you need to have a large number of cultivars that are portable. Two-gallon containers are better, however: garlic grows larger, and the greater amount of soil moderates differences in heat, cold, and moisture.

## HARVEST

Far more than most crops, garlic spends a long time in the soil before it is harvested, typically nine months or even longer. Cool conditions in spring and early summer delay harvest, while hot conditions accelerate harvest. If the temperatures are very warm as harvest approaches, the soil must have ample moisture or the plants will be forced into early maturity and the bulbs will be smaller than desired. Conversely, avoid wet soils at the actual time of harvest. Ideally the plants should have ample water until maximum bulb size is achieved, and then the soil should be allowed to dry for harvest.

Wet soils at harvest increase the chance of root or bulb rot, exposure of the outer cloves, and staining of the outer bulb wrappers. Drying soils facilitate the plant's final maturation and the transition from vegetative growth to storage bulb. It is the natural beginning to the post-harvest process of drying and curing. Dry soil also allows the bulbs to be readily loosened from the soil and lessens the risk of disease and contamination. Harvested garlic needs to be cleaned, and dirt or dust is far easier to remove from a garlic bulb than caked-on mud. If you have control over the soil moisture, reduce and then terminate watering near the onset of harvest. Sometimes we have little control over soil moisture and are reduced to cursing a rain torrent that inconveniently coincides with harvest. If this occurs and conditions permit, delay the harvest until the soil can dry or at least become something

other than mud. If it is well into the time that harvest should occur and rain is expected to persist, you may have little choice other than to harvest in the rain and mud. If so, it is critical to provide conditions that allow the harvested garlic to quickly surface-dry.

Unless your soil is saturated muck, it is probably best to err on the side of too much moisture as harvest nears rather than too little. When I began growing garlic, I was so conscious of the need to allow the soil to dry before harvest that I began the process too early and bulb size suffered as a result. Though not ideal, wet soil at the time of harvest can be acceptable as long as the harvested garlic can be quickly surface-dried.

Garlic harvested prematurely will not have the rich flavor of mature garlic. A garlic bulb continues to grow as long as some green leaves remain, but if garlic is harvested too late, the outer skins will be absent, the cloves will be exposed to the soil and to disease, and the bulb may easily fracture. Such overripe garlic will not store well, and garlic bulbs with exposed cloves and no protective bulb wrappers are not readily marketable.

The best time to harvest garlic is a matter of balance. If all of the leaves are still green it is too early, and if all of the leaves have turned brown it is too late. Garlic should be harvested when the plant has a mix of brown and green leaves. Within this range a variety of factors come into play, including the cultivar, the climate where it is grown, and the intended use of the garlic after harvest.

As discussed in chapter 5, the leaves that we observe on the plant are actually the upper blade of the entire leaf, and what appears to be the aboveground central stem of the plant is actually a pseudostem, comprised of the tightly bundled leaf sheaths. Underground, another part of the same leaf sheaths form wrappers or bulb skins around the garlic bulb. Every aboveground leaf that is

These bulbs have been harvested too late. The bulb on the left is in reasonably good condition, but the remaining bulb skins may not adequately protect the bulb or sustain it in storage. The bulb in the middle has no remaining bulb skins; all the cloves are exposed, and some of the clove skins have worn away, exposing the clove flesh to dirt, disease, pests, and desiccation. The bulb on the right has completely fractured and ceased to exist as a bulb.

green corresponds to a healthy, tight wrapper around the bulb. Leaves wither and die from their tips inward and from the base of the plant upward. As maturity nears, the oldest leaves at the base of the plant wither and die. As they wither, so too does the underground portion that forms the bulb wrappers. The lowermost leaf is the aboveground part of the leaf that corresponds to the outermost bulb wrapper—the underground portion of that same leaf.

We have discussed the extremes of harvesting too early or too late, but within the generally acceptable harvest range there remain trade-offs to

consider. If the garlic is harvested when only one or two leaves have died, it may not have the flavor or size of a more mature plant. If the garlic is harvested when only one or two green leaves remain, the bulb wrappers may not be intact, the bulb will not store well, and the wrappers may be stained, decreasing the garlic's appeal in the market. Even if the wrappers are unstained, there may be too few to withstand the cleaning and preparation for fresh-market garlic.

So, how many green leaves should remain at harvest? There are several rules of thumb based on either the percentage or number of green leaves remaining. One rule of thumb calls for harvesting the bulbs when five or six green leaves remain, and another calls for harvesting when 60% of the leaves are still green. Another rule of thumb calls for harvesting when the plants are "half" green—that is, when the bottom half of the leaves on the plant are mostly all brown and the upper half of the leaves are mostly all green. These principles are predicated on the commercial sale of top-quality bulbs to the gourmet market. The fairly generous number of remaining green leaves means that there will be a similar generous number of sturdy bulb wrappers remaining. Stained or damaged wrappers can be removed, while still leaving an ample number of wrappers to protect the bulb during transportation and storage. This ensures that the garlic will arrive for sale looking its best. If appearance is less critical and some imperfect bulb wrappers are acceptable, the garlic can be harvested with fewer green leaves remaining. The USDA National Plant Germplasm System (NPGS) garlic collection in Pullman, Washington, is harvested when approximately 25% of the leaves remain green. Garlic that will be consumed within a couple of months can be harvested when more mature and "riper." This garlic will require less curing time before it is at its flavor peak, but it will fade fast and not store well. Garlic that is intended for planting stock can also be harvested later since long-term storage is not an issue, and the cloves are easier to separate in the more mature bulbs. Be careful, however, that the cloves are not exposed in the soil, as there is then an increased risk of mold and disease.

As always, there are exceptions to standard practices. For the common softneck cultivars commercially cultivated in California's Central Valley, the number or absence of green aboveground leaves has no direct correlation with the intact wrapper leaves surrounding the bulb. In these circumstances digging a sample of garlic plants helps determine when to harvest. For the commercial cultivars grown in this area, garlic is typically left in the ground until much later, when all of the foliage collapses and begins to die. It is common commercial practice in California to leave harvested garlic to dry in the field for several weeks, the bulbs more or less protected from the sun by the garlic's foliage leaves. Such a practice may be sufficient for large-scale commercial production but is not sufficient for growers of gourmet garlic. For gourmet garlic it is not enough to protect most of the bulbs most of the time from sun scalding and moisture. The careful grower will want to protect all of the harvest, not just most of it halfway. In any case, the practice used by commercial growers in California is not recommended if the growing climate offers rain, dew, or humidity rather than completely dry conditions.

Asiatic and Turban cultivars are another exception, tending to mature abruptly and split their bulb wrappers when only a few leaves have turned brown. Because of this it may be necessary to harvest these cultivars when the very first leaves begin to turn brown. This characteristic is likely climate dependent, however, as I have not experienced a pronounced tendency in these cultivars in my cooler growing conditions where the maturation process is extended over a longer period of time. If you are growing garlic in a climate where the harvest period coincides with significant heat in late spring or early summer, you should examine your Asiatic and Turban cultivars as soon as the first bottom leaves begin to brown. An early harvest will likely be warranted.

In general, nonbolting softneck garlic is more tolerant of being left in the ground too long than is bolting hardneck garlic, but wet soils may diminish any theoretical advantage. Although softnecks are less likely than hardnecks to split apart when overmature, the loss of bulb wrappers makes the bulbs vulnerable to damage and hurts marketability when exterior cloves are exposed. Wet soil conditions make all garlic more vulnerable to disease, particularly if only a very few green leaves remain. Conversely, if many green leaves and bulb wrappers remain, curing conditions need to be optimal and good air circulation is necessary to avoid molds.

Under normal conditions all garlic roots grow below the base of the bulb. If you want to get a sense for how your garlic bulbs are developing, or if you want to compare bulb development with aboveground indicators, you can carefully remove the soil to expose the garlic bulb, but not its roots. It is not necessary to expose a bulb completely when assessing its development; you can feel its size through the last bit of soil that covers it. After examining the bulb, cover it again with soil. Once the soil has been removed and replaced once, it is easier to remove again for subsequent examinations.

If you have a small garden plot it is theoretically possible to harvest every bulb when an exact number or percentage of green leaves remain. For practical purposes, however, and certainly for garlic growers with larger crops to harvest, such precision is neither practical nor necessary. An approximation of the preferred harvest time will suffice.

As a starting point for establishing your own regimen, try harvesting your garlic when approximately five or six green leaves still remain. From that general regimen you can experiment with different harvest times that best suit your growing conditions, cultivars, usage, and storage conditions. In my moderate marine climate, garlic matures very gradually, and I can get away with harvesting when only four or five green leaves remain. On the other hand, this reduced margin shortens storage. If the fall and winter are unusually cold and the house furnace reduces humidity more than usual, storage suffers noticeably, and I inevitably wish I had erred

Soil has been temporarily removed to assess bulb development as harvest approaches.

on the conservative side. For Asiatic and Turban cultivars, as a rule of thumb start harvesting when the first leaf turns brown, but also experiment with leaving the plants in the ground until several leaves turn brown. Depending on your growing conditions it may be possible to leave them in the ground longer before harvesting. As with many factors in growing garlic, start with a general rule of thumb and then make adjustments to find the optimum for your cultivars, growing conditions, and preferences.

When harvesting garlic, do not simply grab it by the neck and pull it from the ground. Depending on the condition of both the soil and the garlic plant, this rough treatment might work, but it risks damage to the bulb and the introduction of soil and disease into the bulb, which might compromise its storage. Moreover, yanking the garlic up by its neck may leave you with a handful of garlic neck, inconveniently separated from the bulb that remains buried in the soil. Before pulling the plant from the soil, loosen the bulb and its roots. On a small scale this is accomplished by digging beneath the bulb with a hand trowel or shovel and lifting the bulb in the soil. It is easy to inadvertently cut into a bulb if you dig too closely to the neck. Sometimes the bulb may be larger than expected or offset slightly in the ground. For these reasons it is best to penetrate the soil slightly away from the bulb, angling beneath the bulb, then lifting upward. The actual process is much simpler than its explanation and will be readily apparent after digging a bulb or two.

On a larger scale, undercutting the bulb is usually accomplished with farm machinery. There are a number of variations on the theme, but the idea is to run a blade beneath the bulbs, loosening the soil and lifting the garlic as the pass is made. Since this operation is accomplished all at once, it is important to have garlic cultivars in each bed that are ready for harvest at the same time.

Fully mechanized harvesting is suitable only for garlic intended for the processed market. Mechanical harvesting tends to damage the outer garlic cloves, subjecting them to decay in storage and making them unappealing and unsuitable for the fresh market.

Treat garlic gently to avoid bruising the bulbs. Bruised bulbs deteriorate more quickly and are at greater risk for infection. Immediately shield freshly harvested garlic from direct sun, which can quickly damage it. In hot-climate areas, some growers begin harvest early in the morning, finishing the day's work by midday. When exposed to the sun for very long, some cultivars also develop green or turquoise blotches on the bulbs.

What about allicin production? For the maximum yield of this compound, does it make a difference what time of day the garlic is harvested? In Native American lore, garlic harvested at midnight has the greatest healing power. Garlic researcher Larry Lawson (1997) conducted a controlled experiment to measure the allicin yield in garlic harvested at five intervals throughout a 24-hour period. The interval closest to midnight was 1:30 a.m. The allicin yield increased by 7.4% from 1:30 p.m. to 1:30 a.m. and then decreased back to its original value at 1:30 p.m. the following day. Lawson suggests that the differences likely occur due to movement of alliin into and out of the bulb from the aboveground portions of the plant. The differences are notable, though perhaps not sufficiently compelling to change one's harvesting habits. Harvesting garlic at night could present dangers, though vampire attacks would not likely be among them.

## CLEANING AND CURING

When garlic is removed from the ground, the skins of the newly harvested bulbs are covered with dust or soil, or, if one is less fortunate, caked with mud. Either way, at some point the bulbs need to be cleaned. Some growers immediately wash the bulbs before putting them up to dry and cure. Others believe that such washing is an unwelcome reversal in the bulbs' natural progression of drying down as their growth cycle is completed, and that washing also increases the risk of molds and other diseases. As with most growers of gourmet garlic, I prefer to leave the bulbs unwashed before curing. After the garlic has cured, the dirt can be brushed off or removed along with the outermost bulb wrapper. If one does decide to wash the bulbs,

it is important to make sure they dry quickly, and to hang the garlic upside down so that any remaining moisture from the washing process can drain from the leaf whorls. If this is not done, botrytis and other diseases can enter the pseudostem and infect the garlic.

Leaving the scapes on the plant will delay drying and curing, and on occasion I have removed the scape just after harvesting to speed the drying process. This practice has not seemed to cause ill effect. However, cutting into any green material risks the introduction of disease and is generally not recommended, particularly if humidity is high.

Garlic should never be dried in the sun, which can quickly deteriorate the bulbs. The harvested plants—with roots, bulb, pseudostem, and leaves all intact—should be dried in a shaded, well-ventilated area sheltered from the rain. They can be bundled in groups of 6 to 12, or even 24 or more in very dry climates, tied with string, and hung to dry, bulb portion downward, in a well-ventilated barn, shed, porch, garage, or the like. One method calls for tying an equal weight of garlic on each end of a string and then looping the middle of the string over nails pounded into the rafters of a barn or shed. A simpler, perhaps more elegant method calls for cutting a section of twine about the length of one's outstretched arms, tying the ends together with a knot to form a loop, putting the twine around the garlic, passing the tied ends through the loop, and then tightening the twine around the garlic bundle. When hanging garlic, make sure the bundles are snug and balanced so that the garlic will not loosen and fall during drying. Vary the length of the loops as needed. The twine loops are reusable.

(top) A bundle of 'Kitab', a bolting hardneck cultivar, hanging to dry. The presence of the rigid scape within the pseudostem causes the garlic to hang more stiffly.

(bottom) A bundle of 'Lorz Italian', a nonbolting softneck cultivar, hanging to dry.

Alternately, garlic can be placed in a single layer on any perforated surface that allows for good air circulation, such as a grate, screen, or even snow fencing. Though it is less ideal, the garlic can be spread out along a countertop or other surface with the leaves suspended in the air and the bulbs and roots in a single layer. I have also angled garlic out of wooden or cardboard boxes with the leaves suspended in the air and the roots and bulbs in a single layer. The boxes can present additional air circulation problems, however, so more attention needs to be paid to any tendency for molds to form. Fans can improve air circulation, reduce the chance of fungal diseases developing, and speed the drying process. If you are drying a lot of garlic in very humid conditions in a confined area, fans may be essential. In dry climates, fans are generally unnecessary. Conditions between the two extremes may or may not dictate the use of fans depending on the volume of garlic for the size of the drying area, relative humidity, and natural air circulation.

How long does it take for garlic to dry? The length of time is dependent upon a number of factors, including temperature, relative humidity, the amount of air circulation, the presence of a scape, the size of the bulbs, the number of clove layers, and so forth. Four weeks is a baseline, but the requisite time may vary from less than two weeks to six weeks or more. The necessary methods and care in drying vary widely. If you grow garlic in a humid climate that fosters molds, considerable care may be warranted, including tying and hanging garlic in bundles of no more than six, and running ventilation fans to circulate the air. On the other hand, if you grow garlic in a hot, dry climate, less attention will be required. You may find that you can dry most garlic cultivars in two weeks, and that you can easily hang 12 or more plants together to dry—or that you can simply lay the plants on a surface to

dry. In general, however, it is best to err on the side of caution, even in favorable conditions.

The curing process actually begins in the ground, as growth slows and leaves wither. Harvest marks the second phase of the curing process. The object at this point is not only to dry the garlic but also to foster a curing process that limits the risk of mold and other infections, conditions the bulb for lengthy storage, and deepens the flavors that we enjoy. The process should be gradual but not so prolonged that the risk of disease is increased. Rapid drying and curing under hot, extremely dry conditions may reduce the time that the garlic can be stored, as separation from the clove wrappers may occur prematurely, and may also cause the cloves and bulbs to shrivel. Prolonged drying and curing under very humid conditions increases susceptibility to molds and other infections, which can reduce the length of storage or make the garlic completely unusable. While this may sound like a difficult balance to achieve, it really is not. A wide range of conditions will work as long as common sense is applied. As a rule of thumb, garlic requires about three to six weeks to cure.

Garlic should not be trimmed until the vegetative material has turned brown. There are exceptions, however. In very humid environments the roots can continue to absorb moisture, hindering the drying and curing process. In such conditions the roots should immediately be pruned to about ¼ in. (0.5 cm). With bolting hardneck cultivars, make sure the scape is dry when it is cut. If it is still moist, the drying process is incomplete and trimming should be delayed. When trimming the scape, leave approximately 1 in. (2.5 cm) extending beyond the height of the cloves. This ensures that the bulb wrappers will continue to encapsulate the cloves. Trimming the scape shorter runs the risk that the bulb wrappers will no longer fully encapsulate the bulb. The scapes of some cultivars can

Trimming and cleaning tools—garden scissors and a toothbrush.

be trimmed shorter without risking a gap in the encapsulation, but 1 in. is a good rule of thumb. For nonbolting softneck cultivars, the leaves are trimmed in a similar fashion so that the bulb remains enclosed by the bulb wrappers. If the softneck garlic will be braided, however, the leaves are left untrimmed.

Choice of trimming instruments is a function of both personal preference and the number of bulbs that need to be processed. After a long stint of trimming, your sore hands will tell you if your tool is marginal for the job, or if it has an uncomfortable handle that causes hot spots and soreness or blistering. Heavy-duty garden scissors and pruning shears are generally the tools of choice. Garden scissors are usually better suited to the finer work of root trimming, while pruning shears offer more cutting power for severing

the heavy pseudostems on hardneck garlic. I use a particularly robust pair of garden scissors for both the roots and pseudostems, though my hand can get a bit sore after a long stint of trimming. Since I do not have any commercial production urgencies, however, I usually only trim a relatively small number of bulbs at a time, extending the process over a number of weeks. In this fashion, as I sit in the shade and let my thoughts wander while I trim, the process becomes less like a chore and more like a relaxing break.

After the roots, scape, and leaves are trimmed, cleaning or removal of the outermost bulb wrappers is the next step in the cleaning process. This can be either a significant or minor chore depending on the dirtiness of the bulbs and their intended purpose or market. Bulbs harvested from dry sandy soil will require little attention, while those harvested from muddy clay may be so dirty as to require removal of multiple outer bulb wrappers. Bulbs that will be used as planting stock or for one's own use can be cleaned more casually than those intended for specialty markets or as gifts. For consumers of gourmet garlics, a dirt-encrusted blob has far less appeal than a jewel-like bulb clearly showing the coloration and delicate patterning of its skins. Well-cultivated specialty garlics are much superior to commercial garlic, but to be economically viable they must necessarily command a higher price than the mass-produced product. Consumers of specialty garlics must perceive and understand this qualitative difference. Since these garlics are worth more, their appearance should reflect that higher standard.

A soft brush, such as a toothbrush, is the basic cleaning tool. It can be used to brush away dirt clinging to the outer wrappers, and can also be tilted at a slight angle so that the edge of it can catch the outer skin and help push it away from the bulb. The brush should also be used to remove any remaining loose dirt particles from the trimmed roots. If the outer wrappers are loose, a brush is unnecessary, and the outer wrappers can easily be removed with slight pressure from the pad of the thumb. Sometimes the outer wrappers are stubborn, coming off in fragments. In these instances a brush is essential for effective removal of the outer wrappers.

How clean should you get your garlic, and at the expense of how many bulb wrappers? Bulb wrappers offer extra protection for the bulb and help it store longer. Ideally you will have harvested the bulb at the perfect time, having left ample bulb wrappers so that removal of the outer wrapper layer during the cleaning process presents no storage issue. If, as sometimes happens, you are left with fewer bulb wrappers, so that the cloves would be exposed, or nearly exposed, if any wrappers were removed, you will generally want to forgo

any wrapper removal unless you will be using the garlic very soon. If you are selling garlic to a specialty market, you should harvest early enough so that you can have a pristine-looking outer wrapper. Sometimes, removal of more than one wrapper layer may be necessary to achieve this. On the other hand, if the garlic is for your own use, you may simply want to remove the loose dirt and the outermost wrapper layer—or whatever part of it sloughs away easily. It is not necessary to have an unstained, uniform outer layer. This cuts down on cleaning time, and may sometimes leave additional wrappers for better storage and protection.

## SIZING AND SORTING

If you are marketing garlic, you may want to sort your harvest by bulb size. A template or jig helps the process. Several variations are possible, including a board with a series of holes of varying sizes. In another method, a sizing jig is made by pounding nails into a board to form a V shape. Nail pairs are positioned opposite each other along the sides of the V. The distance between the nail pairs corresponds to your sizing criteria. You simply slide a bulb down the narrowing V. The first nail pair that is too narrow for the garlic to pass through establishes the bulb size—for example, 2 in. (5 cm) or larger.

Separate any bulb that has any sign of mechanical damage or disease. Diseased bulbs or damaged cloves should never be used for planting stock nor should they be marketed. Diseased bulbs should be isolated from other garlic bulbs and destroyed. Bulbs or cloves with mechanical damage can be used for one's own table, as long as they do not become infected or diseased.

This is also the time when you will be assessing the results of any yield experiments you may have conducted—yield for garlic with and without scape removal, different fertilizer regimens, planting densities, and so forth. If you are growing garlic commercially, you will also want to keep track of harvest yields to help you price your garlic and understand which cultivars are most profitable.

# STORAGE

Storing the garlic harvest for later consumption is a problem for growers. Garlic is usually harvested in the summer, and after a few weeks it is sufficiently cured and ready for the table. At some point garlic reaches its flavor peak and then gradually declines. Eventually the cloves shrivel or sprout, or they deteriorate if molds or other pathogens take hold and spread. Some cultivars store longer than others, but some of the most desirable cultivars do not have a lengthy natural storage period. Although some cultivars can be stored for more than a year, others begin to deteriorate within three to four months of harvest. How well and how long garlic stores is dependent upon the cultivar, growing conditions, and storage conditions.

Commercial garlic is often subjected to a variety of treatments aimed at prolonging storage, such as spraying the plants with maleic hydrazide prior to harvest, irradiating the harvested garlic bulbs, and controlled atmosphere storage. These methods are either not readily available to the small-scale grower, or would be antithetical to the needs of the grower who uses a portion of the crop for replanting, or who sells a portion of the crop to gardeners or other growers as "seed" garlic. In this book we will largely concern ourselves with garlic storage issues in the context of a home gardener or small-scale grower. For those who transport their garlic harvest with fleets of semitrailer trucks, information on chemical treatments and other specialized methods is available elsewhere.

The storage life of garlic depends not only on conditions after harvest but also on conditions while garlic is still in the ground. High temperatures before harvest during the last month of bulb development may inhibit natural dormancy, and bulbs in storage may tend to sprout sooner. In one study this difference in dormancy was observed between garlic grown at 72°F to 86°F (22°C to 30°C) in the last month of bulb development versus garlic grown at 52°F to 68°F (11°C to 20 °C). Other conditions are factors as well. In another study garlic grown without fertilizer amendment in poor soil with little organic matter stored better than garlic grown in soil amended with either organic or inorganic fertilizer regimens. Pumping garlic with nitrogen and water may produce larger bulbs, but they store less well. If you want your garlic to keep well, do not overwater or overfertilize. This does not mean that you should be exceptionally stingy, either. A middle ground is the best course of action.

Harvest and cure the garlic properly, as described earlier in the chapter, making sure to avoid moisture problems or anything else that might encourage mold or spoilage. Small to medium-sized bulbs store best (as long as the bulbs are not small because of disease or plant adversity), so plant or eat the largest bulbs first. Although small bulbs may not be preferred when using garlic in large quantities, they may be ideal when all you want is a few crushed cloves for a salad dressing.

Broadly speaking, the useful storage life of healthy bulbs ends in one of two ways: when the cloves sprout or when they dry out. If storage conditions are too cool and moist, garlic will sprout. If stored too warm and dry, garlic will dry out and shrink. The longer garlic is stored, the more critical the optimal temperature and humidity become. The good news is that garlic lasts reasonably well under a wide range of temperatures, so specialized temperature-controlled storage is not essential.

Garlic produces negligible amounts of ethylene and is not sensitive to ethylene exposure.

Unless one is inducing vernalization with specialized cold-storage methods, garlic should be stored above 50°F (10°C). Garlic stored between 40°F and 50°F (4°C and 10°C) is likely to sprout. Above 68°F (20°C) the rate of shrinkage begins to increase significantly and storage life begins to decrease significantly. Low humidity causes garlic to wither more quickly, but do not store garlic at exceptionally high humidity either. Storing garlic above 70% humidity will cause roots to emerge from the bulb and molds will likely form. In general, garlic stores best at 56°F to 58°F (13°C to 14°C) with a relative humidity of 45% to 50%, conditions fairly similar to those of a good wine cellar. Not everyone can provide these conditions, but even conditions that are less than ideal are generally suitable. We keep our house fairly cool throughout the year, and I have had good results simply keeping garlic in the kitchen area. Nonetheless, if you have access to an area that more closely approximates the ideal, take advantage of it. For example, I no longer have a wine cellar where I live, but the attached unheated garage offers good storage conditions for most of the fall and winter. Depending on what is available, you may find it helpful to change your storage area to take advantage of the best conditions at any given time.

Garlic needs good air circulation to remain healthy in storage and should not be stored in airtight containers. Good air circulation is less critical when the humidity is lower, however. When you purchase seed garlic from specialty growers, the bulbs often arrive in paper bags. For the short term this is generally not an issue, but you should not store garlic in paper bags for lengthy periods. The plastic netted bags for onions and garlic that one often sees in the grocery store are the preferred storage containers. Some specialty growers offer various versions of these bags, or pieces of netted tubing that can be cut in different lengths for various quantities of garlic. The ends of the tubing are knotted to form a bag in the desired size. The cost is usually very reasonable.

Keeping ability varies greatly among the cultivar groups, from Turbans and Rocamboles on the shorter end of the range, which may last only a few months in conditions that are less than ideal, to Silverskins and Creoles on the longer end of the range, which can be stored for more than a year under optimal conditions.

Garlic changes in storage. Immediately after harvest, the cloves are at their juiciest and the clove skins cling tightly to the flesh. Even the easy-peeling Rocamboles require some effort. When you slice through a clove, juices ooze at the surface. Mincing unleashes the sticky juices, which cling to the garlic, knife, cutting board, and fingers. At this newly harvested stage, the garlic is very good, but a bit simple. I usually try to quell my excitement and avoid a culinary plunge into the new crop until two or three weeks go by. Even the short-storing Rocamboles continue to deepen in character during this time.

During garlic's time in storage, its flesh gradually loses some of its moisture. As it does, the clove begins to shrink and draw away from the clove skins, making the clove easier to peel. Toward the end of storage, the clove will have shrunken considerably and the flesh will be somewhat dry and rubbery. Depending on the cultivar and the growing and storage conditions, the cloves may also begin to sprout. Slicing through a clove may reveal the initiation of green growth. In the latter stages of sprouting, the green sprout leaf emerges from the tip of the clove.

When is the optimal time to eat garlic? When is the flavor at its best? The answer depends on the cultivar, the conditions under which the garlic has been grown and stored, and the personal preferences of the eater. After harvest, garlic deepens in flavor for a period of time before reaching its flavor peak—or, perhaps more correctly, before it attains a flavor plateau that continues for a period before flavor and character begin their decline. The flavor plateau may be relatively brief, lasting only a few short months, as with Rocambole cultivars. For these short-storing garlics, a graphical depiction would be a steep curve with a short plateau. For other garlics, such as those from the Creole group, the curve would be much flatter, taking somewhat longer for the flavors to attain their peak, with a very long flavor plateau followed by a slow decline. I have had some cultivars from the Creole group that were still in that long plateau period nearly a year after harvest. Results can certainly vary, however. The same cultivars from another season had sprouted and declined markedly well before a year had elapsed.

Is garlic edible once the green sprout begins to show? Some people do not eat garlic in this condition, some remove the green growth and then eat the garlic, and some simply ignore the change altogether. To my taste, garlic is certainly better before it begins to sprout, but the green hardly makes it unusable. It is reasonably acceptable for sautéing, but it is best to look to other choices for using raw in salad dressings, bruschetta rubs, and the like, where a moister, more succulent garlic is required.

Other factors sometimes intrude on our storage and eating plans. Molds can appear in the harvested heads, causing individual cloves or entire heads to decay. One year, following a particularly wet growing season, the bulbs of some of my Porcelain garlic cultivars began to mold, rapidly changing my plans to eat them toward the latter part of their storage period.

Whether you are purchasing garlic or evaluating your own stock, you can assess its condition by examining the bulb. Ideally the bulb should be firm, with the skins clinging tightly to the bulb and cloves. A slight give when squeezed or looseness to the skins suggests desiccation. This can be further confirmed by removing the skin from a clove to see if it has shrunken and has begun to develop darker spots. If still salvageable, the garlic should be used as soon as possible. More advanced desiccation or mold is likely if the whole head of the garlic has shrunken and the cloves no longer fill their skins. Sometimes only a single clove will be obviously shrunken. Often this suggests mold. The rest of the head may begin to deteriorate, so any cloves that are still mold free and in good condition should be used as soon as possible. If mold is present anywhere in the head, none of the cloves should be used as planting stock even though they may not show evidence of mold. Also, look for any evidence of sprouting. If sprouts have extended from the clove tips, the garlic is well past its prime. It can still be consumed, depending on one's preferences, but it will be considerably less good than garlic in its prime.

Which garlics should you eat first, and which last? Storage longevity is the overriding arbiter of much of this discussion. Turban cultivars have only a brief period of dormancy and store for a very short time. They are also among the first ready for harvest. Although Turbans generally do not have the depth of character of the other cultivar groups, the bulbs and cloves are large and attractive, and the first new garlic of the season is always a joy to eat after miserly sorting through the last cloves from last year's harvest, looking for garlic that is still not too badly past its peak. Turbans are first to my table—their flavors simple and direct, used in abundance to celebrate the new harvest.

Rocambole cultivars have a relatively short storage period and are among my favorites, so I gladly begin eating them as soon as I can, usually soon after I have begun eating the Turbans. Some dishes that call for rich, sweet garlic character are best when prepared with the finest of the Rocambole cultivars, so I also save some Rocamboles as long as possible to use for these dishes.

At the far end of the storage life of Rocamboles, however, their meritorious character declines, at which point it becomes preferable to gravitate to other garlics, such as some of the rich-tasting cultivars from the Purple Stripe group. Purple Stripes store longer than Rocamboles and are very fine all-around garlics. The Creole cultivars store exceptionally well and have fine flavor, but they do not grow very large for me in my cool northern climate. I tend to use them raw for salad dressings and the like toward the end of the storage period, when large quantities of garlic are not called for, but where rich, good character is a requisite. If I grew garlic in a warmer, more southerly climate, I might not be able to grow Rocambole cultivars very well, or at all, but the Creole cultivars would likely grow larger, and I would begin using them much earlier in the storage season when I might otherwise use Rocamboles or Purple Stripes.

This illustrates some of the considerations involved in storing and eating various garlic cultivars. What you decide to grow and when you decide to consume it is dependent upon both personal preferences and growing region. Discovering your own preferences and patterns is part of the enjoyment of growing your own garlic.

## SPECIALIZED STORAGE TREATMENTS

What happens if you store garlic at a very cold temperature? Garlic stored at cold temperatures above freezing eventually begins to sprout. Except for the purposes of induced vernalization, garlic treated in this manner is usually poorly suited for planting stock and does not store very long after removal from cold storage. However, studies have shown that garlic intended for the table can successfully be stored for long periods at temperatures at or below freezing. In one test, garlic stored at approximately 32°F (0°C) and 65% to 70% humidity stored well, though the cloves stored poorly once they were removed from extended cold storage.

Storing garlic slightly below freezing is more effective than storing garlic at the freezing point. A joint study conducted by researchers Gayle Volk and Kate Rotindo of the National Center for Genetic Resource Preservation and garlic grower Walter Lyons demonstrated these results (Rotindo et al. 2004a). A selection of garlic cultivars were stored at 32°F (0°F) and at 27°F (−3°C) for periods of seven to nine months, removed from cold storage, and then kept in brown paper bags in home kitchens at temperatures ranging from 68°F to 86°F (20°C to 30°C). The testers evaluated the garlic for condition and taste at two-week intervals through the fall—more than a year after harvest. Garlic stored at 27°F was firmer with better flavor and stored longer after removal from cold storage than garlic stored at 32°F. After restoration to room temperature, garlic stored at 27°F showed no noticeable difference in quality or taste after up to eight months of cold storage. Additionally, the garlic could be kept at room temperature for at least two months without any degradation in taste or quality. The good news is that it is possible to have top-quality garlic for the table in spring and early summer, normally a difficult time for garlic aficionados, when many favored cultivars from the previous year's harvest are either gone or deteriorated, and when the new year's harvest is not yet ready for the table. The bad news is that most households do not have industrial-grade coolers capable of maintaining a constant temperature of 27°F.

A separate study showed that garlic stored much better at 28°F (−2°C) than at 33°F (0.5°C), but noted that freezing injury was a threat if undried cloves were placed into storage at 28°F to

26°F (−2°C to −3°C) immediately after the harvest. Garlic bulbs that had been dried in the open air for a period of six weeks prior to cold storage suffered no freezing damage at these temperatures. Thoroughly dried bulbs do not suffer injury even if stored at temperatures as low as 18°F (−8°C). However, it is important not to delay cold storage indefinitely if cold storage is the intent. If the bulbs are not still partially dormant at the outset of an extended cold storage, rooting will likely take place.

### Induced vernalization

For various reasons, planting garlic in the normal fall period may not be a viable option. If it is necessary to plant garlic in the spring, then the planting stock must be kept from deteriorating. Garlic stored using conventional methods may remain viable for spring planting, but in many instances specialized cold-storage conditions are necessary for the best results. In a study (Rotindo et al. 2004b) that included eight bolting and two nonbolting cultivars, garlic bulbs were placed in cold storage in the September following the summer harvest at two different temperatures: 32°F (0°F) and 27°F (−3°C). In April of the following year, the garlic was removed from cold storage and planted, then harvested at the end of July and cured. The planting stock that had been stored at 27°F yielded larger, heavier bulbs than the stock that had been stored at 32°F. 'Polish Hardneck', for example, when stored at 27°F had an average circumference of approximately 5 in. (12.5 cm) versus 4 ½ in. (11.25 cm) for bulbs stored at 32°F. However, the most dramatic differences found were between fall-planted garlic and spring-planted garlic. For the average of all cultivars, the spring-planted garlic yielded an average bulb weight of 0.63 oz. (18 g) versus 1.02 oz. (29 g) for fall-planted garlic. Note, as a disclaimer, that

these tests were conducted in Colorado. With some nonbolting cultivars grown in warmer southern climates, planting in late winter or early spring is the norm, and the cultivars are adapted to minimal vernalization requirements. Except for some garlic cultivars grown in warmer, more southerly climates, the test results tell us that fall-planted garlic has by far the highest yields and is clearly preferable. On the other hand, garlic that has been stored under proper cold conditions and planted in the spring can yield a very acceptable crop.

## COMMERCIAL GROWING

Growing garlic commercially can mean anything from an extra-large garden that allows someone to sell garlic and other vegetables at the weekend farmers' market, to the agribusiness world of Gilroy, California, with heavily mechanized, multimillion-dollar garlic processing facilities. Garlic agribusiness is certainly beyond the scope of this book. But while it is not my intent to focus comprehensively on the business and economic processes of garlic farming, some general information on the topic may be in order.

First, let us have a brief look at garlic agribusiness in America. In 2000, California produced approximately 87% of America's commercially grown garlic. Of the approximately 30,000 acres (12,000 hectares) of garlic grown in California, only 20% is for fresh market, and roughly 65% is dehydrated or otherwise processed. Approximately 15% of the crop is used for replanting, though much of California's planting stock comes from Oregon and Nevada. The total California crop value in 2001 was $151,866,000.

'California Early' and 'California Late' are the two most commercially popular cultivars. In

California, where both are grown, the growing period for 'California Early' is one month shorter than that for 'California Late'. 'California Early' is grown primarily for dehydration and processing. 'California Late' has traditionally been favored for the fresh market, but growers are increasingly turning to early-harvest cultivars to help combat the onslaught of imported garlic.

The importation of cheap garlic for the fresh market has heavily impacted commercial garlic growing in the United States. Imported garlic comes from multiple sources, but the garlic from China has been particularly vexing. Very cheap, and vast in quantity, Chinese garlic threatens to bury the American fresh-market industry altogether. Charges of illegal dumping and legal actions follow the ebb and flow of the threat.

If large-scale garlic growing, with all of its inherent efficiencies, can barely compete in the fresh-garlic market, what chance does a small-scale grower have? A very good chance, it turns out, since small-scale growing involves neither the same crop nor the same market. The small-scale grower can focus on the elite culinary cultivars and market to a more discerning clientele—restaurateurs and those who seek out farmers' markets and the like for the finest fruits and vegetables. Better yet, relative to most fruits and vegetables, garlic stores very well and can be easily shipped, opening up the prospect for mail-order and Internet business models to augment other marketing outlets.

As the scale of production increases, some of the concerns and informational needs are much the same as for other crops. Those headed in the direction of commercial garlic farming will want to draw upon traditional farming information for best operational and economic processes. With these caveats in mind, let us look at garlic farming and marketing on something less than an agribusiness scale.

First, and most importantly, do not start big. Start small.

Garlic is unlike any other crop. It is in the ground for nine months. You use the product of this year's crop to plant the following year's crop. How you grow garlic this year will affect your crop for two years or more. Which garlic cultivars grow best in your location? When will you know for sure? Garlic cultivars adapt to local conditions over a period of several years, but climate plays a big role. For example, you are not likely to have good success with Rocambole cultivars in southern Texas, and Creole cultivars are not likely to be highly productive in eastern Canada. Growing garlic is inherently labor-intensive. You may not even think about this when you are growing just a bit of garlic, but when you increase the scale, the labor and attention required become very apparent. Who will do all the work? Will it be you and your family, or will you need to hire labor? If you hire labor, how will this affect the economic picture? Some things can wait, but harvest cannot. Depending on the range of cultivars you are growing, the entire crop may need to be harvested in a relatively short time. Can you do it all yourself? Will the labor be available to take care of this short-term crunch? There are no exact formulas. Experience is the only thing that will teach you about growing and marketing garlic where you live. As you learn more, you can gradually increase production. If you can, talk to other garlic growers in your area. Their own experience can be a major help.

Next, how are you going to sell your garlic? Who is your market and what does your market want? Will your customers pay $1 per pound or $20 per pound? Most of us get into a pursuit such as growing garlic because there is something compelling about it. Sales and marketing are usually an afterthought, yet these matters become a very large part of the garlic-growing business. Did you just

If you want to grow garlic commercially, start small and gradually expand. Each plant must be touched or tended many times during its life cycle. On a large scale, the effort can be daunting.

want to be a farmer in the tranquil countryside? Will you enjoy spending a lot of time selling garlic person to person, or do you want the distance and privacy of selling on the Internet? What is the market like on the Internet? Maybe you should just sell wholesale. What sort of price do you think you can get selling wholesale? How do you build a customer base?

Will all of this work out okay? How will you know? Again, start small. You will have less at risk while you learn the benefits and pitfalls, and while you learn if this enterprise is viable for you. Your learning process will always be more effective if you are not already overwhelmed by more garlic than you can handle. Commercial garlic farming can be very rewarding in a number of ways. If you want to try growing garlic commercially, by all means do so—just start out small. Coping with large-scale failure and lack of sleep for weeks and months on end is not nearly as much fun as expanding and growing a successful small enterprise.

Richard Wrench (1998) has been growing and selling specialty garlic for more than two decades. For well-grown specialty garlic cultivars, he estimates a yield of 4000 to 6000 lbs. or more per acre (730 to 1100 kg or more per hectare). Remember, however, that a portion will need to be returned to the soil for next year's crop. For cultivars with only a few large cloves per head, such as some of the Porcelains, the portion returned to the soil will be substantial. Wrench characterizes anything over 3 acres (1.2 hectares) as a large operation and advises that a plot that is ¼ to ½ acre (0.1 to 0.2 hectare) can yield a nice supplemental income. Like virtually all experienced garlic growers, he also emphasizes the need to start small. If you are new to garlic growing in particular, and to commercial farming and marketing in general, you may want to start with an area that is substantially smaller than ¼ acre just to get a feel for what you will encounter.

If you are growing garlic commercially you will want to keep a record of the number of pounds planted and harvested for each cultivar. This information will help determine net yield and will assist you in setting the prices for your garlic. If you plant 10 lbs. (4.5 kg) of cloves for a given cultivar and harvest 80 lbs. (36 kg) of bulbs, your yield ratio for that cultivar is 8:1. To illustrate further, some Artichoke cultivars produce heads with numerous bulbs, and Artichokes typically produce relatively large heads from moderately sized cloves. At the other end of the spectrum, garlic cultivars from the Porcelain group produce heads with very few but very large cloves, and the size of the bulb is more dependent on the size of the clove planted. With four cloves per head, potentially a fourth of the harvest may be required for planting stock. These differences mean that Porcelain cultivars have a lower effective net yield, requiring a higher portion of the harvest to be devoted to planting stock. On the other hand, consumer demand might mean that Porcelain cultivars can command a correspondingly higher price in the local market—or maybe not. Knowing and understanding these factors will help you determine how to price your garlic and decide which cultivars are most profitable for any given market.

Detailed records will allow you to compare yields from year to year, determine comparative yields for different cultivars, and evaluate the effectiveness of different growing regimens, such as increased fertilizer, different planting densities, and scape retention or removal. Detailed harvest records in conjunction with detailed sales records will give you a more complete understanding of the economics of your operation and what is most profitable for you. Good records will provide answers to many important questions. For example, are the yields of a given cultivar increasing as it adapts to your climate? Is the increased cost of additional fertilizer justified by the resulting yield? What is the effect on yield of scape removal for the various cultivars? Are the increases in yield justified by the additional labor costs? If you sold the scapes as a fresh-market vegetable, how would this affect the economic equation? And so forth. Keeping good records will help you make good decisions.

And by the way, start small.

## GARLIC FROM SEED

Garlic growers sometimes use the word "seed" in reference to cloves reserved for planting. This misnomer grows out of a loose conceptualization that what one plants to later harvest as a crop is the seed, and because for practical purposes true garlic seed simply does not exist for garlic growers. In any case it did not exist until the 1990s or so. Under carefully controlled conditions using fertile cultivars, it is now routinely possible to produce true garlic seed by sexual reproduction.

Although humankind has cultivated garlic for thousands of years, until relatively recently garlic has not been a domesticated crop in the strict sense. Domestication involves selective breeding to meet human needs and preferences. Until the 1980s, when techniques for seed production were developed and subsequently refined, cultivated garlic was exclusively reproduced by vegetative means. No selective breeding was possible. For nearly all of the world's garlic crop, selective breeding still plays no role—but it is now possible.

Over the millennia, many garlic strains have accumulated genetic aberrations that make the production of viable seed virtually impossible. The most common cultivated strains, typical of what we find in the supermarket, have even largely lost their ability to bolt and produce normal flowering structures, let alone produce viable flowers and

seed. Garlic was long thought to be sterile, but in 1875 Eduard Regel described unique flowering characteristics in garlic found in the wild. This raised the prospect that some garlic might still be capable of producing true seed. As early as the 1950s, research groups within the former Soviet Union reported limited success in producing a few seeds from garlic strains originating in Central Asia. Little was known of this research outside of the Soviet Union, but by the 1980s, limited production of garlic seed was reported in Japan, Germany, and the United States. The strains that proved capable of producing true seed had their origins in Central Asia, notably the Tien Shan in Kyrgyzstan and western China (Etoh 1986).

The first garlic seed experiments were highly labor-intensive and yielded very few seeds. Refinements in methodologies and in the selection of suitable strains have vastly improved seed production. In more recent times, the United States and Japan have produced literally millions of viable garlic seeds (Simon 2000). It is now feasible for researchers and commercial enterprises to produce seed in quantities sufficient for plant breeding, experimentation, and the development of new cultivars.

What is the nature of the plants produced from seed? Philipp Simon (2000) reports a wide variation in bulb and plant characteristics and notable differences in culinary quality. Some of the new plants are nonbolting and incapable of establishing flowering structures or producing seed, while others are vigorously bolting producers of seed. Once a cultivar with the desired characteristics is produced from seed, it can be propagated asexually. Alternatively, some seed-propagated cultivars can be handled like onions—producing a new crop from seed that is free of pests, including nematodes and the viruses commonly found in cultivars asexually propagated from cloves. Eliminating viruses and pests can substantially increase yields. For the first time in history, seed production and plant breeding with cultivated garlic are possible.

The ability to produce garlic from seed is important in a number of ways. The absence of genetic refreshment is potentially threatening to a species, or at least constrains its potential. Genetic diversity from sexual reproduction ensures that a species can better adapt to new conditions, such as threats of disease or altered environmental factors. For a species that has largely reproduced vegetatively over a long time, garlic shows remarkable diversity and adaptability. Still, sexual reproduction, whether accidental in nature or through breeding and selection programs, offers the promise of significant benefit. Over the millennia, human cultivation sustained and fostered asexual reproduction to the point that garlic's capacity for sexual reproduction was nearly eliminated. Ironically, it is largely people that are responsible for recovering and preserving what was nearly lost as a result of human intervention. Seed production also opens the way for additional studies in systematics, inheritance, and genetic mapping, which will help us better understand garlic's genetic history and the breadth and depth of its diversity.

In nature, selection occurs randomly over time, and retained characteristics are generally those that benefit the plant's survival in its environment; other retained characteristics are incidental. Plant breeding is more targeted over a much shorter time scale. The ability to sexually reproduce garlic, for example, offers the opportunity to combine desired characteristics in a future strain that can then be reproduced. If one garlic cultivar has excellent storage properties but produces very small bulbs, while another produces very large bulbs but stores poorly, the two cultivars can be used to produce new cultivars that might possess both of the desired characteristics. Among the potential benefits

of garlic breeding are disease-free planting stock and improvements in disease resistance, hardiness, storage longevity, flavor, size, and ease of peeling.

Although garlic seed production has not been observed in the wild, Philipp Simon (2000) concludes that it is highly likely that it does occur. For garlic to set seed in the wild it must be capable of doing so without human intervention. In cultivation even the most productive seed-producing wild garlic strains need controlled manipulation in order to set viable seed—at least that has been the experience so far. Since the early 1980s many fertile garlic strains have been collected in the wild and from bazaars in towns along the Tien Shan in Central Asia. Most of the fertile garlic strains are associated with the Purple Stripes, a group that not surprisingly is genetically the most primordial. This is not to say that all Purple Stripe strains are fertile, however, or that all fertile strains are Purple Stripes. At least two fertile strains, 'Rosewood' (accession number PI 493099) and 'Yampolskij' (PI 540340), are associated with the Porcelain horticultural group. The flowers for most fertile strains have purple anthers. 'Rosewood' and 'Yampolskij' are again exceptions, having yellow anthers.

The garlic commonly found in supermarkets is far removed from its fertile origins. It is generally nonbolting, or occasionally, to the disappointment of the commercial grower, partially bolting—something of a weak gesture toward its primordial fertile vigor. The ability to bolt and produce fully developed flowering structures is an essential precursor for sexual reproduction. Beyond bolting, plants must be able to produce flowers that are capable of anthesis, and capable of producing fertile pollen and setting seed.

Relatively few cultivars are capable of producing seed. In one study of 210 cultivars only 11 produced seed (Pooler and Simon 1994). However, if basic criteria for seed production are included in the selection process, the percentage of seed-producing cultivars increases significantly. In another study of 47 scape-forming accessions from the USDA garlic germplasm, 19 produced seed, ranging from an average of 1.5 to 48.5 seeds per plant (Jenderek and Hannan 2004b). The rate of success in producing seed from previously vegetatively propagated plants is typically rather low, both in frequency and in number of seeds. Seed production in subsequent seed-produced generations generally improves, often dramatically.

Since Purple Stripe garlics are genetically closest to the origins of the species, it is perhaps not surprising that seed production capability is concentrated in the Purple Stripe group, both in terms of the number of seed-producing cultivars and the number of seeds produced per plant. In formal studies, cultivars from the Porcelain, Marbled Purple Stripe, and Rocambole groups have also produced seed. Anecdotal reports indicate that some Glazed Purple Stripe cultivars are also capable of seed production. With a few prominent exceptions, primarily in the Porcelain group, seed production capability in groups other than Purple Stripe appears to be marginal.

Seed production trials have largely been conducted using accessions from USDA and other germplasm collections, rather than cultivars that are in general circulation among growers. This affords a greater level of precision in selection and repeatability, but we are left wondering whether garlic in general circulation is capable of producing seed. This is largely unanswered, but we do know of some cultivars with proven seed production capability. Formal studies have demonstrated seed production from the Purple Stripe cultivars 'Verchnjaja Mcara' (PI 540356), 'Tien Shan' (PI 615416), 'Shvelisi', 'Red Grain', and 'Shatili'; the Porcelain cultivars 'Rosewood' (PI 493099), 'Yampolskij' (PI 540340), and 'Floha'; the Marbled

Purple Stripe cultivar 'Siberian'; and the Rocambole cultivar 'Rocambole Music' (PI 515972). Seed production from a Rocambole may seem surprising. A study conducted in 2004 (Volk et al.) at Fort Collins, Colorado (which I will refer to hereafter as the Fort Collins study), shows that 'Rocambole Music' belongs to the Rocambole group, though it is genetically distinct from other members of that group. Anecdotal unpublished reports have identified additional seed-producing cultivars in all of the aforementioned groups as well as in the Glazed Purple Stripe group.

Early studies on seed production seemed to suggest that only a rare few cultivars were capable of producing seed, but as seed production techniques have become more refined, and as many more formal and informal trials are conducted, it appears that many cultivars are able to produce seed. Although many, or perhaps most, of these may be rather poor seed producers, the ability to include their genetic material in plant breeding trials is a boon in itself.

Accessions in the USDA germplasm that have produced seed include PI 540314, W6 26171, PI 493116, PI 540315, PI 493099 ('Rosewood'), PI 540337, W6 12820, PI 540356 ('Verchnjaja Mcara'), PI 540319, PI 540357, PI 540340 ('Yampolskij'), PI 540316, PI 540335, PI 540327, PI 540362, W6 1885, PI 615416 ('Tien Shan'), PI 615418, PI 515972 ('Rocambole Music'), W6 1861, and W6 26183 (Barbara Hellier, personal communication; Maria Jenderek, personal communication; Jenderek and Hannan 2000, 2004b). This is not a comprehensive list. Broadly speaking, those toward the beginning of the list have been the most productive, but results often vary. For example, in one study W6 12820 was the third most prolific seed producer out of 36 accessions that yielded seed. The following year, in a similar study, W6 12820 did not produce any seed. One effort in the private sector produced seed from 64 different cultivars from various sources, including the USDA germplasm. Accessions from the NPGS are available in small quantities for research purposes.

A garlic plant's umbel is comprised of small separate flowers on pedicels. Except in the case of new genetic crossings, the umbel also always includes bulbils, which compete with the flowers for nutrients. The battle for nutrients is one that the bulbils almost always win, usually leaving the flowers to wither and die before anthesis is achieved. The bulbils and flowers are packed tightly together in a solid mass. As the umbel matures, the bulbils become somewhat more accessible and may begin to fall from the umbel, but by that time the flowers may have withered and died.

Although some researchers have produced first-generation seed without bulbil removal, eliminating competition from the bulbils is a key element in coaxing most potentially fertile garlic clones to produce seed. Subsequent seed-produced generations may not require bulbil removal to produce seed.

Often the spathe must be slit and folded away to expose the bulbils and flowers, so that the bulbils can be removed before they cause the flowers to wither. Removing the bulbils from the umbel without destroying the delicate flowers can seem like a tedious and daunting task. It is certainly tedious, but with a bit of practice it is not particularly daunting.

Various techniques may be viable, but one version calls for using forceps, tweezers, or other

(top) The bulbils have been removed from the umbel of the Rocambole cultivar 'Killarney Red'. Although the ovaries became swollen, this plant did not yield seed.

(bottom) An umbel of PI 540319, a USDA germplasm accession capable of producing seed. Most of the bulbils have been removed so that the flowers can continue their development without withering.

Garlic flowers are small and delicate. Normally a pedicel bears a single flower. A pedicel bearing two flowers and two swollen ovaries, as shown here, is relatively uncommon.

ad hoc tools to remove the bulbils. In a developing umbel, the bulbils and flowers are packed extremely tightly together. Removing the first bulbils is the most difficult task and may initially seem impossible. Start with a bulbil that protrudes somewhat prominently. Try to penetrate down to grasp it at its base or along its full length, and pluck it out if possible. Often the first few bulbils will be squashed and you will lose a flower or two. An alternative is to start at the base of the umbel and either apply the same method or poke the bulbils away, dislodging them with your finger or a nonpenetrating surface of a small tool, such as a small screwdriver or the handle end of tweezers. The idea is to create enough space by removing the first few bulbils so that the rest of the bulbils can be rocked toward the open space to dislodge them. A few flowers are usually lost, particularly when removing the first bulbils. Once there is enough space to rock or pivot the bulbils at their attachment point, they separate from the umbel reasonably easily. At this point it is simply a matter of working your way around the umbel until all of the bulbils are removed, being careful not to rip away the flowers in the process. If an area is particularly troublesome, it can be left alone for a day or two until the bulbils become less compacted and more accessible. Flowers near any remaining bulbils will tend to wither more rapidly. Bulbils that are crushed in the removal process but remain attached to the umbel may continue to develop at the expense of the flowers. Subsequent removal of crushed bulbils is more difficult, so crushing them should be avoided.

After initially removing all visible bulbils, re-examine the umbel within a week and remove any remaining bulbils that might emerge. After a bit of practice, bulbil removal is easy and routine, though still tedious. Unfortunately, seed-producing strains have numerous bulbils and flowers, so you will not be spared from repetitive tedium. In some strains, bulbils may fall away with relatively little coaxing, while the bulbils in other strains may affix themselves tenaciously. Subsequent seed-produced generations often have fewer, less densely packed bulbils, or no bulbils at all, greatly simplifying the process of seed production.

Spraying the green scape with liquid fertilizer once a week helps maintain vigor and longevity during the reproductive process. Some early experiments hypothesized that competition from the bulb could inhibit flower and seed development. The possibility of competition was eliminated by severing the scapes from the plant just above the pseudostem when the scapes were nearly fully elongated. The scapes were then kept in containers of water for pollination and seed development. Although this method was successful, subsequent efforts with intact plants in the ground have generally been more productive. Nonetheless, when outdoor *in situ* conditions are not suitable, the severed-scape method offers an alternative.

Garlic flowers are protandrous. The anthers release their pollen two to four days before the stigma of the same flower is receptive. A stigma remains receptive for one to two days. The flowers in a garlic inflorescence achieve anthesis over a period ranging from five to twenty days (Simon and Jenderek 2003). This means that individual flowers are incapable of fertilizing themselves, but the flowers in an inflorescence are able to provide pollen to other flowers that are in a receptive period. Pollination is ideally accomplished with insect pollinators but can also be accomplished with a small paintbrush and tedious repetition. It can be more carefully controlled by enclosing inflorescences in pollinating cages and introducing insect pollinators such as honeybees, leafcutter bees, houseflies, and bluebottle flies. Bluebottle flies have become a pollinator of choice among garlic seed producers. Honeybees, on the other hand, can damage garlic flowers, which are very delicate.

Environmental conditions can negatively affect seed production or cause complete crop failure. Thrips and mites are a major threat. Wind and rain can interfere with pollination and damage the delicate flowering structures. Heat sensitivity varies among clones, but temperatures exceeding 86°F (30°C) over a period of days during anthesis can cause rapid senescence of the garlic plants, withering flowers, and the decline of pollen viability (Simon and Jenderek 2003). Conversely, daily temperatures in cooler growing regions may be insufficient for seed set. For example, prolonged temperatures below 65°F (18°C) greatly reduce seed set (Pooler and Simon 1993). A daily period of temperatures between at least 70°F and 75°F (21°C to 24°C) may be necessary for effective seed set. In my maritime Northwest climate, minimum temperature requirements are sometimes marginal at best. In some instances it may be possible to sufficiently mitigate negative environmental conditions with shade cloth, wind blocks, and the like, to permit successful seed production.

Garlic seed is black and irregularly shaped, similar in appearance to onion seed but about half the size. Seeds are ready to harvest approximately 45 to 60 days after pollination. They can be treated with a weak solution of household bleach to protect them from disease and contamination. Like many alliums, garlic seed has a period of dormancy that can be reduced with a period of cold treatment. One method calls for keeping seed moist and stored in a refrigerator for four weeks before planting.

Many first-generation garlic seeds may be undersized and nonviable. Subsequent generations are usually larger with a higher rate of viability.

The germination rate for first-generation seeds from plants that were vegetatively propagated is relatively poor, ranging from 10% to 35%. In one study, some seeds were still beginning to germinate a full year after germination conditions had been provided. The germination rate for subsequent seed-produced generations is at least 65% and may be as high as 100%. Usually only a few seeds are produced from plants that have been vegetatively propagated. However, plants that have been produced from seed may subsequently produce more than 600 seeds per umbel (Simon and Jenderek 2003).

The growth of first-generation seedlings is typically slow and weak, and the tiny plants are at risk from diseases and pests over an extended period. Up to four months may pass before the plant forms its first three true leaves. Early generations may exhibit unfavorable characteristics such as stunted growth, deformed leaves, limited root development, and chlorophyll deficiencies. The unfavorable characteristics appear with a higher frequency in self-pollinated plants. Subsequent seed-produced generations from surviving plants usually display increasing vigor, often surpassing traditionally vegetatively propagated garlic. Under ideal conditions, some seedlings are capable of flowering in the first year of growth. More typically, scapes and inflorescences are formed in the second year (Simon and Jenderek 2003, Jenderek 2004). Seed-produced plants exhibit a wide range of phenotypic expression, suggesting significant genetic diversity. Curiously, bolting, seed-producing parents sometimes produce nonbolting offspring.

Researchers have been very successful in selecting seed-produced clones with improved characteristics that facilitate sexual reproduction in subsequent generations. After two or three generations, some of the new cultivars have fewer bulbils that are more easily removed, or even no bulbils. Even if some bulbils are present, bulbil removal is not always necessary for successful seed production in later-generation seed-produced cultivars. Improvement in male fertility is also rapid in subsequent generations. Once sexual reproduction is initiated and fostered, it is typically much easier in succeeding generations.

Traditional commercial agricultural practices that produce virus-free planting stock from tissue culture and isolated growing beds are costly and problematic in terms of preserving and transporting the planting stock. Some seed-produced cultivars have proven capable of yielding large quantities of seed. Growing garlic from seed, similar to the way onions are now grown, offers the potential for significant cost savings, and the relative ease of storing and transporting seed rather than bulbs.

The refinement of sexual reproduction techniques and the ability to produce garlic seed in relatively large quantities have made selective breeding programs possible for the first time. We now have the ability to better understand, preserve, and extend garlic's genetic diversity. Unfortunately, with these potential benefits also comes reason for concern. USDA and other governmental researchers are free and open with research findings and discoveries. Private industry has taken these pioneering research findings and is leveraging them for larger-scale breeding projects. To protect their financial investments, the private sector has largely kept its research and development secretive and proprietary. Some garlic clones are male-sterile but female-fertile, easing the process of F1 hybridizing and proprietary clonal development. The United States Patent and Trademark Office is already listing seed-derived cultivars for propagation by cloves. Propagation of proprietary cultivars can be restricted and controlled by various licensing agreements. DNA fingerprinting is becoming more sophisticated and effective, and plant breeders will be increasingly able to identify proprietary cultivars by DNA fingerprints.

Because of the financial incentive, large-scale seed producers are able to devote the necessary resources to develop new clones with a range of beneficial characteristics that might not otherwise be developed. However, these producers have little incentive to produce open-pollinated cultivars that can easily be propagated by growers. Rather, they have a financial incentive to produce hybrids that require growers to purchase seed anew each year. Widespread commercial adoption of proprietary hybrids could subject garlic to diminished genetic diversity, as has occurred with other crops in our food supply. Increased dependency on seed from a limited range of sources also increases risk.

Garlic seed production and plant breeding are not particularly easy, but neither are they entirely beyond the scope of smaller-scale growers and others who support open-pollinated plants and the commitment to fostering genetic diversity in our food crops. Public-sector research programs could develop open-pollinated seed-producing cultivars. Subsequent generations of seed-produced plants have proven much easier to work with in producing new seed, lessening or eliminating the need for specialized techniques. If some of these subsequent-generation plants began circulating among small-scale growers, the ability to produce garlic from seed could be readily available to many.

All of us can play a role in preserving the genetic diversity of our food crops, including garlic. If an ecological disaster should befall us, broad genetic diversity and open-pollinated crops will have the best likelihood of saving us—not a food supply heavily dependent on a small number of proprietary F1 hybrids from a limited range of sources.

# ∻ SEVEN ∻

# Taxonomy and Diversity

THE WORD GARLIC originates from the Old Anglo-Saxon *garleac*, *gar* meaning "spear" and *leac* meaning "leek," then a general name for allium plants. *Garleac* literally means "spear-leek," a reference to the plant's spearlike leaves. The botanical name for garlic is *Allium sativum*. At one time taxonomists postulated a separate species for wild garlic, *A. longicuspis*, but molecular evidence shows that all garlic belongs to *A. sativum*. Taxonomic placement of alliums has varied over the years but now seems relatively stable. *Allium sativum* is a monocotyledon belonging to the . . .

    subclass Liliidae
    superorder Lilianae
    order Asparagales
    family Alliaceae
    genus *Allium*
    subgenus *Allium*

Various authorities previously included Alliaceae in the families Liliaceae and Amaryllidaceae, but it is now regarded as a separate family. Peter Hanelt (1990) further divides the genus *Allium* into five subgenera and sections within those subgenera. James L. Brewster (1994) summarizes this taxonomic schema as it relates to food crops and identifies two *Allium* subgenera, *Rhizirideum* and *Allium*, which contain our familiar culinary alliums. Included in the subgenus *Rhizirideum* are *A. cepa* (common onion, shallot), *A. fistulosum* (Japanese bunching onion, Welsh onion), *A. chinense* (rakkyo), *A. schoenoprasum* (chive), and *A. tuberosum* (garlic chive). The subgenus *Allium* includes *A. ampeloprasum* (leek, elephant garlic, pearl onion, and kurrat) and *A. sativum* (garlic).

All alliums have a distinctive smell and taste that are characteristic of the genus. Within the genus, the numerous species also have their own characteristic smells and tastes—with *Allium sativum*, for example, significantly differing from *A. cepa*. More subtle variations are also evident within each species, and often among the various horticultural groups and cultivars. Chapter 9 discusses the bases for these differences in greater detail.

What morphological criteria are paramount in garlic taxonomy? As with most plants, the inflorescences—the structural elements of sexual reproduction—are among the most reliable, stable, and telling elements in traditional taxonomy. This is all well and good, except that many garlic strains never flower, and some flower only under certain environmental conditions. Of those that do flower reliably, almost none except subsequent generations of certain select hybrid manipulations are currently known to achieve full development—anthesis and seed set—without mechanical intervention to remove bulbils from the umbel and optimize conditions for development. Nonetheless, nurturing full development of the inflorescence can yield important information for some strains, such as the color, number, and size of flowers and bulbils; anther color; and stigma position.

Other morphological elements are useful in taxonomy, such as bulb shape; number and size of primary cloves; number of leaf axils forming the primary cloves; number of secondary cloves formed in a lateral bud or a primary clove; bulb weight; color and number of protective clove leaves; width, length, and angle of foliage leaves; and plant height. Some of these elements may vary considerably, however, depending on growing conditions. For example, variations in soil nutrients can have a major effect on bulb and clove skin coloration. Physiological and ecological characteristics that are useful in taxonomy include winter hardiness, time of bulbing, time of maturity, and temperature and day length requirements for bulb formation (Takagi 1990).

In the world of taxonomy, molecular markers, particularly plant DNA, have become powerful tools in determining lineage and the ancestral relationships of plants. Unfortunately, since garlic has largely been the product of asexual reproduction in modern history, it is not entirely clear which garlic strains may have arisen as a result of sexual reproduction and which may have arisen

vegetatively. Thus it is not always clear what groupings of strains with similar molecular signatures may mean from an evolutionary standpoint. That is, do the groupings reflect an ancestral and evolutionary relationship, or might recent vegetative sports have similar molecular signatures as strains arising from a completely different lineage? Or is some combination of both factors at play? Regardless of this conundrum, molecular markers such as plant DNA have become exceptionally valuable tools in helping us understand garlic and the similarities and differences among the many garlic strains. As molecular tools and analytical methods become more sophisticated, we can expect that the evolutionary lineages of various garlic strains will become better delineated. For example, using certain models of maternally inherited mutational change, it may be possible to calculate the relative age of mutations and establish an ordered timeline for the origins of the many garlic strains (Christopher Richards, personal communication).

Advancements in genetic research have been rapid and profound. We can look forward to a far more complete understanding of the garlic genome in the years to come, but the advancements in our understanding have already been dramatic and remarkable.

## GARLIC SPECIES

Although some differences of opinion remain, most researchers now conclude that there is only one species of garlic, *Allium sativum*. The relatively recent availability of molecular tools in plant research has helped transform our understanding of garlic. Beginning in the 1990s and continuing into the new millennium, a series of studies employing molecular markers and increasingly sophisticated

DNA analyses have affirmed that garlic is a single species.

*Allium longicuspis* had been postulated as a separate species of wild garlic, the presumed progenitor of *A. sativum*, the garlic we know in cultivation. *Allium sativum* was long thought to be sterile, and in 1875 Eduard Regel first described *A. longicuspis* as the fertile ancestral species from which the cultivated *A. sativum* originated. In more recent years, fertile garlic strains have been collected in the wild and from bazaars in towns along the Tien Shan in Central Asia. Since Regel's description of the ancestral species, there have been numerous scattered reports of *A. longicuspis* populations. Some authorities have speculated that *A. longicuspis* might simply be an old garlic strain that became naturalized in locally favorable growing sites.

The characteristics that distinguished *Allium longicuspis* proved difficult to define. Plants supposedly representing *A. longicuspis* and *A. sativum* were very similar with respect to overt morphological characteristics. Characteristics of *A. longicuspis* that purportedly distinguished it from *A. sativum* varied, and reported differences from various sources were often conflicting. Some of the distinguishing characteristics of *A. longicuspis* that were proffered included anthers exserted from the perianth (Vvedensky 1946), stamens with longer filaments, yellow anthers, longer leaf internodes, taller scapes, elongated cloves, and small bulbils. However, both collectively and individually, these characteristics are also present in numerous strains of *A. sativum*. Conversely, plants that are putatively *A. longicuspis* do not always have open flowers, and thus one of the presumably key identifying morphological characteristics, anthers exserted from the perianths, does not always apply. The notion of a separate wild garlic species has been put to rest to the satisfaction of most researchers by vari-

ous studies of biochemical and molecular markers conducted since the 1990s. None have sustained *A. longicuspis* as a separate species. Karyotype, isozyme, randomly amplified polymorphic DNA (RAPD), and amplified fragment-length polymorphism (AFLP) analysis show that the variations in the markers for *A. longicuspis* are also within the range found in *A. sativum* (Etoh and Simon 2002). Neither overt morphological characteristics nor molecular marker studies support a separate species of wild garlic. *Allium longicuspis* is simply *A. sativum*.

The perceived need for a separate species of wild garlic grew out of the assumption that all cultivated garlic was sterile, and the logical necessity that cultivated garlic must have come from somewhere—an ancestral fertile species. When garlic with viable flowers was discovered in the wild, it was assumed that this was the wild ancestral predecessor to *Allium sativum*. However, we now know that numerous cultivated garlic strains are capable of flowering and anthesis, and that many are also fertile in varying degrees, though they may need the assistance of bulbil removal and other manipulations so that the plant can redirect its energy toward seed production. Conversely, in Central Asia, the region of garlic's origins, both fertile and sterile strains are found in the wild. If there ever was a distinct species of wild garlic, it has been lost to the passing millennia. The apparent logical need for a separate species of wild fertile garlic has been obviated by the finding that many strains of *A. sativum* are fertile. Had this been known earlier, the notion of a separate species of wild fertile garlic may not have been posited.

Strains formerly classified as *Allium longicuspis* have many characteristics in common, though they are shared with other strains that are also genetically proximate to garlic's origins. Characteristics may include exserted purple anthers, a higher rate of flowering and seed production, relatively small bulbils in the inflorescence, and elongated cloves. Again, most researchers now conclude that *A. longicuspis* is not distinct from *A. sativum*. *Allium sativum* is the botanical name for all garlic, both cultivated and wild. A number of alliums growing in the wild have a garlicky smell and taste. They are sometimes erroneously called wild garlic, but all garlic belongs to *A. sativum*. The garlic strains that had previously been regarded as representative of *A. longicuspis* remain some of the more interesting and compelling plants in the garlic world. They exhibit the widest range of genetic diversity and are among the most primitive ancestral strains. Many retain the capacity for sexual reproduction and the prospect of generating new cultivars with unique characteristics.

## SUBSPECIES VARIATION

The classification of garlic below the species level remains a challenging and problematic endeavor. If our only exposure to garlic has been at the grocery store, we might well conclude that there is no variation of note. However, as garlic enthusiasts, researchers, and farmers-market shoppers know, garlic cultivars vary considerably in their characteristics. If you grow a variety of garlic cultivars in your own garden, the differences are even more evident. We can also observe that various cultivars have differences yet share common characteristics.

The single species of garlic, *Allium sativum*, exhibits substantial variation. Some of the variations are independent of environmental conditions, some are partially dependent upon environmental conditions, and others still are represented by their response to environmental conditions. Some of the overt differences in garlic include bulb shape; number, size, and coloration of the clove skins;

number of leaf axils that form the primary cloves; width and angle of foliage leaves; plant height; size, shape, and coloration of the spathe; flower and anther color; number, size, and coloration of the bulbils; thickness and texture of the protective clove leaves; and variation in the sulfur compounds in the cloves. These are not merely academic differences. Many define or reflect the particular characteristics we seek when we grow and eat garlic: the size of the bulbs and cloves, how they taste, how easy they are to peel, and how well they store. The response to environmental conditions among the garlic variations also has a direct bearing on the garlic we grow. For example, some garlic cultivars require minimal cold exposure to grow and produce well, and are far better suited to warmer climates. Others require a pronounced period of cold to grow and produce well, and are best suited to colder climates.

Because of the richness of subspecies variation, garlic grows very successfully in regions where success might have otherwise been minimal or nonexistent. Subspecies variation also offers us a choice of characteristics in the garlic we choose to grow, store, and eat. Ideally, one might say, we might choose to grow only one garlic—the one that tastes the best, produces the biggest bulbs and cloves, peels the easiest, stores the longest, is the most tolerant of heat and cold and drought and wet and soil conditions and day length and temperature and sunlight—and so on. Of course, no such single variant exists that exhibits the best of every feature for every location. For that matter, there is not always a single best. In taste, for example, we may all have strong general preferences, but different cultivars are best suited to different culinary uses. There is no single best way for garlic to taste.

Do we then choose a single cultivar that is the best compromise? Maybe, if we want to grow only one cultivar, but that would exclude us from the very richness of the diversity that is available. In the case of grocery store garlic, the compromise is even greater (although, hearteningly, I have occasionally seen a few real choices in grocery stores in the past few years). The garlic sold at the supermarket is the garlic that is the easiest and cheapest to grow, ship, store, and market in large quantity—forget any considerations of taste or other preferential subtleties.

If we had a cultivar that tasted very good and stored a long time, and another cultivar that did not store very long but tasted even better, would we not want both? After the best-tasting garlic had exceeded its storage limits, we would still have the garlic that tasted very good. If we had a cultivar with a hot, aggressive taste that produced very large cloves, would we not also want that garlic for times when the cuisine called for that taste characteristic or for times when we wanted to quickly prepare a large quantity of garlic? If we had only poor planting soil or if we lived in a very warm or very cold growing area, would we not also want choices that would best suit those conditions? Once one begins combining these and other preferences and characteristics, we quickly become thankful that we have such diversity. A single cultivar does not satisfy, but many do.

As we come to a better understanding of what is available, we naturally desire to buy or grow and eat a variety of cultivars. We also find a need to understand not only the differences but also the similarities among the numerous garlic cultivars, so that if we dislike or like the characteristics of one cultivar we might avoid or seek a cultivar that offers similar characteristics. Beyond the needs of the informed grower and consumer, if we are allium researchers or aficionados, we are further compelled to understand the subspecies taxonomy of this remarkable plant—how different morpho-

logical manifestations might logically be grouped, and how the various strains are related in evolutionary ancestry.

So, good then, what are these subspecies groups? Here lies the conundrum. It is very clear that garlic exhibits significant diversity at the subspecies level. It is also arguably clear that the degree of diversity and repetition of occurrence in numerous cultivars validate the merit of subspecies classification. However, overlapping shared characteristics sometimes make natural or logical grouping boundaries unclear—and sometimes untenable. Provisional groupings at the subspecies level have often seemed to be just that—provisional. Provisional, however, does not mean meaningless. Even if imperfect, subspecies groupings help us understand the similarities and differences among cultivars. Genetic studies with DNA markers have helped make the provisional groupings far less provisional, and we are coming to a clearer understanding of garlic's subspecies diversity.

Before we address garlic specifically, let us first review how plants in general can be grouped at the subspecies level. In 1753, with the publication of *Species Plantarum*, Carl Linnaeus promulgated the fundamental unit of naming that remains in use to this day: a binomial name consisting of the genus and the specific member of the genus. For example, the binomial *Allium sativum* consists of the genus, *Allium*, and a modifier that designates the specific member of the genus, *sativum*. The species name is the binomial *A. sativum*. The naming of plants of wild origin is now under the sanction of the *International Code of Botanical Nomenclature* (*ICBN*). The *Code* permits the identification and naming of variations within the species, at the subspecies level. Subspecies distinctions can be employed as warranted. The subspecies groupings, in descending order of significance, are subspecies (ssp.), variety (var.), and form (f.).

Plants of cultivated origin that are variations within the species are under the sanction of the *International Code of Nomenclature for Cultivated Plants* (*ICNCP*). Because of their nature and purpose, the *ICNCP* subspecies classification categories are not as unbendingly hierarchical as the *ICBN* subspecies categories. The principle cultivated plant categories include cultivars, hybrids, and groups. Cultivars may be propagated vegetatively or from seed. A cultivar may consist of plants that may or may not be genetically identical but which nonetheless have characteristics that distinguish them from other cultivars (Griffiths 1994). A hybrid is the product of sexual reproduction of two plants that are not genetically identical; it typically differs in some notable way from the parent plants. A hybrid may occur naturally in the wild, may arise spontaneously in cultivation without human intervention, or may be the product of human intervention and manipulation. A group is a category that designates two or more cultivars or hybrids that share common distinguishing characteristics. The *ICBN* and *ICNCP* have different but somewhat overlapping responsibilities, and the lines of distinction are not always clear. For many plants the distinction between wild and cultivated forms at the subspecies level is sometimes blurred. For garlic this is especially so.

Which applies when it comes to subspecies differences in garlic, the nomenclature for wild plants or the nomenclature for cultivated plants? Or do both apply in some combination? This is part of the conundrum, and it is not simply a matter of deciding which semiarbitrary naming system to apply. The absence of a clear indication of which system of nomenclature applies to garlic at the subspecies level points to more fundamental issues germane to the species and its remarkable history of adaptation, evolution, and cultivation. We have said that garlic exhibits substantial variation at the subspecies level. Let us take a general look at some of the differences and how some of them may have come about.

Garlic with new and distinctive characteristics can arise either vegetatively from somatic mutation or from sexual reproduction in both wild and cultivated plants. Unlike most plants in the wild, even wild garlic (at least in modern times) reproduces primarily vegetatively. For the most part, for the past many centuries and perhaps longer, cultivated garlic has rarely been reproduced sexually from seed but has almost always been reproduced vegetatively from bulb, cloves, or bulbils. Except for a few earlier experiments, only since the 1990s has cultivated garlic (again?) been manipulated to reproduce sexually from seed. With respect to garlic, the boundaries between wild and cultivated plants are not always clear. Garlic may have been cultivated for as long as 10,000 years, since the end of the last Ice Age. Much of the cultivation, particularly in earlier times, has been at the hand of nomadic or seminomadic peoples in Central Asia. Some of the cultivated plants may have been essentially wild. Conversely, some of the apparently wild plants may have once been cultivated and returned to the wild, resulting in feral reproduction. Such may have occurred within the last century, or perhaps as long as 10,000 years ago. Perhaps we would still consider a plant that has been returned to the wild within the last decade, or last century, a cultivated plant. Would we still consider a plant that returned to the wild 5000 years ago a cultivated plant? Likely not. And over the course of 5000 years it may have changed enough to be a different plant, in any case. Over time, in the course of reproduction, either sexually or vegetatively, these plants, too, would likely have generated new forms, and they in turn other new forms. In the wild, garlic reproduces vegetatively as well as sexually from seed. Differences can and do arise from vegetative sports. In these instances, differences may arise without a clear genetic path of parental lineage.

Let us look at a hypothetical example. Many garlic strains that are thought to exhibit the most primitive ancestral characteristics tend to have elongated cloves. Let us say, and this is purely hypothetical, that for every 10,000 or so plants that are reproduced vegetatively, garlic has a propensity to generate a vegetative sport that yields squat cloves and that this propensity applies to all or most garlic strains. This would mean that if one of our criteria for a subspecies grouping of garlic was squat cloves, many unrelated strains might fit under this grouping. Let us also hypothesize that long ago, through sexual reproduction, a line of garlic emerged that produced squat cloves in a percentage of plants. Let us add that from these squat-cloved plants, additional genetic variations emerged and established their own branched lineages with differing characteristics such as leathery clove skins, infertile pollen, yellow anthers, and fewer but larger cloves. Let us also say that the character of fewer but larger cloves periodically emerges as a vegetative sport in some strains but not others. So, to simplify, say we have 10 different garlic cultivars that differ in various ways, but all have squat cloves and fewer but larger bulbs. Are they related? And what does "related" mean? If it means sharing a common ancestry, some of the 10 cultivars are related and others are not.

Even if the cultivars do not share a common ancestry, is it still meaningful to group them and ascribe relationship by virtue of shared morphological characteristics? Probably, but since the plants may look alike for different reasons, the boundaries of the groups are likely to be unclear (as indeed they sometimes are in garlic), and variations within the groups may not be as logical or orderly as they might be had the group members all shared a common ancestry. Though fraught with

problems, placing garlic into subspecies groups still seems to be a worthwhile enterprise. How then should we decide upon the groups?

In the hypothetical example, characteristics of potential groups are already overlapping and there are many more potential identifying characteristics that may be shared or not shared in various combinations. If we are to form logical groupings, which characteristics are most meaningful? Squat cloves? Infertile pollen? Yellow anthers? For most of us, squat cloves is a more meaningful characteristic than yellow anthers. At least it is something that we can relate to better—nice fat cloves to peel, mince, and cook. Squat cloves might also be a good defining characteristic from a scientific point of view, though nonmolecular taxonomic assessments typically give more weight to morphological differences in reproductive structures than to other morphological differences. For garlic, where might this take us? Do we group based on anther color, clove shape, or something else? Or do we group based on some combination of elements?

Even if we decided that anther color was the most important criterion for a subspecies group, anther color could not always serve as a distinguishing characteristic since flowers and anthers are not always present in many garlic strains. Some garlic strains do not routinely bolt and do not generate external reproductive structures of any kind, let alone flowers and pollen. And here is another possible defining element in subspecies classification: the ability or inability to bolt and generate flowering structures. The inability to generate reproductive structures could itself be a subspecies delimiter, defining two broad categories of garlic at the subspecies level. In the vernacular of garlic growers and aficionados, these categories are called hardneck (bolting) and softneck (nonbolting). Such a schema has also been posited in the scientific community, dividing garlic into two major subspecies groups, with other groupings falling below them in the hierarchy. Here too, however, the taxonomic boundaries are less than clear. Many presumed nonbolting cultivars do bolt, with varying degrees of ease, in more northerly growing regions. To some extent the ability or inability to bolt is a matter of degree, and the distinction is at least partially dependent upon environmental conditions. This gradation along a continuum, and dependency upon environmental conditions, is hardly what we would like to see for a criterion that is to define a bifurcation of the species. This further illustrates the taxonomic conundrum we are facing with respect to garlic. We like to have things placed in neat, hierarchical categories. Nature is sometimes rudely uncooperative.

Since the 1990s, molecular techniques have given researchers new tools for assessing garlic's genetic diversity and subspecies groupings. As is often the case when new tools open new avenues for exploration and understanding, the first results have revealed greater complexities and generated as many questions as answers. Advancements have been substantial, however, and new tools and methods are beginning to bring some of our conceptual conundrums to resolution.

## Classification proposals

Before we leap to the contemporary findings of genetic research, let us take a closer look at some of the subspecies classification proposals that have been offered over time, noting what they reveal and where they tend to break down. An understanding of where we have journeyed will help us better understand where we are now—and we are not yet at an end point. We are still on the journey.

In 1827, in a monograph on alliums, George Don described two forms of garlic: nonbolting (softneck) and bolting (hardneck). This distinc-

tion was doubtlessly made much earlier by others, certainly by indigenous peoples who encountered the overtly different forms. However, the first description of the two forms in Western scientific literature begins an odyssey that will see the distinction repeatedly surface and repeatedly prove itself as problematic as it is useful.

In 1930 J. Prokhanov first described *Allium pekinense* as a separate species, believing it to be a mutation of cultivated garlic grown in Asia. In his description, *A. pekinense* was differentiated primarily by its broad, drooping leaf blades. Subsequently *A. pekinense* was treated as a variety of garlic, *A. sativum* var. *pekinense*, rather than as a separate species. In 1956 Johannes Helm described three botanical varieties of garlic: *A. sativum* var. *sativum*, *A. sativum* var. *ophioscorodon*, and *A. sativum* var. *pekinense*. Presumably *A. sativum* var. *ophioscorodon* denoted bolting garlic and *A. sativum* var. *sativum* denoted nonbolting garlic, but according to Henry Jones and Louis Mann (1963) the description promulgated for *A. sativum* var. *pekinense* could equally apply to more common strains such as 'California Early', a very common nonbolting cultivar. Jones and Mann stated that plant material obtained from Japan as *A. sativum* var. *pekinense* showed no clear distinctions justifying treatment as a separate species or variety, but they did note that the plants bolted freely—something that 'California Early' does not do.

In a 1978 paper that included a review of garlic taxonomy, Soviet researcher A. A. Kazakova noted that P. F. Zagorodskij in 1935, A. V. Kuznetsov in 1954, and M. V. Alekseeva in 1960 all independently divided garlic into two subspecies groups: bolting and nonbolting. Kuznetsov divided each major subspecies group into three subgroups. The bolting subgroups were Central Asian, Caucasus, and East Caucasus. The nonbolting subgroups were Continental, South, and South Coast of

Russia. Kazakova, however, rejected the findings of these researchers. In field trials, Kazakova found that bolting was an unstable characteristic with substantial dependence on environmental conditions. Instead Kazakova proposed a subspecies classification based on geographic origin, *Allium sativum* subsp. *sativum* representing a Mediterranean group with large bulbs and cloves, and *A. sativum* subsp. *asiae-mediae* representing a Central Asian group with small bulbs and cloves. Both subspecies included strains with both bolting and nonbolting tendencies.

In 1985 Takeomi Etoh addressed the variance in bolting propensity by characterizing some garlic strains as complete bolters that always develop scapes, nonbolters that never develop scapes, and incomplete bolters that exhibit an intermediate bolting response.

Hideaki Takagi (1990) broadly describes garlic groups as complete bolting, incomplete bolting, and nonbolting. The complete-bolting strains are characterized by long, thick scapes that bear topsets with many flowers and bulbils. Cloves are normally formed in the axils of the youngest two foliage leaves. Incomplete-bolting strains usually produce scapes, but they are thinner and shorter than those of the complete-bolting strains, and their topsets often remain clustered within the plant's pseudostem and bear no flowers. Sometimes the abbreviated scapes remain within the bulb, and the garlic looks like a nonbolting strain. Some incomplete-bolting strains form cloves in the axils of the youngest two foliage leaves, as in the manner of the complete-bolting garlic strains, while others form cloves in the axils of the youngest three or more foliage leaves, more akin to the nonbolting strains. The nonbolting strains do not normally produce scapes. They form cloves in the axils of the youngest five or more foliage leaves. Takagi's findings suggest that there may not be

discrete categories of bolting propensity, but rather a continuum of bolting propensities and a corresponding morphological continuum in the manner in which new cloves are formed—in the axils of two foliage leaves for the strains with the strongest bolting propensity, and in the axils of up to five or more foliage leaves for strains with weaker bolting propensity.

Acknowledging the wide range of variation among garlic strains and the overlap of characteristics that has plagued attempts to classify the strains into subgroupings of the species, Takagi concluded that attempting to classify garlic into varieties of the species was not productive. He suggested, instead, a focus on the individual strains, citing criteria for distinguishing among them. Of the useful morphological characteristics, Takagi included bolting type, number and size of the primary cloves, number of leaf axils forming the primary cloves, number of secondary cloves formed in a lateral bud or a primary clove, bulb weight, color of the outer protective clove leaf, number of protective leaves, width and length of the foliage leaves, plant height, and the tenderness of the green leaves. He also cited distinguishing physiological and ecological characteristics, including time of bulbing and maturity, temperature and day length requirements for bulb formation, winter hardiness, and bulb dormancy. Additionally, Takagi cited the taste of the cloves and adaptation to agroclimatic zones. Storage properties, the thickness and texture of the outer clove leaves, and ease of peeling can also be added to the list of distinguishing characteristics. At the time of Takagi's writing, the variation in the flowering structures was less well known, but flowering structures may provide the clearest and most defining set of overt morphological indicators, including the size, shape, and coloration of the spathe; beak length; number and coloration of the flowers; anther color; number, size, and coloration of the bulbils; height and curling pattern of the scape; and capability for anthesis and seed production.

In 1990 Peter Hanelt concurred with Jones and Mann that *Allium sativum* var. *pekinense* did not merit a separate group but should be included with others of the common garlic group. *Ophioscorodon* was named as a second garlic group. In *A Review of* Allium *Section* Allium, Brian Mathew (1996) indicates that the eastern Asiatic variant *A. sativum* var. *pekinense* should be regarded as another garlic cultivar, not as a separate botanical variety.

In 1991, Ron Engeland proposed division of garlic into two subspecies: *Allium sativum* subsp. *sativum*, corresponding to nonbolting garlic; and *A. sativum* subsp. *ophioscorodon*, corresponding to bolting garlic. Engeland characterized subspecies *sativum* as primarily clove producers and subspecies *ophioscorodon* as primarily bulbil producers. Engeland aligned his views with those of Kuznetsov in advocating that the two types should be accorded subspecies distinction and not merely be described as varieties. He proposed a "tentative classification of cultivated garlic varieties." In this schema the "varieties" of *A. sativum* subsp. *sativum* included Artichoke and Silverskin, and the "varieties" of *A. sativum* subsp. *ophioscorodon* included Rocambole, Continental, and Asiatic. The distinctions among the groups are detailed later in this section, but briefly, in Engeland's schema, Artichoke cultivars are described as maturing earlier in the season than Silverskin cultivars and having larger bulbs with a slightly flattened shape. Artichoke cultivars may produce bulbils in partially bolting false stems. Silverskin cultivars mature very late, have a more teardrop-shaped bulb, and may fully bolt in northern growing regions. Rocambole cultivars have scapes of moderate length that coil tightly. Continental cultivars produce very tall scapes with numerous tiny bulbils. As of 1991, Engeland had not yet been able to obtain a good representation of Asiatic cultivars with the broad drooping leaves, but he tentatively grouped them with Rocambole and Continental in subspecies *ophioscorodon*.

Most researchers today would not accord *sativum* and *ophioscorodon* subspecies status, and Engeland's "varieties" might better be regarded as groups or subgroups. A garlic grower, and by his own declaration not a taxonomist, Engeland nonetheless had a thirst for researching information and combining it with his own intensive observations of the growing habit and morphology of a broad range of garlic cultivars. His conclusions led him to establish garlic groupings and to anticipate additional groupings that would prove prescient of subsequent molecular research findings.

In the late 1980s and early 1990s, several researchers employed relatively new molecular tools to assess garlic variations. The studies attempted to correlate isozyme patterns with morphological traits. They were not fully successful, hampered as they were by a limited number of strains that did not reflect the diversity of the species, or by the limitations of a single enzyme system for determining patterns. However, the potential value of the studies was evident, and in 1993, Margaret Pooler and Philipp Simon analyzed 110 garlic strains using four enzyme systems. Other enzyme groups showed variation but were not sufficiently consistent for inclusion. The study also included an assessment of morphological traits, including number of cloves per bulb, bulb weight, skin color, number of flowers, number of bulbils, flower color, time of anthesis, anther color, and scape length. The study sought to determine if isozyme groups corresponded to morphological traits.

The results were highly informative. Each of the 110 strains fell into one of 17 isozyme patterns, and the 17 isozyme patterns fell into four major groupings. Not unexpectedly, the study found that morphological traits associated with the bulb, including size, number of cloves, and skin color, were partially dependent upon environmental factors, including soil and moisture content. Although growers and garlic aficionados focus keenly on bulb characteristics, these characteristics are less stable and less reliable than other morphological traits, notably the characteristics of the flowering structures. The study's morphological assessment showed that flowering structures varied significantly among the strains and effectively reflected the diversity of the species. As hoped, the flowering structures also correlated very well, if not perfectly, with the isozyme groupings. Given the undetermined genetic base with inclusion of strains arising, at least in part, from somatic variation, the study did not attempt to ascertain evolutionary relationships. The study results, however, were quite telling with respect to phenotypic similarities. Based on the relative differences among the 17 groups, a phenogram of the study results showed four major branches with additional branching under some of the main branches. The study showed no correlation between isozyme groups and geographic origin. At the time of the study *Allium longicuspis* was posited as a separate species of wild garlic, but the study found that strains that were putatively *A. longicuspis* did not fall into a distinct isozyme group, nor did they exhibit unique morphological characteristics, thus suggesting, as is now generally accepted, that wild garlic is not a separate species. As in previous studies and schemas, some strains, presumably including those that had been previously described as Asiatic or *A. sativum* var. *pekinense*, did not clearly resolve, falling into the group with nonbolting garlic strains with no external flowering structures. These "Asiatic" strains, however, did produce flowering structures and flowers in the study.

Ron Engeland had been an astute observer of the morphology and growing habits of his more than 400 garlic cultivars. The results of the Pooler and Simon study affirmed much of what Engeland had postulated. However, the study also shed additional light on logical groupings and prompted Engeland to revise his previous conclusions. The group that Engeland had called Continental corresponded to one of four major branches identified in the Pooler and Simon study. The study identified two subbranches of the major branch. In 1993 Engeland abandoned the Continental descriptor of the major branch in favor of designations for the two subbranches. He called the two subbranches Purple Stripe and Porcelain. The Pooler and Simon study identified a major branch of "nonbolting *sativum* type" garlic and two subbranches. The subbranches corresponded to Engeland's Artichoke and Silverskin groups. However, the strains that Engeland had called Asiatic and had placed in the larger *ophioscorodon* group of bolting garlic strains had an isozyme pattern that placed them in Pooler and Simon's "nonbolting *sativum* type" group, specifically in the subgroup that Engeland had termed Artichoke. In 1995 Engeland revised his classification schema and moved his Asiatic group from *ophioscorodon* to his Artichoke group in *sativum*. He concluded that "Asiatic garlics, despite being a distinct type of bolting garlic, were actually genetic softneck Artichokes that apparently bolt (produce stalks) in response to environmental conditions."

In his 1991 book, Engeland made passing mention of a group of *ophioscorodon* garlic cultivars that exhibited particular characteristics and performed better in warmer southern climates than in more northern climates. He informally referred to these cultivars as "Southern Continental." In his 1995 publication, Engeland concluded that the Pooler and Simon study results showed that the Southern Continental cultivars were a type of what Engeland had called Silverskin. He dropped the name "Southern Continental" in favor of "Creole." However, only one of the 110 strains in the study appears to be from this Southern Continental or Creole group. The morphology of that strain differs from the other strains that have the same isozyme signature.

Unlike most of Engeland's other naming distinctions that had some basis in correlation of isozyme pattern and morphological characteristics, the Pooler and Simon study results did not reveal a distinctive isozyme pattern for the Creole group corresponding with its morphology. Engeland concluded that the Creole group was a type of Silverskin garlic, but another conclusion could be that the four enzyme systems used in the study, and the limited representation of the putative Creole group, were simply not sufficient to resolve all of the logical groups, most notably the Creole group. Creole may be a taxonomically viable group, but it may not necessarily prove to be a subgroup of the Silverskin group. Subsequent studies will show that the Creole group is resistant to resolving well into a tightly defined group with unambiguous boundaries.

Based on his observations and the results of the Pooler and Simon study, Engeland went on to describe additional subgroups. He had labeled a group of garlic cultivars "variety unknown," and these had flowering structures similar to Purple Stripe cultivars but a bulb morphology that somewhat resembled Rocambole cultivars, with fewer but larger cloves. The Purple Stripe cultivars were comprised of four isozyme patterns and Engeland's "variety unknown" cultivars all fell under a single pattern. Engeland named this group Marbled Purple Stripe for the marbling pattern on their bulb wrappers. He noted that the differences between the Marbled Purple Stripe group and the standard Purple Stripe group were much greater than the differences in other subgroups and that the Marbled Purple Stripe group appeared to have many members. He speculated that further testing might reveal Marbled Purple Stripes to be a distinct group of its own and not just a subgroup of the Purple Stripes.

Engeland noted two Purple Stripe cultivars that exhibited somewhat different bulb morphology from the others in their group. Both were most notably distinguished by bulb and clove coloration. The bulbs were described as a "royal, glazed purple blush" tinged with gold. Later descriptions would include silver as well as gold hues. Neither of the two cultivars were included in the Pooler and Simon study, but Engeland regarded them as sufficiently distinctive to assign them a new group, Glazed Purple Stripe.

The flowering structures of plants are typically the most taxonomically informative. Engeland identified a group of garlic cultivars with a distinctively shaped umbel capsule, which he described as turbanlike. These cultivars typically mature very early in the growing season. Many came from Asia and were nonbolting when acquired, but subsequently exhibited a bolting habit. Engeland named this the Turban group. Like the Asiatic group, the Turban group seemed to bolt only in response to environmental conditions, and also like the Asiatic group, Engeland regarded the Turban group as a "genetic softneck" subgroup within the Artichoke group. Although some diagrams published by Engeland and Filaree Farm appear to place the Turban group in a specific isozyme group, Engeland (1995) stated, "So far as we can tell, no Turban strains have been included in electrophoretic enzyme tests by USDA researchers."

Engeland (1995) noted that the garlic group he had known as Rocambole equated to one of Pooler and Simon's four major isozyme groups. The major isozyme group was comprised of three different isozyme patterns, suggesting the prospect of additional taxonomic groups that might correlate with morphological traits. Engeland had observed that the Rocambole cultivar 'Carpathian' had straight leaves that seldom bent down at the tips. Later he identified other Rocambole cultivars with similar leaf characteristics and noted that the straight-leaved Rocamboles tended to produce more flowers than other Rocamboles, and that their flowers also tended to remain longer without withering. The uniqueness and the boundaries of other characteristics, however, was less than certain, and with the information at hand, Engeland did not posit a separately named group. He speculated that further research and the inclusion of tropical and semitropical strains in the studies would reveal additional garlic groups.

Other studies in the 1990s employed various molecular methods, and morphological and physiological characteristics in garlic classification scenarios (Etoh and Simon 2002). A study of Argentinean garlic, representing typical South American cultivars, concluded that they were of the "Mediterranean type" of nonbolting or incomplete-bolting strains. Another study applied a chemotaxonomic approach, comparing mitochondrial DNA in selected cultivars. The study results suggested five garlic groups. Most of the fertile cultivars were classified in the "Russian" group comprising Central Asia and the Caucasus. Strains from Central Asia showed the greatest genetic variation. Another study of 65 garlic cultivars from 25 countries (Lallemand et al. 1997) correlated isozyme types with morphological and physiological characteristics. The results were comparable to those of similar studies, showing definite though sometimes incomplete correlation of isozymes and morphological and physiological characteristics. Nine cultivars from Japan and northern China shared an isozyme pattern that differentiated them from other cultivars, notably those from Europe, Africa, and America, yet the nine cultivars did not display a homogeneous morphology.

Employing both isozyme and RAPD markers, Helga Maaß and Manfred Klaas (1995) proposed four groups for Old World garlic strains: *sativum* from the Mediterranean, *ophioscorodon* from central and eastern Europe, *longicuspis* from Central Asia, and a southern Asian subtropical group. The *longicuspis* group is regarded as the most primitive. In this schema, *longicuspis* includes a subgroup *pekinense* of bolting plants with coiling scapes from eastern Asia. The subtropical group may have originated from the *pekinense* subgroup in the distant past in northern India. The *ophioscorodon* group may have originated from the *longicuspis* group in Transcaucasia and the area north of the Black Sea. The *sativum* group may have originated from the *longicuspis* group in western Asia. It includes both nonbolting and incomplete-bolting types, which also showed distinctly in the molecular results. The strains in the study, however, showed relatively high genetic homogeneity, suggesting that a more diverse representation of strains might have revealed more.

## Identifying and preserving genetic diversity

Before moving forward in our survey of garlic research and the various proposals for subspecies classification, it is worth noting that there is a shifting emphasis in the purposes of these studies, particularly by researchers involved with germplasm preservation. Rather than focusing on establishing hierarchical categories for similarities, the thrust of traditional taxonomy, the focus has shifted to identifying genetic differences for the purposes of recognizing and preserving genetic diversity. The two objectives are not antithetical. One could argue that the end result will essentially be the same, though the pathways to that result may differ. This distinction may seem somewhat obscure, so let us explore it a bit further.

Contemporary research, and the application of molecular methods in assessing variation in garlic, has not focused so much on evolutionary relationships and taxonomy as on identifying and understanding the diversity within the species. Why is this so important? Subspecies diversity of garlic is well recognized but is less well understood. The world's food supply is highly dependent upon intensive cultivation of crops that have a relatively high degree of genetic uniformity. This places our food at increased risk from pests, diseases, and environmental changes and stresses. Preserving the genetic diversity of the world's crop plants is a vital need. A richer plant and gene pool ensures a greater ability to adapt to current and future conditions, and provides genetic material that may prove beneficial for some unknown future need.

Germplasm repositories, including the USDA National Plant Germplasm System (NPGS), maintain collections of plants representing the genetic diversity. Maintaining a collection of certain food crops, notably garlic, is particularly problematic. Garlic must be replanted every year to perpetuate the strain. Every germplasm accession must be planted in the fall, harvested in the summer, and planted again in the fall. The garlic germplasm is at perpetual risk from invasion by pathogens or other calamities. Although the likelihood of complete crop failure is very small, the risk is high. Unlike most seed crops, if there were a complete garlic crop failure, one could not simply replant next year—there would be nothing to replant. Cryopreservation offers promise but is time-consuming, expensive, and not yet broadly applicable. Ideally a germplasm should represent comprehensive genetic diversity without duplica-

tion, but germplasms inevitably have duplicate accessions. Particularly with respect to garlic, duplicate accessions are costly to maintain, and may divert attention from acquisition and maintenance of strains reflecting additional genetic diversity. Given the informal way in which garlic has been asexually propagated and extensively transported, traded, and retraded over many millennia, some garlic cultivars inevitably carry multiple names for the same cultivar. In any large collection of garlic, some duplication is likely. Conversely, genetically different cultivars sometimes have the same name. Names such as "Italian Red" and "Italian Purple" have become all but meaningless, except perhaps within a given locale where they might happen to refer to the same cultivar.

How does one eliminate duplicate accessions but ensure that species diversity is fully represented? Traditionally, plant morphology and phenotypic characteristics have been the basis for assessing the garlic germplasm. Although this sometimes works relatively well, garlic can exhibit a high degree of phenotypic plasticity. The same garlic clone may express itself differently under different environmental conditions. Genetically identical garlic may look and act differently depending upon where it is grown, giving further impetus to the generation of multiple names for the same clone. Garlic's phenotypic plasticity also brings confusion to the subspecies classification of garlic. The "Asiatic" group of partially bolting strains is an example in point, rarely bolting in some growing regions, while rarely not bolting in others.

## Molecular tools

Traditional methods for determining taxonomic diversity relied on differences among a relatively small number of characteristics, which could be mutable and dependent on local growing conditions. Molecular methods employ a large array of discrete, identifiable characteristics independent of growing conditions, offering a mechanism for assessing the diversity of the germplasm apart from environmental influences. In some instances, molecular techniques have revealed differences that were not overtly evident in morphological or physiological assessments. In other instances, however, molecular tools failed to identify important differences that were readily evident from physical observation. As molecular tools and the ways they are used become more sophisticated, they are increasingly valuable in assessing garlic's subspecies diversity. Let us now look in more detail at some of these methods and what they show us.

The landmark 1993 Pooler and Simon isozyme study of garlic diversity found a strong correlation of isozymes with flower-related morphological traits, but traits associated with the garlic bulb or with geographic origin did not show correlation (Ipek et al. 2003). The Pooler and Simon study, and subsequent studies using isozymes or RAPD, showed that the putative wild garlic species, *Allium longicuspis,* is not a distinct species but that all garlic belongs to one species, *A. sativum.* In general the isozyme and RAPD studies were effective in assessing relationships at the species level and generally correlated well with morphological observations, particularly those associated with flowering structures. However, the two systems were less successful in delineating finer relationships, and in particular, discriminating between individual clones. Better tools were needed for assessing the diversity of the species and ensuring that germplasm collections fully reflect genetic diversity with minimal duplication. Better tools would also help determine authentic genetic diversity apart from differences merely arising from response to local growing conditions. Beyond these needs, now that seed production and

hybridization have become possible, better tools could help match plants for breeding to achieve desired characteristics.

Isozyme and RAPD offer a relatively limited number of molecular markers. A clearer assessment of garlic subspecies diversity requires a greater array of molecular markers to better discriminate closely related strains and identify duplication. Another molecular tool, AFLP, better meets the need. AFLP is capable of generating relatively large numbers of molecular markers. Plant studies that included other molecular methods as well as AFLP found that AFLP was better able to distinguish variation in closely related plants. The capability of the markers to render finer distinctions was a factor, in addition to the greater number of them. Would AFLP prove similarly effective with garlic? Meryem Ipek, Ahmet Ipek, and Philipp Simon (2003) applied all three molecular methods to a diverse subset of the garlic strains used in the Pooler and Simon study. A random selection of 80 AFLP markers was matched with the 80 RAPD markers. The study found that where the RAPD system lumped individual strains together without identifying distinction, AFLP, with the same number of markers, readily distinguished individual strains. When all 183 AFLP markers were used, additional strains could be distinguished. For example, three strains happened to share all 80 of the randomly selected AFLP markers, but when all 183 AFLP markers were examined, the three strains shared more than 90% of them—but not all. This shows that the strains are very similar but not identical, and AFLP was able to distinguish among them. Like the RAPD and AFLP markers, the isozymes generally grouped the 48 strains in a similar manner, but were less in accord than RAPD and AFLP. The ability of isozymes to distinguish individual strains within the groups was also much more limited.

Like the Pooler and Simon study, the study by Ipek, Ipek, and Simon showed no association between groupings and geographic origins, but the authors noted that other studies have suggested geographic associations, and they speculated that the country of collection of the various clones may not be the same as the country of origin. Given the free and frequent trading and migration of garlic cultivars through the millennia, it is logical to assume that many cultivars may have been widely distributed. It is quite likely that the country of collection of the various cultivars may not reflect their country of origin. There indeed may be a correlation between garlic groupings and geographic origin, but those associations may not lend themselves to ready discernment.

Previous isozyme and RAPD studies showed that the putative wild garlic species, *Allium longicuspis*, was not distinguishable as a separate species. The AFLP study results agreed with the earlier studies, showing that the wild garlic strains were clustered with the strongly bolting groups of *A. sativum*, but that there was no indication of a separate species of wild garlic.

One might also wonder if all the diversity of the species has been adequately represented in these studies. Might there have been omissions or underrepresentation of strains that would have shed more light, or revealed more questions, about relationships and categorizations? Some of the studies included numerous cultivars, but how do we know whether these cultivars represent the full diversity of the species? Most of the studies draw heavily upon subsets of germplasm collections from various academic or governmental sources. Ideally germplasm collections should, and largely do, reflect a broad range of diversity—which is, after all, a fundamental precept of a germplasm collection. The garlic cultivars in circulation among growers are often not included in the studies, though many are likely some of the same cultivars, carrying more appealing names than the number and letter codes attached to the germplasm accessions.

The study by Ipek, Ipek, and Simon demonstrated the value of the AFLP methodology in distinguishing finer differences among garlic strains that other molecular methods would have indicated were identical. The study also showed that AFLP offers a mechanism for assessing possible common identity of putatively different strains, independent of differences that are merely the result of environmental factors rather than genetic difference. Of the 48 strains in the study, 16 strains in 6 different clusters shared 100% of the 183 AFLPs. Morphological examination of the duplicate strains corroborated the AFLP findings. This shows that AFLP is a very powerful tool in identifying different cultivars that might otherwise be regarded as identical, and in identifying cultivars that are the same but carry different names. By employing these tools, a germplasm collection can be refined, ensuring full representation of different cultivars while eliminating cultivars that are identical to others in the collection. We are increasingly, if yet imperfectly, growing closer to identifying sameness, similarity, and difference within the garlic germplasm. And in a more informal manner, garlic gardeners and growers will be able to do the same.

A major caveat here is that while AFLP can distinguish differences that other molecular markers cannot, AFLP studies have also demonstrated that there are still substantive differences that AFLP methodologies have so far been unable to adequately resolve. Morphological observation and common sense still have a role in the assessment of garlic diversity, even as newer and better molecular tools are developed.

## Genetic diversity

American germplasm collections have generally not placed accessions into detailed subspecies groupings. Meanwhile, at least in North America, the subspecies groupings posited by Ron Engeland in 1991 and 1995 have been broadly, though not universally, adopted in one form or another by garlic growers and enthusiasts. Although there are many hundreds and perhaps thousands of local names for cultivars, many cultivars are widely classified in accord with the subspecies groupings proposed by Engeland. Germplasm collections and the widely recognized commercial cultivars assuredly contain genetic duplicates among their number, both within the individual collection systems and among the numerous collections and systems around the world. What would be desirable, of course, would be the reconciliation of all the systems, elimination of all duplication, and inclusion of all distinct genetic variants. We are a far distance from that goal, but the new molecular tools are helping steer us in that direction.

What would be a good next step? How about an AFLP study with a large number of accessions from the NPGS and inclusion of commercial cultivars in broad circulation among growers, perhaps also with a look to see how the subspecies groupings posited by Engeland might coincide with the clustering that would emerge from the study? Gayle Volk, Adam Henk, and Christopher Richards at the National Center for Genetic Resources Preservation in Fort Collins, Colorado, published just such a study in 2004, titled "Genetic Diversity Among U.S. Garlic Clones as Detected Using AFLP Methods."

Volk and her colleagues developed cryogenic methods for germplasm preservation as a backup to field-planted garlic, but such methods are labor-intensive and success is somewhat dependent on genotype. Whether the garlic is field-planted or cryogenically preserved, maintaining duplicate cultivars is time-consuming and expensive. Garlic cultivars are phenotypically and morphologically plastic; that is, depending on their growing environment, they may look and act differently. It is not always possible to discern identical, different, or similar clones with certainty, based on observable characteristics alone. Characteristics that remain the same, independent of environmental conditions, are needed to discern, or at least corroborate, observable characteristics—which takes us back to AFLP molecular markers and the primary reason for the Fort Collins study.

The landmark study included 211 garlic accessions from the NPGS and cultivars from commercial sources. To test if cultivars carrying the same name but obtained from different commercial sources were genetically identical, the study also included duplicates from different commercial sources. Forty-seven clones represented 20 of the named cultivars. Previous studies sometimes included commercially available cultivars, but Volk and her colleagues were the first to explore not only a large, broad cross section of germplasm accessions but also a large, broad cross section of commercially available cultivars. Additionally, the study assessed the correlation of Engeland's phenotypic classification system with the genetic findings emerging from the AFLP analysis. For the first time popular cultivars, germplasm accessions, and a widely used phenotypic classification system were brought under the scope of a genetic study that employed advanced molecular tools.

Many commercially available garlic cultivars in the United States have been classified according to the schema proposed by Engeland. Use of his classification system by commercial growers and garlic aficionados has spread to other parts of the world as well. Although Engeland made an effort to gather information about the phenotypic characteristics of the same cultivars grown elsewhere, most of his observations were necessarily of garlic that he grew in Okanogan, Washington. He modified his taxonomic schema once the results of the Pooler and Simon isozyme study were available, though the study generally corroborated the schema he had proposed—at least to the extent and degree of specificity that the isozyme markers then permitted. It would be interesting to see how Engeland's phenotypic system would correspond with AFLP findings.

The NPGS collection has some 233 garlic accessions. The collection includes 14 accessions identified as *Allium longicuspis* and 219 accessions identified as *A. sativum*, which are further classified at the subspecies level into two varieties, *A. sativum* var. *sativum* and *A. sativum* var. *ophioscorodon*. Broadly speaking, the two varieties represent nonbolting and bolting accessions. The NPGS garlic accessions are not classified by Engeland's system or any similar system. Among its objectives, the Fort Collins study would assess genetic support for the division of garlic into the two varietal groups, assess genetic evidence that would affirm or refute the thesis of a separate species of wild garlic, *A. longicuspis*, and assess the correlation of the molecular diversity with phenotypic classification schemas.

A modest degree of correlation and cross-referencing exists between the commercial cultivars carrying common names and the accessions in the NPGS germplasm. For example, 'Chet's Italian Red' corresponds to PI 540368 in the NPGS system. Unfortunately, such correlation and cross-referencing information is relatively sparse. The absence of nomenclature correlation and cross-referencing between commercial cultivars and germplasm accessions, and the absence of Engeland's classification schema in the germplasm collection, makes uniform assessment of a nonuniform study subject all the more challenging. On the other hand, part of the purpose of the Fort Collins study was to bring more uniformity and comprehensive rationale where there is now relatively little.

For this study, the clones were classified as hardneck or softneck in type by the presence of a stem in the cross-sectional images of the NPGS accessions and by the classification of the growers submitting the commercial samples. Artichoke cultivars almost never bolt and form a hard neck, but Silverskin, Creole, Turban, and Asiatic cultivars bolt under certain conditions. As a result, there was some inconsistency in how cultivars associated with the Silverskin, Creole, Turban, and Asiatic groups were designated—whether softneck or hardneck. The results, nonetheless, were independent of the ad hoc designations.

The results of the study were analyzed using several different models to reveal different aspects of genetic similarity and difference. One statistical method, principle component analysis, looked for broad patterns of differentiation. For this portion of the analysis, 53 of the 211 garlic clones were excluded because of ambiguity in the data. The remaining 158 clones clustered into four groups.

Hardneck types clustered into three groups: Porcelain, Rocambole, and the assorted types that remained. Softneck types clustered into one group, but that group also included Silverskin, Creole, and Turban clones that bolt under certain conditions. Asiatic clones also bolt only under certain conditions, but they clustered unambiguously with the hardneck group. The softneck types showed far less genetic diversity than the hardneck types. Apart from the exception of the Asiatic group, the results are generally consistent with previous studies.

As previous studies have indicated, there appears to be a garlic group that includes all Artichoke and nonbolting cultivars, but that also includes cultivars that bolt and produce hard necks under certain conditions. If one is to call this group by a defining name, a name other than the colloquial "softneck" might better reflect its nature.

Studies that include a taxonomic mission frequently depict the results using some sort of hierarchical or treelike diagram, often called a cladogram, or at the subspecies level, and more generically, a dendrogram. Such a hierarchical tree is particularly common and useful above the species level for showing inherited relationships and divergences from ancestral forms. This kind of analytical model is often somewhat less on the mark at the subspecies level. This is particularly true for garlic, where differences include phylogenetic relationships and differences, as well as differences that have arisen vegetatively through somatic variation over many millennia. In other words, differences in garlic have arisen not only from sexual reproduction and evolution but also from vegetative sports. Similarities and differences are not wholly attributable to genetic lineage and ancestral descent. Differences and relationships among garlic clones do not fit readily into a tidy hierarchy but are more akin to a mulligan stew. Dendrogram hierarchies are certainly useful, but other analytical models may be more suitable and revealing for garlic.

Christopher Richards, the molecular geneticist in the Fort Collins study, employed a three-dimensional spanning network analytical model. Instead of a two-dimensional fixed hierarchy, relationships are arrayed in a three-dimensional network of interconnected nodes. One node—in this instance, a garlic cultivar or group of cultivars—may have many reticulations (genetic connections or associations) with other cultivars or groups of cultivars, not just a single hierarchical relationship. Additionally, genetic similarities are represented by the proximity of the interconnected nodes to one another. This type of statistical model, called a minimum spanning tree, can accommodate multiple interrelated hierarchies in the same model. It can represent many relationships and their genetic proximities in a single minimum spanning distance diagram.

The results proved fascinating. Although the NPGS accessions are not classified by Engeland's phenotypic schema, thereby limiting the ability to assess their correlation with the schema, most widely available commercial cultivars have been. Many of the regions in the minimum spanning tree closely corresponded to Engeland's phenotypic categories, including Artichoke, Rocambole, Porcelain, Purple Stripe, Marbled Purple Stripe, and Asiatic. With rare exception, all of the accessions within a group of genetically indistinguishable accessions belonged to the same classification group in Engeland's system. The minimum spanning tree showed that Purple Stripe accessions formed the basal region of the network and had the most reticulations. In other words, more garlic strains are genetically related to the Purple Stripe group than to any other garlic group, and genetic diversity and manifold interrelationships are greatest within the Purple Stripe cluster. This indicates that the Purple Stripe cluster contains the most primary ancestral forms.

The Marbled Purple Stripe group is often described as a subtype of the Purple Stripe group, as the names suggest. Engeland provisionally described them as such, but also allowed that subsequent research might show that Marbled Purple Stripes are a separate group. A decade later the Fort Collins study showed that the Purple Stripe group is basal for all other garlic groups, not just Marbled Purple Stripe, and that Marbled Purple Stripe cultivars form a distinct group apart from the Purple Stripes.

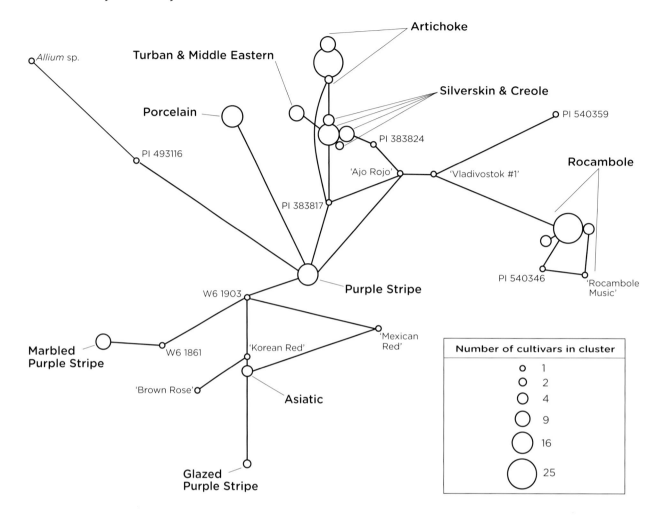

Figure 6. This diagram is based on the minimum spanning distance diagram in the study "Genetic Diversity Among U.S. Garlic Clones as Detected Using AFLP Methods" (Volk et al. 2004). Horticultural group annotations have been added, and the diagram has been simplified by eliminating some cultivar nodes, primarily those with missing data elements that precluded precise placement. Those wishing to explore this topic in greater depth are encouraged to review the original publication and its more detailed diagram.

Based on his phenotypic observations, Engeland placed Asiatic garlics with the *ophioscorodon* or hardneck group, which he later revised based on the findings of the Pooler and Simon isozyme study that grouped Asiatic cultivars with the Artichoke and Silverskin groups—"*sativum*/softnecks." The Fort Collins study, using more advanced molecular tools, showed that the Asiatic cultivars clustered strongly with the Rocambole, Purple Stripe, Porcelain, and Marbled Purple Stripe groups—"*ophioscorodon*/hardnecks." Moreover, the Asiatics clustered at a greater genetic distance from the softneck cultivars than many other well-established hardnecks.

The Fort Collins AFLP findings further revealed the conundrum of classifying garlic into two major subspecies groups based on nonbolting (*Allium sativum* var. *sativum*) and bolting (*A. sativum* var. *ophioscorodon*) behavior. In previous attempts to make this scenario somehow fit, it became necessary to include strains that bolted "infrequently, incompletely, or weakly" with the nonbolting strains, so that one could have a strain that bolted (for example, a Silverskin cultivar) but still group it with the nonbolting garlic group. But the AFLP study showed that the Asiatic group—a poster child for the contingent of infrequent, incomplete, or weak bolters—genetically belongs with the hardnecks.

In the Fort Collins study the Silverskin and Creole cultivars, which are infrequent, incomplete, or weak bolters, clustered with the softneck garlic cultivars, as they had in previous molecular studies. Engeland concluded that Creoles were likely a type of Silverskin. Previous studies and morphological observations are in general accord that Silverskin and Creole cultivars are closely related, but their exact relationship remains unclear. The AFLP study showed at least four distinct but tightly grouped clusters comprised of Silverskin and Creole cultivars. Each of the four clusters contained both Silverskin and Creole cultivars. The clusters were arrayed at a threshold separating bolting and nonbolting strains. Since the Silverskin and Creole cultivars can be described as infrequently, incompletely, or weakly bolting, their positioning at the threshold of hardneck and softneck strains would be a logical expectation.

One would have expected that Creole cultivars would cluster together and that Silverskin cultivars would also cluster together, with no or minimal cross-membership, but this was not the finding. It may be that the existing phenotypic groups Silverskin and Creole are not monophyletic, even in the broader, looser sense of garlic strains, and that alternate groupings and nomenclature are warranted. I have, for example, observed major differences in leaf width and bulb and clove shape among cultivars that are commonly accepted as belonging to the Creole group. Some Silverskin and Creole cultivars closely resemble prototypic members of the other group, while other cultivars are obviously at variance. It may be that the number of molecular markers used in the study, or perhaps the AFLP tool itself, are not sufficiently granular to fully resolve the genetic distinctions among these tightly clustered strains. This could be an explanation for the generalized cross-membership among the clusters and would leave open the prospect that Creoles could be a subgroup of Silverskins, or perhaps some other more manifold grouping, as might be suggested by the four clusters. Interestingly as well, 'Ajo Rojo', putatively a Creole cultivar, was arrayed some distance from the other four clusters, further contributing to the puzzle.

The Fort Collins study included only two cultivars commercially identified as Turbans. These clustered with two NPGS accessions that, at least on cursory appearance from NPGS bulb photographs, appear consistent with the Turban group. Curiously, a commercially available Purple Stripe cultivar clustered with the four Turban cultivars. The bulb of another accession in the NPGS photograph appears deformed, making assessment of it more problematic. Contributing more to the puzzle, the NPGS accession W6 10473 was also clustered with the Turbans. In this book I have listed W6 10473 under the cultivar name 'Egyptian' and provisionally placed it in a new group: Middle Eastern. (The proposed Middle Eastern group is discussed in more detail in chapter 10.) The bulb morphology of W6 10473 and others in the Middle Eastern group differs from the bulb morphology of Turban (and Purple Stripe) strains.

The Middle Eastern strains have numerous smaller cloves arrayed in multiple clove layers. Most or all members of the group appear to grow very poorly in temperate North America. The study also included an NPGS accession, PI 543049, called 'Jomah', which was arrayed in very close proximity to the cluster. Although I have not had direct experience with that accession, a cross section of the bulb indicates a morphology associated with the Middle Eastern group. More precise positioning was unavailable for 'Jomah' because of missing data at one of the molecular markers. No other members of the putative Middle Eastern group were included in the study, but it seems likely that further molecular research with additional accessions might validate a distinct but closely related group. Phenotypically, Turban cultivars grow happily and productively in much of North America, whereas the genetically proximate Middle Eastern cultivars decidedly do not. The inclusion of at least one Purple Stripe cultivar in the cluster seems a bit of a puzzle, but perhaps it is not unexpected that members of the genetically most basal group, the Purple Stripes, might appear in a cluster that is not fully resolved.

It appears that the cluster that includes Turban and Middle Eastern cultivars, and some Purple Stripe cultivars, is not monophyletic, and that further genetic study is needed to resolve distinctions within the group. Phenotypically, the Turban group has been characterized as infrequently, incompletely, or weakly bolting. The study's spanning network diagram shows that the cluster that includes the Turban cultivars is arrayed along a threshold that separates bolting and nonbolting strains.

All of the study's 211 garlic clones were included in the minimum spanning distance diagram, including 53 that had incomplete data for one of the 27 loci (genetic measuring points). Inclusion of the 53 clones affords a more complete overview,

though at a cost in precision in the positioning of the 53 clones. The study employed two other statistical models to determine major differences and larger groupings. The 53 clones with incomplete data were excluded from these statistical models, the principle component analysis previously discussed, and parsimony analysis. Parsimony analysis of the 158 remaining clones collapsed the arrays and groupings of the spanning network into a simplified topology of fewer but larger clusters, or clades. This analytical model would be expected to reflect the larger, more basal similarities and differences among the garlic clones. The findings were indeed interesting.

Ron Engeland's phenotypic groups, Rocambole, Artichoke, Porcelain, and Turban, formed separate distinct clades. Interestingly, Purple Stripe, Marbled Purple Stripe, Asiatic, Silverskin, and Creole cultivars collapsed into a single large clade. The parsimony analysis showed that the infrequently, incompletely, or weakly bolting Silverskin, Creole, and Asiatic cultivars grouped not with the softneck Artichoke cultivars but with the stalwart hardnecks.

The study by Ipek, Ipek, and Simon initially employed 80 molecular markers and then included additional markers for a total of 183. Increasing the number of markers to 183 revealed additional genetically distinct strains. The Fort Collins study employed only 27 molecular markers. However, 34 of the accessions that showed no genetic difference when tested with the 27 molecular markers were further tested with 80 additional markers to determine if additional markers would make a difference in resolving additional genetic differences. The increase in the number of markers to 107 yielded negligible difference in the results. Whereas Ipek, Ipek, and Simon pooled multiple clones of a single accession, the Fort Collins study did not pool samples. The Fort Collins study also included

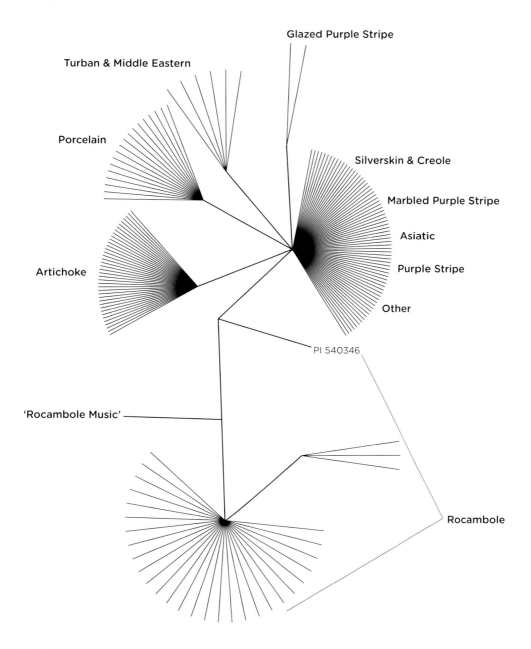

Glazed Purple Stripe

Turban & Middle Eastern

Porcelain

Silverskin & Creole

Marbled Purple Stripe

Asiatic

Artichoke

Purple Stripe

Other

PI 540346

'Rocambole Music'

Rocambole

Figure 7. This diagram is based on the parsimony analysis diagram in the study "Genetic Diversity Among U.S. Garlic Clones as Detected Using AFLP Methods" (Volk et al. 2004). Horticultural group annotations have been added. Those wishing to explore this topic in greater depth are encouraged to review the detailed analysis in the original publication.

replicate samples obtained from different sources. One might speculate that the additional rigor in the Fort Collins study eliminated false findings of distinction. However, it might also be the case that employing additional markers throughout a greater range of samples would have revealed additional genetic difference.

The Fort Collins study included an extensive selection from the USDA germplasm and commercial sources. The breadth and depth of the study's scope and the application of advanced molecular tools and analysis make the study exceptionally valuable for scientist and garlic aficionado alike. And as is often the case, something good makes us want even more. Seventy-nine NPGS accessions could not be included because of an unacceptable error rate in the test results. Turban, Middle Eastern, Creole, and Asiatic cultivars were underrepresented. Additional study of these could further clarify relationships and distinctions. Some clones held unique positions in the spanning network. These may be solitary clones, or they may be representatives of additional groups that may offer further insight into links and relationships in the spanning network. Some groups in the study results contained only NPGS members and no commercial cultivars. Some of these groups may or may not be sufficiently distinct to merit separate consideration and phenotypic classification. One also wonders what unique cultivars or groups may not have been included in the study. Though the study was exceptionally broad, other allium germplasms throughout the world likely include additional genetically distinct accessions. Inclusion of tropically grown garlic may reveal additional extensions in the spanning network.

The AFLP study identified many genetically unique garlic clones. It also identified 18 groups of clones with no evident genetic difference among members of the group. The size of the groups ranged from two differently named clones to 30 differently named clones. In one group of Rocamboles the study found no genetic difference among the 27 clones. Does this mean there is no genetic difference in this group? Not necessarily. In some instances we may indeed have the exact same genetically identical cultivar with two or more different names attached to it. In other instances, however, it is likely, perhaps certain, that existing molecular tools and methods are not yet fully able to resolve all genetic differences.

Again, in the context of morphological difference, a plant's flowering structures are among the most taxonomically defining. The study results identified no genetic difference between 'Pyongyang' (syn. 'Pyong Vang') and 'Sakura' (syn. 'Japanese'). Does this mean that there is no genetic difference? In my garden both cultivars display the classic Asiatic scape, with a broad, elongated, hollow beak area and very few but exceptionally large bulbils. However, even when viewed on a casual walk through my garlic beds, the scapes of 'Sakura' are obviously unique and readily distinguishable, not only from 'Pyongyang' but from all other Asiatics in the garden. (See the photos in chapter 10.) The differences are consistently present year after year in plants growing next to each other, and cannot be attributed to different growing conditions. There are other differences between the two cultivars as well, but the scape is the most obvious and telling. This is one example among many. No matter how sophisticated our molecular tools become, plant morphology is always a good "gut check." We should think of plant morphology and molecular analysis as complimentary. In the words of plant taxonomist C. M. A Stapleton (1997), "Even if technology provides a hand-held DNA extractor and sequencer and access to vast data banks of known sequences for identification of plants, someone is still going to ask, 'What do they look like?'"

Garlic has one of the largest genomes (1.59 × 10¹⁰ base pairs) among all cultivated plants (Ori et al. 1998), and genetic analysis is difficult, even with today's remarkably powerful molecular tools. We need to be mindful that the tools and methods for genetic analysis are actually very new and in the longer view relatively primitive. Though the current molecular tools are richly informative, we are really only at the initial pathways of a lengthy journey.

The Fort Collins study has richly added to our understanding of garlic, showing the interrelationships and genetic proximity of numerous clones and their correlation with phenotypically identifiable groups. The study has also directly served a targeted key purpose. Cryopreservation of garlic is costly and complex. Now, armed with the results of the study, it is readily possible to prioritize cryopreservation efforts, first including accessions that have been identified as genetically unique as well as at least one representative of each genetic group of accessions.

As molecular tools and our ability to use them become even more powerful, additional genetic differentiation will come to light. Some clones that are now lumped together without evident genetic difference will be shown to stand apart as genetically unique. At the same time, we will be able to say with even greater confidence that some differently named clones are indeed genetically identical. Spanning network models will become more ramified and extended, showing additional interrelationships among genetically unique garlic clones and clusters of clones. The complexity of the garlic genome and the intermingling of changes arising from vegetative sports and sexual reproduction over many thousands of years make an assessment of lineage and phylogeny highly problematic. New molecular tools and analytical models offer great promise here as well. Using a model of mutational change known as the coalescent, it may be possible to determine the relative age of mutations and derive an ordered timeline for the origin of each garlic cultivar (Richards 2004, personal communication). Our knowledge of the garlic genome has increased dramatically since the 1990s and will only continue to accelerate. This is a golden era for researchers and enthusiasts alike.

## Species bifurcation versus subequal groups

Does molecular evidence support a longstanding hypothesis of a species bifurcation into *ophioscorodon* (hardneck, bolting, flowering) and *sativum* (softneck, nonbolting or bolting weakly or infrequently, nonflowering)?

Is this even the right question?

Rather than asking if new molecular evidence is compatible with a longstanding hypothesis, a better question might be what taxonomic model best fits the information that the new molecular evidence shows us. Some of the molecular evidence could be used to support a species bifurcation into *ophioscorodon* and *sativum*—but it may not be the most accurate taxonomic model. Moreover, such a taxonomic model could well cloak a more accurate and informative understanding.

Let us first look at the findings that seem to support the species bifurcation. The 2003 study by Ipek, Ipek, and Simon showed that the weakly or infrequently bolting clones included in the study clustered with the nonbolting clones. The strongly bolting clones clustered unambiguously together. These results correlated with previous molecular studies regardless of the molecular system employed—isozyme, RAPD, or AFLP. For example, the 1993 Pooler and Simon study arrived at this finding using isozymes. In 1997, M. Al-Zahim, H. Newbury, and B. Ford-Lloyd employed RAPD markers to separate bolting and nonbolting clones. In this study, RAPD markers associated with 'Burgundy', a weakly bolting cultivar that is nominally in the Creole group, clustered 'Burgundy' with nonbolting softneck cultivars. Using RAPD markers, K. F. Bradley, M. A. Rieger, and G. G. Collins (1996) reported that bolting forms of garlic clustered separately from nonbolting and intermediate-bolting forms.

Essentially, molecular marker studies have tended to cluster clones having infrequent, incomplete, or weak flowering structures with nonbolting clones. Concomitantly, studies generally have shown that strongly bolting clones that routinely and reliably produce fully developed flowering structures cluster together. Characteristics such as the number of cloves, shape of cloves, leaf width, skin coloration, and so forth, may define more granular distinctions and groupings, but the grouping of strongly bolting clones separate and apart from clones that are not strongly bolting have appeared to be a superordinate distinction.

These findings would seem to validate the long-standing inclination to divide garlic into two major groups: *sativum* (nonbolting—or in the studies, nonbolting or bolting infrequently, incompletely, or weakly) and *ophioscorodon* (strongly bolting). This would also seem to validate the colloquial division of garlic into two main groups: softneck (*sativum*, nonbolting) and hardneck (*ophioscorodon*, bolting). The findings of these studies suggest that bolting propensity is a defining attribute, despite the fact that for some clones environmental conditions play a major role in the expression of this attribute.

Such a high degree of phenotypic dependency in defining the superordinate taxonomic division of a species is hardly desirable. Ideally such a taxonomic division would be defined or supported by morphological and genetic attributes, independent of environmental conditions. The study results,

however, have seemed to point us in a different, more problematic direction. The conclusion that infrequently, incompletely, or weakly bolting garlic clones cluster not with bolting clones but with nonbolting clones, creates a taxonomic conundrum. Descriptively minimizing the bolting behavior of these clones, or categorizing the bolting behavior as somehow different, seems to be an attempt to rationalize our way out of the taxonomic conundrum. That is, we are trying to say that when these clones bolt, it is really not the same as when "real" bolting garlic clones bolt.

Some garlic clones that the studies showed as clustering with nonbolting clones (for example, those that are nominally in the Creole group, such as the 'Burgundy' cultivar previously referenced in Al-Zahim, Newbury, and Ford-Lloyd's study) almost always bolt and generate flowering structures under certain growing conditions—mine, for instance. It can and has been argued that these are nonetheless weakly bolting and thus should be regarded differently than strongly bolting clones. It is true that they may not have a scape that is as thick and vigorous as the scapes of the strongly bolting clones, but their bolting expression is hardly inconsequential, displaying fully developed flowering structures, with umbels filled with bulbils and flowers. For that matter, one could also describe cultivars in the Rocambole group—a group whose credentials as strong bolters are unquestioned—as weakly bolting, relative to some of the towering flowering structures and massively sturdy scapes of cultivars in the Porcelain or Marbled Purple Stripe groups. The flowers and bulbils in the umbels of these latter groups are far more numerous than they are in the umbels of the Rocambole group. Dismissing the bolting behavior of cultivars in the Creole group as something somehow categorically different seems a problematic distinction at best. One might suggest that "weakly bolting" is more

Flowers and bulbils in the fully developed umbel of the "weakly bolting" Creole cultivar 'Burgundy'.

of a weakly hoped-for distinction than a defining taxonomic distinction. Even if we concluded that garlic should be divided into two main subspecies groups, *ophioscorodon* and *sativum*, defining the groups principally by their bolting propensity seems increasingly untenable.

When various statistical models are applied to DNA study results, the taxonomic model of a species subdivision into *sativum* and *ophioscorodon* fairs even less well. In the Fort Collins study conducted in 2004, a parsimony analysis of molecular variance showed that the garlic clones included in the analysis clustered into large clades. The nonbolting Artichoke clones formed a distinct clade. Instead of joining with the Artichoke clones in the same clade, as might be expected, or even forming a separate clade or clades, the "weakly bolting" Silverskin, Creole, and Asiatic clones helped comprise a clade that includes the "strongly bolting" Purple Stripe and Marbled Purple Stripe clones. If one is looking for support of a species bifurcation based on bolting propensity, this is hardly it—unless one wants to draw the line separating the Artichoke clones from all others, a division not supported by other molecular evidence.

The minimum spanning distance diagram in the Fort Collins study is even more telling. A three-dimensional minimum spanning tree arrays clones according to genetic distance values. The spanning tree shows that Silverskin, Creole, and Turban clones are separate from but generally proximate to the Artichoke clones. The Asiatics, the other weakly bolting clonal group, clusters at a considerable genetic distance from the Artichoke, Silverskin, Creole, and Turban groups, on an entirely different and nearly opposite genetic vector. The weakly bolting Asiatic clones cluster strongly with the bolting clones and far distant from the Artichoke clones, further weakening the species bifurcation thesis.

Let us look a bit more closely at the topology of the minimum spanning distance diagram (figure 6). The basal group, the Purple Stripes, is located at an approximate center. What would the topology look like if the species were bifurcated into two main groups? We might see the basal Purple Stripe group, then two separate genetic vectors leading away from the basal group in two different directions. Alternatively, we might see the basal Purple Stripe group comprising one group, and a genetic vector extending from the Purple Stripes comprising the other group. We see neither. Instead we see genetic variation vectors radiating from the basal group in nearly all directions. We do not see a species divided into two main groups, but a species with many subequal groups.

Examining the minimum spanning distance diagram further, the nonbolting Artichoke clones are among the furthest away from the basal Purple Stripe group, garlic's genetic center. The Artichoke clones are located near the top of the diagram, along one of many genetic vectors. Along this general vector, but closer to the basal Purple Stripe group, are some of the groups with less vigorous or less certain bolting characteristics: Silverskin, Creole, and Turban groups. What does this suggest? Along this genetic vector, the bolting propensity of the garlic clones diminishes the further the clone is from the genetic center. What we see is a progressively diminishing propensity for a particular phenotypic expression—the ability to bolt and produce fully developed flowering structures. Even Artichoke clones, the most nonbolting of the nonbolting or weakly bolting garlics, occasionally bolt and produce developed flowering structures. A progressive and variable phenotypic propensity is not a sound basis for a taxonomic bifurcation.

In their classic 1963 work, *Onions and Their Allies*, Henry Jones and Louis Mann stated, "Our

Basing a major taxonomic distinction on a varying and unstable phenotypic propensity is problematic at best. Even the most nonbolting of the so-called nonbolting cultivars sometimes bolt, as seen in this photo of the Artichoke cultivar 'Lorz Italian'.

preliminary data show, that while some of the clones fit into var. *sativum* or var. *ophioscorodon* reasonably well, so many show combinations of characteristics of both varieties that we feel no purpose is served by recognizing these two varieties or by designating horticultural groups to replace them." Now, many years later, and armed with highly sophisticated DNA tools and analytical models, our conclusion would seem to be much the same.

A species bifurcation into *sativum* and *ophioscorodon* is not a taxonomic model that fits very well. A good taxonomic model should grow out of what we discover about nature. We should not be trying to fit what we discover about nature into a preexisting taxonomic model that was promulgated at a time when we knew much less about what nature is presenting us. It may well be that further study will validate such a taxonomic bifurcation, but for now it is my view that neither morphological, phenotypic, nor genetic evidence supports or sustains such a taxonomic model.

If a species bifurcation into two subspecies or two varieties, *sativum* and *ophioscorodon*, is not a fitting taxonomic model, what is? Rather than a species comprised of two superordinate divisions, we seem to have a species comprised of multiple subequal groups. Morphological, phenotypic, and genetic evidence all show clustered clonal groupings within the species. The minimum spanning network analysis in the Fort Collins study is exceptionally revealing and instructive in many ways, including, in my view, its implications regarding our taxonomic thinking. The topology of the spanning network shows a basal region with significant genetic diversity and the greatest number of reticulations with the rest of the network. This basal region is comprised of clones associated with the phenotypic group, Purple Stripe. Purple Stripe clones are among those that generate the most complete and fertile flowering structures, and some

Purple Stripe clones have retained the capability (generally with assistance) for sexual reproduction and the production of seed. Purple Stripe clones are the most proximate to the originating genetic source of the species.

The Purple Stripe region is garlic's genetic Rome—all roads, all reticulations, all pathways lead back to this genetic center. What we see in the spanning network's topology is not a simple bifurcation of the species into two groups, but rather a multitude of extensions of broadly equivalent hierarchical value extending in multiple directions from a genetic center. To the extent that the spanning network suggests hierarchies, they would be manifold in nature and not branches of a simple, and simplistic, bifurcation of the species. The spanning network topology suggests that the primary subspecies division is not dichotomous, but manifold, and generally corresponds to the phylogenetic groupings posited by Ron Engeland: Purple Stripe, Marbled Purple Stripe, Rocambole, Porcelain, and the like.

Much of the genetic research on garlic has been conducted by those interested in genetic identity and difference in the garlic germplasm, rather than by taxonomists per se. We should defer to specialists in taxonomy and systematics to say whether or not any of the subspecies groupings merit assignment of subspecies, variety, or form in accord with the *ICBN*. Such a prospect might have been readily dismissed at one time, but it seems quite possible that some of the variation and the genetic clustering we are seeing in the garlic germplasm have occurred in the wild and not just in cultivation, and that subspecies differences could be sufficient for *ICBN* attribution. For now it is sufficient for our purposes to treat the subspecies groupings simply as horticultural groups. We can expect that additional genetic research will further refine and likely reorder some of these groups, but their general legitimacy is now solidly grounded in genetic evidence.

## Horticultural groups

How many garlic horticultural groups are there? How many should there be? These questions take me back to one of my earliest conversations with Richard Hannan, then a research leader and supervisory horticulturist at the USDA Agricultural Research Service in Pullman, Washington. After patiently listening to my ramblings about garlic horticultural groups, the difficulties with defining boundaries and membership, and my search for the "true" answer, he sagely described two groups: splitters and lumpers. These are not horticultural groups but people groups. Splitters are those of us inclined to split description and classification into numerous smaller groups, which inevitably end in overlap and contradiction, while lumpers are inclined to lump everything together and treat differences as individual rather than as characteristics of a group. So, what is one to do with garlic cultivars that share common characteristics? If we endlessly divide the garlic germplasm into ever-smaller unique groups, we will end up with as many groups as clones—groups of one, the effective equivalent of no groups. Splitting, at its most extreme, turns upon itself and becomes lumping. Long before that extreme, however, we would run into contradiction and increasing overlapping of characteristics. There is probably no "true" answer, but the most viable conceptual approach no doubt lies somewhere in between the extremes of lumping and splitting. Attentive phenotypic observation, preferably under a variety of growing conditions, in conjunction with well-designed genetic research and analysis, will help us come to informed conclusions.

It is best to think of garlic horticultural groups not as absolute categories but as clusters of genetically and phenotypically similar cultivars. The minimum spanning distance diagram in figure 6 depicts genetic clustering. At the periphery of a cluster, it may be less clear whether or not a cultivar ought to be included as a member. The likeness of one cultivar to another is not always a matter of absolute demarcation, but is sometimes a matter of gradation. What we have, then, are clusters of cultivars that share similarities. Cultivars at the outer boundaries of a cluster (horticultural group) will share fewer similarities than cultivars nearer the center of the cluster.

Some clusters are genetically and phenotypically far apart from other cultivars or clusters of cultivars, and thus seem more tightly defined and unambiguous. Other clusters may have more extended peripheries—cultivars that may have significant differences from the cultivars at the core of the cluster, yet be more similar to those cultivars than to any other cluster. Where one draws the boundaries on these clusters in naming a horticultural group is a matter of judgment and a function of the current state of our knowledge and understanding. And there are other conundrums. Does a cultivar at the periphery represent a new and separate cluster? Would it be the sole member, or would we see many more members if we had greater knowledge of the world germplasm? If two clusters are genetically and phenotypically very close to each other, but distant from any other clusters, should we regard them as two horticultural groups or as a single group? Would treating them as two groups or as one group be most meaningful and useful to a researcher, garlic grower, or germplasm preservationist? These are the questions we face as we propose an analytical construct—a horticultural group—to represent a cluster of cultivars, which is itself an analytical construct representing genetic similarity and proximity.

We very much prefer clearly defined categories with simple yes or no membership. Nature, however, is not always cooperative in this regard, sometimes offering similarities and differences as manifold gradations that resist reductions to rigidly demarcated categories. This certainly applies in the context of garlic horticultural groups, where membership is not always tightly or simply defined. Yet, genetically, morphologically, and phenotypically, garlic cultivars with shared characteristics do cluster into groups of like kind. Although membership boundaries may not be absolute, horticultural groups do help us see and understand relationships and differences. Assigning groups to cultivars with clustered similarities can be highly useful and informative as long as we do not become so fixated on the groups and group names that we ignore greater nuance in the cultivars themselves.

As we have wound our way through garlic's taxonomic journey we have seen how genetic research generally supports, if not defines, the subspecies groups described by Ron Engeland (1991, 1995): Purple Stripe, Marbled Purple Stripe, Glazed Purple Stripe, Rocambole, Porcelain, Artichoke, Asiatic, Creole, Silverskin. For some groups, such as Porcelain and Rocambole, genetic support is strong and unambiguous. For others, such as Creole and Silverskin, genetic relationships are evident but not fully resolved. Further genetic research promises to tell us more.

The horticultural groups included in chapter 10 are substantially those described by Engeland. I have made only minor adjustments and proposals based on phenotypic observation and genetic research findings that have become available since Engeland first proposed the groups. As genetic studies reveal more about garlic, it is likely that additional reordering and refinement of the horticultural groups will be in order. Rather than contribute to confusion by proposing interim changes, which surely would be modified yet again, I have elected to be rather conservative in proposing change in areas that seem to be in flux. Nonetheless, a few adjustments seem to be in order at this juncture, and I have proposed them as the need has arisen.

In my view, genetic research does not support a fundamental bifurcation of the species into *sativum* and *ophioscorodon*, softneck and hardneck, or other variations on the theme. Accepting this avoids such tortured linguistics and mental gymnastics as having a bolting cultivar with a hard neck that we nonetheless proclaim to be a genetic softneck. Of course, genetic difference would override any phenotypic expression that we might observe, but it appears that attempting to fit genetic findings into such a species bifurcation is a tortured exercise as well. One can use a large hammer to pound a square peg into a round hole, but that does not mean that it really fits. So, differing from Engeland's descriptions and the thinking of the time, I have not proffered *sativum* and *ophioscorodon* as subspecies, varieties, or horticultural groups.

Engeland used the *ICBN* designation "variety" to refer to some subspecies groups and used the terms "subvariety" and "horticultural group" to refer to other groups. For example, Purple Stripe was termed a variety and Marbled Purple Stripe and Glazed Purple Stripe were variously called subvarieties or horticultural groups. Until specialists in taxonomy and systematics evaluate garlic in light of contemporary genetic research, it seems wise to avoid formal *ICBN* nomenclature at the subspecies level and let horticultural groups suffice for now.

Based on his own observations and molecular evidence available at the time, Engeland described some garlic groups as subgroups of other groups. While subsequent genetic research largely supports the garlic groups themselves, the understanding of the group interrelationships has changed—or, at least, the research findings seem to suggest that the understanding ought to change. For example, Engeland variously described Marbled Purple Stripe and Glazed Purple Stripe as subvarieties or horticultural groups of the Purple Stripe variety. Genetic research now shows that Purple Stripe strains comprise the basal group for all garlic. All garlic groups, not just Marbled Purple Stripe and Glazed Purple Stripe, have a derivative genetic relationship with the Purple Stripe group.

Let us look a bit further into what the genetic studies have shown. In the Fort Collins study, a principle component analysis collapsed garlic into four groups. Rocambole and Porcelain cultivars each formed separate groups; Artichoke, Creole, Turban, and Silverskin tended to fall into another group; and Marbled Purple Stripe and Glazed Purple Stripe grouped with Purple Stripe. However, Asiatic also grouped with Purple Stripe. One might surmise that in an analysis that reduces garlic to four groups, many cultivars that are not sufficiently separated would tend to fall with the basal group Purple Stripe. In the same study, a minimum spanning distance diagram depicting genetic relationships and genetic distance showed multiple groups extending in multiple directions from the basal Purple Stripe group, not just Marbled Purple Stripe and Glazed Purple Stripe. Interestingly, too, the Asiatic group showed greater genetic proximity to Purple Stripe than did Marbled Purple Stripe and Glazed Purple Stripe. Describing Marbled Purple Stripe and Glazed Purple Stripe as subgroups of Purple Stripe does not accurately depict what genetic evidence now seems to show.

The names Marbled Purple Stripe and Glazed Purple Stripe are not ideal, as they help perpetuate the notion that these are subgroups of Purple Stripe with a closer relationship to Purple Stripe than, for example, the Asiatic group, which genetic evidence shows is not the case. However, chang-

ing the horticultural group names at this juncture would likely create further confusion, so it seems best to leave the nomenclature as it is. We can, however, stop referring to Marbled Purple Stripe and Glazed Purple Stripe as subgroups of Purple Stripe.

Engeland described Artichoke and Silverskin as varieties of the subspecies *sativum*. He also described Turban and Asiatic as subvarieties or subgroups of Artichoke, and Creole as a subvariety or subgroup of Silverskin. The Fort Collins study revealed some interesting differences. More robust than previous molecular studies, it showed that the Asiatic group is genetically very distant from Artichoke, Silverskin, Creole, and Turban cultivars. Turban cultivars had limited representation in the study, but a parsimony analysis (figure 7) grouped Artichoke and Turban cultivars into separate clades. Curiously, Silverskin and Creole cultivars grouped with a large clade that included the basal Purple Stripe group. In this type of analysis, collapsing the array into large clades is expected, but what is one to make of the result that Artichoke and Turban cultivars clustered separately while Creole and Silverskin cultivars were collapsed into association with the basal Purple Stripe group? A minimum spanning distance diagram (figure 6) depicting genetic relationships and genetic distance generated from the study findings suggests some interesting conclusions. Creole and Silverskin cultivars are arrayed in at least four separate but very closely clustered groups. Along this genetic vector, they are the closest groups to the basal Purple Stripe group. Beyond these groups, along the same vector but genetically more distant, are groups of Artichoke cultivars. The Creole and Silverskin cultivars are in groups that are at the genetic threshold for bolting, where environmental conditions play a major role in dictating whether bolting will occur. Further out on this genetic vector are Artichoke cultivars, which bolt only by exception. The Turban cultivars branch away from one of the main Creole and Silverskin groups in a different vector from the Artichoke cultivars. Rather than regarding any of these groups as a subgroup of Artichoke, as was previously the inclination, it would actually be more accurate to say that Turban and Artichoke are subgroups of the Creole and Silverskin group, though thinking in terms of subgroups is probably not the most accurate conceptual model for understanding the relationships. It is notable that Creole, Silverskin, and Turban cultivars still retain substantial capacity for bolting and are genetically much closer to the basal Purple Stripe group than is the Artichoke group, whose members have all but lost the ability to bolt and form flowering structures. All of this suggests that at least some of the Creole and Silverskin groups are basal to the Artichoke groups and that Artichoke cultivars are likely more recent in origin, having further lost their ability to bolt and form complete flowering structures. In any case, we can conclude that neither Turban nor Asiatic is a type or subgroup of Artichoke.

What of Creole and Silverskin? The minimum spanning distance diagram places these cultivars in at least four separate but closely arrayed clusters. Clearly Creole and Silverskin cultivars are very closely related, but so far, it does not appear that either has an unambiguous genetic identity. I have personally noted differences in bulb morphology among Silverskin cultivars and differences in bulb and plant morphology among Creole cultivars, but my observations are only sufficient to pique interest, not to draw conclusions. It seems likely that these two horticultural groups will require reordering and redefinition. Additional genetic research and more careful morphological observation are needed to better resolve the Silverskin and Creole cluster.

The minimum spanning distance model is revealing not only in terms of the association of clusters with horticultural groups but also in terms of the association of individual cultivars with the clusters. As discussed previously, there are genetic differences within groups, and cultivars at the periphery of a group vary more from those at the core of the group. For the purposes of growers and aficionados, a separate horticultural group would be merited by observable meaningful difference in conjunction with measurable genetic difference.

In the minimum spanning distance diagram, the Rocambole group stands well on its own from other groups, though it shows significant genetic diversity, and is comprised of several distinct cultivar clusters and additional individual cultivars. The 1993 Pooler and Simon isozyme study suggested several distinct Rocambole groups. Ron Engeland (1995) cited phenotypic differences in some Rocambole cultivars, notably 'Carpathian', a widely available commercial cultivar, which he described as having straight leaves that rarely bent downward at the tips, producing more flowers that withered less quickly, and maturing 7 to 10 days later than most other Rocambole cultivars. Engeland also observed additional Rocambole cultivars that shared various combinations of these characteristics, but he was unable to delineate the boundaries of additional possible subgroups. The Rocambole clusters in the minimum spanning distance diagram radiate in multiple directions, not along a single genetic vector. For now there does not seem to be a compelling reason or sufficient basis for establishing additional Rocambole horticultural groups. We can simply make note of the genetic diversity within the group.

The Marbled Purple Stripe cluster exhibits genetic variation but does not suggest a need for alternate or additional horticultural groups. However, at least two cultivars that have been placed in the Marbled Purple Stripe group in commercial catalogs appear to belong elsewhere. In the minimum spanning distance diagram, 'Brown Rose' did not cluster with the Marbled Purple Stripe cultivars and had no reticulations with cultivars of that group. Where it might otherwise belong is also unclear, however, so for the purposes of this book I have placed it in an unclassified listing. Further genetic research could reveal reticulations to the Marbled Purple Stripe group or a separate clustering elsewhere. The placement of 'Pskem' is also problematic. 'Pskem' has relatively few, large cloves and superficially suggests membership in the Marbled Purple Stripe group, where it has appeared in commercial catalogs. In the Fort Collins study it was one of the 53 clones with a missing data element, so its genetic placement is less precise than it otherwise would be. Nonetheless, 'Pskem' has no reticulations with the Marbled Purple Stripe group and is genetically distant from it. However, 'Pskem' is reticulated with the Purple Stripe group. The bulb morphology of 'Pskem' is distinctive, with typically four large cloves when developed. The cloves are somewhat elongated and in this aspect resemble Purple Stripes more closely than Marbled Purple Stripes. Until more is known about 'Pskem', I have placed it in an unclassified listing.

The Glazed Purple Stripe group that Engeland proposed has seemed rather tenuous. Its phenotypic description is heavily dependent upon bulb coloration, which is among the more mutable and less reliable descriptors. Even the description of the coloration seems tenuous—bulbs with a "royal, glazed purple blush with tinge of gold" are subsequently described as sometimes including silver hues. The cloves are described as fewer and less elongated than in Purple Stripes. Engeland ini-

tially included two cultivars in the group. The Fort Collins study included one of Engeland's original Glazed Purple Stripe cultivars, 'Purple Glazer'. Remarkably, 'Purple Glazer', along with a noncommercial germplasm accession, formed a distinct cluster substantially apart from Purple Stripe and Marbled Purple Stripe, validating Engeland's observations. Subsequently, at least two additional Glazed Purple Stripe cultivars have come into commercial circulation. All of the cultivars in the group need further genetic study to validate their membership and shed more light on their genetic interrelationships. We are also in need of additional phenotypic descriptors to supplement the tenuous descriptors that currently define the group. In this book I have included four commercial cultivars that have been described as Glazed Purple Stripe. One hopes that further genetic study will affirm that they all belong to the Glazed Purple Stripe group and not elsewhere.

In the Fort Collins study, Porcelain cultivars formed a distinct cluster, and in the principal component analysis, even "survived" as one of four unique groups, along with Rocambole. All other clones and horticultural groups collapsed into the two remaining groups. The study included 11 different Porcelain cultivars, some with duplicates from separate sources. With one exception, the study uncovered no genetic difference, indicating a high degree of similarity among the clones. In the Fort Collins study, the exception 'Leningrad' showed reticulation with the Porcelain cluster, but was arrayed some distance from it. However, 'Leningrad' was among the 53 cultivars with missing data at one of the molecular markers, making placement less precise. In this book I have continued to include it in the Porcelain group.

The Pooler and Simon study arrayed garlic clones into 17 isozyme groups. One of the groups consisted of a single member, 'Kisswani' (PI 497951), obtained from Syria. This cultivar grows very poorly in North America, at least in temperate-climate regions. It has numerous tiny cloves arranged in multiple clove layers. A subsequent study by Ipek, Ipek, and Simon (2003) using AFLP markers showed this cultivar clustering with only one other clone, 'Rojo de Cuenca' (W6 1961) from Cuenca, Spain. 'Rojo de Cuenca' appears to belong to the Creole group, sharing that group's characteristics, including a (usually) single clove layer and far fewer, far larger cloves than 'Kisswani'.

'Kisswani' shares bulb morphology and the phenotypic disposition for miserably weak growth in North America with several other cultivars (Sorensen and Pelter 1998). These include 'Syrian' (W6 10472) from Syria, 'Yabroudi' (PI 540321) from Syria, 'Egyptian' (W6 10473) from Egypt, and 'Jomah' (PI 543049) from Pakistan. In the Fort Collins study, 'Egyptian' clustered with what appear to be Turban cultivars in the minimum spanning distance diagram. 'Jomah', from Islamabad, clustered separately but very near. (It was one of the 53 cultivars with a missing data element, making placement less precise.) Turban cultivars have relatively large cloves clustered in a single layer around a scape—a very different bulb morphology from the Middle Eastern cultivars. The weak growth and bulbing of the Middle Eastern cultivars have made it difficult to assess their morphological characteristics with the assurance that they have fully expressed themselves, but even at a very small bulb size, they produce numerous cloves in multiple layers. This suggests a kinship with the Silverskin group, yet the cloves are more separated, with rounded sides and an inner surface that is curved but not flattened or concave as is typical of Silverskin cultivars. The narrow leaves are a characteristic shared with most Silverskin cultivars, though not Turban cultivars nor most

Creole cultivars. After growing 'Egyptian' and 'Syrian' for a number of years, I was finally able to observe a single 'Syrian' plant bolt and form a mature flowering structure. The single modest example did not exhibit a defining morphology, at least to my untrained eye, but I am ever hopeful that these cultivars will reveal more of their nature as I grow and observe them. Additional molecular study of this group is certainly needed as well.

These cultivars from (mostly) the Middle East appear to share a common bulb morphology and a phenotypic disposition to grow poorly at northern latitudes. Most come from the same general geographic area in the Middle East, though with the extensive east-to-west trade routes over the millennia, it is not surprising to find geographical dispersion as well. Molecular studies that have included these cultivars are informative but inconclusive. The molecular tools currently available suggest associations and general spanning network positioning along the transitional region of bolting and nonbolting clusters—a transitional region that includes Creole, Silverskin, and Turban. Various molecular studies have placed these cultivars in different groups along this transitional region, but their bulb morphology is decidedly different from all of the rest, even given the limits of observable phenotypic expression.

Although additional phenotypic information from different growing regions would be very helpful in evaluating these cultivars, they nonetheless appear to form a distinct horticultural group, which I have called the Middle Eastern group. In most of North America, from a grower's standpoint, the Middle Eastern cultivars appear to be of little consequence. To my knowledge, none are available commercially. They typically produce tiny bulbs with numerous tiny cloves in multiple clove layers. Even if these cultivars could be grown larger, the numerous, relatively small cloves would hardly be desirable in the marketplace. For the scientist, collector, and aficionado, however, these cultivars remain intriguing.

So, after our long taxonomic journey and our venture into garlic horticultural groups, where are we now? The horticultural groups that Ron Engeland first proposed in 1991 and 1995 have largely become de facto standards in North America, with broad though not universal acceptance among growers and enthusiasts. These horticultural groups are in use in other parts of the world as well, at least among small-scale commercial growers and enthusiasts. It may be too strong of a statement to say that genetic research has verified these groups, since the groupings are analytical constructs, as

are the analytical models used in genetic research; clearly, however, genetic research has validated the viability and cogency of Engeland's phenotypic groups. These groups are closely mapped to genetic findings and effectively reflect the nature and diversity of the garlic genome. The degree of correlation among the groups that Engeland proposed and the clonal clustering that subsequently emerged from genetic research is really quite remarkable.

Additional research will help us further refine our understanding of garlic's horticultural groups, relationships, and lineage. We have a long way to go in our journey, but we have come a long way as well.

## ~ EIGHT ~

# Diseases and Pests

AS WE KNOW, when garlic is mechanically disturbed the disruption of the cells causes the enzyme alliinase to interact with nonvolatile sulfur compounds to produce volatile sulfur compounds, including allicin and other thiosulfinates. These transformations occur in the aboveground parts of the plant as well as in the bulb. The pungent sulfur compounds effectively defend garlic against many plant-eating pests and are toxic to many pathogenic fungi and bacteria. In addition to garlic protecting itself, its extracts or emulsions are effective in protecting other plants from pests and diseases. This does not mean that garlic is immune, however. Some pests and diseases are not entirely deterred, and some are unaffected by the sulfur compounds. Garlic is a relatively trouble-free crop, but like all crops it bears its own set of risks. Good cultural practices require that we exercise care in our stewardship to stave off the pests and diseases that threaten garlic.

Planting garlic or other alliums in the same soil year after year increases the risk of a variety of diseases and pests. This can be avoided by rotating garlic with other crops that do not have the same susceptibilities. Planting alliums in the same bed every other year may be sufficient in many growing areas, but if diseases or pests become evident or begin to build, extended rotations may be warranted. For more details on crop rotation, refer to "Soil" in chapter 6.

If you introduce new garlic cultivars to an established garlic-growing or -farming operation, it is a good idea to grow the new introductions in a separate area to isolate any disease or pest contamination problems that might emerge. This may not be practical or essential in a home garden or small-scale operation, but it is a good practice for larger-scale operations.

Good general cultural practices can go a long way in keeping your garlic crop healthy and minimizing the risk and impact of diseases and pests. Many of the preventative measures for each of the diseases and pests described in this chapter are the same. The following good cultural practices should be employed whether or not diseases or pests are immediately present: crop rotation; carefully inspecting planting stock; selecting the most healthy and vigorous bulbs; excluding bulbs with signs of infection or physical injury; thoroughly curing and drying garlic after harvest; providing good air circulation during curing and storage; avoiding excess nitrogen; avoiding soils that are too dry, too wet, or poorly draining; removing culls and plant debris from the garlic beds; and excluding allium plant debris from compost that will be used for garlic beds.

# DISEASES AND PHYSIOLOGICAL DISORDERS

## Basal plate rot (fusarium, bottom rot)

Basal plate rot is caused by the soil-borne fungus *Fusarium oxysporum*. Symptoms include yellowing leaves that begin to curve, leaves that begin to die back at the tips, or wilting of the entire plant. The infection begins in the underground stem plate and progresses into the cloves. The stem plate may show a brown discoloration and white mycelium may be observable. Eventually the roots will rot. Inflected cloves have brownish watery flesh.

Signs of infection may be minimal at harvest but progress during storage. Infection may occur at any time, but plants are particularly susceptible during periods of warm, wet weather prior to harvest. Mechanical damage to the bulb or stem plate, including damage caused by pests, increases the likelihood of infection. The threat of infection spreading to other bulbs during storage is negligible. The fungus can remain viable in the soil for extended periods by way of chlamydospores. If soil is heavily infested and growing conditions are problematic, the soil should be planted with nonsusceptible plants for four or more years.

In general, however, the impact on the crop can simply be minimized by excluding infected bulbs from planting stock, managing pests, and planting healthy, vigorous cloves.

## Basal rot (fusarium, bottom rot)

Basal rot is similar in effect to basal plate rot and the two are often lumped together in descriptions of garlic diseases. Basal rot was first discovered in California in 1976 and has subsequently spread to distant growing areas. It is caused by *Fusarium culmorum*, a soil-borne fungus that infects garlic through the underground stem plate. Elephant garlic is only moderately susceptible to the fungus, and onions are unaffected. The strains of the fungus that are harmful to cereals are not harmful to garlic, but garlic strains are harmful to cereals.

The stem plate and cloves of infected garlic can show decay at any stage of growth through harvest and storage. Lesions may have a reddish fringe, though the coloration is not always present. Symptoms of infection are not always evident in infected plants, and infection may be present for successive generations of plantings before the infection flares and disease is evident. Plant leaves can carry the infection even though they may not show any evidence of infection. Plant debris, soil, and runoff water can be vectors for spread of the infection. The fungus can remain viable in the soil for extended periods. Crop rotation regimens should not include cereals, since they are also affected by this strain of the fungus. Chemical and hot water treatments have generally proven ineffective. Risk can be managed by thoroughly curing and drying the bulbs after harvest, excluding bulbs with evidence of infection from planting stock, and planting healthy, vigorous cloves.

## Blue mold

Blue mold is caused by various species of *Penicillium*. It is the familiar blue-green mold common on many fruits and vegetables, including garlic. *Penicillium* molds are common in the soil, growing on plant and animal debris. Blue mold affects garlic through wounds to the bulb or cloves during harvest, storage, or separation of the cloves from the bulb prior to planting. Infected cloves may fail to grow, or new plants may be very weak, with yellowing leaves. Vigorous plants may be able to outgrow the disease. Blue mold is a common problem during storage, typically affecting individual cloves, or adjacent cloves in a bulb.

Blue mold can be managed simply by handling garlic bulbs and cloves with care to prevent mechanical damage. Carefully separating the cloves prior to planting and planting the cloves soon after separation will help prevent infection. Do not use any infected bulbs or cloves for planting stock. Immediately remove infected material from the area where cloves are being separated for planting, and wash your hands before separating any more bulbs into cloves. Blue mold is common, but it should only be an incidental occurrence and not a major threat.

## Leaf blight

Leaf blight is caused by the fungus *Botrytis squamosa*. It is more of a problem for onions than garlic, but garlic plants can be affected, particularly during periods of prolonged high humidity late in the growing season. Symptoms are circular or elliptical, whitish or grayish spots surrounded by a light green halo. If infection is severe, the halo may disappear as the spots expand, blighting the leaf. Control leaf blight by removing cull material and leaf debris from the field, particularly debris

from onions. Avoid excessive irrigation that keeps leaves wet or humidity high, and rotate the crop with nonsusceptible crops. Damage to garlic by leaf blight is usually not prevalent or sufficiently severe to cause concern.

## Neck rot (botrytis)

Neck rot is caused by several species of *Botrytis*, including *B. porri*. The fungus affects garlic in some growing regions more than others, notably on fall-planted garlic in western North America, Europe, and New Zealand. Symptoms first appear on the pseudostem near the soil line. The disease can spread rapidly under moist conditions, causing the pseudostems to have a water-soaked appearance. Infection can move into the bulb and persist through storage. Preventative measures include good air circulation in the field and in storage, avoiding injury to the plant and bulb, thorough drying prior to storage, and avoidance of excess nitrogen and irrigation, particularly late in the season. Mulch can also foster neck rot, particularly in chronically damp conditions. The "Mulch" section of chapter 6 discusses the trade-offs of mulching in more detail.

## Pink root

Pink root is caused by the fungus *Phoma terrestris*, which is primarily active when temperatures are above 75°F (24°C). It attacks garlic roots, causing them to turn pink and die. Replacement roots also become infected and die. The only aboveground symptoms are browning of the leaf tips. Pink root affects onions more severely than garlic. Although it is not commonly a problem on other plants, pink root has a wide range of hosts and can persist in the soil for three or more years. Because the fungus only flourishes in warm conditions, it is a significant problem only in certain growing regions. Infection generally means reduced yields rather than plant death.

## Rust

Garlic rust is caused by the fungus *Puccinia porri*. Although it is rarely a problem for garlic, an outbreak of rust in California in the late 1990s resulted in 100% infection in some fields and up to a 75% reduction in crop yield. Symptoms include small yellow to white spots or streaks on leaves that develop into orange pustules comprised of orange urediospores. Severely infected leaves may be almost entirely covered with pustules. If the disease progresses further, darker teliospores can form black pustules on the same leaves. Both spores can overwinter. Urediospores are windborne and can spread long distances. High humidity and low rainfall favor the disease. Temperatures above 75°F (24°C) or below 50°F (10°C) inhibit infection. Plant stress significantly increases susceptibility and damage. Avoid excess nitrogen and soil that is too dry, too wet, or poorly draining.

## Viruses

Virtually all commonly available garlic planting stock is infected with one or more viruses. Although most of the viruses are symptomless and do not cause disease, some viruses impact health and vigor. Onion yellow dwarf virus (OYDV) affects garlic as well as onions and is particularly problematic. Because almost all garlic is vegetatively propagated, perpetuation of virus-infected plants is virtually assured. The identity of all the many viruses that affect garlic is unknown, and many cultivars are likely infected with multiple viruses. Plants with viruses typically show reduced vigor and yield. Comparisons with virus-free plants generated from tissue have shown that viruses can result in crop reductions of 25% to 50%. Virus-free plants retain their vigor longer. Studies show that senescence in virus-free garlic may be delayed up to five weeks.

Virus-infected plants are most affected when under stress from poor growing conditions such as dry and infertile soil. The effects are mitigated by good cultural practices that optimize conditions for the plant. Because nearly all planting stock is affected by viruses, we have come to accept certain plant behavior as the norm. Visible symptoms may include leaves with chlorotic mottling, striping, or streaking, or stunted or crinkly leaves. The entire plant may appear stunted compared to plants without virus infection.

Virus-free plants can be produced through tissue culture or by planting from seed rather than cloves. They must be kept isolated from infected plants, since aphids and thrips can transmit the virus to healthy plants. Some viruses are not spread by aphids and thrips but can be spread by mites. Virus-free commercial planting stock is sometimes multiplied in isolated growing areas. The virus-free cloves are then used as planting stock for the commercial growing fields, which are replanted with the virus-free stock each year.

## Waxy breakdown

Waxy breakdown is a physiological disorder, not a pathological disorder. It can begin in the later stages of growth and is associated with high temperatures as harvest approaches. Poor ventilation and low oxygen levels after harvest and during storage also contribute to the problem. The first symptoms are small, light yellow areas in the clove flesh that become darker yellow or amber over time. Eventually the clove, or portions of the clove, becomes translucent and waxy. The outer clove skins typically look normal. The first signs of waxy breakdown are usually not evident in the field but only appear later, after the harvest.

## White rot

White rot is the most serious and threatening of all garlic diseases. It is caused by *Sclerotium cepivorum*, a fungus that is highly destructive to alliums, though other crops are unaffected. White rot is responsible for major garlic and onion crop losses throughout the world, including Africa, Australia, Central and South America, Europe, the Middle East, Asia—and the United States.

Early signs of infection include the appearance of fluffy mycelium on the underground stem plate. As infection spreads, the mycelium moves upward and into the plant bulb. Older (lower) leaves yellow and die prematurely (not to be confused with the normal withering of the lower leaves as harvest nears), and plant growth is stunted, followed by the rapid death of all foliage. Individual plants, clusters, or whole fields may suddenly die, depending on the degree of infestation. The death of plants in clusters is an indicator of possible infection by white rot. Typically the plants in the center of a cluster are the first to die. The fungus does not reproduce from spores but from poppy-seed-like sclerotia that are capable of remaining viable in the soil for decades. An abundance of sclerotia may be visible on decaying tissues.

The fungus is most active when soil temperatures are below 75°F (24°C). Control is highly problematic. If infection is noticed on isolated plants, removing the surrounding soil, locally fumigating the soil, and removing and burning plant material may control or eliminate the fungus. Flooding an infected field during warm weather can reduce if not eliminate the fungus. Unfortu-

nately, once widespread infection occurs, garlic and other alliums can no longer be grown on the site.

# PESTS

## Armyworms

Armyworm infestations are highly cyclic in nature. Armyworms are green-gray to black with yellow striping. Heavy infestations can cause rampant plant defoliation but are seldom a problem for garlic. By the time armyworms are ascendant, garlic has finished most of its growth and is nearing harvest. If necessary, these pests can be controlled with *Bacillus thuringiensis* (Bt), which is deadly to caterpillars but otherwise harmless. Later-stage infestations can be controlled with more aggressive chemical means.

## Bulb mites

Various mites can affect garlic. They are introduced through infested material, typically planting stock, and survive on infested plant debris left after harvest. They cause damage by penetrating the bulb tissue and creating a vector for diseases. Heavy infestations may destroy cloves or whole bulbs. Mites have a wide host range. Green manure crops can sustain and increase populations. Hot water treatment regimens with planting stock may reduce the likelihood of infestation, but good cultural practices including careful selection of planting stock, debris removal, and crop rotation are generally sufficient for control.

## Gophers

Gophers are enthusiastic garlic consumers and can devastate a crop. Richard Smith (1999) recounts the year he planted 110,000 cloves of garlic only to have 45,000 of them destroyed by gophers over the course of the winter, wiping out nearly half of his expected income. Author Chester Aaron protects his garlic from gophers by planting in raised redwood boxes with chicken-wire bottoms (described in more detail under "Bed Configuration and Spacing" in chapter 6). Coated hardware cloth is a more expensive but longer-lasting alternative to chicken wire. Depending on one's propensities and local conditions, various forms of gopher eradication are likely the most practical and cost-effective solution.

## Grasshoppers

Devastating numbers of grasshoppers are not a common threat for most growers. However, if you live in an area that is subject to cyclic grasshopper infestations, your garlic will not be not immune. In central Texas, Bob Anderson (2004) has witnessed heavy infestations of grasshoppers that not only ate his garlic crop to the ground but also pursued the garlic into the ground to eat the bulbs. In less than a week, 24,000 plants were lost. Attempts to protect the crop with floating row covers proved unsatisfactory for Anderson's extreme conditions. Some grasshoppers chewed through the row covers to get at the crop, and the row covers also retained heat, resulting in early maturity and small bulbs.

Floating row covers can be effective in less extreme conditions and when left covering the plants for shorter time periods. Screening materials may be a good alternative. Grasshopper infestations produce a great deal of grasshopper manure, which they further augment with their bodies as they die. The soil is enriched the year following an infestation.

## Leek moth

Leeks are the preferred victim of the leek moth (*Acrolepiopsis assectella*), but other alliums, including garlic, are targets as well. Distributed in Europe, Asia, and Africa, this small moth made its way to North America in the early 1990s when it appeared in Ontario. In North America it is confined to a localized area in eastern Ontario and western Quebec and has not yet made its way to other parts of Canada or to the United States.

The leek moth causes damage by tunneling into garlic leaves, scapes, and sometimes bulbs, and feeding on the tissue. Information from Europe indicates that pyrethroids and Bt products may provide effective control. Bt can be applied at intervals of 10 to 14 days when larvae are present. Removal and destruction of infested tissue, destruction of pupae and larvae, and crop rotation can help manage infestation.

## Nematodes (eelworms)

Nematodes are microscopic wormlike animals that migrate by swimming in films of water on the surface of the plant or between soil particles. Several species of this parasite attack garlic, but *Ditylenchus dipsaci* is by far the most common. There are many strains of *D. dipsaci*. Most are specific to their hosts, but the extent to which they may migrate to alternate hosts is not entirely clear. The strain that attacks garlic is also hosted by onions, leeks, and chives, as well as an unusual combination of other hosts such as celery, parsley, salsify, Shasta pea, and miner's lettuce.

Nematodes are spread primarily through infected planting stock. Diseased cloves generally show no symptoms, and the presence of the tiny wormlike pests can only be detected with a microscope. In the field the upper leaves of infected plants may prematurely yellow and die. Infection typically occurs at the basal plate, the underground stem. If infection is severe, the bulb may separate from the basal plate, and the bulb may deteriorate into a spongy mass, leaving only traces of itself by harvest time. Infected plants may show little or no symptoms under cool growing conditions, but symptoms become quickly apparent at elevated temperatures. The pests move through the tissues of infected plants, breaking down cell walls and consuming the cell contents.

Nematodes can survive in stored plant tissues for at least nine years. Unlike some other threats to garlic, nematodes are more likely to remain in plant tissue than in the soil. Using chemicals in the field or treating cloves with hot water prior to planting can be effective controls for nematodes, but routine cultural practices may be sufficient. These include rotating crops with nonsusceptible crops, carefully removing plant debris and volunteer plants from fields with a nematode problem, never returning composted garlic debris to the planting field, and excluding from planting stock all cloves from any bulb showing deterioration or abnormality.

## Onion maggots

These creamy white, legless maggots are approximately ½ in. (1.25 cm) long. They are the larvae of *Delia antiqua*, a gray fly somewhat smaller than a housefly. Although primarily an onion pest, onion maggots occasionally cause damage to garlic, particularly in coastal climates. The maggots bore into the bulb, bringing bacteria with them, causing rot and stench. The plant is stunted, and the aboveground growth yellows. Damage to garlic is usually incidental. Infected bulbs should be culled and destroyed.

## Thrips

Onion thrips (*Thrips tabaci*) are more of a problem for onions than garlic, but garlic plants can be affected as well. Adult thrips are small, slender, pale yellow to light brown insects with feathery wings. Young thrips are pale yellowish green and wingless. Both feed on garlic leaves, creating whitish specks that may expand to larger blotches if infestation is severe. Thrips thrive in hot, dry weather and have a wide range of hosts. They can multiply in cereal crops in the spring, then migrate to nearby garlic fields. Chemical sprays and insecticidal soap can be employed to control severe thrip infestation, but overhead sprinkling may be sufficient for suppression.

## Wireworms

Wireworms are the larvae of the click beetle (*Limonius* species). Click beetles cause no damage themselves, but their larvae feed on garlic roots and bulbs. The jointed larvae are typically light brown and approximately 1 in. (2.5 cm) in length when fully grown. Wireworms are most commonly a problem when planting garlic in fields that were previously in sod. After converting a field from sod, it is generally recommended to wait a year before planting garlic, although wireworms can live in the soil from two to six years. Wireworms tend to multiply in weedy fields or where grain and vegetable crops are grown. Avoid planting garlic in fields recently converted from sod or fields with a known wireworm problem.

# ~ NINE ~

# Composition and Chemistry

A DISTINCTIVE alliaceous odor, largely the product of organic sulfur compounds, characterizes all *Allium* species. Onions, leeks, chives, and garlic taste similar to but also distinctively different from one another. The number of sulfur compounds, their relative ratios, and their interactions with enzymes and other compounds create the complex taste chemistry characteristic of alliums.

If the cells of alliums are undisturbed, they essentially have no odor. However, once the cells are disrupted, the enzyme alliinase interacts with the existing sulfur compounds to produce the volatile sulfur compounds that characterize the taste and smell of alliums. An undisturbed onion is benign, but cutting into it generates volatile sulfur compounds—and sometimes a well of tears. As briefly discussed in chapter 3, an undisturbed garlic bulb has essentially no odor, but cutting or crushing the bulb or one of its cloves immediately generates the characteristic aromatic pungency. A deteriorating garlic bulb may have aromas from cellular breakdown, but the aroma from a healthy undisturbed bulb is virtually nil.

We will delve more deeply into the complexities of garlic's composition and taste chemistry, but if some of this is more than you care to absorb, you only need to keep in mind a few basics. The key elements in the composition and taste of garlic are as follows:

**Alliin.** S-allyl cysteine sulfoxide, a flavor precursor in garlic essential for the creation of allicin. It does not have the aroma, flavor, or health benefits associated with garlic.

**Alliinase.** The enzyme responsible for interacting with alliin and other non-volatile (nonaromatic) sulfur compounds to produce allicin and other volatile sulfur compounds. These volatile sulfur compounds characterize garlic's taste and smell. Heat, freezing, and strongly acidic conditions can permanently inactivate alliinase.

**Allicin.** The sulfur compound responsible for much of garlic's therapeutic benefit and characteristic smell and taste. Allicin is not present in whole cloves but is rapidly created when garlic is chopped or crushed, bringing alliin into contact with alliinase. Heat destroys allicin.

Let us now look further into garlic's composition and taste chemistry. The basis for the pungent flavors and aromas associated with alliums are sulfur compounds that are themselves nonvolatile. Collectively these nonprotein sulfur amino acids are known as S-alk(en)yl cysteine sulfoxides. Because they do not produce the characteristic flavors and aromas without enzymatic interaction, they are called flavor precursors. Catalytic action by alliinase, however, generates many volatile sulfur compounds. This enzymatic interaction with the S-alk(en)yl cysteine sulfoxides is key to the taste chemistry of alliums. The volatile sulfur compounds that are the product of these interactions characterize alliums and have made them highly valued as foods and medicines throughout human civilization.

There are four naturally occurring S-alk(en)yl cysteine sulfoxides. The first of these to be identified was S-allyl cysteine sulfoxide, commonly called alliin, which was first isolated from garlic. The other three S-alk(en)yl cysteine sulfoxides are S-methyl cysteine sulfoxide, S-propyl cysteine sulfoxide, and S-propenyl cysteine sulfoxide (Lancaster and Boland 1990). The presence and relative quantity of the flavor precursors varies among alliums and is responsible for the general flavor and aroma of each species. The common onion (*Allium cepa*), for example, has a very high proportion of S-propenyl cysteine sulfoxide and no alliin, while garlic (*A. sativum*) has a high proportion of alliin and no S-propenyl cysteine sulfoxide. Chive (*A. schoenoprasum*) has no alliin, but garlic chive (*A. tuberosum*) has a high proportion of alliin. Although elephant garlic is not true garlic but belongs to the species *A. ampeloprasum*, the ratio of the four S-alk(en)yl cysteine sulfoxides in elephant garlic is very similar to the ratio of the compounds in garlic. Alliin is present in abundance in only a few other alliums, including *A. moly*, *A. ursinum*, *A. victoralis*, and *A. vineale*.

Alliinase occurs in most if not all members of the genus *Allium* and is fundamentally responsible for the development of flavor and aroma compounds in these plants. Our knowledge of allium taste chemistry and the critical role of alliinase is relatively new. Alliinase was first extracted from garlic in 1947 but was not purified until the late 1970s. It is approximately 10 times more abundant in garlic cloves than garlic leaves. Onions isolate alliinase and other compounds in separate compartments of the same cell, but the alliin and alliinase in garlic are isolated in different cells. In garlic, alliinase is located in the vascular bundle sheath cells. Alliin is concentrated in the storage mesophyll cells.

For an enzyme, alliinase is present in unusually large amounts in garlic cloves, comprising at least 10% of the total clove protein. A fresh garlic clove contains approximately equal amounts of alliin and alliinase. The abundance of alliinase may help explain the exceptionally rapid conversion of alliin into allicin and other sulfur compounds. At room temperature, when garlic is cut or crushed, the transformation is completed within 10 seconds. Even oven-dried commercial garlic powders, when moistened, rapidly complete the transformation: half of the alliin is converted to allicin within 6 seconds, and the transformation is complete within 30 seconds. Alliinase is quite stable. The alliinase in garlic powders that have been stored for up to five years retain their ability to convert alliin to allicin with little loss in viability.

Garlic alliinase is most effective within a pH range of 5.0 to 8.0. At a pH of 3.5 or lower, alliinase activity is destroyed. At a pH of 3.0 or lower, alliinase activity can no longer be restored by neutralizing the pH. When empty, the stomach has a highly acidic pH of 1.5, increasing to about 3.0 after a light meal. A heavy, high-protein meal can increase the pH to as much as 4.5, but in general if one were to swallow a whole clove of garlic, stomach acids would destroy the alliinase and no allicin would be produced. Alliinase is most effective in a temperature range of 91°F to 99°F (33°C to 37°C), though there is still effective enzyme activity near freezing. Freezing inactivates alliinase and may substantially destroy it, but the conditions of freezing play a major factor. In one study of commercially frozen onion, alliinase activity was only 6.6% compared to fresh onion. However, laboratory-frozen onion had 18% activity and freeze-dried onion 45%.

The role of alliinase in allium taste and aroma is as important as it is short lived. The products of the interaction of alliinase and the flavor precursors are themselves unstable and are immediately transformed into other compounds that ultimately comprise the flavor and aromas that characterize the allium. When ingested, most of the compounds are quickly absorbed in the intestinal tract and are rapidly and extensively metabolized. Virtually none of the original compounds remain intact in the body. More than 80 different volatiles, primarily from onions and garlic, have been reported in allium studies.

What are the primary interactions that generate the characteristic taste and smell of garlic? The main flavor precursor is alliin. Bringing alliin and alliinase together (typically by chopping, crushing, or chewing) produces allyl sulfenic acid, which im-

mediately rearranges to form diallyl thiosulfinate (allicin). In shorthand form, the enzyme alliinase interacts with alliin to produce allicin. The amount of alliin decreases with storage, though a parent compound of alliin appears to act as a reserve for alliin during storage and sprouting.

Allicin is the primary volatile in freshly crushed garlic and characterizes the taste and smell we associate with garlic. However, allicin also undergoes rearrangements to other compounds, including diallyl disulfide and a thiosulfinate. Diallyl disulfide may further rearrange to trisulfides and polysulfides. The flavor precursors S-methyl cysteine sulfoxide and S-propyl cysteine sulfoxide, though present to a lesser degree in garlic than in other alliums, also undergo transformations that contribute to the array of flavor and aroma, giving rise to methyl and propyl disulfides and some polysulfides (Augusti 1990). The rearrangements and transformations are greatly accelerated by heat. Twenty-five different sulfur compounds have been identified in the oil of steam-distilled garlic. Although the bulb is the primary source of flavor precursors that form the basis for this tumultuous riot of flavor and aroma transformation, the precursors are also present in leaf blades and garlic roots.

The stability of allicin is heavily dependent on temperature and its inclusion in a solvent. At 73°F (23°C) allicin has a half-life of 16 hours. In water it has a half-life of 30 to 40 days. Water is a particularly effective stabilizing solvent because the hydrogen in water bonds with an oxygen atom in allicin. In ethanol, for example, the half-life is only 24 hours. Refrigeration increases stability approximately 20-fold. If frozen to −94°F (−70°C), allicin has a half-life of 25 days. In water, frozen to this temperature, there is no loss after two years. The allicin in crushed garlic is not as stable as pure allicin (Lawson 1996).

The total sulfur compounds in garlic comprise nearly 1% of its dry weight, or approximately 0.35% of its fresh weight. Some studies have indicated protein content at up to 6.3%, but these findings were based on total nitrogen, and garlic contains an abundance of nonprotein nitrogen compounds, including the cysteine sulfoxides. The actual protein content of fresh garlic is approximately 1.5%.

The alliin content of garlic, and thus the allicin yield potential, is dependent upon a variety of factors, including soil, weather, location, harvest time, and cultivar. Various studies have shown up to a 5-fold difference in allicin yield, but some of the variance is likely attributable to the differing analytical methods used in the various studies. In a separate study (Lawson 1996), a number of different cultivars grown in the same location showed a variation in alliin content of up to 2.7-fold among the various cultivars. Artichoke cultivars generally yielded the least amount of allicin, Porcelain cultivars the most. The Artichoke cultivar 'Inchelium Red' yielded the least at 2.8 mg/g. The Porcelain cultivar 'Romanian Red' yielded the most at 7.7 mg/g. However, sometimes there were substantial differences within the horticultural groups. The Porcelain cultivar 'Rosewood', for example, yielded only 3.3 mg/g of allicin in the study.

Although we typically only think of the garlic bulb as a source for allicin, the other parts of the plant can yield allicin as well. One study (Lawson 1997) showed that approximately 70% of allicin yield comes from the bulb, 15% from the leaves, 5% from the scape, 9% from the umbel (which is similar to the bulbs on a per weight basis), and 1% from the roots.

Garlic is often consumed cooked rather than raw. Heating garlic before it has been crushed or chopped prevents formation of important sulfur compounds, including allicin. Heat inactivates alliinase, thus preventing enzymatic action on alliin to form allicin and other volatile sulfur flavor compounds. Microwaving whole garlic cloves for 30 seconds inactivates all alliinase. Boiling an unpeeled clove for 15 minutes totally inactivates the alliinase, though a modest amount of volatile sulfur compounds are formed, likely as a result of minor mechanical impacts during boiling, which cause alliinase and alliin to come together before the alliinase is destroyed by the heat. In one study (Lawson 1993), heating crushed garlic to boiling temperature in a closed container for 20 minutes caused complete conversion of allicin and other thiosulfinates to diallyl trisulfides and other sulfides. In an open container, 7% of the thiosulfinates remained, but 97% of the sulfides dissipated. Frying crushed garlic cloves in hot cooking oil eliminated all allicin and 94% of the sulfides.

In a series of studies, up to 60 volatile compounds were identified when sliced garlic cloves were baked, fried, or microwaved, but only 16 compounds were identified when whole cloves were boiled. The studies once again demonstrated the importance of bringing the enzyme alliinase into contact with alliin by slicing, chopping, or crushing, thus generating a cascade of chemical transformations. Diallyl disulfide was the dominant volatile in all of the studies. Diallyl trisulfide was present in abundance only in garlic slices that had been baked or microwaved. Garlic slices fried in oil had significant amounts of other compounds, including allyl methyl disulfide, allyl alcohol, and vinyldithiins (Lawson 1993). In another study, glucose added to alliin yielded a different set of compounds and produced a meatlike flavor. New volatile compounds continue to be discovered. For example, S-allyl thiohexanoate was found when chopped garlic and vegetable oil were heated together—the sort of transformation likely to be found every day in a good garlic kitchen.

We launch these complex chemical interactions in our culinary laboratories—our kitchens—when we crush fresh garlic for a salad dressing, mince it and sauté it with vegetables, or chop it and throw it into the roasting pan with other vegetables. Although we know a great deal about the cause and effect of these interactions, the multitude of volatiles, and their effect on taste, smell, and therapeutic effects, we still have much more to learn.

# PART TWO

# THE ESSENTIALS

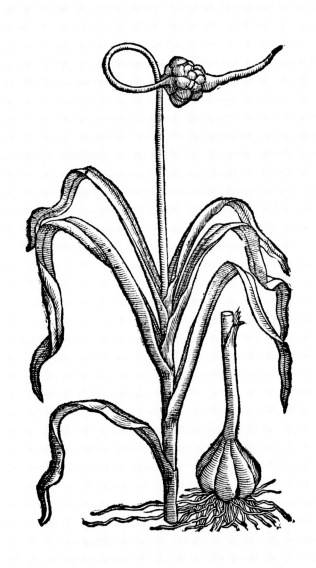

# ~: TEN :~

# Garlic Groups and Cultivars

IN THIS CHAPTER we will focus on garlic horticultural groups and garlic cultivars more from the standpoint of grower and consumer than from that of scientist, though a bit of the latter emphasis is certainly useful here as well. We will also be a bit looser in our terminology, sometimes employing the terms "softneck" for nonbolting cultivars and "hardneck" for bolting cultivars, except where greater precision is required. For a more technical discussion of garlic horticultural groups and taxonomy, refer to chapter 7.

Because of its adaptability and propensity for new variants, garlic grows happily throughout a large part of the world. Enthusiasts can enjoy garlic cultivars that exhibit a wide range of characteristics, with differences in ease of peeling; flavor, whether the garlic is raw or cooked; cold hardiness; clove number and size; and storage properties. Since strength in one characteristic sometimes means limitation in another, the garlic aficionado will likely want a number of cultivars. Ease of peeling, for example, is very desirable, but cultivars that peel easily do not store very long. One might want

a cultivar that peels easily for immediate consumption and a cultivar that is more resistant to easy peeling for longer storage. When all of the features of the various cultivars are thrown into the mix, the possibilities are manifold.

In addition to culinary properties, other distinguishing characteristics are directly related to ecological adaptation, such as the response of vegetative growth, bulbing, and flowering to temperature, day length, dormancy, and hardiness. In regions with severe winters, softneck Artichoke cultivars or Creole cultivars are more difficult to grow successfully, but Porcelain and Purple Stripe cultivars grow well in such conditions. In regions with exceptionally warm winters, most Purple Stripe and Rocambole cultivars fare poorly, while many Artichoke and Creole cultivars excel. Although the garlic horticultural groups frame general group characteristics, individual cultivars have their own expression. For example, bolting hardneck cultivars are generally better suited to more northerly regions with cold winters, but Bob Anderson (1999) reports that the hardneck Marbled

Purple Stripe cultivars 'Metechi' and 'Siberian' are very well suited to his growing region, located 75 miles (121 km) southeast of Abilene, Texas.

If supermarket garlic is all you have ever seen and experienced, the cultivars pictured and described in this chapter will be quite a revelation—at least they were very much a revelation to me when I first encountered them. Grow garlic if you are able to do so. As with any vegetable or fruit—or any food, for that matter—the more you are involved, the greater will be the depth of your experience and appreciation. Discovering your own favorites and using part of your harvest for next year's planting stock is a wonderful ritual of discovery and culinary pleasure. If you cannot grow your own garlic, seek out the better cultivars at farmers' markets. Do not be alarmed if the names you encounter differ from those in this book; cultivars often take on new names at different localities. Ask the grower for the name of the cultivar's horticultural group. If nothing else, this will help raise awareness about garlic horticultural groups. Awareness is rapidly spreading, however, and if you inquire you may find out that "Uncle Ned's North Forty Special" is a local name for a Rocambole cultivar. Growers at farmers' markets are sometimes very familiar with the horticultural groups but do not display that information for fear of confusing the customer. If you express interest and knowledge, you may be able to find out much more about the garlic that is being offered. If you cannot grow garlic and your local farmers' market does not offer an adequate selection, do not despair: some of the garlic sources listed in the back of the book sell garlic for the table as well as for planting.

Garlic cultivars adapt to local growing conditions over time. It is common for garlic to grow better and produce larger bulbs after several years at the same location. Growing conditions and adaptation can shape performance but not fundamental morphological traits. That is not to say that there will be no differences in appearance or behavior resulting from different growing conditions. Climate, soil nutrients, and the presence of viruses, for example, can significantly alter the coloration of the clove and bulb skins. Variations in latitude and winter temperature can cause some cultivars to bolt—or not. These are all phenotypic expressions of the plant. Core morphological traits such as the shape of the umbel capsule, spathe color, flower color, and anther color are largely independent of growing conditions. Other characteristics, such as bulb shape, clove shape, and relative number of cloves, are generally stable. These exhibit somewhat greater plasticity, such as when growing conditions produce a small bulb that develops only two cloves, or conversely, when conditions produce an exceptionally large bulb that begins forming an additional clove layer and cloves. Other characteristics may also be distinctive indicators but exhibit a higher degree of plasticity. The color of bulb and clove skins is one such example. Even in the same garden plot in the same year, bulb and clove skin coloration sometimes varies from bulb to bulb. Variation is all the more possible when garlic is grown under different conditions in different growing regions. When describing a cultivar or horticultural group, one looks to characteristics that are less plastic (flowering structures, for example) to supplement those that are more overt (clove coloration, for example) but more plastic. Should the more plastic indicators be dismissed altogether? No. All indicators are helpful in identification—just look at the photographs of the Creole cultivars to see how intense and distinctive the coloration can be. Large, well-grown bulbs that have had a normal development cycle offer the best comparisons among horticultural groups and cultivars. Distinguishing characteristics are more readily apparent, and characteristics that might have resulted from abnormal development or limited size are eliminated.

How many garlic cultivars are there? On the one hand, many cultivars undoubtedly have not yet made their way to widespread circulation. On the other hand, particularly when one includes farmers' markets and locally traded cultivars, the number of named cultivars exceeds the actual number of distinct cultivars. Accession designators from allium germplasms, such as PI 540368, do not roll off the tongue with ease, nor do they readily affix in memory or capture a meaningful mental association. It is not surprising, then, that the grower of a newfound favorite garlic will give it a new, more evocative name. If a "large" or prominent garlic grower does the naming, something of a de facto nomenclature may be established, but inevitably different names are chosen by different growers for the same garlic accession, leading to multiple names for the same cultivar—and sometimes the same name for a different cultivar. Other factors contribute to duplication of named cultivars. Garlic that is sold, traded, or passed down to others over the years inevitably acquires a variety of names from new growers in new locations as the original name is forgotten or abandoned.

Among the garlic cultivars in widespread cultivation, there is certainly some duplication in naming, and the differences among some cultivars may be relatively minor. Nonetheless, among hundreds of genuinely distinct cultivars in widespread cultivation, there is substantial diversity. Some names may refer to any number of cultivars, sometimes spanning horticultural groups. Names such as "Italian Red" or "Italian Purple," for example, have been applied to a wide range of garlic cultivars. At best, they may have some sort of consistent meaning within a locality, but they are otherwise not par-

ticularly useful and only contribute to confusion. Cultivars from the Silverskin group are sometimes called Italian garlic in some locales and Egyptian garlic in other locales. Again, such imprecise and overlapping groupings further confuse an already confusing subject.

Genetic research with increasingly sophisticated DNA tools has revealed and affirmed extensive genetic diversity in the garlic germplasm. It has also revealed and affirmed clusters of similar garlic types—horticultural groups within the species. Molecular research is relatively new, and as the tools and techniques become more sophisticated, they will be able to resolve more complex differences and interrelationships among cultivars and cultivar groups. Although the naming and grouping of garlic cultivars is sometimes a bit muddled, it should not detract from the horticultural and culinary enjoyment of the differences that the numerous cultivars offer.

The inclination to draw distinctions among crop plant cultivars, including garlic, is a relatively new one—at least, there is no evidence of such a focus in earlier times. Within the last thousand years, we begin to see distinctions drawn between garlic types cultivated in southern Europe, notably distinctions between bolting and nonbolting (hardneck and softneck) cultivars. Only within the last several hundred years do we see more detailed descriptions and finer distinctions made among crop plants in general. Garlic is a bit late in this regard, carrying on with only broad distinctions when other crop plants sported hundreds or perhaps thousands of named cultivars. The realization that numerous distinct garlic cultivars exist, and the inclination to identify, name, and appreciate them, are relatively recent developments.

Henry Jones and Louis Mann's 1963 benchmark work on alliums acknowledges that garlic-growing regions generally have their own distinct cultivars. The authors describe three cultivars in California: 'California Early', 'California Late', and "Creole," the latter being of lesser importance and primarily grown in the hot southern interior of the state. Mexico is described as having five cultivars and the Philippines as having two—a large-bulbed cultivar from the Batanes that does not bulb if grown in most of the rest of the country to the south, and a poorly producing, small-bulbed, early cultivar that is grown in its stead. France, Italy, Brazil, and Japan, among others, are cited as having several cultivars each. A 1976 leaflet from the University of California (Sims et al.) indicates that 'California Early' and 'California Late' accounted for approximately 95% of the garlic grown in the state. "Creole" was listed at less than 5%, with other incidental "varieties," including "Chilleno" and "Formosan," described as resembling "Creole" and grown in the desert regions of Southern California. Another cultivar grown in the region was called "Egyptian," which was described as differing from the other three in its larger size, with white rather than purple bulbs. The "Creole" that was described as a single cultivar in the 1976 leaflet is now generally regarded as a horticultural grouping of many cultivars.

In the decades following Jones and Mann's 1963 work, allium explorers collected many hundreds of strains from around the world, from the wild, and from markets, bazaars, and the germplasm collections of other countries. John Swenson introduced numerous cultivars to North America and shared more than 400 of his accessions with enthusiasts and specialty garlic growers through Seed Savers Exchange and other venues. USDA allium researchers and plant explorers such as Richard Hannan, Philipp Simon, and Barbara Hellier made collecting trips to remote areas of Central Asia and elsewhere to bring back garlic strains previously unknown in cultivation. Books

by Ron Engeland and Chester Aaron, among others, raised awareness of the various cultivars and stimulated interest in them. The emergence of specialty garlic growers has heightened awareness of the numerous cultivars and their merits, raising demand and stimulating emergence of more specialty growers—and yet more awareness and interest, in an expanding spiral. We are in the midst of a garlic renaissance. Never before have more garlic cultivars been more widely available or more widely appreciated.

The cultivars listed in this book are primarily those with broad North American circulation, but the list is not intended to be comprehensive—you will undoubtedly encounter many cultivars not listed here. In no way should unlisted cultivars be regarded as inherently less desirable. One day we may have a way to comprehensively list all genetically distinct cultivars and systematically identify cultivars with duplicate names. Until then, unfamiliar names and duplicate names are inevitable. In any case, discovering favorite new cultivars is part of a garlic enthusiast's enjoyment.

For the cultivars listed in this book, I have included alternate names when known. Some of the cultivars originated from germplasm collections, and I have included the germplasm accession numbers when available. The National Plant Germplasm System (NPGS) accessions are designated by a plant introduction (PI) number, such as PI 493098, or may carry a provisional introduction number such as W6 8417, indicating introduction at the Western Regional Plant Introduction Station's allium germplasm in Pullman, Washington. Some of the cultivars originated from the Leibniz Institute of Plant Genetics and Crop Plant Research in Gatersleben, Germany. These are designated by a prefix of either ALL or K followed by a number, such as ALL 7204. Undoubtedly I have missed numerous alternate cultivar names and germplasm accession references, but this is at least a small step in the direction of a more uniform and universal nomenclature.

In my view, all of us—writers, growers, and enthusiasts—should always include reference to a germplasm accession number in conjunction with the common name whenever the accession number is known. This is not to say that we need to entangle ourselves with arcane accession numbers every time we speak of garlic, but if, for example, we are selling "Uncle Ned's North Forty Special" at a farmers' market, the label or information that gets passed on to the buyer should include an accession number whenever possible.

Some of the cultivars listed here are also available in other countries, though one is more likely to encounter regional or country-specific cultivars or names. If you know a cultivar's horticultural group, it will give you a general idea of its character. A grower who is offering an unfamiliar cultivar may nonetheless be able to tell you the horticultural group, or you may be able to determine it yourself by looking at the bulb. Growing the unfamiliar cultivar and observing the plant, of course, will give you more information about its horticultural group and merit.

The horticultural groups listed in this section are substantially those described by Engeland in 1991 and 1995, with some updating and revision, as detailed in chapter 7. Chapter 7 also details the molecular research and DNA fingerprinting supporting the horticultural groups. Molecular research will likely further refine the horticultural groups presented here, but in general, if you encounter an unknown cultivar, it will likely belong to one of eleven horticultural groups: Artichoke, Asiatic, Creole, Glazed Purple Stripe, Marbled Purple Stripe, Middle Eastern, Porcelain, Purple Stripe, Rocambole, Silverskin, or Turban.

These groups reflect the broad diversity of the species. Cultivars in the Purple Stripe group are genetically the closest to wild garlic and garlic's ancestral roots. Many Rocambole cultivars offer the unique, rich sweetness that, along with their tendency to peel easily, makes them a favorite in the culinary world. Some Porcelain cultivars are especially high in sulfur compounds that are healthy for the body, and their huge cloves make for quick work in the kitchen. And so on.

Not unexpectedly, differences within horticultural groups are generally more subtle than the differences among horticultural groups. If you are able to do so, try growing or sampling at least one cultivar from each group. This is a fine way to begin exploring the world of garlic, since each group offers unique properties worthy of investigation. As you venture along in your journey, you will come to your own discoveries and develop your own favorites.

## ARTICHOKE

Artichoke cultivars are among the most productive and least problematic. They are ready for harvesting earlier, readily develop very large bulbs, and adapt to a wide range of growing conditions and soils. Most cultivars bolt rarely, if ever, and so direct more energy toward bulb development rather than to reproductive mechanisms. Bolting cultivars often require removal of the scape to achieve the largest bulbs and greatest productivity. From the standpoint of a large-scale commercial grower, an easily grown, heavily producing garlic that does not need the additional labor-intensive step of scape removal is highly desirable. This quickly rules in Artichoke garlics and rules out all bolting hardneck garlics. Artichoke cultivars are by far the most commonly favored and grown commercial garlics. Most of the garlic in the supermarket is from the Artichoke group.

Although the common commercial Artichoke cultivars are less than optimal from a flavor standpoint, other Artichoke cultivars have better culinary properties. At their worst, Artichoke cultivars can taste simple and vegetative. The best, however, have very good flavor. Broadly speaking, they may not have the rich, sweet depth of the best Rocambole cultivars, or the complex flavor intensity of Purple Stripe cultivars, but at their best they offer fairly complex, milder, more high-toned flavors of their own. For many culinary purposes, Artichoke cultivars have a more pleasing flavor than the often more aggressively sulfurous Silverskin cultivars.

Unlike late-maturing Silverskins, Artichokes tend to mature very early in the season. Artichokes are generally larger with a flattened bulb shape. Some cultivars have a bulb that is rounded and relatively smooth, while others have a knobby, irregular bulb. Silverskins tend to have more of a teardrop-shaped bulb and are generally smaller. Artichoke bulb skins are relatively thick and coarsely textured. Outer cloves are typically fat and blocky with sides and edges that are often squared and angular. Inner cloves are usually, though not always, smaller and narrower, with some angular edges and irregular shapes. The cloves sometimes have a wide "tail" at the tip, formed from the clove skin.

The plants are short with very broad yellow-green leaves that are angled relatively horizontally and arrayed with only a semblance of bilateral symmetry. These shorter, less statuesque plants, nevertheless, typically produce large bulbs with relative ease. Under certain conditions, such as cold winters or other stress, Artichoke cultivars may partially bolt, forming bulbils within a pseudostem. This activity may take place at the top of the bulb within the bulb wrappers, or several inches up the pseudostem. When present, the bulbils are large and often dark reddish purple. Very rarely the plants may form a complete flowering structure with a fully developed scape. The scape is typically straight or drooping without the radical curling of the vigorously bolting horticultural groups. Ron Engeland (1995) reports that in cold-winter climates 5% to 20% of the plants produce bulbils, but plants originating in southern climates react to an exceptionally cold winter by forming bulbils in as much as 50% to 75% of the plants. The propensity to partially bolt and produce bulbils varies from cultivar to cultivar. The formation of bulbils and partial bolting are undesirable characteristics from the standpoint of the large-scale commercial garlic industry. The industry controls expression of these characteristics by growing garlic in more southerly regions with moderate winter temperatures, and by focusing on a very few cultivars that have limited propensity for producing bulbils. As most of us know, Gilroy, California is the commercial "garlic capital of the world"—or at least the United States. 'California Early' and 'California Late' are the commercial cultivars of choice.

Artichoke cultivars have lost their ability to produce seed, and thus the capacity for genetic diversity is significantly diminished. Nonetheless, vegetative sports over the millennia ensure that there are differences within the horticultural group. If you have only had supermarket Artichoke garlic, try some of the more characterful Artichoke cultivars such as 'Lorz Italian', 'Tochliavri', and 'Kettle River Giant'.

Artichoke cultivars have multiple clove layers and numerous cloves, though not typically as many as Silverskin cultivars. Although the inner cloves are usually smaller, cultivars such as 'Trueheart' and 'Machashi' are exceptions to the rule. The bulb wrappers are off-white, but many cultivars exhibit purple coloration, ranging from an occasional blush to pronounced color throughout the entire wrapper. The clove skins are off-white to light tan,

This 'Chamiskuri' plant is partially bolting. The large purple bulbils have burst through the pseudostem.

A partially bolting plant may form bulbils within the bulb, at the top of the bulb, or anywhere along the pseudostem.

This bulb from a partially bolted Artichoke plant shows the abbreviated scape and bulbil swelling.

with reddish or purplish tones in some cultivars. The commercial cultivars 'California Early' and 'California Late' are less likely to exhibit coloration in bulb wrappers and clove skins than most other Artichoke cultivars.

Artichoke cultivars are the most widely adapted garlics, growing well in a wide range of climates. Although they are not well suited to climates with exceptionally harsh winters, they are tolerant of hotter southerly climates. They also store well, though not nearly as well as Silverskin cultivars.

## 'California Early'

Over 80% of the commercial garlic grown in the United States is grown in California, and most Californian garlic is 'California Early' or 'California Late'. 'California Early' has white skins, a flattened bulb shape, and light tan clove skins. Its bulb is rougher in appearance than 'California Late', and its inner clove layers are generally fairly large. 'California Early' bulbs can be huge when grown under optimal conditions. It is the garlic most often processed into powders, salts, seasonings, and is used in all manner of canned and frozen convenience foods. It is a high-volume producer and the mainstay of the Gilroy garlic industry.

'California Late' on the left, 'California Early' on the right.

'California Early' adapts to a wide range of climates, matures early, and is more tolerant of southern climates and hot spring weather than 'California Late'. In northern climates it is far less prone than 'California Late' to producing bulbils in the pseudostem. In California, 'California Early' is typically planted in November for harvest the following June. The taste is relatively mild but rather simple and vegetative.

## 'California Late'

Another staple of the garlic business in Gilroy, 'California Late', when grown in the same conditions as 'California Early', produces smaller, more rounded bulbs, with more numerous but smaller cloves. Its clove skins are pinkish to pinkish brown. Its leaves are narrower than those of 'California Early', and it does less well than 'California Early' in the hotter growing regions of California. 'California Late' has a higher content of solids and stores much better than 'California Early'. In California it is typically planted in December for harvest in July or August. In northern climates it has a tendency to partially bolt, and often produces bulbils in the pseudostem.

'California Late' has a hotter, more aggressive taste than 'California Early'. Since it stores very well, it is available for the table after some of the more preferred garlic cultivars have deteriorated.

'Chamiskuri'.

Citing the merit of 'California Late', a publication on commercial garlic production in California speaks of the cultivar's long-storing virtues, which allow it to have a lengthy marketing season as well as the flexibility of keeping the crop off the market during intervals of lower garlic prices. The cultivar's culinary merit relative to other, more desirable cultivars was not mentioned in the article.

## 'Chamiskuri' (ALL 778, K 6035)

'Chamiskuri' was collected in 1983 at Chamiskuri in the Republic of Georgia. It is a productive cultivar but sometimes yields bulbs with smaller and more numerous cloves than other Artichoke cultivars. It stores well. In my garden 'Chamiskuri' shoots early, well before other Artichoke cultivars, and is more prone to partial bolting.

## 'Chet's Italian Red' (PI 540368)

Now widely distributed, 'Chet's Italian Red' was discovered in the 1960s at an abandoned garden site in Tonasket, Washington, by Chet Stevenson. It may have up to four clove layers, and the interior cloves can be relatively small. 'Chet's Italian Red' has qualitatively good, but rather mild, garlic flavor. It is not particularly biting even when raw, though severe winter cold may sharpen its character and make it hotter.

## 'Chilean' (PI 540379)

The taste of 'Chilean' is generally mild, though with vegetative echoes of supermarket garlic. It keeps only moderately well. It is not bad, but other choices are readily available.

### 'Early Red Italian'

Selected for earlier maturity, 'Early Red Italian' may be a selection of 'Chet's Italian Red' from the 1980s by Telowa Farms in southern Oregon.

### 'Inchelium Red'

'Inchelium Red' comes from a garden located along the Columbia River in Inchelium, Washington, a small community on the Colville Indian Reservation, near the Canadian border. It was the top-rated softneck garlic at a 1990 Rodale Kitchens taste test and has also shown well in various other tastings. 'Inchelium Red' has good, but not particularly intense or complex, garlic flavor. Its pleasant mildness undoubtedly accounts for its success in tastings. In a study of more than 20 garlic cultivars, 'Inchelium Red' yielded the least allicin. Tasting raw garlic can very quickly become rather brutal, and a mild, less assertive garlic such as 'Inchelium Red' can provide an abused palate a measure of relief. From a culinary standpoint, however, a garlic with more assertive character may well be more desirable in many recipes and preparations.

'Inchelium Red' has a flattened bulb shape and many smaller inner cloves, though on a large head, the inner cloves are relatively large. It is capable of producing very large bulbs with up to four or five clove layers, though it seems to grow much smaller in cooler growing areas with mild winters. It remains a very popular favorite.

### 'Kettle River Giant'

'Kettle River Giant' is highly productive. It has exceptionally large heads, and its large cloves are arrayed in no more than two layers. It is among the more flavorful Artichokes and stores well. It is an heirloom cultivar from the Kettle River area in northeastern Washington State near the Canadian border.

'Inchelium Red'.

'Kettle River Giant'.

'Lorz Italian'.

### 'Loiacono'

This cultivar from the Loiacono family of New York State is believed to have been brought to America when the patriarch of the current generation emigrated from Europe. It yields large bulbs with large, squat cloves.

### 'Lorz Italian'

A Northwest heirloom and a very fine garlic cultivar, 'Lorz Italian' was brought from Italy to Washington State's Columbia Basin in the 1800s by the Lorz family. It is productive and well adapted to summer heat, though it also does well in cooler climates. Although the typically large bulbs yield numerous cloves in multiple layers, there are relatively few small inner cloves.

Compared with most hardneck cultivars, many Artichoke cultivars are either mild with modest flavor complexity, or else display aggressive, vegetative, or other less desirable flavor characteristics. However, all but the most ardent hardneck proponents would agree that some Artichoke cultivars have very fine taste characteristics as well. 'Lorz Italian' is one such cultivar. It has strong complex flavors and is devoid of vegetative or other less optimal flavor characteristics. Its flavors are more high-toned than Rocambole or Purple Stripe cultivars, but that simply means that one has more culinary choices in one's repertoire. It also keeps well. Under certain growing conditions, 'Lorz Italian' has a propensity for partial bolting.

### 'Lukak'

'Lukak' comes from New York grower Boris Andrst's collection of Czech garlic cultivars. It produces large bulbs with mild but good flavor.

'Machashi'.

### 'Machashi' (ALL 759, K 5873)

This cultivar was collected in 1982, at an elevation of 1640 ft. (500 m), between the Caucasus Mountains and the Black Sea, at Machashi in the northwestern Republic of Georgia. It frequently partially bolts in some climates and sometimes has large cloves arrayed in a single circle around a center. When inner cloves are formed they tend to be larger, similar to 'Trueheart'. The Fort Collins study (Volk et al. 2004) suggests that 'Machashi' may be genetically distinct from other Artichokes, but a missing data element in the study did not permit more precise genetic placement.

### 'Madrid'

Acquired from a market in Madrid in 1992.

### 'Okrent'

'Okrent' produces good yields and stores well. The bulbs sometimes show a reddish blush.

### 'Olomuk'

Another Artichoke from Boris Andrst's collection of Czech garlic cultivars. The name may be derived from the city of Olomouc in the eastern Czech Republic.

### 'Oregon Blue'

'Oregon Blue' is an old Northwest heirloom. The coloration does not quite live up to the name, but under some conditions the bulbs have a slight purple blush on a white background. Multiple cultivars may be carrying the name 'Oregon Blue'. One report indicates that 'Oregon Blue' may be a variant of 'Chet's Italian Red'. One large commercial grower indicates that it is a variant of 'California Late'.

## 'Polish White' ('New York White')

From grower Ron Bennett of the Holly, New York, area, near Lake Ontario, 'Polish White' is more tolerant of colder winters than many Artichoke cultivars. It produces bulbs with few or no small cloves. The clove skins often have a slight purple blush.

## 'Purple Cauldron'

From France by way of Oregon grower Horace Shaw, 'Purple Cauldron' generally shows more purple coloration than most Artichoke cultivars, and a stronger tendency toward partial bolting.

## 'Sicilian Artichoke'

Previously from Ronniger Potato Farm and subsequently offered by Filaree Farm, 'Sicilian Artichoke' produces and stores well.

'Sicilian Artichoke'.

## 'Simoneti' (ALL 763, K 5878, 'Simonetti')

'Simoneti' was collected in 1982, at an elevation of 820 ft. (250 m), from the small village of Simoneti in the western Republic of Georgia and introduced to the United States by Philipp Simon. It adapts well to a range of climates. It is productive even in poor soils and is capable of producing exceptionally large bulbs in rich soils. The bulb and clove wrappers have a pinkish blush under certain growing conditions. 'Simoneti' has good flavor but is rather mild and less intense than some other Artichoke cultivars.

## 'Susanville'

'Susanville' is generally regarded as a selection of 'California Early'. The USDA accession listing (PI 540373) states that 'Susanville' resembles 'California Late' and also lists it as a bolting cultivar. Richard Hannan indicates that the 'Susanville' introduced to the collection in the 1980s initially did not bolt but bolted in subsequent years (personal communication). It appears that two different cultivars may be carrying the same name. The cultivar in commercial circulation typically does not bolt and has a large, flattened bulb shape most closely resembling 'California Early'.

## 'Thermadrone'

'Thermadrone' is a productive commercial cultivar that was imported from France for commercial testing.

'Tochliavri'.

### 'Tochliavri' ('Red Toch')

'Tochliavri' was obtained from Peter Hanelt at the Gatersleben Seed Bank in eastern Germany. In 1988 Hanelt collected the garlic from the tiny village of Tochliavri in the Republic of Georgia, the same village where the father of garlic writer Chester Aaron was born. It is commonly marketed under the name 'Red Toch'. Both Aaron and Darrell Merrell, garlic grower and organizer of national garlic symposiums, praise its character highly. Merrell describes it as a garlic by which he judges other garlics, with a flavor that is "not too mild, not too hot" that has "a mellow spicy tang with a fragrant aroma."

The taste is complex yet delicate and without a great deal of heat. The flavors may be less rich and intense than some of the better bolting cultivars, and it is a somewhat mild garlic, but its more high-toned character is nonetheless flavorful and fairly complex in its own way. 'Tochliavri' typically has 12 to 18 cloves per bulb. The cloves on the inner layers can be fairly small.

### 'Transylvanian'

Despite what the name might conjure, 'Transylvanian' is a mild-tasting garlic with little raw heat. It was purchased in the historic Transylvania region of Romania by Professor Feur of Brandeis University and acquired by Chester Aaron. Aaron reports that the original heads consisted of numerous tiny cloves, but as the cultivar acclimated over the years, it produced increasingly larger heads and fewer cloves. Nearly lost in the first few years, it

'Trueheart'.

'Tzan'.

is now fully acclimated and produces some 6 to 10 large cloves with several smaller cloves. Somewhat unusually, the bulb is elongated horizontally. Other cultivars with the same name may also be in circulation.

## 'Trueheart'

For those who do not like to deal with the smaller inner cloves on Artichoke garlic cultivars, 'Trueheart' offers an alternative. It is named for its typical large center clove as opposed to an array of small cloves. 'Trueheart' is hot when raw but has good character without the vegetative elements that are characteristic of some Artichoke cultivars.

## 'Tzan' ('Mexican Red')

'Tzan' reportedly comes from Shandong Province, China, where it is commercially grown, and is marketed in Mexico as 'Mexican Red'. It is usually listed as a Turban in commercial catalogs, but the plant I obtained from one of the commercial sources is an Artichoke.

The cloves are mounded upward toward the bulb center, giving the bulb somewhat of a teardrop shape, albeit a teardrop with a flattened or indented bottom. The bulb and clove shape are Artichoke, not Turban. In my growing environment, Turbans easily and reliably bolt, but 'Tzan' has never bolted, and also unlike Turbans, 'Tzan' stores very well. Curiously, a grower's accession report from the early 1990s indicates that only some of the plants bolted and that the plants that bolted had different-looking cloves. One suspects that a mix-up occurred in identification of the planting stock. It is possible that there are also Turban cultivars named "Tzan" in circulation. The 'Tzan' in my collection is an exceptionally large-bulbed Artichoke garlic.

## 'Zahorsky'

From Boris Andrst's collection of Czech garlic cultivars.

# ASIATIC

Asiatic cultivars are readily identifiable by their distinctive umbel capsule. When fully developed, the capsule has an exceptionally long beak that is broad and hollow for a substantial portion of its length. Ron Engeland (1995) describes it as looking like a long, wrinkled bean pod. The bulbils are also distinctive. They range from large to huge in some cultivars and are often very dark reddish purple. For some Asiatics the umbel capsule may have as few as two to four bulbils. If planted, the bulbils are large enough to produce a small multicloved bulb at harvest. Unlike most bolting cultivars, Asiatics do not require scape removal to produce normal large bulbs, though scape removal may yield slightly larger bulbs in some growing conditions.

The scape is typically short and drooping rather than strongly coiling. Asiatics routinely bolt in northerly climates but may not routinely do so in more southerly climates. Early molecular studies indicated that Asiatic cultivars were genetically similar to nonbolting Artichoke cultivars, but more advanced DNA studies have shown that Asiatics are genetically quite distant from Artichokes and are much closer to Purple Stripes and other strongly bolting groups. The Asiatics display considerable variation in bulbil size—and in the case of 'Sakura', bulb morphology—suggesting that the group may be comprised of several closely related groups or subgroups. Asiatic cultivars have been underrepresented in genetic research and would benefit from additional study.

I am quite taken with Asiatics. Previously regarded, along with Turbans, as a subgroup of the Artichokes, Asiatics were often overlooked by many people, including myself, as anything particularly special. In my early days of exploring garlic,

I tended to lump these cultivars with Turbans and focused my interest on other horticultural groups. I know now that they are genetically, phenotypically, and organoleptically far different from Turban and Artichoke cultivars. Some of the Asiatic cultivars—'Pyongyang' and 'Asian Tempest', for example—have exceptionally fine flavor, far more closely resembling Purple Stripes than Artichokes or Turbans, and some Asiatics also store very well. The distinctive Asiatic umbel capsule also adds interest to the garden and can be left to grow without inordinately diminishing the size of the bulb.

Though clove coloration is partially dependent on growing conditions, the cloves of some Asiatics display a brown to deep reddish purple coloration that can rival Creole cultivars in terms of intensity. The clove skins are thick and substantial. The cloves are generally similar in shape to Purple Stripe cloves but are perhaps even more similar to the somewhat shorter cloves of Glazed Purple Stripes, a group with which, according to DNA studies, Asiatics appear to share genetic proximity. Asiatic cloves are typically arrayed in a single layer around the scape. The bulb wrappers often display a pronounced purple striping. Curiously, the mild-tasting 'Sakura', which has the most exaggerated Asiatic umbel capsule shape, has less typical bulb and clove characteristics, to the extent that the bulb and cloves have even been described as resembling elephant garlic on a smaller scale. Despite its appearance, however, DNA studies place 'Sakura' in the Asiatic group, as does its distinctive umbel capsule.

Asiatic leaves are yellow-green and relatively broad. Maturity can come quickly in warmer growing climates, and the bulb wrappers will split if the garlic is not harvested as soon as one or two leaves begin to turn brown, in contrast to other garlic cultivars that can and should be left longer to fully develop. On the other hand, in my marine-

A 'Pyongyang' umbel capsule.

(above) On the left, a huge 'Russian Redstreak' bulbil. On the right, three tiny bulbils from 'Romanian Red', a cultivar in the Porcelain horticultural group.

(left) A huge bulbil and tiny flower burst through a 'Russian Redstreak' spathe.

influenced climate, maturation is more gradual, and I have noticed only modest differences in the propensity to split bulb skins. My harvesting regimen with Asiatics varies only slightly from other cultivars. If long storage is a goal, harvesting a bit early is advisable. A little experimentation will show you the harvesting regimen best suited to your growing conditions.

'Asian Tempest'.

### 'Asian Tempest'
(PI 615431, 'Seoul Sister', W6 12911)

From South Korea by way of Horace Shaw of Oregon's Sweetwater Farm, 'Asian Tempest' is the best-known Asiatic garlic cultivar. It is very productive and reliable, producing relatively few but large cloves with good garlic character. The cloves are hot when raw but tamed and flavorful when cooked. Though large, the bulbils are smaller than those of some other Asiatic cultivars. Along with 'Wonha' and 'Pyongyang', 'Asian Tempest' is one of the last cultivars to shoot in my garlic garden. Clove coloration is often deep purple.

'Asian Tempest' has excellent depth of character that may approximate the best of the Purple Stripes. If harvested somewhat early, it stores exceptionally well for a bolting cultivar, and I enjoy eating it after other favored cultivars are past their prime.

### 'French Red Asian'

The unstable Rocambole cultivar 'French Red' has reportedly generated a number of sports, including 'French Red Asian' in 1990.

An 'Asian Tempest' scape and umbel capsule. The beak of the umbel capsule is beginning to swell.

With further development this 'Asian Tempest' umbel capsule shows more of the prototypic Asiatic look, with its broad, swollen beak.

A split 'Pyongyang' spathe reveals the extended bulbil sheaths that force their way into the beak of the umbel capsule, swelling and extending it.

A rambunctious 'Pyongyang' umbel capsule.

## 'Pyongyang'
### (ALL 819, K 7041, 'Pyong Vang')

'Pyongyang' comes from an area near the North Korean capitol of Pyongyang. It is hot when raw and has a crisp texture, becoming nutty and richly flavorful when cooked to a straw to light tan color. 'Pyongyang' stores exceptionally well. I have consumed bulbs in good condition in late June following the year of harvest, though typical storage is not as lengthy.

Some growers describe the cloves as light brown with a rosy purple blush. My examples have shown clove coloration more akin to the rich reddish purple of some of the Creole cultivars. The bulbils are large, with deep purple coloration. 'Pyongyang', 'Asian Tempest', and 'Wonha' are among the last cultivars to shoot in my garlic garden. Richard Hannan reports that it can be planted in spring very successfully (personal communication). 'Pyongyang' is a characterful, rich-tasting cultivar that is very worthy of the garden and the table.

Bulbils and flowers in a 'Pyongyang' umbel.

'Pyongyang'.

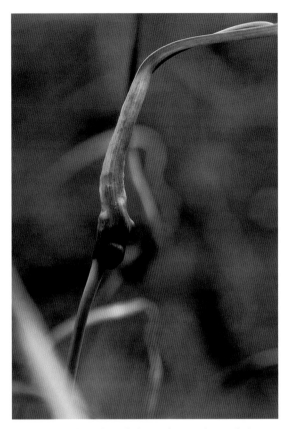

A 'Russian Redstreak' umbel capsule—another variation showing the characteristic extension of the capsule and broad, hollow base of the beak.

'Russian Redstreak'.

## 'Russian Redstreak'

'Russian Redstreak' originates from Filaree Farm in Washington State. In 1988 it reportedly arose as a mutation of the Rocambole cultivar 'Russian Red'. Unlike Rocamboles, 'Russian Redstreak' grows well in southern climates with warm winters as well as in more northerly climates. The spathe sometimes displays pronounced reddish tones. The umbel capsule is typically lumpy and unsymmetrical, reflecting large, unevenly distributed bulbils within. 'Russian Redstreak' is tolerant of drought and stores well.

## 'Sakura' ('Japanese')

'Sakura' is an unusual Asiatic. The umbel capsule is the most exaggerated and dramatic of the Asiatic group, with a very broad, elongated, hollow beak. The bulb, however, looks quite different from most Asiatics. The bulb wrapper is typically off-white with little or no purple striping. The tannish cloves are fat and large. At a casual look, some bulbs are reminiscent of elephant garlic. The flavor is good but rather mild. It shoots earlier than other Asiatic cultivars and stores less well. As with other Asiatics, the size of the bulb is not particularly dependent on scape removal, so the rather unusual scape can be left on the plant and enjoyed for its unique appearance.

'Sakura' was originally brought to the trade by Giannangelo Farms, who obtained it from an elderly Japanese farmer in western Washington. It is widely marketed under the name 'Japanese'.

A 'Sakura' umbel capsule. The exaggerated bulbil sheaths coil their way into the wide, hollow base of the beak.

A split spathe offers a glimpse at the exaggerated bulbil sheaths in the 'Sakura' umbel capsule.

'Sakura'.

A 'Wonha' umbel capsule.

On the right, bulbils and a few sparse flowers in a 'Wonha' umbel. On the left, one of the bulbils has been removed to show the exaggerated sheath, extending many times the bulbil's length.

'Wonha'.

### 'Wonha' (ALL 785, K 6801)

'Wonha' was collected in 1985 about 19 miles (31 km) north of Pyongyang, North Korea. It was introduced to the United States by way of Gatersleben, Germany, and John Swenson. 'Wonha' has a good, rounded flavor without sulfurous overtones.

'Creole Red', showing the long, narrow profile of the developing umbel capsule.

## CREOLE

The Creole group is well suited to hot southern growing climates and is tolerant of early-season heat and drought. At one time Creoles were called Southern Continental. Many of the cultivars in circulation in the United States originated in Spain. In the Southwest they are sometimes called Mexican Purple. In a 1976 leaflet from the University of California (Sims et al.), a Creole was described as a "common variety in Mexico and South America." The "variety" was further described as having cloves with deep purple skins that are smaller than the cloves of 'California Early' or 'California Late'. The

keeping quality and level of solids were described as being between that of 'California Early' and 'California Late'. We now know that Creole represents not just a single cultivar, but multiple cultivars with shared characteristics. One might speculate that the Central and South American Creole cultivars made their way to the New World by way of the Spanish explorers and settlers. In America's large-scale garlic industry, Creole cultivars play an insignificant role. However, for the specialty garlic grower, gardener, or consumer, Creoles offer fine taste and lengthy storage properties. Even in ideal

Numerous flowers among the bulbils in a 'Creole Red' umbel.

growing environments, the bulbs are only moderate in size, but their quality more than compensates.

Creoles are very beautiful. The clove skins are vividly and deeply colored, in a range of shades of red and purple, making Creoles arguably among the most distinctive and overtly identifiable cultivars. At one time Creoles were regarded as a subgroup of Silverskins, but the status of both groups is not entirely clear. The Fort Collins study (Volk et al. 2004) shows multiple clusters of Creole and Silverskin cultivars in close proximity, but the Creole and Silverskin cultivars are intermixed within the clusters. Further genetic study as well as attentive physical observation are needed to better understand the interrelationships and the boundaries of the existing, or perhaps new, horticultural groups.

Creoles have a reputation as sweet-tasting garlics, though some cultivars can be quite hot as well. Garlic growers in hot southerly climates may not be able to grow Rocamboles successfully, but Creoles are compensation, thriving in such climates and tolerating drought. Rocamboles have a magnificent taste but store poorly, whereas Creoles have very fine character and store exceptionally well, some nearly as long as Silverskins. Creoles do not grow as well in more northerly climates, typically yielding small bulbs. However, garlic does acclimate and adapt to local conditions over a period of seasons. Filaree Farm in north central Washington State reports that after many years of acclimatization, their Creole cultivars now produce relatively large bulbs.

Creoles typically bolt in the temperate growing regions of North America, but the bolting impulse is not as insistent as it is with the strongly and steadfastly bolting Purple Stripes or Rocamboles. The scapes droop in an upside-down U shape or curl gently without the exaggerated coiling and looping of the strongly bolting cultivars. Creole umbels develop slowly, and the umbel capsule is long and narrow as development progresses. Allowing the scape to remain through maturity can significantly reduce bulb size. Creole bulbils have white to pink and purple coloration. They are small to medium-sized. The weak flowers are numerous among the bulbils. Most Creole cultivars have broad leaves.

The number and array of cloves vary with the cultivar and size of the bulb. The cloves may be very large with as few as four per bulb, or more numerous with double or more the number, even on relatively small bulbs. The cloves are sometimes arrayed in a single layer around the scape but may include inner cloves as well, with the inner cloves enveloped by a separate leaf. The cloves are generally uniform in size when arrayed in a single layer around the scape but more variable in size when the bulb has multiple layers and inner cloves.

The variations in the bulb structure as well as the variations in leaf size are likely phenotypic expressions paralleling the DNA studies. We have more variance and intermixing of attributes than can be adequately described by the existing Creole and Silverskin horticultural groups. As our understanding grows, we will likely see a reordering of these two groups, and perhaps the emergence of additional horticultural groups as well.

In the meantime we can enjoy and explore the variation found among the Creoles. If you can grow these garlic cultivars, you should do so. They are arguably the best-tasting cultivars for long-term storage. In spite of their generally smaller size when grown in my cool northern garden, Creoles play a key role in my garlic repertoire. No other garlic that lasts this long tastes this good.

A curling 'Burgundy' scape drapes the umbel capsule across a broad leaf.

'Burgundy'.

## 'Burgundy'

'Burgundy' made its way into broader commercial production from Davis, California, by way of Horace Shaw. It is a beautiful garlic, the cloves typically displaying more of a deep purple than the red tones of some Creole cultivars. The bulbs are also squatter and the cloves less elongated than some others in the group. 'Burgundy' is among the more mild-flavored Creoles, but having said this, one should not mistake its more moderate character for dullness. It has an excellent, sweet, rich character and is a good producer. 'Burgundy' has a well-established place in my garlic repertoire.

## 'Creole Red'

'Creole Red' made its way into market circulation by way of a California virus-free program in the 1980s. In some 50 tastings that Chester Aaron (2002) conducted around the United States, 'Creole Red' has generally ranked among the top two or three. It is indeed a fine cultivar, performing very well in warm southern climates, though like most Creole cultivars it does less well in northern climates.

## 'Labera del Obispo'
('Labera Purple', W6 8413)

'Labera del Obispo' is a 1991 introduction from Cordoba in southern Spain. In my limited experience with the cultivar, it has been somewhat hotter and less sweet than the best of the Creoles.

'Creole Red'.

'Labera del Obispo'.

'Manuel Benitee'.

'Morado de Pedronera'.

### 'Manuel Benitee'
('Spanish Benitee', W6 8414)

'Manuel Benitee' was introduced to the United States from Cordoba, Spain, in 1991. In my limited experience with it, it is among the richer, sweeter Creoles.

### 'Morado de Pedronera'
('Spanish Morado', W6 8415)

Another of the larger-cloved Creole cultivars, 'Morado de Pedronera' was introduced to the United States from Cordoba, Spain, in 1991. The leaves are quite broad compared to some other Creole cultivars, while the bulb and cloves are classically Creole in appearance.

Unlike most Creoles, 'Morado de Pedronera' is quite hot when eaten raw. Late in the storage season, I no longer grab any handy Creole when a dish calls for raw garlic. After a time or two of exchanging wide-eyed looks across the dinner table, my wife and I have excluded 'Morado de Pedronera' from raw garlic duty. Nonetheless, it is quite fine for sautéing, has large cloves, and stores well, so it remains in my repertoire.

The split spathe shows the densely packed bulbils and flowers in an umbel of 'Morado de Pedronera'.

'Pescadero Red'.

'Rojo de Castro'.

## 'Pescadero Red'

'Pescadero Red' comes to the commercial market by way of California. In my garden this cultivar tends toward red more than purple. It is beautiful, if slightly less intensely colored than some Creoles. It is also sweet and rich, and stores well.

## 'Rojo de Castro'
('Cuban Purple', W6 8417)

'Rojo de Castro' was introduced to the United States from Cordoba, Spain, in 1991. Although this cultivar originated in Spain and not Cuba, the marketability of a garlic that seems to be associated with Fidel Castro has apparently been too much to bear—and understandably so, as the market is often unkind to good cultivars with less appealing names. In a convoluted twisting of nomenclature, this Spanish cultivar is now commonly marketed under the name 'Cuban Purple'.

Regardless of the name it bears, it is a fine cultivar, with sweet, rich character and minimal heat. It grows very well in some of the hottest southern growing regions where other garlic cultivars struggle.

A 'Blanak' umbel with bulbils and numerous flowers.

## GLAZED PURPLE STRIPE

Glazed Purple Stripe has been described as a subgroup of Purple Stripe. However, the Fort Collins study (Volk et al. 2004) shows that Purple Stripe is the basal group for all garlic. Thus, all garlic groups, not just Glazed Purple Stripe, have a derivative genetic relationship with the Purple Stripe group. Glazed Purple Stripe is no more a subgroup of Purple Stripe than are, for example, the Asiatic or Rocambole horticultural groups. Like them, Glazed Purple Stripe stands on its own.

Glazed Purple Stripe cloves are generally more squat and fewer per bulb than those of Purple Stripes, but more numerous than those of Marbled Purple Stripes. The cloves are perhaps most similar to Rocambole cloves in proportion, if not appearance. Glazed Purple Stripes are strongly bolting hardneck cultivars.

The name "Glazed Purple Stripe" is a good descriptor. The bulb wrappers have a glazed, matte metallic appearance and are silvery purple with occasional gold tones. The clove skins are smooth and shiny with a purple blush over a tannish background. Although useful as taxonomic descriptors, bulb and clove coloration can be heavily influenced

A curling 'Vekak' scape.

'Vekak' umbels bursting through their spathes.

least one of the purported Glazed Purple Stripes, 'Brown Tempest', belongs elsewhere. The cultivars in this group need further genetic study to affirm their membership and shed more light on their genetic interrelationships. We are also in need of additional phenotypic descriptors to supplement the tenuous bulb and clove color descriptors that currently largely define the group. Interestingly, an analysis of DNA information shows that the Asiatic group and the Glazed Purple Stripe group are closely related along the same genetic vector. Both groups are much in need of additional study.

Glazed Purple Stripes are well worth exploration. The bulb coloration is certainly attractive, and these are very fine culinary garlics as well. My own preference leans more toward full-flavored garlics, and for that reason, 'Red Rezan' is less of a favorite, though others may find it a perfect match. I am quite taken with 'Vekak', which is neither vegetative nor sulfurous but offers rich, rounded garlic flavor.

## 'Blanak'

'Blanak' features purple coloration and satin silver undertones. It comes from Boris Andrst's collection of Czech garlic cultivars.

'Blanak'.

by environmental conditions and are not as reliable as one might wish. In terms of observable characteristics, the Glazed Purple Stripe group is heavily dependent on bulb and clove coloration. For this reason I was initially a bit skeptical of the validity of the Glazed Purple Stripe group. The Fort Collins study, however, included a member of the group, 'Purple Glazer', and the analysis clearly showed that it is genetically distinct and well separated from other horticultural groups.

Ron Engeland originally proposed the group and included two cultivars, 'Purple Glazer' and 'Red Rezan'. At least five putative Glazed Purple Stripe cultivars are in commercial circulation. However, the Fort Collins study showed that at

'Red Rezan'.

'Vekak'.

### 'Purple Glazer' (ALL 830, K 7092, 'Mcadidzhvari #1', 'Mchadijvari #1')

'Purple Glazer' was collected in 1986 at Mcadidzhvari near the town of Dusheti, Mtskheta-Mtianeti, east central Republic of Georgia. It is an attractive garlic with a satiny finish. Depending on growing conditions, it may display deep purple hues with silver undertones.

### 'Red Rezan' (ALL 850, K 7205)

'Red Rezan' was collected by Klaus Pistrick in 1986 from Rezan, Russia, southeast of Moscow. It has good garlic flavor, completely devoid of vegetative characteristics, but is somewhat mild. Depending on growing conditions, it displays a satiny, glazed purple and silver coloration.

### 'Vekak'

This highly productive cultivar from Boris Andrst's Czech collection is increasingly popular. The flavors have a more intense character than some of the other cultivars in the group, such as 'Red Rezan' and 'Purple Glazer'. It is particularly rich and good when sautéed. I always plant plenty of this cultivar, and it has become a mainstay in my kitchen.

## MARBLED PURPLE STRIPE

As with Glazed Purple Stripe, Marbled Purple Stripe has been described as a subgroup of Purple Stripe, and earlier molecular studies seemed to suggest such an association. Again, however, the Fort Collins study (Volk et al. 2004) shows that Purple Stripe is the basal group for all garlic. All garlic groups, not just Marbled Purple Stripe, have a derivative genetic relationship with Purple Stripe. Despite the implications of the name, we should not think of Marbled Purple Stripe as a subgroup of Purple Stripe, but as a separate horticultural group of its own, in the same way that we think of Porcelain as a separate group. The name, nonetheless, is a good descriptor of the coloration. The bulbs of these cultivars are purple striped and marbled or dappled with purple. The large, squat, fat cloves are tan to brown and sometimes have varying degrees of dark purple coloration. Because of their size, there are fewer cloves per bulb of an equivalent size than Purple Stripe, but generally more than Porcelain. The cloves are arrayed in a single layer around the scape. The shape and number of cloves are well defined through the bulb wrappers.

The leaves are relatively wide, and the plants are very vigorous and tall. Marbled Purple Stripes are strongly bolting cultivars. The thick scapes curl dramatically before straightening and becoming erect, reaching up to 6 ft. (1.8 m) tall for some cultivars when grown under optimal conditions. The large umbels contain numerous medium-sized purple bulbils and numerous purple flowers. The anthers are yellow or purple. The scapes generally must be cut if bulb size is not to suffer, but I like to let a few scapes fully develop to see the large umbel filled with purple flowers and bulbils perched atop the towering scape—a delightful sight.

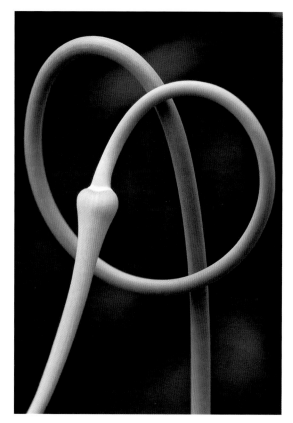

A curling 'Northe #3' scape.

A 'Siberian' umbel's bulbils and flowers burst through the spathe.

As the 'Siberian' umbel matures, the flowers and bulbils become more purple.

The spathe has dropped away, revealing a 'Siberian' umbel in its entirety. The flowers in this umbel have not yet turned purple.

Marbled Purple Stripes store reasonably well, and the large cloves are relatively easy to peel. The taste can be quite hot when raw. When these garlics are sautéed, the taste can be somewhat more sulfurously garlicky and not as nutty and rich as Purple Stripe cultivars. After cooking, some cultivars can taste mealy and a bit bland, though the best Marbled Purple Stripes more closely approximate Purple Stripes in flavor and character. From a culinary standpoint, one might describe Marbled Purple Stripes as somewhere between Porcelains and Purple Stripes in character. For many culinary uses, Marbled Purple Stripes are a fine alternative to Porcelains. The cloves are not quite as large, but a relatively few cloves still provide a good quantity of garlic. The Marbled Purple Stripe character works better with some cuisines than the typically more sulfurously aggressive character of Porcelains. Al-though Marbled Purple Stripes thrive in climates that provide a period of vernalization in winter, they are among the better of the strongly bolting hardneck cultivars for growing in hotter southern climates with early warm springs. Texas grower Bob Anderson (1999) reports that the Marbled Purple Stripe cultivars 'Metechi' and 'Siberian' have given him some of the best results of the hardneck cultivars.

I have not grown all of the Marbled Purple Stripes listed here, and it is possible that some may belong in another group such as Purple Stripe. Seed catalogs include 'Brown Rose' and 'Pskem' in the Marbled Purple Stripe group, but the Fort Collins study shows that they belong elsewhere; until more is known, I have listed them under "Unclassified."

A close-up of 'Siberian' flowers. If the bulbils had not previously been removed, the flowers would have withered.

'Bai Pi Suan'.

'Bogatyr'.

'Brown Vesper'.

### 'Bai Pi Suan'

'Bai Pi Suan' originated in China, possibly from Xinjiang Uygur, an autonomous region in northwest China that is sometimes referred to as Chinese Turkistan.

### 'Bogatyr' (ALL 7204)

From the Moscow area by way of the Gatersleben Seed Bank in eastern Germany, 'Bogatyr' produces very large, long-storing bulbs. It has a strong, clarion garlic taste and is very hot when raw, particularly when grown in hot southern climates, where it also produces among the largest hardneck bulbs. For taste and performance in hotter growing climates, it is regarded by some as equal to 'Metechi'. As is typical of hardneck cultivars, 'Bogatyr' also performs well in cooler northerly climates. In my own garden, I have found it superior in flavor and texture to 'Metechi'.

### 'Brown Tempest' (PI 493098)

From the Moldavian Institute for Research in Irrigated Agriculture and Vegetable Growing by way of Poland, 'Brown Tempest' was introduced to the United States in 1984. Its cloves are typically brown with pinkish overtones. It is hot when raw, with good garlic character that carries through in cooking.

### 'Brown Vesper'

'Brown Vesper' was introduced from the former Soviet Union to the United States by garlic researcher Maria Jenderek. It is hot when raw but mild and sweet when baked.

### 'Bzenc'

Named for a town in the Czech Republic not far from the Austrian border, 'Bzenc' made its way to commercial availability by way of Boris Andrst and his collection of Czech garlic cultivars.

### 'Choparsky'

'Choparsky' was obtained from the Siberian Botanical Garden. Like many Marbled Purple Stripe cultivars, it is hot when raw but mild and starchy when baked.

### 'Duganskij' (ALL 130, 'Dunganskij', K 1020, 'Mestnyj')

'Duganskij', from Kazakhstan, is a productive, long-storing, late-maturing Marbled Purple Stripe with good, strong garlic flavor.

### 'Jovak'

'Jovak' made its way to commercial availability by way of New York grower Boris Andrst's collection of Czech garlic cultivars.

### 'Khabar'

Collected from Khabarovsk, Russia, by Alaskan garlic grower Bob Ellis.

'Metechi'.

### 'Metechi'

'Metechi' is a late-maturing garlic that is highly productive in a wide range of climates and growing conditions. In both southern and northern growing regions, it produces very large heads and cloves, and is long storing. It is among the better hardneck cultivars for regions with warm winters and early springs.

Views on the culinary merit of 'Metechi' vary widely. In my experience it is not particularly notable when raw, and I find its cooked texture mealy and its flavor lacking. Others, however, regard 'Metechi' very highly, extolling the virtues of its hot, strong flavor—characteristics I have not found in the plants grown in my garden. The Fort Collins study (Volk et al. 2004) included 'Metechi' from two different commercial sources. 'Metechi' from one of the sources clustered with Purple Stripes, not the Marbled Purple Stripes. This could suggest that more than one cultivar carries the name.

The spathe begins to split on this 'Northe #3' umbel capsule.

The senescing spathe drops away from a 'Northe #3' umbel.

'Siberian'.

## 'Monshanskij' (ALL 131, K 1021)

From Kazakhstan in the former Soviet Union by way of Czechoslovakia, where it had been accreted to the allium germplasm in 1954.

## 'Northe #3' ('Northe')

'Northe #3' is among the earliest-sprouting Marbled Purple Stripes. It is also among the earliest for harvest, and it stores moderately well. It made its way to commercial production by way of the Beltsville Agricultural Research Center in Maryland.

## 'Siberian'

'Siberian' is an impressive cultivar. Although it does not excel in any individual aspect, it performs well in nearly all respects. It is vigorous and does well even in hotter southern climates that usually do not favor hardneck garlics. It produces large cloves and large heads that store quite well. While its flavor and cooked texture are not quite in the same league as the best Purple Stripes, such as 'Shvelisi', 'Shatili', and 'Samarkand', it is among the better-tasting Marbled Purple Stripes. In hotter climates 'Siberian' is said to have a milder character than 'Metechi', though my own experience in the cool Pacific Northwest has been just the opposite.

'Siberian' made its way to commercial production from Alaska, where it was obtained from fishermen who had acquired it when trading green leafy vegetables with subsistence farmers from eastern Siberia who grew only root crops. Unlike many cultivars that have a narrower growing range for quality and productivity, 'Siberian' does very well in both cold and hot climates. It has produced true seed in formal trials, though it is not among the better seed producers.

# MIDDLE EASTERN

Perhaps productive in their native environments, the Middle Eastern cultivars are as interesting as they are ill suited for garlic growing in most of North America. You are unlikely to find them at your local farmers' market or even from specialty growers. I am not aware of any that are commercially available.

I have grown some of these cultivars for a number of years, gradually increasing the size of their bulbs, from miniscule to tiny. My best luck comes from cloves that fail to produce multicloved bulbs and instead yield a single, relatively large round. The following year a round will yield a somewhat larger bulb, but fully differentiated into numerous tiny cloves, the largest of which is still much smaller than the previous round, and generally incapable of producing a subsequent bulb of greater diameter. A joyful Sisyphus, I continue to experiment with these cultivars with considerable interest, though with little hope of winning a blue ribbon at the county fair.

In a Washington State University germplasm evaluation of 46 garlic cultivars (Sorensen and Pelter 1998), only eight failed to reach an average bulb diameter of 1 ½ in. (3.75 cm). At least three of the eight, 'Kisswani', 'Yabroudi', and 'Egyptian', were from the Middle Eastern group. It is quite possible that these cultivars may grow larger in some of the warmest southern growing regions of the United States, but the Middle Eastern cultivars, with their numerous, relatively small cloves, would still not be looked upon with great favor by most growers and consumers, absent any other compelling attribute.

The relative smallness of the plants has made it difficult to assess their morphological characteristics with the assurance that the cultivars have fully expressed themselves. The multiple clove lay-ers and numerous cloves might suggest a kinship with the Silverskin group, though the cloves of Middle Eastern cultivars are more separated, with rounded sides and an inner surface that is curved but not flattened or concave as is typical of Silverskins. The narrow leaves are a characteristic shared with most Silverskins.

Molecular studies that have included these Middle Eastern cultivars are inconclusive but informative. With the molecular tools currently available, differences and duplication among cultivars and cultivar groups have not been fully resolved. Although not uniform, molecular studies usually suggest a distinct group clustered in general proximity to other weakly bolting cultivar groups: Silverskin, Creole, and Turban. In the Fort Collins study (Volk et al. 2004), 'Egyptian' clustered with Turban cultivars, and 'Jomah' clustered nearby, though a missing data element for 'Jomah' diminished the accuracy of its placement. The Middle Eastern and Turban cultivars are both in need of further genetic study. The two groups clearly have a very different bulb morphology and a very different phylogenetic response.

## 'Egyptian' (W6 10473)

'Egyptian' was collected from a bazaar in Cairo in 1992. I have had even worse fortune trying to increase the bulb size of this cultivar than I have had with 'Syrian'. In a DNA study of garlic strains, 'Egyptian' clustered with the Turban strains, though its manifold cloves and clove layers set it apart.

## 'Jomah' (PI 543049)

'Jomah' was collected at the Jomah market in Islamabad, Pakistan. In the Fort Collins study (Volk et al. 2004) it clustered very near the Turban group.

'Syrian'.

A weakly growing 'Syrian' plant produces a scape.

Because of a missing data element, a more precise genetic placement was not possible. The multiplicity of cloves and clove layers sets it morphologically apart from the Turban group.

### 'Kisswani' (PI 497951)

Collected in Syria, 'Kisswani', like others of this group, steadfastly resists sizing up. It was the only cultivar of the Middle Eastern group included in the 1993 Pooler and Simon study, in which it was arrayed as the sole member of an isozyme group, clustering with no other cultivars.

### 'Syrian' (W6 10472)

'Syrian' was collected in 1992 from a large bazaar in Aleppo, northwestern Syria. One of the world's oldest inhabited cities, Aleppo is located on an arid plateau less than 100 miles (160 km) from the Mediterranean. After years of growing this cultivar, I finally had a plant bolt and produce fully formed flowering structures.

### 'Yabroudi' (PI 540321)

Collected in Syria and introduced to the USDA germplasm repository in 1988.

## PORCELAIN

Porcelains are impressive, statuesque plants reaching up to 7 ft. (2.1 m) tall. The leaves are thick, broad, and spreading, and the pseudostem and scape are correspondingly thick and sturdy in support of the plant's height and vigor. The bulbs are impressive as well. They are large and typically all white, hence the name "Porcelain," although purple or copper streaking may sometimes appear depending on growing conditions and cultivar.

Porcelain bulbs generally have four to six cloves arrayed in a single layer around a sturdy scape. It is quite common for a bulb to consist of only four cloves. Since the cloves are so few and the bulbs so large, the cloves are exceptionally large as well. They are fat, but more elongated than Marbled Purple Stripe cloves. The clove skins range from yellowish tan to brown to reddish purple in both background color and streaking. The coloration can be vivid but is often muted, particularly when the plants have been grown in unstressed conditions. The skins cling tightly to the clove, and Porcelains reportedly store quite well, though my own experience has not been as positive. Because of the clove size, Porcelains are not particularly difficult to peel, and one need only peel a few cloves to have a substantial quantity of garlic.

As a group, Porcelains have among the highest yields of allicin, the sulfur compound most associated with garlic's therapeutic benefits. The trade-off is that they can taste a bit sulfurous and unsubtle. Porcelains have intensity, but most of them are less generous in flavor complexity and depth than Purple Stripes or even Marbled Purple Stripes. Nonetheless, they work well with dishes that call for a more direct aggressive garlic character. As a group, Porcelains are more appealing than Silverskins, which can be sulfurously aggressive to

A 'Romanian Red' umbel capsule.

a crude and unkind degree. In my experience, the character among the Porcelains is relatively homogeneous, though cultivars like 'Romanian Red' and 'Polish Hardneck' seem to have more complexity and nuance. The relative homogeneity of the group is also affirmed by DNA studies. Porcelains cluster well apart from other cultivars but are genetically very similar within the group.

When planted, a clove of garlic yields a garlic bulb. For Porcelains, this means that if you have bulbs with four cloves, a fourth of your harvest must be replanted to generate next year's crop. In this light, Porcelains are relatively expensive to grow. For a commercial grower this can be a concern, though the impressive bulbs and huge cloves of Porcelains have considerable market appeal,

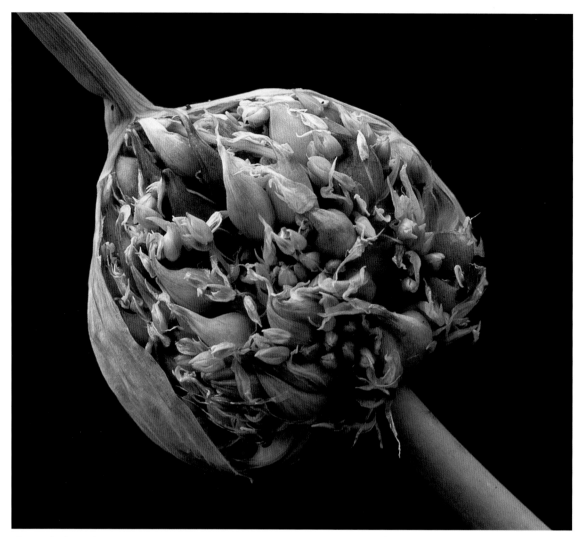

The spathe has split, revealing the 'Romanian Red' umbel's flowers and bulbils.

which may more than compensate for the added growing expense. Porcelain cultivars are very cold hardy and are a mainstay for many Canadian garlic producers. They are more adaptable than many other strongly bolting cultivars and grow reasonably well in warmer southerly climates. Spring and early-summer heat stress and drought can cause problems, however, and growers in more southerly climates must moderate these effects to the extent possible. Like most strongly bolting hardneck cultivars, Porcelains need good garden soil to produce their best. They seem more sensitive than other cultivars to spring growing conditions and to conditions just prior to harvest. One must ensure that they have ample moisture. As garlic is readied for harvest, the soil is usually allowed to dry. For Porcelains, however, it may be advisable to err on the side of more moisture.

On the left, the spathes on the 'Georgian Crystal' umbel capsules are about to split. The bumpy outlines of the swelling bulbils are readily visible. On the right, the spathe has split, revealing the small pinkish bulbils. More developing bulbils remain nestled in the umbel.

Porcelain scapes curl and coil before straightening. As with all strongly bolting hardneck cultivars, the scape usually must be cut to prevent the bulb size from suffering as the plant's energies are directed away from the bulb to produce the thick, towering scape and bulbil-filled umbel. Porcelains are affected more than most in this regard, and leaving the scapes untrimmed is an invitation to highly diminished bulbs at harvest. One can wait until the scapes begin to uncoil before trimming them, so that the sight of the twisting scapes can be enjoyed in the garden. I usually leave a few scapes untrimmed just so that I can see these largest of all garlics fully express themselves, with their tall scapes and towering umbels. As the scapes straighten, the umbel capsules have the appearance of a long-beaked bird with a long, graceful neck. This look is common to all bolting cultivars but seems most striking with Marbled Purple Stripes and Porcelains.

Porcelains are the largest garlic plants and have the largest cloves, but the bulbils are the smallest of any garlic cultivar. Porcelain umbels may be filled with hundreds of tiny to small, white to pinkish purple bulbils. The pinkish flowers are numerous as well. They usually have yellow anthers and sterile pollen, though at least two cultivars, 'Rosewood' and 'Yampolskij', are capable of producing seed under carefully controlled conditions.

## 'Armenian'

From the Armenian community of Hadrut, Nagorno-Karabakh, near Azerbaijan, 'Armenian' made its way to the commercial market via Chester Aaron and subsequently achieved broader distribution through Filaree Farm in Washington State.

## 'Blazer' (PI 250662)

An old accession to the USDA germplasm, 'Blazer' was introduced to the United States from the former Soviet Union in 1958. As is typical of Porcelain cultivars, it is hot when raw, and mild and starchy when baked.

## 'Fish Lake #3' ('F3', 'Ted Maczka's F3')

Developed in Ontario by noted garlic grower and proponent Ted Maczka, 'Fish Lake #3' is a robust cultivar. One grower reported a plant that produced a ½ lb. (0.23 kg) bulb in 2002. 'Fish Lake #3' has also adapted well to more temperate conditions in British Columbia.

## 'Floha' (ALL 264)

'Floha' comes from an area near Floha, Germany, by way of the Gatersleben germplasm.

## 'Georgian Crystal'
(ALL 791, 'Cichisdzhvari #1', K 6819)

'Georgian Crystal' was collected in 1985 at Cichisdzhvari in the intermountain region of the central Republic of Georgia. A vigorous garlic, it typically produces large white bulbs. It is less pungently biting than most Porcelain cultivars.

'Georgian Fire'.

'Leningrad'.

### 'Georgian Fire'

(ALL 794, 'Cichisdzhvari #4', K 6822)

'Georgian Fire' was collected in the same area as 'Georgian Crystal', but when eaten raw it is more pungently biting than 'Georgian Crystal'. It tends to yield slightly more cloves per bulb.

### 'German White' ('German Extra-Hardy', 'German Porcelain', 'German Stiffneck')

A popular Porcelain cultivar in America's Northeast. 'German White' and its synonyms are becoming somewhat generic descriptors and may embrace multiple similarly performing cultivars that are robust and cold hardy.

### 'Kyjev'

Made commercially available by Filaree Farm, 'Kyjev' comes from the collection of Czech garlic cultivars of New York grower Boris Andrst.

### 'Lapanantkari'

An introduction from the Republic of Georgia by John Swenson. According to some reports, 'Lapanantkari' may produce somewhat smaller bulbs than other Porcelain cultivars.

### 'Leningrad' (ALL 684)

Although this cultivar actually comes from Belarus, it carries the name 'Leningrad' in the United States, and no doubt suffers in appeal from its unearned nomenclature. In the Fort Collins study (Volk et al. 2004), 'Leningrad' clustered along the same genetic vector as the Porcelain group, but a significant distance apart. Unfortunately, a missing data element for 'Leningrad' did not permit more precise placement. In my very brief experience with it in my own garlic garden, I have not noticed any overt morphological distinctions between it and other Porcelains.

### 'Majestic'

A large, robust cultivar developed at Beaver Pond Estates in Ontario, 'Majestic' also grows very large in the more temperate, marine-influenced climates of British Columbia.

'Music'.

'Polish Hardneck'.

"Romanian Red'.

## 'Music'

'Music' was introduced to Ontario from Italy in the 1980s by Al Music. A robust and healthy grower, it performs very well in cold climates and is a mainstay of garlic producers in parts of Canada. As is typical of Porcelain cultivars, it is hot and pungent when raw, starchy when baked. Note that a less widely distributed Rocambole cultivar, 'Rocambole Music', is similarly named.

## 'Polish Hardneck'

Widely distributed by Filaree Farm and other growers, 'Polish Hardneck' comes from Ontario garlic grower John Yovanov. It has somewhat greater flavor complexity and manifests less aggressive raw heat than many other Porcelain cultivars—though this is only a matter of degree and may vary according to growing climate. 'Polish Hardneck' is widely grown in America's Northeast and Northwest.

## 'Romanian Red' ('Red Elephant Garlic')

Introduced to British Columbia from Romania, 'Romanian Red' may have been among the first Porcelain cultivars introduced to North America. It is the prototypic Porcelain, a robust grower with large bulbs, usually with only four or five cloves per bulb. Its taste is prototypic as well—pungent and hot when raw. In a study of more than 20 garlic cultivars, 'Romanian Red' yielded the greatest amount of allicin. When cooked, 'Romanian Red' has good, straightforward garlic character and perhaps a bit more complexity than the average Porcelain garlic.

In poor soils or stressed conditions 'Romanian Red' may display substantially more coloration than is typical for a Porcelain cultivar, perhaps giving rise to its anecdotal name, 'Red Elephant Garlic'—an inadvertent and unfortunate pejorative, if one's view of elephant garlic is less than positive. 'Romanian Red' is a robust, statuesque plant. Several growers have observed that it appears to be among the more disease-resistant cultivars.

### 'Rosewood' (PI 493099)

From the Moldavian Institute for Research in Irrigated Agriculture and Vegetable Growing by way of Poland, 'Rosewood' was introduced to the United States in 1984. It is capable of producing viable flowers and true seed under carefully controlled conditions. Most garlic strains capable of producing true seed have purple anthers, but 'Rosewood' anthers are yellow.

### 'Russian Giant'

In good growing conditions, 'Russian Giant' yields exceptionally large bulbs with as many as six to eight cloves per bulb. Smaller bulbs will have fewer cloves.

### 'Susan Delafield' ('Susan D')

'Susan Delafield' is grown in British Columbia and is well adapted to wet growing conditions.

### 'Vostani'

'Vostani' was obtained from a longtime resident near the border of British Columbia and Washington State. Filaree Farm brought it into commercial circulation.

### 'Wild Bluff'

'Wild Bluff' comes from the Beltsville Agricultural Research Center in Maryland and was introduced to the commercial market by Filaree Farm.

'Zaharada'.

### 'Yampolskij' (ALL 149, 'Jampolskij', K 1042, PI 540340)

'Yampolskij' comes from north Moravia, Czech Republic. Relatively few garlic strains are capable of producing true seed. Most of the known strains with seed-producing capability have inflorescences with purple anthers. 'Yampolskij' is an exception. It has yellow anthers, yet can produce seed under carefully controlled conditions.

### 'Yugoslavian Porcelain'

'Yugoslavian Porcelain' is an heirloom from the Kootenay and Okanagan regions of western Canada.

### 'Zaharada'

From the Czech collection of New York grower Boris Andrst, 'Zaharada' was introduced commercially by Filaree Farm.

## 'Zemo' (ALL 784, K 6307)

'Zemo' was collected in 1984, at an elevation of 1560 ft. (475 m), at Zemo Surebi in the western Republic of Georgia, about 35 miles (56 km) from the Black Sea. 'Zemo' gained heightened attention when *Cook's Illustrated* magazine's America's Test Kitchen evaluated eight garlic cultivars and picked 'Zemo' and the Rocambole cultivar 'Carpathian' as the panel's favorites. Like most Porcelain cultivars, 'Zemo' performs very well in climates with cold winters and large seasonal temperature variations but does less well in warmer southern climates.

## PURPLE STRIPE

Genetically closest to the origins of the species, Purple Stripes are the ancestors and antecedents of all other garlic cultivars, and as the Fort Collins study (Volk et al. 2004) showed, they are the basal group for all garlic. Purple Stripes are strongly bolting, hardneck cultivars. Some Purple Stripes, with assistance, remain capable of sexual reproduction and the production of seed. Not surprisingly, they also exhibit the greatest genetic diversity.

Purple Stripes would be inherently special even if their primal origins were their only notable feature, but they are also splendid culinary garlics. In general, the taste of Purple Stripes is strong, complex, and richly garlicky, without being overly sulfurous. They do not have the sweetness of Rocamboles, but some of the best may be even more characterful. Many regard Purple Stripes as the tastiest and best garlics for roasting.

Purple Stripes are named for the vivid purple coloration and striping on the bulb wrappers and clove skins. The cloves are generally arrayed in a single layer around the scape, though very large bulbs may have inner cloves. For a similarly sized bulb, the cloves are more numerous and thus

A 'Shvelisi' scape and umbel capsule.

somewhat smaller than Rocambole cloves and are considerably smaller than Marbled Purple Stripe cloves. Purple Stripe cloves are tall and crescent-shaped with somewhat angular edges and an elongated tip. They are not particularly difficult to peel, but their clove skins tend to be thinner and more tightly attached, making them more resistant to peeling than Rocamboles and somewhat more resistant to peeling than Marbled Purple Stripes or Glazed Purple Stripes. Because the clove skins are more tightly attached, Purple Stripes last longer in storage than Rocamboles, becoming easier to peel as time passes. After the harvest, for dishes that have garlic in the forefront, I usually focus first on Rocamboles, and then as they fade from time in storage, I shift my emphasis to Purple Stripes. Conveniently, the Purple Stripes are then in their

A 'Samarkand' umbel. The spathe has been shed but remains clinging to the base of the umbel.

prime for taste. For medium-term storage and taste quality, the Purple Stripes are easily among the best.

Purple Stripe leaves are medium in width. The lower leaf blades are typically closer to the soil surface and flop out more horizontally than those of other horticultural groups. The plants are somewhat delicate in appearance compared to Marbled Purple Stripes or Porcelains. Purple Stripe scapes coil vigorously before uncurling and becoming erect. The umbel capsule contains numerous small to medium-sized purplish bulbils and numerous pink to purple flowers. The flower anthers are usually purple—a color associated with fertile pollen in garlic, though by no means are all cultivars with purple anthers capable of producing seed. Sprouting time and maturation vary considerably among Purple Stripe cultivars. Befitting the group's ancestral origins in the harsh environment of Central Asia, Purple Stripes need exposure to cold to grow well and develop large bulbs, though they can still produce reasonably well in some southern regions. They are hardy survivors in poor soils and harsh conditions but respond to rich garden soil with more vigorous growth and larger bulbs.

Allium explorers have collected many Purple Stripes from the wild, and some of these garlics have made their way from germplasms to the commercial market. Because Purple Stripes are genetically close to garlic's primal wild origins, they behave as one might expect of plants that have not been extensively pampered in cultivation. As survivors in a harsh environment, they are quick to react to adverse conditions to ensure their survival. When they bolt, Purple Stripes rapidly divert their energies to the reproductive structures and away from the bulb. Bulb size suffers if the scape is left uncut. If the scape is allowed to fully develop, the result will be a fine umbel filled with flowers and bulbils, but a very small bulb. I usually allow the scapes to remain on a few plants so that I can see these primal garlics fully express themselves, knowing that I am sacrificing the bulb in the ground. If you are in a climate where you can grow Purple Stripes, do—no garlic garden should be without at least one Purple Stripe cultivar.

### 'Belarus' (PI 540355)

Collected in Belarus during the Soviet Union era, this cultivar is among Richard Hannan's favorites. It emerges early in spring, forming large, hearty bulbs. It does not store quite as well as some Purple Stripes but can be harvested and enjoyed earlier. It is an excellent cultivar in both taste and appearance.

### 'Ferganskij' ('Ferganski', W6 1862)

'Ferganskij' was collected in 1989 by John Swenson at a village market in Samarkand, Uzbekistan.

### 'Red Grain'
(ALL 792, 'Cichisdzhvari #2', K 6820)

'Red Grain' was collected in 1985, at an elevation of 5350 ft. (1631 m), in the intermountain region of the central Republic of Georgia. The popularity of this productive and well-established cultivar may be diminished by its somewhat odd name.

### 'Samarkand' ('Duganskij', 'Persian Star')

Acquired in 1989 at a bazaar in Samarkand, Uzbekistan, by John Swenson. It has fine garlic character similar to 'Shvelisi' and 'Shatili'. Some reports indicate a relatively short storage life, but that has not been my experience. The local name for the garlic is 'Duganskij', though it appears that several other cultivars may also carry that name. It is commonly marketed under the name 'Persian Star'.

'Belarus'.

'Red Grain'.

'Samarkand'.

A 'Shatili' umbel.

'Shatili'.

'Shvelisi'. The huge bulb on the right has developed an inner clove layer.

### 'Shatili' (ALL 841, K 7108)

'Shatili' was collected in 1986, at an elevation of 4750 ft. (1448 m), at Shatili in the Republic of Georgia. It is a fine, rich-tasting garlic similar in taste to 'Samarkand' and 'Shvelisi'. It stores longer than the Rocambole cultivars and makes a good transition as the Rocamboles begin to wane. Under controlled conditions it has produced true seed.

### 'Shvelisi' (ALL 790, 'Chesnok Red', K 6811, 'Schvelisi')

'Shvelisi' was collected in 1985 in the village of Shvelisi in the southern Republic of Georgia. A deservedly popular cultivar, it is commonly marketed under the name 'Chesnok Red'. It is highly productive and capable of producing exceptionally large bulbs if growing conditions are favorable. It has also produced true seed in formal trials.

'Shvelisi' is excellent for baking, though the flavors and depth of character really shine when it is chopped and sautéed to a straw color or light tan. Starting in January, after my short-storing Rocamboles are consumed, this becomes one of my favorite garlic cultivars. By then the skins have become easier to peel, and it has some of the rich sweetness that had made the Rocamboles so appealing. 'Shvelisi' is also excellent raw in an oil and vinegar salad dressing.

### 'Skuri #2' (ALL 780, K 6038)

'Skuri #2' was collected in 1983, at an elevation of 1080 ft. (329 m), at the village of Skuria, Republic of Georgia, between the Black Sea and Caucasus Mountains. Northern cold-climate growers report that when 'Skuri #2' is eaten raw it has a mild, earthy taste. Southern hot-climate growers report that it is extremely strong and hot.

A small spider makes its way through a thicket of bulbil sheaths and sprouts in this 'Tien Shan' umbel.

A 'Tien Shan' bulb kept in storage has begun to sprout.

### 'Tien Shan' (PI 615416, W6 1890)

'Tien Shan' was collected in the wild, at an elevation of 4300 ft. (1311 m), in the eastern Tien Shan, Chatkal, Uzbekistan, and donated to the USDA germplasm in 1989. Under carefully controlled conditions it is capable of producing true seed. Its umbel capsule is distinctive. The bulbils develop exceptionally elongated sheaths and sometimes shoots, which fill and expand the upper portion of the umbel capsule, elongating it and sometimes producing a secondary bulge.

A 'Tien Shan' umbel capsule. The elongated bulbil sheaths have created a secondary bulge.

'Verchnjaja Mcara'.

## 'Verchnjaja Mcara' (ALL 766, K 6017, PI 540356, 'Red Czar', 'Verchnyava Mcara')

'Verchnjaja Mcara' was collected in 1983, at an elevation of 1020 ft. (311 m), in Verchnjaja Mcara, northwestern Republic of Georgia, between the Black Sea and the Caucasus Mountains. Under controlled conditions it is capable of producing true seed.

## ROCAMBOLE

For many people, the name "Rocambole" is synonymous with hardneck garlic and culinary supremacy. Rocamboles are among the most widely known and grown hardneck garlic cultivars. Back in the dark ages when I thought garlic was just garlic, without distinction, I purchased a few heads of garlic at a farmers' market. It was the Rocambole cultivar 'Spanish Roja'. I tried it and knew then that all garlic was not the same. A new world opened, and I have not looked back. Although I have come to appreciate many different garlic cultivars, the Rocamboles remain a special favorite.

In the views of many, Rocamboles are the finest-tasting garlic of all. The best cultivars have a rich, deep, complex flavor palate. As soon as one whacks a clove with the edge of a knife to break the skin, the rich aroma infuses the air. Rocamboles are sweet as opposed to aggressively sulfurous, and they are devoid of vegetative overtones. While they certainly have garlic's heat when eaten raw, they are relatively moderate in that regard, and the heat is balanced by a fine depth of character. Rocamboles are my favorite cultivars when raw garlic is called for, such as for crushing and mixing with vinegar or lemon and olive oil for salad or vegetable dressing. These garlics are at their juiciest just about the time that fresh corn becomes available. Crush a few Rocambole cloves through a garlic press, add salt and briefly mash with a spoon to a slurry, add olive oil, stir, and drizzle or paint over each ear of cooked fresh corn. The taste is ambrosial.

Rocamboles are also among the top choices when the character of the garlic will be a prominent feature in the cuisine. This is not to say that all Rocambole cultivars are equally excellent tasting. For a time I grew a cultivar called 'Korean' that I purchased at a farmers' market, but the flavor was consistently disappointing, at least relative to what I had come to expect from the best Rocambole cultivars. Most Rocamboles, however, are excellent, and many are truly sublime. For some dishes, one might want a garlic that is more assertive than a Rocambole, or one might find a Purple Stripe better suited for baking, but for many culinary purposes, Rocamboles are always among the top choices.

Unfortunately, Rocamboles have a few practical downsides. They store poorly and are more demanding of growing conditions. They require a period of winter cold to grow well, and they may not grow at all in southern climates with warm winters and springs. After I harvest my Rocamboles, I struggle to restrain myself as I impatiently wait for them to cure and mature, and then I eat them greedily before they pass their prime.

Rocambole cloves peel exceptionally easily, which is part of the reason for their short storage

A coiled 'Montana Giant' scape.

life. Ease of peeling is a boon in the kitchen, however, and one can quickly peel a good number of cloves with little effort. The cloves are arrayed in a single layer around the scape. They are plump, but more numerous than Marbled Purple Stripe for an equivalent bulb size. Relative to Purple Stripes, the cloves have less angular edges and are more blunted and rounded at the tip. Double cloves are common for some cultivars (see "Selecting Planting Stock" in chapter 6 for more details). The cloves are tan to brown with some purple and red tones and occasionally more pronounced purple coloration. The color and finish of the clove skins are typically a bit dull looking. The bulb wrappers are not very colorful, either—off-white with varying degrees of purple blushing or striping, but seldom very distinctive.

The bulb may not be particularly distinctive in appearance, but the scape certainly is. It curls more tightly than the scapes of any other garlic horticultural group, sometimes completing as many as three complete curls before straightening and becoming erect. As with most strongly bolting cultivars, the scape should be removed or bulb size will likely suffer. However, one can wait until the scapes begin to uncoil before removing them, so it is still possible to have these coiling, serpentine scapes grace one's garden.

Although not much of a concern, at least in North America, the name "Rocambole" and the more colloquial "serpent garlic" have historically had ambiguous meanings. The names have erroneously been applied to the nongarlic *Allium scorodoprasum*, a plant that also has coiling scapes. "Rocambole"

(above) A 'Russian Red' umbel.

(below) The spathe peels away from a 'Brown Saxon' umbel.

(left) As maturity approaches, the 'Carpathian' umbel capsule changes from yellowish to white, a characteristic of Rocamboles.

On the left, 'Russian Red' bulbils. On the right, 'Spanish Roja' bulbils.

has also erroneously been applied to other garlic horticultural groups with coiling scapes. These are largely historical ambiguities, however, and the name has long been accepted as referring to the horticultural group we are discussing here.

The Rocambole spathe is distinctive, turning from yellowish to whitish at maturity, in contrast with the spathes of other horticultural groups, which remain yellowish. The umbel capsule's beak is relatively short. The plant's leaves are broad and closely spaced. Some cultivars have erect leaf tips; others are drooping. The plants are not particularly tall, but the wide, closely spaced, blue-green leaves give a substantial look, topped by the drama of the tightly curling scape. The bulbils range in size from medium to large. Their coloration varies from yellowish brown to brownish to purple. The flowers range from very few to moderately numerous and from whitish to pinkish purple. As a general rule, a cultivar with smaller and more numerous bulbils will have more numerous flowers.

The variations in the reproductive and vegetative parts reflect the genetic diversity within the Rocambole group. The Fort Collins study (Volk et al. 2004) showed that Rocamboles are well separated from other horticultural groups but demonstrate notable variation within their own cluster.

'Carpathian', for example, is a widely available commercial cultivar that stands apart in DNA studies. An excellent-tasting garlic, it matures slightly later than some other Rocambole cultivars, has more erect leaf tips, and has less of a propensity to produce double cloves. These are notable though relatively subtle differences, and 'Carpathian' is otherwise very much in the Rocambole mainstream.

Many of the Rocambole variations in the DNA studies are germplasm accessions that may or may not be in commercial circulation under different names. The special nature of the Rocambole group makes one eager to know more about the variations, including the prospect that certain clusters within the group might be associated with richer and sweeter flavor, longer storage, or other attributes. Regardless of the more subtle variations, Rocamboles remain gourmet garlic's hallmark.

### 'Baba Franchuk's'

'Baba Franchuk's' migrated from Winnipeg to British Columbia, where it is increasing in circulation. Growers report that it is similar to 'German Red', tending toward the stronger, less sweet end of the Rocambole spectrum.

### 'Belgian Red'

'Belgian Red' comes from Belgium by way of a western Washington herb farm.

### 'Brown Saxon' (ALL 847, K 7116)

'Brown Saxon' was collected in 1986, at an elevation of 5580 ft. (1700 m), at Gudani, a village in the Caucasus Mountains north of Tbilisi, Republic of Georgia. It is among the more late-harvesting and long-storing Rocamboles. The typically brownish cloves are plumper, larger, and fewer in number than most Rocambole cultivars. Double cloves are rare. 'Brown Saxon' has a strong, rich garlic flavor that is perhaps a bit less sweet than some other Rocamboles.

## 'Carpathian'

'Carpathian' is an interesting cultivar that represents some of the variation within the Rocambole group. Relative to some of the other Rocamboles, its leaves tend to be more upright and fan-shaped without curling downward at their tips. Double cloves are uncommon. The bulb wrappers sometimes show thin copper-colored striping along with purple blotching.

'Carpathian' is an excellent-tasting garlic, its flavors rich, strong, and sweet. It comes from the Carpathian Mountains in southwest Poland. It gained heightened attention when *Cook's Illustrated* magazine's America's Test Kitchen evaluated eight garlic cultivars and picked this one among its favorites.

## 'German Brown'

This cultivar came to Filaree Farm, where it was originally offered, mixed with 'German Red'. As suggested by the name 'German Brown', the cloves are more distinctively brown. Taste characteristics are generally similar to 'German Red'. Growers report that 'German Brown' reliably produces large bulbs.

## 'German Red'

Different sources cite different origins for 'German Red', and it is possible that different cultivars carry the same name. In my garden it readily produces large, reddish bulbs. The cloves are light brown but may have a faint tinge of purple at their base. When raw, this is among the more hot-tasting Rocamboles. When cooked it has strong garlic flavor,

'Brown Saxon'.

'Carpathian'.

but the sweet richness associated with the classic Rocambole cultivars is not as evident. Nonetheless, it is a good garlic on its own terms. Double cloves are common.

A 'Killarney Red' scape completing its uncoiling.

'Killarney Red'.

### 'Killarney Red' ('Killarney Roja')

A very productive cultivar with the classic rich, sweet Rocambole taste. Its origins are unclear. Some reports suggest that it may be a selection of 'German Red'. Others indicate that it is a selection of 'Spanish Roja' from Killarney Farm in Idaho. 'Killarney Red' has outstanding flavor and in my experience is much more similar to 'Spanish Roja' than 'German Red'. It consistently produces larger bulbs for me than 'Spanish Roja' in my marine-influenced climate, and is also very productive in dry climates.

A 'Killarney Red' umbel bursting through the spathe. A few flowers are nestled among the large bulbils.

'Maxatawny'.

'Montana Giant'.

### 'Maxatawny'

Although cultivated garlic has a long history, the history of most named garlic cultivars is relatively short. In this regard 'Maxatawny' is exceptional. It was introduced to Pennsylvania in the 1740s from a part of Silesia that is now western Poland. Food researcher and author William Woys Weaver discovered the cultivar among the Mennonites in Pennsylvania, where it is used locally in making pickles.

'Maxatawny' is a characterful garlic—relatively aggressive for a Rocambole, with less of the rich sweetness that is the hallmark of some cultivars from this group. Its flavor profile perhaps tends somewhat toward the Purple Stripe spectrum, which in itself is hardly a bad thing.

### 'Montana Giant'

A selection of 'Montana Roja' that consistently produces bulbs exceeding 2 in. (5 cm) in diameter for some growers. It may be that this cultivar requires hotter summers or cooler winters, as my bulbs initially tended to range more toward "Montana Average" in size. However, they have adapted and are now among the larger of the Rocamboles that I grow. Regardless of bulb size, 'Montana Giant' is a good and characterful Rocambole.

### 'Montana Roja' (W6 12912)

'Montana Roja' was developed over the course of a decade by Richard Wrench, near Kalispell, Montana, and donated to the USDA germplasm system in 1993. The USDA donor notes indicate that the cultivar was planted in March or April for an early September harvest, yielding bulbs that weighed an average of ¼ lb. (0.11 kg) when cured.

### 'Ontario Giant' ('Puslinch')

A cultivar from Puslinch, Ontario, in Canada's Great Lakes region, 'Ontario Giant' is hardy and robust. In Canada it is in circulation as 'Puslinch', a name that may be dear to local residents but is perhaps not a marketer's dream.

### 'Pitarelli'

Introduced to America from Czechoslovakia in the 1920s, 'Pitarelli' matures later and stores longer than many Rocamboles. To my taste, although it is a good garlic, it does not have the sweet, rich character associated with the prototypic Rocamboles.

### 'Rocambole Music' ('Music', PI 515972)

Most garlic growers know 'Music' as the Porcelain cultivar from Canada. Although not as widely known or distributed, a Rocambole cultivar also named 'Music' is included in the USDA germplasm collection (PI 515972). This cultivar is an heirloom obtained from Steve Music, located near Pullman, Washington (Richard Hannan, personal communication). Locally known as 'Music' and cultivated for more than 70 years, it was placed into the USDA germplasm collection in 1988. I have taken the liberty to term this cultivar 'Rocambole Music' to mitigate confusion with the more widely known Porcelain cultivar.

Since 'Rocambole Music' has had minimal distribution, listing it might hardly seem worth the effort, but it is notable in several respects. The Fort Collins study (Volk et al. 2004) shows that this cultivar clusters with the Rocambole group but is genetically distinctive. 'Rocambole Music' has also produced true seed under controlled conditions—highly unusual for a Rocambole garlic.

'Ontario Giant'.

This large 'Ontario Giant' clove shows divisions within the clove skin. If planted it would likely produce a double or triple bulb—separate bulbs growing tightly adjacent to each other and flattened where they face.

'Russian Red'. The base of the clove shows the development of two basil plates, indicating a double clove.

A 'Spanish Roja' umbel. The flowers have withered among the bulbils, and the extended bulbil sheaths have created a tangle.

## 'Russian Red'

'Russian Red' is among my favorite garlic cultivars. To my palate, it is the equal of 'Spanish Roja', 'Killarney Red', and 'Carpathian', with its deep character and sweet, full taste. It reliably produces good-sized bulbs. Double cloves are common. Cloves are typically all brown but sometimes exhibit a pronounced reddish purple coloration.

The Doukhobors, a communal pacifistic religious sect of Russian origin, introduced this garlic cultivar to Canada in the late 1800s or early 1900s while fleeing Russia to escape persecution. The earliest evidence of 'Russian Red' in North America is associated with British Columbia, but it is likely that it came to Saskatchewan first.

## 'Spanish Roja' ('Greek', 'Greek Blue')

Introduced to the Portland, Oregon, area prior to 1900, 'Spanish Roja' is the prototypic Rocambole, with its rich, sweet, complex, full-bodied character devoid of vegetative overtones. It is a well-known heirloom, and for many people its name is synonymous with "Rocambole." In some 50 tastings that Chester Aaron (2002) conducted around the United States, 'Spanish Roja' generally ranked among the top two or three.

This cultivar may be a bit more finicky about growing conditions than some other Rocamboles, and it performs less well in mild winters. In my marine-influenced Pacific Northwest climate, other

'Spanish Roja'.

'Wisconsin German Red'.

Rocamboles typically grow larger, though 'Spanish Roja' has adapted over the years and now grows larger. Arguably, Rocamboles such as 'Killarney Red', 'Russian Red', and 'Carpathian' may equal its flavor, but none surpass it.

### 'Vietnamese' (PI 615432, W6 16275)

Collected in Vietnam, this cultivar has a spathe shape and coloration characteristic of Rocambole cultivars. Other characteristics are also consistent with the Rocambole group. As with most Rocamboles, the flavor is warm, rich, and very good, although in my experience it is not quite in the same league as the best-tasting cultivars of the group.

### 'Wisconsin German Red'

A number of different cultivars may carry variations of this name, so confusion is likely to abound. The particular cultivar cited here is a Rocambole that has been cultivated in Wisconsin for some 150 years, originating near Kewaskum. It readily generates double cloves. 'Wisconsin German Red' may not have quite the sweet richness of the very best Rocambole cultivars, but it is a reliable producer and exhibits fine Rocambole character.

### 'Youghiogheny Purple'

'Youghiogheny Purple' has been grown in the Youghiogheny River valley in Pennsylvania since about 1920. It is among the more large-bulbed Rocamboles.

### 'Yugoslavian'

'Yugoslavian' was introduced into the American market by way of the Dacha Barinka seed company in Chilliwack, British Columbia. The cloves are dark brown, and double cloves are common.

## SILVERSKIN

Silverskins are among the most long-storing garlic cultivars. In various regions of the United States they are called Italian garlic and Egyptian garlic. If storage conditions are favorable, well-grown bulbs can be stored for up to a year or more. On the negative side, the taste of these cultivars can be hot, sulfurously aggressive, acrid, and lacking in nuanced complexity. Longer storage may exaggerate the more aggressive characteristics. Having said that, cooking methods can make a significant difference in appeal. I once briefly sautéed some minced Silverskin garlic, then added moist, cooked greens. The garlic steamed a bit under the blanket of greens, and the resulting dish had a sulfurous character that was not particularly appealing. This method is normally an excellent way to prepare garlic and greens, though it is by far the best when the garlic is cooked to a straw or tan color before adding the wet greens. When I have undercooked other garlic before adding greens, the flavor has not been optimal, but the dish has not suffered from unpleasant sulfurous overtones. On the other hand, I later minced and cooked the very same Silverskin garlic until it reached the straw to tan color, and the flavor was quite fine—a bit aggressive to be sure, but this cooking method brought out tasty, caramelized, nutty overtones.

In matters of taste, opinions vary widely, and undoubtedly there are garlic enthusiasts that regard Silverskins as their favorite. I am certainly not in that category, but I always have some Silverskin bulbs in my garlic garden repertoire. For long storage, however, I primarily focus on the Creole cultivars, many of which store nearly as well as Silverskins and have a more appealing taste. Interestingly, Silverskin and Creole cultivars are genetically very closely related, and the demarcation of the two horticultural groups is not fully defined.

A 'Locati' scape straightens. The umbel capsule is only partially swollen.

Silverskins are generally quite productive and tolerant of a wide range of growing conditions, though they grow best where the growing season is long and winters are mild. Like Artichoke cultivars, Silverskins are generally nonbolting and softneck, at least when grown in more southerly climates. Some cultivars routinely bolt in more northerly regions. If Silverskins are grown in warm southern climates and then planted in northern temperate climates, most of the crop will bolt. Artichoke cultivars tend to mature early in the season, while Silverskins are among the most late-maturing of all garlic cultivars. Silverskins are more likely than many other cultivars to produce bulbs of an acceptable size when planted in spring. This is likely attributable to later maturation and a lesser need for vernalization.

The 'Locati' umbel capsule continues to swell, and the outlines of the lumpy bulbils are now clearly visible.

While Artichoke cultivars tend to be larger with a flattened bulb shape, Silverskins are generally smaller and tend to have a teardrop shape. Comparing similarly sized bulbs, Silverskins have more cloves than any other horticultural group. The cloves are arrayed in multiple layers. Many of the inner cloves are often tall, slender, and small. The outer cloves are relatively large, flattened on the interior side, and tallish, with rounded corners and a graceful curvature that helps form the teardrop shape of the bulb. The outer cloves may be quite thin and wide in some cultivars. Conversely, Artichokes tend to have fat, blocky outer cloves with more squared sides and angular edges.

The bulb wrappers are white but may have yellow or tan veining. Clove skins range from white to tan, prominently pink-blushed, or even reddish or purplish. The bulb and clove skins adhere very tightly, contributing to exceptional storage longevity.

Silverskin leaves are narrow and blue-green. They are more vertically angled than Artichoke cultivars and have a pronounced bilateral symmetry. The thin, sturdy leaves remain pliable after drying. The leaf characteristics of Silverskins, combined with their compact, teardrop-shaped bulbs and long storage ability, make these cultivars the chosen garlic for braiding.

A 'Locati' umbel.

'Locati'.

### 'Idaho Silver'

Relative to other Silverskin cultivars, 'Idaho Silver' is well adapted to colder winter climates. Depending on growing conditions, the cloves can show pronounced reddish pink overtones.

### 'Locati'

This cultivar from Milan has fewer small inner cloves than most Silverskins. Like others in its group, clove coloration can be rather striking, in this case a vivid pinkish red. Although 'Locati' is visually attractive, its taste can be a bit acrid and not entirely pleasant in some culinary preparations. Particularly after long storage (which is raison d'être for Silverskins), it is at its best when chopped and sautéed to a straw to light brown color. This preparation tames the aggressive sulfurous characteristics and emphasizes nutty, caramelized flavors.

### 'Mexican Red Silver' ('Mexican Red')

Originally from Mexico, this cultivar made its way into commercial circulation in the United States by way of G & G Spanish American Grocery in Highwood, Illinois, and John Swenson. Multiple cultivars carry the name 'Mexican Red', including cultivars outside the Silverskin group.

### 'Mild French'

This cultivar comes from Porter and Sons in Texas and is well adapted to hot southern climates. Contrary to the name, the taste can be hot and aggressive, particularly when grown in more northerly climates. 'Mild French' grows taller and matures earlier than most Silverskins.

### 'Nootka Rose'

'Nootka Rose' comes from Steve Bensel of Nootka Rose Farm on Waldron Island in Washington State. The cloves are brown with red streaking and have red tips. The highly distinctive coloration is more pronounced in poorer soils. A large bulb may have five clove layers and numerous smaller inner cloves. The taste is strong and aggressive. Given the general similarity in climate between this cultivar's origins and my own garlic garden, 'Nootka Rose' should grow well for me, but it has proven to be a bit finicky.

### 'Prim' (PI 493115)

'Prim' came from the Institute of Experimental Botany in Olomouc, North Moravia, Czech Republic, by way of Poland, in 1984.

'Nootka Rose'.

'Prim'.

'Rose du Var'.

### 'Rose du Var'

'Rose du Var' was imported from France for commercial testing in California. It is an attractive Silverskin with rose to red cloves, depending on

'Silver White'.

growing conditions. The inner cloves are relatively large. Even in warmer growing climates, the taste is strong and hot.

### 'S & H Silver'

The cloves of this cultivar from S & H Organic Acres in California are brownish at the bottom, changing to tan or beige with a pinkish tip.

### 'Sicilian Silver'

Growers report that 'Sicilian Silver', from Sicily, is very hot tasting even for a Silverskin, but that it retains more flavor interest than most garlic cultivars when baked.

A 'Wedam' umbel.

### 'Silver White'

A productive cultivar that is adapted to a wide range of climates, 'Silver White' is a good producer in warmer southern climates, northerly climates with cold winters and hot summers, and temperate maritime climates. From Harmony Farm Supply in California, it is now widely distributed. As is typical of Silverskins, 'Silver White' stores well but has many small inner cloves.

### 'St. Helens'

'St. Helens' is an heirloom garlic from the marine-influenced climate of western Washington State.

### 'Wedam'

'Wedam' made its way into commercial production by way of Filaree Farm in Washington State and its namesake, Nora Wedam, in Montana. In my experience with it in a more temperate climate, 'Wedam' has proven to be among the more productive Silverskins.

'Wedam'.

# TURBAN

This group is named for the flattened turban shape of the umbel capsule. Turban cultivars are among the first ready for harvest; have the shortest dormancy, and thus the shortest storage ability; and are the first to sprout after planting. Everything about them is quick and early. The bulbs are quite attractive and can be sold at farmers' markets before other cultivars appear on the scene.

Turbans have been called the garlic world's summer apple. Their taste is typically simple and direct. They can be very hot when raw, but mild and not particularly distinctive after cooking. Nonetheless, I like them and continue to grow them. Not only are they the first ready to harvest, but I also do not feel bad about eating them a bit early, before they have fully cured, because I know that I am not sacrificing a great deal. (Conversely, if I greedily eat Rocambole cultivars before they have fully cured, I feel I am committing a sacrilege for which I will somehow be punished.) After many weeks of gleaning the last of last season's harvest in search of garlic that is not too dried up or sprouted, the juicy fresh cloves from the newly harvested Turbans are quite welcome. A favorite Thai restaurant that I once frequented used large quantities of barely chopped garlic in some of their dishes, so that garlic was not only a flavoring but also a vegetable. I often use Turbans in this way in spicy cuisines.

Turban plants do not look very robust. They are not very tall, and their medium-sized leaves are spaced relatively far apart. As harvest approaches, the pseudostems often weaken and the plant may bend at ground level and fall over. In spite of these weak-kneed histrionics, most cultivars readily produce large bulbs. The bulb wrappers are typically heavily blotched or striped with purple. The cloves are usually arrayed in a single layer around the

A 'Luster' umbel capsule. Here, the prototypic turban shape is upside down.

scape. Because they are fairly numerous on large bulbs, the cloves are more slender than squat and fat. They are also more rounded and less angular than the cloves of other cultivar groups. The clove skins are typically tan to satiny pink, but they may have purple, red, or brown tones in some instances. Turbans are weakly bolting and sometimes refuse to bolt. The scapes droop but do not curl. The turban-shaped umbel capsule has a relatively short beak and contains numerous small to medium-sized bulbils. Unlike most horticultural groups, Turban bulb size is not greatly affected if the scapes are left on the plant.

Turbans should be harvested when the first one or two leaves brown, otherwise the short period of dormancy and storage period will be

The swollen umbel of this plant of 'Uzbek Turban' has split the spathe.

further shortened. Bulb wrappers also deteriorate in the ground if left too long. These admonitions are most important in hot climates where maturity comes quickly. In more moderate climates the harvest timing is not as critical.

Ron Engeland (1995) suggested that the Turban group may include more than one type. Turban cultivars have been underrepresented in genetic studies, and the genetic and phenotypic boundaries of the group are not entirely clear. The Turban group is in need of further genetic study and phenotypic observation.

### 'Blossom'

'Blossom' was introduced to the United States by Greg Czarnecki, who purchased the cultivar in a market at the Temple of Heaven in Beijing.

### 'Chengdu'

Different collection scenarios have been reported for 'Chengdu' garlic. It is not entirely clear whether all garlic bearing the name 'Chengdu' is the same cultivar. All of the scenarios, nonetheless, indicate that the cultivar was obtained from markets in Chengdu, China.

### 'China Stripe'

Purchased at a market in Beijing by Greg Czarnecki.

### 'Chinese Pink'

Exceptionally early maturing and productive, 'Chinese Pink' brings an early, pleasant-tasting bounty to the table and market while one waits for more characterful cultivars to mature.

### 'Chinese Purple'

'Chinese Purple' grows very well in warm southern climates. It ripens very early. When tasted raw it has immediate heat. Turban cultivars generally store poorly, but growers report that 'Chinese Purple' is among the more long-storing cultivars of the group.

### 'Dushanbe' (ALL 691, K 6299)

'Dushanbe' was collected in 1984 in Dushanbe, Tajikistan's capital city. The name is rather more appealing than the city's previous Stalin-era name of Stalinabad.

### 'Lotus'

'Lotus' was purchased at a market in Kowloon, Hong Kong, by Greg Czarnecki.

### 'Luster'

'Luster' is among the more flavorful and long-storing Turban cultivars. It was obtained by Greg Czarnecki at the Hongqiao Market in Beijing.

### 'Maiskij'

This cultivar was purchased in 1989 by John Swenson at a bazaar in Ashkhabad, Turkmenistan. The name means "May." 'Maiskij' has sometimes been associated with the USDA accession W6 1883, 'Maiski', but accession notes indicate that accession was collected at a Tashkent market in Uzbekistan.

'Luster'.

'Red Janice'.

### 'Red Janice' (ALL 776, K 6030)

'Red Janice' was collected in 1983, at an elevation of 460 ft. (140 m), at Narazeni, a village about 20 miles (32 km) from the Black Sea, in the Republic of Georgia.

A ladybug makes its way down a 'Red Janice' scape.

### 'Shandong'

Originally from Shandong Province but purchased in Beijing by Greg Czarnecki. Like many Turban cultivars, 'Shandong' has a good but rather simple garlic character. Its clove wrappers are pinkish purple to dark tan.

### 'Sonoran'

From Sonora, Mexico, 'Sonoran' is adapted to warmer climates, though it grows well in cooler northerly climates as well.

### 'Thai Fire'

'Thai Fire' comes from a Bangkok market by way of Salt Spring Seeds in British Columbia. As is typical of Turbans, it sprouts early, whether in storage or in the ground.

### 'Uzbek Turban'

From the former Soviet Union, 'Uzbek Turban' was introduced to America by Richard Hannan.

'Shandong'.

'Thai Fire'.

'Uzbek Turban'.

The base of a 'Xian' umbel as it sheds its spathe.

'Xian'.

## 'Xian' ('Xi'an')

This storied cultivar is among Chester Aaron's favorites, although its sources and nature are rather muddy. In *Garlic Kisses* (2001) Aaron relates how he obtained 'Xian' in San Francisco's Chinatown for $30 per bulb from an unknown woman who allegedly smuggled the garlic into the United States from Xi'an, China. 'Xian' is described as having a brief period of searingly intense heat when tasted raw, followed by a rich, earthy, mushroomy finish. Other references describe garlic from the same source as not too hot but very rich. Filaree Farm is sometimes cited as a source, but according to the farm's records 'Xian' was obtained in 1992 from Greg Czarnecki. In the 1999 *Seed Savers Yearbook* Czarnecki indicates that 'Xian' was purchased at the Northwestern Polytechnical University in Xi'an.

Xi'an is an ancient city built upon layers of predecessor cities and settlements, including a village from the late Neolithic period. It was a source of silk for trading along the Great Silk Road, likely a trade route for garlic as well. It appears that multiple cultivars may be carrying the 'Xian' name. The 'Xian' in my garden is perhaps slightly less hot and a bit more complex than most Turbans, though not remarkably so. As is typical of Turbans, it has a short period of dormancy before it begins to sprout.

## UNCLASSIFIED

Garlic horticultural groups are far from resolved. Some of the preceding groups will likely be changed and reordered as molecular tools and our understanding of their use become more refined. In some instances I have continued to include cultivars in familiar groups even when their membership has become somewhat suspect. In other instances DNA evidence or morphological observation are sufficiently compelling to exclude a cultivar from existing groups. Further study may show that the cultivar belongs in an existing group after all—or may show that the cultivar is a representative of a new horticultural group. In the meantime we can enjoy these "other" cultivars as further confirmation of garlic's wonderful diversity.

### 'Ajo Rojo'

'Ajo Rojo' has long been among my favorite Creole cultivars. It has a fine flavor, stores exceptionally well, and grows more productively in my northern climate than most other Creoles. Ironically, however, it may not actually belong to the Creole group.

The Fort Collins study (Volk et al. 2004) shows 'Ajo Rojo' clustering some distance from other Creole and Silverskin cultivars. The boundaries of the Silverskin/Creole complex are unclear, and the entire aggregate is likely in need of reordering. Until more is known of the group, I had been tempted to leave 'Ajo Rojo' with the Creoles, where it is generally found in commercial listings. However, 'Ajo Rojo' is different enough that temporarily labeling it as unclassified better reflects its status. The multilayered bulb, the clove shape, and the clove coloration more closely resemble prototypic Silverskins than Creoles, but the fla-

On the left, narrow-leaved plants of 'Ajo Rojo'. On the right, broad-leaved plants of the Creole cultivar 'Morado de Pedronera'.

vor is sweet and nonsulfurous, more akin to the sweeter Creoles than the typical aggressive bite of the Silverskins.

Whatever its horticultural group, 'Ajo Rojo' is an excellent cultivar. It was brought into the United States from Spain in the early 1990s via Nevada and a virus-free program. Broadly adapted, it produces very well in warmer southern growing regions and better than expected in northern growing regions with cool springs and summers. The cloves are sometimes quite red, though they often exhibit lighter, less intense coloration than typical Creoles. The bulb, cloves, and narrower leaves of 'Ajo Rojo' are more similar in appearance to Silverskin cultivars than most Creoles.

'Ajo Rojo'.

'Brown Rose'.

'Ajo Rojo' is among my favorite garlic cultivars for long-term storage. The taste is excellent, sweet and strong, particularly after the flavors have deepened with storage.

### 'Brown Rose'

Introduced to the United States from Central Asia by Maria Jenderek. The cloves tend to have a rose-brown blush, evoking the cultivar's name. 'Brown Rose' stores well, has good garlic character, and sprouts early.

Although 'Brown Rose' is usually classified as a Marbled Purple Stripe, the Fort Collins study (Volk et al. 2004) did not show a genetic connection to that group. More information is needed, but this cultivar appears to be a branch off of a genetic trunk that includes Asiatics and Glazed Purple Stripes. 'Brown Rose' sometimes has double cloves.

(below) A 'Brown Rose' umbel bursts through the spathe.

'Himalayan Red'.

## 'Himalayan Red'

A highly unusual cultivar from Nepal, where it is grown at elevations of more than 8000 ft. (2438 m) above sea level. 'Himalayan Red' is a difficult garlic and is not recommended for either the commercial grower or casual garlic gardener. It is, however, a fascinating cultivar for garlic aficionados and collectors.

For many years in my Pacific Northwest garden, 'Himalayan Red' produced only two-cloved bulbs at best, occasionally with a poorly developed third clove. It is finally producing bulbs that are somewhat better developed, if not yet fully developed. All of the plants are partially bolting. The most fully formed bulbs are multilayered with smaller inner cloves. The purple-skinned cloves are wide at the base, but tapering and notably elongated. Raw, 'Himalayan Red' is one of the hottest garlic cultivars I have ever tasted, burning from the tip of the tongue to the back of the throat. Cooking eliminates the sulfurous heat, leaving a pungent garlic flavor. The bulbs store poorly. Darrell Merrell reports a similar phenotypic expression in his much warmer Oklahoma climate.

'Himalayan Red' is among the more unusual garlic cultivars. It would be fascinating to see what a DNA assessment would reveal about its genetic relationships.

A 'Kitab' umbel splitting the spathe.

A 'Kitab' umbel.

'Kitab'.

## 'Kitab'

John Swenson (1999a) recounts the 1989 allium-collecting expedition that took him, Philipp Simon, and others to Central Asia. Flights from Moscow to Ashgabat, then from Ashgabat to Samarkand, were made at night, presumably so that these potential "spies" could not photograph strategic oil fields. The collecting party drove to Kitab but decided against staying at a roadside hostel after observing long, thin, transparent worms in the local drinking water. They decided instead to camp on a mountainside overlooking the city. This proved fortuitous. Two in the party discovered garlic growing in a dry, rocky streambed. The bulbs were buried so deeply in the rocks that they could not be extracted, so the party resorted to collecting a few handfuls of bulbils. These were later planted and grown into bulbs. This is the garlic we now call 'Kitab'.

There may be some mixing of 'Kitab' and 'Pskem' in the commercial market. An oblique reference in the records of one commercial grower suggests that 'Kitab' and 'Pskem' may have been deemed identical and subsequently marketed together as 'Pskem'. In my garden, the cultivars that I obtained as 'Kitab' and 'Pskem' look essentially the same. Both are among the latest to sprout and among the earliest to bolt—habits, one speculates, that ensure survival in harsh climates with short growing seasons.

The bulbs are comprised of few, but very large, elongated cloves, somewhat reminiscent of garlic from the Porcelain group, but the purple patterning of the bulb wrappers, and of the inflorescences in particular, are more typical of Purple Stripes than Porcelains. The flowers and bulbils have purple coloration, and the bulbils, while not large, are larger than the grain-sized bulbils typical of Porcelain cultivars. The 'Kitab' in my garden somewhat resembles Marbled Purple Stripe cultivars, but its cloves are more elongated. One grower reports that 'Kitab' has produced true seed under controlled conditions.

'Kitab' is a fine-tasting garlic with strong depth of character, if perhaps less complexly rich than some Purple Stripes. When sautéed, it does not have the mealy, bland tendencies that one sometimes encounters with Marbled Purple Stripes. 'Kitab' is an excellent garlic on its own merit and is all the more special given its wild origins and the intriguing tale of how it was brought to cultivation and the culinary world.

## 'Marino'

Originating in New York State from a grower with the surname Marino. Growers report that this cultivar is among the more vigorous and less demanding Rocamboles. Curiously, the Fort Collins study (Volk et al. 2004) places the example tested unambiguously in the Marbled Purple Stripe group. Having never grown the cultivar myself, I cannot comment further.

## 'Mexican Red'

Other cultivars carry the name 'Mexican Red', including a Silverskin and a Turban. This 'Mexican Red' is generally listed as a Purple Stripe, but the Fort Collins study (Volk et al. 2004) indicates that it is genetically unique and differs from the core of the Purple Stripe group. It is adapted to warmer growing areas.

## 'Pskem'

'Pskem' was collected in 1989 by John Swenson from the mountains of the Pskem River valley near Pskem, Uzbekistan. 'Pskem' and 'Kitab' were collected some 250 miles (400 km) apart in separate river drainage systems. In my garden, 'Pskem' and 'Kitab' appear to be virtually identical. Some evidence indicates that in the mid 1990s, in commercial circulation and trade, 'Kitab' may have been deemed identical and combined with 'Pskem'.

Note the secondary pseudostem and leaves at the upper left of the plant. 'Pskem' has an unusual propensity for generating leaf blades from lateral buds at the time of clove formation, sometimes producing secondary scapes in the leaf axils.

'Pskem' has relatively few large cloves and superficially suggests membership in the Marbled Purple Stripe group, where it has appeared in commercial catalogs. However, the Fort Collins study (Volk et al. 2004) showed no direct link with the Marbled Purple Stripes and showed a direct link and apparent genetic proximity to the Purple Stripes. Unfortunately, a missing data element in the study did not permit more precise genetic placement. The bulb morphology of 'Pskem' differs from what is typical of either the Marbled Purple Stripes or Purple Stripes, with generally four large, somewhat elongated cloves. The bulb somewhat resembles those of Porcelain cultivars, but the more telling inflorescence and bulbils are very dif-

'Pskem'.

ferent, more closely resembling those of the Purple Stripe group.

'Pskem' is quite hot when raw but has good depth of character to go with the heat. Its large cloves and full flavor make it a desirable addition to the garlic repertoire and an appealing alternative to the other large-cloved cultivars of the Porcelain and Marbled Purple Stripe groups. It is all the more special for its unique morphology and wild origins.

### 'Single Garlic' ('Chengdu #2')

This cultivar was obtained in an open market in Chengdu, China, by Greg Czarnecki. 'Single Garlic' is the name given to the cultivar by the Chinese. It often lives up to its name by resisting formation of multicloved bulbs, frequently yielding enormous undivided rounds. 'Single Garlic' is usually grouped with Asiatic cultivars, though the umbel capsule and bulbils suggest a closer similarity with the Turban group. The cloves have the angularity of the Asiatic cultivars rather than the more rounded angles characteristic of Turbans, but they are squatter than typical Asiatic cloves. It is a unique cultivar in many respects, and its genetic affiliation is unclear.

### 'Tai Cang' ('White Garlic')

'Tai Cang' comes from the China National Seed Foundation in Beijing by way of Greg Czarnecki. In the trade it is generally grouped with the Asiatics, and it may well belong in that group, but it seems sufficiently different to merit temporary placement with the unclassified cultivars. It shoots earlier than other Asiatics and appears to be less cold hardy than most cultivars, readily showing leaf tip burn from frosts. The umbel capsule is more like a Turban than a typical Asiatic, though the bulb and clove shape are consistent with most Asiatics. The flavor is more aggressive than some Asiatics and somewhat less sweet.

'Single Garlic'. In the center is an enormous round.

'Tai Cang'.

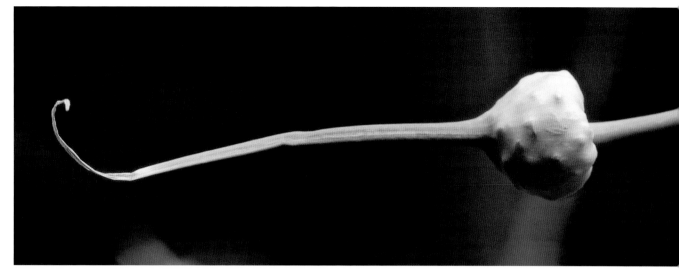

A 'Single Garlic' umbel capsule.

A 'Tai Cang' umbel capsule.

## OTHER GARLICLIKE ALLIUMS

### Allium canadense

Native to North America, *Allium canadense* is variously called Canadian garlic, meadow garlic, meadow onion, wild garlic, and wild onion. The bulb is covered with a distinctive mat of fibers. The flavor is strong and more onionlike than garliclike. *Allium canadense* was widely consumed by many Native Americans as well as by subsequent European settlers.

### Allium macrochaetum

*Allium macrochaetum* is found in parts of Iran, Iraq, and Turkey. It smells like garlic when crushed and is allied to *A. tuncelianum*, another allium with characteristic garlic aroma. Both may be ancestral precursors to garlic, though their current geographic distribution at some distance from garlic's origins in Central Asia is an argument against the hypothesis.

### Allium scorodoprasum

Like the *Allium sativum* cultivars of the Rocambole group, *A. scorodoprasum* has a prominently coiled scape and is generally similar in appearance. Since pre-Linnaean times, Rocamboles and *A. scorodoprasum* have been confused. The common names rocambole and serpent garlic properly refer to *A. sativum* with prominently coiled scapes, not to *A. scorodoprasum*. The name "sand leek" has also been applied to both. *Allium scorodoprasum* is distributed in Europe, Bulgaria, Turkey, southern Ukraine, Georgia, Azerbaijan, and Armenia. Its typical habitats include low-altitude, cultivated or abandoned fields, scrub areas, and vineyards, where it can rapidly multiply and spread vegetatively. It is cultivated for food on a minor scale.

### Allium tuberosum

*Allium tuberosum* is commonly known as garlic chive or Chinese chive. Its bulbs are negligible, and the species name, *tuberosum*, meaning "enlarged" or "swollen," likely refers to the plant's rhizomes. The plant spreads by its rhizomes and forms dense clumps. It can be propagated from sections of a clump or from seeds, which it produces in abundance. Garlic chive grows wild over a wide range in Asia, from Mongolia to Japan in the north, to Thailand and the Philippines in the south. Because it readily naturalizes, its initial center of origin is unclear.

Like chive (*Allium schoenoprasum*), garlic chive is cultivated for its leaves, which are grasslike, flat on one surface, and slightly keel-shaped on the other. The garlicky part of its garlic-onion character comes from the sulfur compound alliin. Among the common food alliums, only garlic, garlic chive, and elephant garlic contain alliin. Garlic chives are sometimes blanched by shielding them from the sun. They may be encountered in Asian markets, either blanched or unblanched, under various names, including *nira* (Japanese) and various Chinese transliterations, including *kiu ts'ai, jiu tsai,* and *gau tsoi,* as well as other country-specific names.

### Allium tuncelianum

*Allium tuncelianum* appears to be closely allied to garlic, *A. sativum*. It smells like garlic and is used as such in its native Turkey. Its inflorescences are fully fertile and devoid of bulbils. The bulbils in garlic inflorescences compete with the flowers causing the flowers to senesce. *Allium tuncelianum* scapes coil prominently prior to maturity. The similarities between *A. tuncelianum* and *A. sativum* are suffi-cient to prompt some to speculate that the fertile *A. tuncelianum* may be garlic's ancestor. Others question the likelihood of the hypothesis, noting that garlic is a Central Asian species, while *A. tuncelianum* is currently found in Turkey. Genetic research will likely one day resolve the matter.

## Allium ursinum

Most alliums compete poorly with other vegeta-tion. *Allium ursinum* is one of the few woodland alliums. It is sometimes called wild garlic and is used as a substitute for garlic in cuisine and health preparations. As with the other garliclike alliums, the abundance of the sulfur compound alliin gives the plant its distinctive garliclike character.

## Allium vineale

*Allium vineale* was introduced to the United States from Europe, where it is sometimes harvested for its garlicky character. Although sometimes called wild garlic, *A. vineale* is not a garlic, as readily evidenced by its leaves, which are rounded and hollow, unlike the solid, V-shaped leaves of garlic. This allium has an unsavory reputation. Common in pasturelands, it can impart an unwelcome onionlike or garliclike flavor to milk products or to the meat of livestock and poultry. The flavor can also taint grain if the bulbils from the inflorescence are inadvertently harvested along with the grain. *Allium vineale* is listed as a noxious weed in many states.

## Elephant garlic

The common name "elephant garlic" does not refer to a species but to a horticultural group within a species, and for this reason the plant is listed here by its common name. Elephant garlic belongs to the great-headed garlic group of *Allium ampelopra-sum*, and "great-headed garlic" is another common name for the plant. Leek, kurrat, and pearl onion constitute the three other groups in *A. ampelopra-sum*. Elephant garlic was likely part of the basis for Linnaeus' 1753 description of the species. The name "elephant garlic" was promulgated by Luther Burbank in 1919. The plant closely resembles *A. sativum*, true garlic, and it is not surprising that both home gardeners and popular culture confuse the two, assuming that elephant garlic is a type of garlic—which it is not. Unfortunately, the popular name "elephant garlic" propels and perpetuates the confusion.

The sulfur compound alliin, which is respon-sible for the flavor characteristics of true garlic, is also responsible for the garliclike flavor of elephant garlic. Some people are fans of elephant garlic. I am not one of them. It forms very large heads and cloves and has a somewhat garlicky character, but to my palate the garlic character is weak and muddled with unwelcome earthy overtones and off-flavors. I might object less if it was proffered under a more honest common name, such as garlic leek, which would suggest a leek with some garlic character. As it is, the common name of this plant defames *Allium sativum*.

Elephant garlic plants are large and robust. They flower readily, produce large umbels, and shed their spathes at maturity. True garlic produces smaller umbels, and at maturity, the spathe splits but typically remains attached to the base of the umbel. Elephant garlic flowers are more globular than those of true garlic. Except for new genetic crossings, bulbils are always present in *Allium sa-tivum* inflorescences, but bulbils are usually absent from the inflorescences of elephant garlic. Garlic scapes sold on the fresh market are sometimes el-ephant garlic scapes rather than true garlic scapes. Elephant garlic typically produces a cluster of large cloves around a central scape. Unlike true garlic, there may be small bulblets around the main bulb. If the elephant garlic does not produce a scape, its bulb typically consists of a massive single clove or round. Garlic rounds are typically relatively small and are produced from bulbils, or when the plant is too small, weak, or otherwise unable to produce a fully developed bulb. With respect to less overt taxonomic differences, *A. sativum* has a diploid chromosome count of 16, while elephant garlic has a diploid chromosome count of 48.

## ~ ELEVEN ~

# Quick Guides

**THESE QUICK GUIDES** are condensed references summarizing a topic. They offer a quick start, but by no means do they tell the whole story. Generalizations are inevitably incomplete, and there is always the risk of introducing distortion or misunderstanding. Nonetheless, these guides can serve as a good starting point. As time and interest permit, the more detailed sections in this book offer additional information.

## GROWING GARLIC

The basics of growing garlic are very easy. You can successfully grow garlic under conditions that are far from ideal. What is ideal for your growing area and the cultivars that you grow may differ from what is indicated here, but these criteria will serve as a good beginning point. If you live in an area with exceptionally cold winters or exceptionally warm winters, you will want to refer to chapter 6 for important additional information. For any generalization, there are always exceptions, and often

'Killarney Red' plants.

more than one good way to do something. Caveats aside, here are some of the basics:

Obtain good-quality planting stock. Avoid garlic from a grocery store, which may have been treated with growth suppressants or stored in a way that will be detrimental to your garlic crop. Obtain planting stock from a local grower or one of the many specialty producers of "seed" garlic through mail order or the Internet. Some are listed in the garlic sources section in the back of the book.

Separate the cloves and discard any that look unhealthy. The biggest cloves will produce the biggest bulbs. One clove produces one bulb at harvest.

Plant the cloves in the fall in a sunny location at least three weeks before the ground freezes. October is a good planting month for most North American climates. Plant cloves with the root end down, pointed tip up, 2 to 3 in. (5 to 7.5 cm) deep, at a spacing of 10 in. (25 cm) between rows and 6 in. (15 cm) within the rows. As you gain more experience, you can determine the row spacing that works best for you and your growing climate. Make sure you can reach all areas of the bed without stepping into the bed.

Garlic will grow in poor soil, but for the best crop, plant in loose, loamy soil with near neutral pH. In general, good garden soil is good garlic-growing soil. Garlic is not a heavy nitrogen feeder, but composted manure worked into the soil at planting adds both tilth and fertilizer. Feed again in early spring with liquid fertilizer or foliar spraying. Fertilizer regimens can be much more elaborate and optimized, but the basics will produce a successful crop.

If your winters are very cold or very dry, add a layer of mulch to your beds to protect the garlic against freezing or drying, or from being heaved out of the ground by heavy frosts. A loose mulch such as straw works well. If you have wet springs, remove the mulch to prevent problems with mold, slugs, and snails. If you do not have wet springs, leave the mulch in place to suppress weeds.

The aboveground plant will appear in early spring, or in late fall or winter in mild climates, depending on the cultivar. Keep weeds from shading the garlic and from stealing moisture and nutrients.

As you would with any garden crop, keep the garlic well watered but not suffocating in mud. Allow the soil to dry for about a week before harvest. Garlic bulbs develop rapidly in the period before harvest, so do not cut off water too soon. Unless you are dealing with muddy conditions, it is best to err on the side of ample moisture rather than too little. You can refine your practices as you gain experience.

Hardneck (bolting) garlic produces scapes—flower stalks that emerge from the top of the plant, curl down, then uncurl and grow straight up. For most cultivars in most growing conditions, leaving the scapes on the plant will reduce the size of the bulb. To avoid this, cut off the scapes after they have curled downward but before they uncurl to grow straight up. Softneck (nonbolting) garlic has no scapes.

As harvest nears, the plant's leaves will begin to die from the tip inward and from the lowermost leaf upward. Harvest the garlic bulbs when approximately five to six leaves remain green. Do not try to pull the garlic from the ground without first loosening the soil with a spade, garden fork, or other tool. Pull the bulb from the ground and loosely rub the soil out of the roots. Keep the harvested garlic out of direct sunlight. Do not wash it with water.

Garlic needs to dry and cure in a well-ventilated area out of the sun. With twine, tie the garlic in bundles of six to twelve and hang to dry and cure, bulb portion downward, for several weeks until the vegetative material above the bulb is completely dry. Large bulbs with many clove layers will take longer to dry.

Trim off the vegetative material to approximately 1 in. (2.5 cm) above the bulb. If the vegetative material is still moist, the garlic needs more drying time. Trim the roots, leaving about ¼ in. (0.5 cm). Brush the soil from the roots with a toothbrush and remove the outermost dirty bulb wrapper with your thumb or the edge of the toothbrush.

Use netted bags, such as those typically used for onions, shallots, and garlic, to keep your harvested garlic sorted and stored so that air can circulate. These storage bags are often available from specialty garlic growers.

Store garlic in a cool, well-ventilated area. Do not store it in the refrigerator or below 50°F (10°C) or it will sprout. In general, ideal conditions are a temperature of 56°F to 58°F (13°C to 14°C) and a relative humidity of 45% to 50%, similar to the conditions of a good wine cellar. Do not worry if these idealized conditions are not available to you, unless your storage area is very hot or low in humidity. Garlic stores reasonably well under a wide range of conditions, including ambient room temperature.

## BUYING GARLIC

Avoid purchasing garlic from your local supermarket. With occasional exception, the garlic will likely be a commercial cultivar of mediocre culinary merit. Quite likely it will have been stored or chemically treated in a manner that is detrimental to its use for planting stock, and it may not store well after purchase.

Support specialty garlic growers, who know a lot about garlic and have made a commitment to garlic and its diversity. You can find specialty growers at farmers' markets, on the Web, and through mail order. A few are listed in the garlic sources section in the back of the book. Do not be concerned if the garlic cultivars that are offered are not named in this book; many cultivars are not included in this book, and many cultivars are grown under different names.

The major garlic horticultural groups reflect much of garlic's diversity. Trying garlic from each group is a good way to begin exploring and enjoying the variety that garlic has to offer.

This Creole cultivar does not look much like the garlic commonly found at the supermarket. Trying garlic from different horticultural groups is a good way to explore and enjoy garlic's diversity.

## RECOMMENDED GARLIC CULTIVARS

The following recommendations are examples of garlic cultivars that meet different needs. The lists are subjective and far from exclusive. As much as possible, the recommendations reflect my own experience—and I continually revise my own preferences.

Climate, cultural practices, and storage conditions are all variables that help determine how garlic performs. Porcelain cultivars reportedly have a moderately long storage life, but those that I have grown have not stored well. On the other hand, some Asiatics store very well for me, beyond what

is sometimes reported. Many cultivars besides those listed may work as well or even better for your particular situation.

Treat these recommendations as a point of departure for your own garlic explorations rather than a point of conclusion. As you live with garlic over a number of harvests, you will develop your own list of favorites.

### Excellent tasting, short storing

Many garlic growers and enthusiasts think that cultivars from the Rocambole horticultural group are the best-tasting garlics of all. I am among that contingent. Some Rocamboles taste better than others. Although there are undoubtedly others of equal merit, I offer the following as examples of Rocamboles that I grow and like a great deal: 'Carpathian', 'Killarney Red', 'Russian Red', and 'Spanish Roja'.

## Excellent tasting, medium storing

Cultivars from the Purple Stripe and Glazed Purple Stripe groups are not as sweet as those from the Rocambole group, but their flavors are intense and complex. Some aficionados prefer them to Rocamboles, and they store longer. Widely available cultivars from the Purple Stripe group include 'Samarkand', 'Shatili', and 'Shvelisi', and from the Glazed Purple Stripe group, 'Vekak'.

## Excellent tasting, medium to long storing

Some Asiatic cultivars, such as 'Pyongyang' and 'Asian Tempest', have a qualitative intensity similar to Purple Stripes and store longer. Artichoke cultivars generally store longer than most bolting cultivars but have a less rich, sometimes vegetative character. 'Kettle River Giant', 'Lorz Italian', and 'Tochliavri' are examples of Artichoke cultivars that have the more high-toned flavors characteristic of the Artichoke group, but still have good flavor complexity without vegetative notes.

## Excellent tasting, long storing

Many cultivars in the Creole group store very well and have excellent taste. I have eaten Creoles that had been in storage for more than a year, and though not in their prime, they still had good flavor. I have had particularly good results from the Creole cultivars 'Burgundy', 'Creole Red', 'Manuel Benitee', 'Pescadero Red', and 'Rojo de Castro', though many other cultivars in this group may be equally good.

'Ajo Rojo' is another excellent-tasting, long-storing cultivar. Although it is commonly included with the Creole group, it is genetically distinct.

## Exceptionally long storing

Garlic cultivars from the Silverskin group can be stored the longest. Flavors may vary, depending on growing conditions and storage, but are typically hot and aggressive without the complexity and nuance associated with other horticultural groups. Nonetheless, like most garlic, Silverskins taste their best when minced and sautéed to a light straw color, and can be quite satisfying when prepared in this fashion. 'Locati', 'Nootka Rose', 'Rose du Var', 'S & H Silver', 'Silver White', and 'Wedam' are among the more widely available Silverskins.

## Exceptionally large cloved

Porcelain cultivars rule in this category, since all Porcelains have exceptionally large cloves. Good examples include 'Leningrad', 'Music', 'Romanian Red', 'Rosewood', and 'Zemo'. Some Marbled Purple Stripe cultivars also produce very large cloves, though not quite as large as the Porcelains, and are arguably better tasting than the Porcelain cultivars. Good examples include 'Bai Pi Suan', 'Bogatyr', and 'Siberian'. The unclassified cultivar 'Pskem' also has very large cloves and fine character.

## Early harvesting

Turban cultivars are among the most early-harvesting garlics. 'Luster', 'Shandong', and 'Uzbek Turban' are a few examples of early-harvesting cultivars, though many others are equally early. As a group, Turbans may not have the richest or most complex flavor, but after weeks of gleaning the last of the past season's harvest in search of garlic that is not too far past its prime, one will likely find the juicy cloves of the newly harvested Turbans most welcome.

## Tolerant of severe winters

In general, the vigorously bolting hardneck cultivars are best suited to regions with harsh winters. These cultivars are generally the same as, or most closely related to, the wild garlic strains of Central Asia, and are better adapted to survive harsh winter conditions. Cultivars from the Purple Stripe, Porcelain, Marbled Purple Stripe, and Rocambole groups are among those best suited to climates with severe winters.

## Tolerant of hot climates

Garlic needs a period of cooler temperatures in order to develop bulbs. For some cultivars the need is quite modest. For others it is significant. Cultivars from the Artichoke group are among the best performers in growing regions with warm winters and springs, such as the warmest southernmost regions of the United States. Cultivars from the Creole group are also well suited, though their bulbs are generally smaller.

In general, the vigorously bolting hardneck cultivars have a greater requirement for a period of colder growing conditions than nonbolting cultivars. Of the vigorously bolting hardneck cultivars, Rocamboles are among the worst performers in hot climates, while Marbled Purple Stripes are among the best.

# FLAVOR CHEMISTRY AND CULINARY METHODS

The sulfur compound allicin is responsible for much of the flavor and therapeutic benefits associated with garlic.

Allicin is not present in whole garlic heads or cloves. It is created when the enzyme alliinase comes into contact with the sulfur compound alliin, a process that takes place when garlic is chewed, cut, chopped, or crushed. This interaction initiates a cascade of transformations that result in the creation of many volatile sulfur compounds that contribute to garlic's complex taste and therapeutic effects.

Many people eat raw garlic only for health purposes, but it is also an excellent match for some culinary preparations. Refer to "Cooking, Taste, and Health" in chapter 3 for more information.

Heat destroys allicin, but chopping or crushing garlic prior to heating generates numerous volatile sulfur compounds and the rich, complex flavors associated with garlic.

If garlic is cooked whole, no allicin and very few flavor compounds are produced. The flavor is not only milder but also simpler, and very much different from garlic that has been chopped or crushed prior to cooking.

Roasted garlic is essentially cooked whole, without chopping or crushing. It has a mild, sweet, caramelized taste that has broad appeal, but without the interaction of the enzyme alliinase with alliin, the broad range of aromatic flavor compounds is not produced.

Chopping garlic and sautéing it in oil until it begins to turn straw-colored to light tan produces rich, complex, nutty flavors. Lightly salting helps enhance the character. This method is simple and easy. It brings out the best flavors from even the blandest cultivars and helps even the most sulfurous and aggressive cultivars taste rounded and nutty. This preparation is excellent on its own with crusty bread. It can also readily be incorporated into other dishes or serve as a step in the preparation of vegetables or sauces.

Sautéed garlic should not simply steam or the flavors will be more sulfurous without the rich, nutty character.

Do not cook garlic to a dark brown, or worse yet, burn it, or it will taste acrid and unpleasant.

Throughout the world, in numerous cuisines, whether for sauces, stews, curries, or stir-fries, chopping or crushing garlic and then cooking it in oil is a fundamental culinary building block. Chopping or crushing garlic generates the volatile aromatic flavor elements, and cooking it in oil enhances its character and helps distribute its flavors for the culinary preparation.

# Garlic Sources, Organizations, and Newsletters

## GARLIC SOURCES

This list, though far from exhaustive, includes a number of specialty garlic growers that accept mail and Web orders. Many garlic growers do not accept mail or Web orders but can be found at your local farmers' markets. Increasingly, general seed catalogs are offering more garlic cultivars, and I have included a few that offer a good selection. Search the Web and check your local farmers' markets for the most current information and additional sources.

**Ashley Creek Farm**
9221 Littlerock Road SW
Olympia, Washington 98512
www.ashleycreek.com

**Beaver Pond Estates**
3656 Bolingbroke Road
Maberly, Ontario
Canada K0H 2B0

**Bobba-Mike's Garlic Farm**
P.O. Box 261
Orrville, Ohio 44667
www.garlicfarm.com

**Boundary Garlic Farm**
Box 273
Midway, British Columbia
Canada V0H 1M0
www.garlicfarm.ca

**Charley's Farm**
Charley and Ginny Hein
54 E. Stutler Road
Spokane, Washington 99224
www.charleysfarm.com

**Filaree Farm**
182 Conconully Highway
Okanogan, Washington 98840
www.filareefarm.com

A long-established major vendor of specialty cultivars from all of garlic's horticultural groups, offering a wide range of cultivars, growing supplies, books, and an informative catalog.

**Freeman Farms**
2371 Rotter Road
Rice, Washington 99167
www.freemanfarms.biz

**Garlicsmiths**
967 Mingo Mountain Road
Kettle Falls, Washington 99141
www.garlicsmiths.com

**The Garlic Store**
5313 Mail Creek Lane
Fort Collins, Colorado 80525
www.thegarlicstore.com

A large selection of garlic cultivars, food items, cooking supplies, books, videos, newsletters, and information.

**Gourmet Garlic Gardens**
12300 FM 1176
Bangs, Texas 76823
www.gourmetgarlicgardens.com

A Texas grower with experience growing a range of cultivars in a warmer climate.

**Hood River Garlic**
P.O. Box 1701
Hood River, Oregon 97031
www.hoodrivergarlic.com

**Irish Eyes—Garden City Seeds**
www.gardencityseeds.net

**Laughin' Farms Garlic**
1399 Palm Avenue
Kalona, Iowa 52247
www.laughinfarmsgarlic.com

**Maple Bay Garlic**
6462 Pacific Drive
Duncan, British Columbia
Canada V9L 5S7
www.mbgarlic.com

**Montana Gourmet Garlic**
The River Bottom Ranch
15999 E. Mullan Road
Clinton, Montana 59825
www.montanagourmetgarlic.com

**Nature's Wisdom Garlic**
195 Bolster Road
Oroville, Washington 98844
www.natureswisdomgarlic.com

**Nichols Garden Nursery**
1190 Old Salem Road NE
Albany, Oregon 97321
www.nicholsgardennursery.com

**Revolution Seeds**
204 North Waverly Street
Homer, Illinois 61849
www.revolutionseeds.net

**Seed Savers Exchange**
3094 North Winn Road
Decorah, Iowa 52101
www.seedsavers.org

A nonprofit organization dedicated to the preservation of genetic diversity and heirloom seed. They offer a general sales catalog as well as the membership-only *Seed Savers Yearbook*. Both include a selection of garlic cultivars.

**Seeds of Change**
One Sunset Way
Henderson, Nevada 89014
www.seedsofchange.com

**Territorial Seed Company**
P.O. Box 158
Cottage Grove, Oregon 97424
www.territorial-seed.com

**Three Oaks Farm**
32993 Saginaw Road E.
Cottage Grove, Oregon 97424
www.threeoaksfarm.com

# ORGANIZATIONS AND NEWSLETTERS

*The Garlic News*
Beaver Pond Estates
3656 Bolingbroke Road
Maberly, Ontario
Canada K0H 2B0

Edited by Paul Pospisil, the newsletter focuses on garlic growing in Canada, but much of the information is applicable south of the border in the United States and elsewhere.

**Garlic Seed Foundation**
Rose Valley Farm
Rose, New York 14542
www.garlicseedfoundation.info/index.htm

Founded and maintained by David Stern and Bob Dunkel, the organization describes itself as "educational, not-for-profit, informal, unofficial, unrecognized association created in 1984 over our love of good garlic food and desire to find profitable crops and production for small and family farms." The Garlic Seed Foundation is a clearinghouse for garlic information and publishes *The Garlic Press*, an irregularly released, informative newsletter. The first newsletter was mailed to 125 farmers in New York State. The 42nd issue, *The Best of the Press* (2006), was mailed to 1200 recipients in 10 countries.

**Seed Savers Exchange**
3094 North Winn Road
Decorah, Iowa 52101
www.seedsavers.org

This nonprofit organization with some 8000 members is dedicated to the preservation of genetic diversity and heirloom seed. Seed Savers Exchange produces three publications a year, including a yearbook listing some 12,000 varieties of vegetables and fruits available to members. The listing includes numerous garlic cultivars.

# Bibliography

Aaron, C. 1996. *Garlic Is Life: A Memoir with Recipes*. Berkeley, California: Ten Speed Press.

———. 1997. *The Great Garlic Book: A Guide with Recipes*. Berkeley, California: Ten Speed Press.

———. 2001. *Garlic Kisses: Human Struggles with Garlic Connections*. Milan, Ohio: Mostly Garlic.

———. 2002. Growing, cooking, and eating great garlic. In *Seed Savers 2002 Harvest Edition*. Decorah, Iowa: Seed Savers Exchange. 22–29.

Admati, E. 1979. Recommendations for garlic cultivation for exports. Israeli Ministry of Agriculture, 3.

Alekseeva, M. V., and M. G. Sokolova. 1984. Growth and productivity of winter garlic in relation to clove orientation at planting. *Horticultural Abstracts* 55: 1063.

Allen, J. 2005. Tip burn in garlic. *The Garlic News* (Fall) 5: 8.

———. 2006. What is pyruvate analysis and how is it used to determine the pungency or flavor of garlic? *The Garlic News* (Spring) 7: 10.

Al-Zahim, M., H. Newbury, and B. Ford-Lloyd. 1997. Classification of genetic variation in garlic (*Allium sativum* L.) revealed by RAPD. *HortScience* 23: 1102–1104.

American Botanical Council. 2007. Stanford University garlic trial published in Archives of Internal Medicine finds no cholesterol-lowering effect. http://www.herbalgram.org/default.asp?c=stanfordugarlic. Accessed 17 March 2007.

Anderson, B. 1999. Garlic with a southern accent: A guide to growing the superb herb south of the Mason-Dixon Line. *Mostly Garlic* (1998/1999 Winter): 14–16, 37.

———. 2004. GSF letters to the press. *The Garlic Press* (Early Spring) 43: 8.

Angell, W. T., and L. A. Ellerbrock. 1993. 1992–93 New York experiments. *The Garlic Press* (Fall) 18: 8.

Augusti, K. T. 1990. Therapeutic and medicinal values of onions and garlic. In *Onions and Allied Crops*, vol. 3. Edited by J. L. Brewster and H. D. Rabinowitch. Boca Raton, Florida: CRC Press. 93–108.

Bacon, F., and L. Bacon. 1999. Move over, maple syrup . . . here comes garlic! *Mostly Garlic* (Summer): 16–19, 23, 45.

Barthel, M. 2002. The garlic collection and commercial production at Heritage Farm. In *Seed Savers 2002 Harvest Edition*. Decorah, Iowa: Seed Savers Exchange. 35–39.

Block, E. 1985. The chemistry of garlic and onions. *Scientific American* 252: 114–119.

———. 1996. Foreword. In *Garlic: The Science and Therapeutic Application of* Allium sativum *L. and Related Species*. Edited by H. P. Koch and L. D. Lawson. 2d ed. Baltimore, Maryland: Williams and Wilkins. v.

Bradley, K. F., M. A. Rieger, and G. G. Collins. 1996. Classification of Australian garlic cultivars by DNA fingerprinting. *Australian Journal of Experimental Agriculture* 36: 613–618.

Brewster, J. L. 1994. *Onions and Other Vegetable Alliums*. Oxon, England: CAB International.

Brewster, J. L., and H. D. Rabinowitch. 1990. Garlic agronomy. In *Onions and Allied Crops*, vol. 3. Edited by J. L. Brewster and H. D. Rabinowitch. Boca Raton, Florida: CRC Press. 147–157.

Buwalda, J. G. 1986. Nitrogen nutrition of garlic (*Allium sativum* L.) under irrigation. Components of yield and indices of crop nitrogen status. *Scientific Horticulture* 29: 69.

Callow, C., H. Fraser, and J. F. Landry. 2003. The leek moth. Ontario Ministry of Agriculture, Food and Rural Affairs. http://www.omafra.gov.on.ca/english/crops/facts/leekmoth.htm. Accessed 15 August 2007.

Cantwell, M. 2002. Recommendations for maintaining postharvest quality. *The Garlic Press* (Spring) 40: 13–14.

Cavallito, C. J. 1996. The discovery of allicin in garlic. *The Garlic Press* (Winter) 26: 15.

Cavallito, C. J., and J. H. Bailey. 1944. Allicin, the antibacterial principle of *Allium sativum*. *Journal of the American Chemical Society* 66: 1950–1951.

Celetti, M. 2005. Managing the bulb and stem nematode menace in garlic. *The Garlic News* (Fall) 5: 9.

Cook's Illustrated. 2001. *The America's Test Kitchen Cookbook*. Brookline, Massachusetts: Boston Common Press.

Crawford, S. 1992. *A Garlic Testament: Seasons on a Small New Mexico Farm*. New York: HarperCollins.

———. 1999. Six thousand feet, two acres and patience: A small commercial garlic farm in New Mexico. *Mostly Garlic* (Fall): 20, 42–43.

Crowe, F. 1995a. Fusarium basal rot of garlic. In *Compendium of Onion and Garlic Diseases*. Edited by H. F. Schwartz and S. K. Mohan. St. Paul, Minnesota: APS Press. 11.

———. 1995b. Garlic and mosquitoes. *Science* 269: 1806.

———. 1995c. White rot. In *Compendium of Onion and Garlic Diseases*. Edited by H. F. Schwartz and S. K. Mohan. St. Paul, Minnesota: APS Press. 14–16.

Crowe, F., S. K. Mohan, and H. F. Schwartz. 1995. Other botrytis diseases. In *Compendium of Onion and Garlic Diseases*. Edited by H. F. Schwartz and S. K. Mohan. St. Paul, Minnesota: APS Press. 19–20.

Czarnecki, G. 1999. Garlic. *Seed Savers 1999 Yearbook*. Decorah, Iowa: Seed Savers Exchange. 173–186.

Das, A. K., M. K. Sadhu, M. G. Som, and T. K. Bose. 1985. Effect of time of planting on growth and yield of multiple clove garlic (*Allium sativum* L.). *Indian Agriculture* 29: 177.

Davis, R. M. 1995a. Diseases caused by viruses and mycoplasmalike organisms. In *Compendium of Onion and Garlic Diseases*. Edited by H. F. Schwartz and S. K. Mohan. St. Paul, Minnesota: APS Press. 40–42.

———. 1995b. Penicillium decay of garlic. In *Compendium of Onion and Garlic Diseases*. Edited by H. F. Schwartz and S. K. Mohan. St. Paul, Minnesota: APS Press. 27–28.

De Candolle, A. 1886. *Origin of Cultivated Plants*. Reprint. New York: Hafner, 1967.

Don, G. 1827. A monograph of the genus *Allium*. *Memoirs of the Wernerian Natural History Society* 1: 1–102.

Dunkel, B. 2002. Garlic leaves, slowly. *The Garlic Press* (Spring) 40: 12.

Dunn, C. 1999. Garlic in New Mexico. *Mostly Garlic* (Fall): 18–19, 42.

Ellis, D. D., D. Skogerboe, C. Andre, B. Hellier, and G. M. Volk. 2006. Implementation of garlic cryopreservation techniques in the National Plant Germplasm System. *CryoLetters* 27: 99–106.

Engeland, R. L. 1991. *Growing Great Garlic: The Definitive Guide for Organic Gardeners and Small Farmers*. Okanogan, Washington: Filaree Productions.

———. 1995. *Supplement to Growing Great Garlic*. Okanogan, Washington: Filaree Productions.

———. 1998. How does your garlic taste? *Mostly Garlic* (Fall): 11.

Ershov, I. I., and L. L. Gerasimova. 1984. Position of cloves in the bulb and the quality of spring garlic planting behavior. *Sel. Semenovod* 9: 37.

Etoh, T. 1985. Studies on the sterility in garlic, Allium sativum *L. Memoirs of the Faculty of Agriculture of Kagoshima University* 21: 77–132.

———. 1986. Fertility of the garlic clones collected in Soviet Central Asia. *Journal of the Japanese Society for Horticultural Science* 55: 312–319.

Etoh, T., and P. W. Simon. 2002. Diversity, fertility and seed production of garlic. In *Allium Crop Science: Recent Advances*. Edited by H. D. Rabinowitch and L. Currah. New York: CAB International.

Fellner, M. 1998. Gibberellic acid suppresses production of vegetative topsets and promotes development of flowers *in vitro* in garlic (*Allium sativum*) inflorescences. Allium *Improvement Newsletter* 8: 22–23.

Fenwick, G. R., and A. B. Hanley. 1990. Processing of alliums; use in food manufacture. In *Onions and Allied Crops*, vol. 3. Edited by J. L. Brewster and H. D. Rabinowitch. Boca Raton, Florida: CRC Press. 33–72.

Fitzsimmons, J. P., and L. C. Burrill. 1993. Wild garlic: *Allium vineale* L. Pacific Northwest Extension Publication, PNW 444.

Fulder, S. 1997. *The Garlic Book: Nature's Powerful Healer*. Garden City Park, New York: Avery Publishing Group.

———. 1998. Yes, but how safe is it? *Mostly Garlic* (Fall): 8.

Fulder, S., and J. Blackwood. 2000. *Garlic: Nature's Original Remedy*. Rev. ed. Rochester, Vermont: Healing Arts Press.

Gardner, C. D., L. D. Lawson, E. Block, L. M. Chatterjee, A. Kiazand, R. R. Balise, and H. C. Kraemer. 2007. Effect of raw garlic vs. commercial garlic supplements on plasma lipid concentrations in adults with moderate hypercholesterolemia: A randomized clinical trial. *Archives of Internal Medicine* 167: 346–353.

Garlicworld. 2007. http://www.garlicworld.co.uk/index.html. Accessed 23 February 2007.

Gerard, J. 1633. *The Herbal or General History of Plants*. Reprint. New York: Dover, 1975.

Giradin, J. M. 1995. Midwest garlic growers: Minnesota garlic field day and potluck picnic. *The Garlic Press* (Fall) 24: 9.

———. 2004. Garlic. *Seed Savers 2004 Yearbook*. Decorah, Iowa: Seed Savers Exchange. 141–158.

Griffith, L., and F. Griffith. 1998. *Garlic, Garlic, Garlic: Exceptional Recipes for the World's Most Indispensable Ingredient*. New York: Houghton Mifflin.

Griffiths, M. 1994. *Index of Garden Plants*. Portland, Oregon: Timber Press.

Grubben, G. J. H. 1994. Constraints for shallot, garlic, and welsh onion in Indonesia: A case study on the evolution of allium crops in the equatorial tropics. *Acta Horticulturae* 358: 333–340. (Abstract)

Hahn, G. 1996a. Botanical characterization and cultivation of garlic. In *Garlic: The Science and Therapeutic Application of* Allium sativum *L. and Related Species*. Edited by H. P. Koch and L. D. Lawson. 2d ed. Baltimore, Maryland: Williams and Wilkins. 25–36.

———. 1996b. History of folk medicine, and legendary uses of garlic. In *Garlic: The Science and Therapeutic Application of* Allium sativum *L. and Related Species*. Edited by H. P. Koch and L. D. Lawson. 2d ed. Baltimore, Maryland: Williams and Wilkins. 1–24.

Halligan, M. 2000. Growing garlic in Wisconsin. *Mostly Garlic* (1999/2000 Winter): 28–29, 34.

Hanelt, P. 1990. Taxonomy, evolution and history. In *Onions and Allied Crops*, vol. 1. Edited by H. D. Rabinowitch and J. L. Brewster. Boca Raton, Florida: CRC Press. 1–26.

Hannan, R. M. 2004. Germplasm collection in Turkmenistan. In *Seed Savers 2004 Summer Edition*. Decorah, Iowa: Seed Savers Exchange. 22–24.

Hannan, R. M., and D. Garoutte. 1995. Cryopreservation of garlic germplasm as meristems in LN for long-term storage. From the National Onion Research Conference, Madison, Wisconsin, December 6–9. Allium *Improvement Newsletter* 5: 76. (Abstract)

Hannan, R. M., and E. J. Sorensen. 2002. Crop profile for garlic in Washington. Washington State University Extension Bulletin.

Haque, M. S., T. Wada, and K. Hattori. 1997. Longer cold growing season can increase bulb size of garlic cv. Bangladesh local. Allium *Improvement Newsletter* 7: 50–51.

Harris, Linda J. 1997. Garlic: Safe methods to store, preserve, and enjoy. University of California Division of Agricultural and Natural Resources Publication 7231.

Harris, Lloyd J. 1991. *The Book of Garlic*. 3d ed. San Francisco: Panjandrum Press, 1974. Reprint, Aris Books.

Havey, M. J. 1995. Fusarium basal plate rot. In *Compendium of Onion and Garlic Diseases.* Edited by H. F. Schwartz and S. K. Mohan. St. Paul, Minnesota: APS Press. 10–11.

———. 1999. Advances in new alliums. In *Perspectives on New Crops and New Uses.* Edited by J. Janick. Alexandria, Virginia: ASHS Press. 374–378.

Hellier, B. C. 2004. The garlic collection of the USDA, ARS National Plant Germplasm System. *The Garlic Press* (Fall) 44: 1.

Hellier, B. C., and M. Pavelka. 2005. Summary of fertility characteristics of the USDA garlic collection when grown in Pullman, Washington. *HortScience* 40: 1039. (Abstract)

Helm, J. 1956. Die zu Wiirz- und Speisezwecken kultivierten Arten der Gattung. *Allium* L. *Kulturpflanze* 4: 130–180.

Higazy, M. K., S. A. Shanan, M. Billah, and H. M. El-Ramadan. 1974. Effect of soil moisture levels on postharvest changes in garlic. *'Egyptian' Journal of Horticulture* 1: 13.

Hill, J. P. 1995. Rust. In *Compendium of Onion and Garlic Diseases.* Edited by H. F. Schwartz and S. K. Mohan. St. Paul, Minnesota: APS Press. 24–25.

Hong, C. J. 1999. Fundamental studies on cross-breeding in garlic, *Allium sativum* L. Ph.D. Thesis, Kagoshima University, Kagoshima, Japan.

Hsu, J. P., J. G. Jeng, and C. C. Chen. 1994. Identification of a novel sulfur compound from the interaction of garlic and heated vegetable oil. *Chemical Abstracts* 121: 81, 405.

Hughes, B. G., and L. D. Lawson. 1991. Antimicrobial effects of *Allium sativum* L. (garlic), *Allium ampeloprasum* (elephant garlic), and *Allium cepa* L. (onion), garlic compounds, and commercial garlic supplement products. *Phytotherapy Research* 5: 154–158.

Hughes, B. G., B. K. Murray, and L. D. Lawson. 1989. Antiviral constituents from *Allium sativum. Planta Medica* 55: 114.

Ipek, M., A. Ipek, S. G. Almquist, and P. W. Simon. 2005. Demonstration of linkage and development of the first low-density genetic map of garlic based on AFLP markers. *Theoretical and Applied Genetics* 110: 228–236. (Abstract)

Ipek, M., A. Ipek, and P. W. Simon. 2003. Comparison of AFLPs, RAPD markers, and isozymes for diversity assessment of garlic and detection of putative duplicates in germplasm collections. *Journal of American Society for Horticultural Science* 128 (2): 246–252.

Jain, R. C. 1976. Onion and garlic in experimental cholesterol induced atherosclerosis. *Indian Journal of Medical Research* 64: 1509.

Jenderek, M. M. 2004. Development of S1 families in garlic. In *Proceedings of the XXVI International Horticultural Congress: Advances in Vegetable Breeding.* Edited by J. D. McCreight and E. J. Ryder. Toronto, Canada. *Acta Horticulturae* 637.

Jenderek, M. M., and R. M. Hannan. 2000. Seed producing ability of garlic (*Allium sativum* L.) clones from two public U.S. collections. In *Proceedings of the Third International Symposium on Edible Alliaceae.* Athens, Georgia: University of Georgia. 73–75.

———. 2003. Phenotypic characteristics of open pollinated garlic progenies. *HortScience* 38: 673. (Abstract)

———. 2004a. Tolerance to rust (*Puccinia allii*) in seed derived garlic progenies. *HortScience* 39: 775.

———. 2004b. Variation of reproductive characteristics and seed production in the USDA garlic germplasm collection. *HortScience* 39: 485–488.

Jenderek, M. M., K. A. Schierenbeck, and R. M. Hannan. 1997. Random amplified polymorphic DNA analysis of garlic (*Allium sativum* L.) germplasm collection. *HortScience* 32: 452. (Abstract)

Johnson, A. W., and P. A. Roberts. 1995. Diseases caused by nematode. In *Compendium of Onion and Garlic Diseases*. Edited by H. F. Schwartz and S. K. Mohan. St. Paul, Minnesota: APS Press. 35–40.

Jones, H. A., and L. K. Mann. 1963. *Onions and Their Allies*. New York: Interscience Publishers.

Josling, P. 1998. A clove a day: The cardio-protective properties of garlic. *Mostly Garlic* (Fall): 6–8.

———. 1999a. The anti-fungal and anti-viral effects of garlic. *Mostly Garlic* (Fall): 6–7, 43.

———. 1999b. Garlic and cancer. *Mostly Garlic* (Spring): 20.

———. 1999c. Nature's antibiotic: The antimicrobial properties of garlic. *Mostly Garlic* (Summer): 6–7, 41.

———. 2000a. Blood pressure effects of garlic. *Mostly Garlic* (1999/2000 Winter): 8–9, 38.

———. 2000b. Cholesterol and lipid-lowering effects of garlic. *Mostly Garlic* (Spring): 6–7.

Kamenetsky, R., and H. D. Rabinowitch. 2001. Floral development in bolting garlic. *Sexual Plant Reproduction* 13: 235–241.

Kazakova, A. A. 1978. *Allium*. In *Flora of Cultivated Plants*, vol. 10. Edited by D. D. Brezhnev. Kolos, Leningrad.

Keller, E. R. J. 2002. Cryopreservation of *Allium sativum* L. (garlic). In *Cryopreservation of Plant Germplasm II* (*Biotechnology in Agriculture and Forestry*) 50. Edited by L. E. Towill and Y. P. S. Bajaj. Berlin: Springer-Verlag. 37–47.

Kline, R. 1990. *Garlic*. Report 387. Rose, New York: Cornell University and the Garlic Seed Foundation.

Koch, H. P. 1996a. Biopharmaceutics of garlic's effective compounds. In *Garlic: The Science and Therapeutic Application of* Allium sativum *L. and Related Species*. Edited by H. P. Koch and L. D. Lawson. 2d ed. Baltimore, Maryland: Williams and Wilkins. 213–220.

———. 1996b. Non-medical applications of garlic and curiosities. In *Garlic: The Science and Therapeutic Application of* Allium sativum *L. and Related Species*. Edited by H. P. Koch and L. D. Lawson. 2d ed. Baltimore, Maryland: Williams and Wilkins. 229–233.

———. 1996c. Toxicology and undesirable effects of garlic. In *Garlic: The Science and Therapeutic Application of* Allium sativum *L. and Related Species*. Edited by H. P. Koch and L. D. Lawson. 2d ed. Baltimore, Maryland: Williams and Wilkins. 221–228.

Koch, H. P., and L. D. Lawson, eds. 1996. *Garlic: The Science and Therapeutic Application of* Allium sativum *L. and Related Species*. 2d ed. Baltimore, Maryland: Williams and Wilkins.

Koike, S., R. Smith, M. Davis, and J. Nunez. 2001. Garlic rust outbreak in California, June 1998. University of California Vegetable Research and Information Center. http://vric.ucdavis.edu/veginfo/commodity/garlic/garlicrust.html. Accessed 15 August 2007.

Lacy, M. L., and J. W. Lorbeer. 1995a. Botrytis leaf blight. In *Compendium of Onion and Garlic Diseases.* Edited by H. F. Schwartz and S. K. Mohan. St. Paul, Minnesota: APS Press. 16–18.

———. 1995b. Botrytis neck rot. In *Compendium of Onion and Garlic Diseases.* Edited by H. F. Schwartz and S. K. Mohan. St. Paul, Minnesota: APS Press. 18–19.

LaGasa, E. H., J. Agnesani, S. Tipton, and D. Bowden. 2003. 2002 pheromone-trap detection survey for leek moth, *Acrolepiopsis assectella* (Zeller 1893) (Lepidoptera: Acrolepiidae), an exotic pest of *Allium* spp. Plant Protection Division, Pest Program, Washington State Department of Agriculture. WSDA PUB 082 (N/04/03).

Lallemand, J., C. M. Messian, F. Briand, and T. Etoh. 1997. Delimitation of varietal groups in garlic (*Allium sativum* L.) by morphological, physiological, and biochemical characters. *Acta Horticulturae* 433: 123–132. (Abstract)

Lancaster, J. E., and M. J. Boland. 1990. Flavor biochemistry. In *Onions and Allied Crops,* vol. 3. Edited by J. L. Brewster and H. D. Rabinowitch. Boca Raton, Florida: CRC Press. 33–72.

Lawson, L. D. 1993. Bioactive organosulfur compounds of garlic and garlic products: Role in reducing blood lipids. In *Human Medicinal Agents from Plants (ACS Symposium Series)* 534. Edited by A. D. Kinghorn and M. F. Balandrin. Washington, D.C.: American Chemical Society Books. 306–330.

———. 1996. The composition and chemistry of garlic cloves and processed garlic. In *Garlic: The Science and Therapeutic Application of* Allium sativum *L. and Related Species.* Edited by H. P. Koch and L. D. Lawson. 2d ed. Baltimore, Maryland: Williams and Wilkins. 37–107.

———. 1997. Effect of harvest day on allicin yield of garlic bulbs. *The Garlic Press* (Summer/Fall) 32: 13.

———. 1999. The health effects of garlic: A list of annotated resources. *Mostly Garlic* (1998/1999 Winter): 6–8.

Lawson, L. D., and Z. J. Wang. 1993. Pre-hepatic fate of organosulfur compounds derived from garlic (*Allium sativum*). *Planta Medica* 59: A688.

Leino, M. E. 1992. Effect of freezing, freeze-drying, and air-drying on odor of chive characterized by headspace gas chromatography and sensory analyses. *Journal of Agricultural and Food Chemistry* 40: 1379–1384.

Linnaeus, C. 1753. *Species Plantarum*, vol. 1. Reprint. London: Ray Society, 1957.

Lot, H., V. Chovelon, S. Souche, B. Delecolle, T. Etoh, and C. M. Messiaen. 2001. Resistance to onion yellow dwarf virus and leek yellow stripe virus found in a fertile garlic clone. *Acta Horticulturae* 555: 243–246. (Abstract)

Lucier, G., and B. H. Lin. 2000. Agricultural outlook, June–July. USDA Economic Research Service. ERS-AO-272.

Lyons, W. 1998. Green garlic—secret garlic. *Mostly Garlic* (Summer): 16–17.

———. 1999. Bulbils . . . ignored for too long. *Mostly Garlic* (Fall): 34, 43.

————. 2000. The great escape: Escape the garlic blues with scapes, the new kid on the culinary block. *Mostly Garlic* (Spring): 14–15.

Maaß, H. I. 1993. What are the true *Allium sativum* L. var. *ophioscorodon* (Link) Döll? Allium *Improvement Newsletter* 4: 12–14.

Maaß, H. I., and M. Klaas. 1995. Infraspecific differentiation of garlic (*Allium sativum* L.) by isozyme and RAPD markers. *Theoretical and Applied Genetics* 91: 89–97.

Maczka, T. 2003. No, to the mechanical removal of scapes! *The Garlic Press* (Early Spring) 41: 9.

Maggioni, L., J. Keller, and D. Astley, eds. 2002. European collections of vegetatively propagated *Allium*. *Report of a Workshop, 21–22 May 2001, Gatersleben, Germany*. Rome: Biodiversity International.

Mann, L., and P. Minges. 1958. Growing and bulbing of garlic (*Allium sativum* L.) in response to storage conditions of planting stocks, day length, and planting date. *Hilgardia* 27: 385–419.

Mathew, B. 1996. *A Review of* Allium *Section* Allium. Kew, England: Royal Botanic Gardens.

Merrell, D. 1999. Garlic. *Seed Savers 1999 Yearbook*. Decorah, Iowa: Seed Savers Exchange. 173–186.

————. 2000a. Growing garlic and festivals in . . . Oklahoma. *Mostly Garlic* (Spring): 16–17, 20, 38.

————. 2000b. Garlic. *Seed Savers 2000 Yearbook*. Decorah, Iowa: Seed Savers Exchange. 159–171.

Meyers, J. M., and P. W. Simon. 1998. Continuous callus production and regeneration of garlic (*Allium sativum* L.) using root segments from shoot tip-derived plantlets. *Plant Cell Reports* 17: 726–730.

————. 1999. Regeneration of garlic callus as affected by clonal variation, plant growth regulators and culture conditions over time. *Plant Cell Reports* 19: 32–36.

Mitchnik, Z. 1972. Garlic. In *Israeli Encyclopaedia of Agriculture*, vol. 2. Edited by H. Halperin. 383.

Moerman, D. E. 1998. *Native American Ethnobotany*. Portland, Oregon: Timber Press.

Moon, W., and B. Y. Lee. 1985. Studies on factors affecting secondary growth in garlic (*Allium sativum* L.): I. Investigations on environmental factors and degree of secondary growth. *Journal of the Korean Society for Horticultural Science* 26: 103.

Moore, J. F., L. Campbell, W. P. Mortensen, and A. J. Howitt. 1954. Growing garlic in western Washington. Circular 247, State College of Washington, Institute of Agricultural Sciences, Western Washington Experiment Station, Puyallup, Washington.

Mtenga, D. J., D. G. Msuya, and T. A. Mtaita. 1993. Garlic (*Allium sativum*) production system in a mountainous farming center in Morogoro, Tanzania. Allium *Improvement Newsletter* 3: 39–46.

Nekola, J. 2006. Heirloom vegetable archive: Garlic. University of New Mexico. http://sev.lter-net.edu/~jnekola/Heirloom/plantlist.htm. Accessed 19 January 2007.

Nunez, J. 2001. Kern County garlic rust trial—1998. University of California Vegetable Research and Information Center.

Ogawa, T., N. Mori, and N. Matsubara. 1975. The studies on the ecological distribution and bulbing habit of garlic plants. (Japanese.) Nagasaki Agricultural Forestry Experimental Station. 3: 3.

Ori, D., R. M. Fritsch, and P. Hanelt. 1998. Evolution of genome size in *Allium* (Alliaceae). *Plant Systematics and Evolution* 210: 57–86.

Parente, F. 2006. *Garlic! Grow West of the Cascades.* Freeland, Washington: Frank Parente.

Parkinson, John. 1629. *Paradisi in Sole Paradisus Terrestris.* Reprint. Amsterdam: Theatrum Orbis Terrarum; Norwood, New Jersey: Walter J. Johnson, 1975.

Pathak, C. S. 1993. Flowering and fertility studies in garlic (*Allium sativum* L.). Allium *Improvement Newsletter* 3: 15–16.

Pentz, R., and C. P. Siegers. 1996. Garlic preparations: Methods of qualitative and quantitative assessment of their ingredients. In *Garlic: The Science and Therapeutic Application of* Allium sativum *L. and Related Species.* Edited by H. P. Koch and L. D. Lawson. 2d ed. Baltimore, Maryland: Williams and Wilkins. 109–134.

Pooler, M. R., and P. W. Simon. 1993a. Characterization and classification of isozyme and morphological variation in a diverse collection of garlic clones. *Euphytica* 68: 121–130.

———. 1993b. Garlic flowering in response to clone, photoperiod, growth temperature, and cold storage. *HortScience* 28: 1085–1086.

———. 1994. True seed production in garlic. *Sexual Plant Reproduction* 7: 282–286.

Pospisil, P. 2005. The 2005 garlic crop in eastern Ontario. *The Garlic News* (Fall) 5: 7.

———. 2006a. Garlic maturity chart 2004 harvest. *The Garlic News* (Summer) 8: 7.

———. 2006b. Living with the garlic leek moth—an organic approach. *The Garlic News* (Spring) 7: 8.

Prokhanov, J. 1930. A contribution to the knowledge of the cultivated alliums of China and Japan. (English summary.) *Bulletin of Applied Botanical Plant-Breeding* 24 (2): 123–188.

Rahim, M. A., M. N. A. Chowdhury, H. R. M. M. Anwar, and M. S. Alam. 2003. Effect of planting dates on the growth and yield of garlic germplasm. *Asian Journal of Plant Sciences* 2: 171–174.

Rahim, M. A., and R. Fordham. 1994. Control of bulbing in garlic. *Acta Horticulturae* 358: 369–374. (Abstract)

Rahim, M. A., M. A. Siddique, and M. M. Hossain. 1984. Effect of time of planting, mother bulb size and plant density on the yield of garlic. *Bangladesh Journal of Agriculture* 9: 112.

Regel, E. 1875. Alliorum adhuc cognitorum monographia. *Acta Horti Petropolitani* 3: 1–266.

———. 1887. *Allii species Asiae centralis in Asia media à Turcomania desertisque aralensibus et caspicis usque ad Mongoliam crescentes.* Petropoli.

Rekowska, E. 1997. The estimate of growth and the yielding of garlic according to some agrotechnics measures. Allium *Improvement Newsletter* 7: 47–49.

Reuter, H. D., H. P. Koch, and L. D. Lawson. 1996. Therapeutic effects and applications of garlic and its preparations. In *Garlic: The Science and Therapeutic Application of* Allium sativum *L. and Related Species.* Edited by H. P. Koch and L. D. Lawson. 2d ed. Baltimore, Maryland: Williams and Wilkins. 135–212.

Richards, C. M. 2004. Molecular technologies for the management and use of genebank collections. In *The Evolving Role of Genebanks in the Fast-Developing Field of Molecular Genetics (Issues in Genetic Resources)* 11. Edited by M. C. de Vicente. Rome: International Plant Genetic Resources Institute. 13–18.

Rosen, C., R. Becker, V. Fritz, B. Hutchison, J. Percich, C. Tong, and J. Wright. 2007. Growing garlic in Minnesota. University of Minnesota Extension Service. http://www.extension.umn.edu/distribution/cropsystems/DC7317.html. Accessed 19 February 2007.

Rosen, C., and C. Tong. 2001. Yield, dry matter partitioning, and storage quality of hardneck garlic as affected by soil amendments and scape removal. *HortScience* 36 (7): 1235–1239.

Rotindo K., G. M. Volk, and W. Lyons. 2004a. Fresh garlic in the spring: Cold storage may be the answer. *The Garlic Press* (Early Spring) 43: 16.

———. 2004b. Spring planting of garlic. *The Garlic Press* (Early Spring) 43: 17.

Sainani, G. S., D. B. Desai, N. H. Gorhe, S. M. Natu, D. V. Pise, and P. G. Sainani. 1979. Effect of dietary garlic and onion on serum lipid profile in Jain community. *Indian Journal of Medical Research* 69: 776.

Salomon, R. 2002. Virus diseases in garlic and the propagation of virus-free plants. In *Allium Crop Science: Recent Advances.* Edited by H. D. Rabinowitch and L. Currah. New York: CAB International.

Schwartz, H. F. 1995. Noninfectious abiotic conditions. In *Compendium of Onion and Garlic Diseases.* Edited by H. F. Schwartz and S. K. Mohan. St. Paul, Minnesota: APS Press. 44–46.

Schwartz, H. F., K. Mohan, M. J. Havey, and F. Crowe. 1995. Introduction. In *Compendium of Onion and Garlic Diseases.* Edited by H. F. Schwartz and S. K. Mohan. St. Paul, Minnesota: APS Press. 1–6.

Senula, A., and E. R. J. Keller. 2000. Morphological characterisation of a garlic core collection and establishment of a virus-free *in vitro* genebank. Allium *Improvement Newsletter* 10: 3–5.

———. 2001. Diversity in a clonally propagated crop: Morphological characters in garlic compared with existing molecular classifications. In *Proceedings of a Symposium Dedicated to the 100th Birthday of Rudolf Mansfeld, Gatersleben, Germany, 8–9 October 2001.* Gatersleben, Germany: Leibniz Institute of Plant Genetics and Crop Plant Research (IPK).

Shadbolt, C. A., and L. G. Holm. 1956. Some quantitative aspects of weed competition in vegetable crops. *Weeds* 4: 111–123.

Shah, J. J., and I. L. Kothari. 1973. Histogenesis of garlic clove. *Phytomorphology* 23: 162.

Silenzi, J. C., A. M. Moreno, and J. C. Lucero. 1985. Effects of irrigation with saline water on sprouting of cloves of garlic (*Allium sativum* L.) cv. Colorado. *IDIA* 17: 433–436.

Simon, P. W. 1993. Breeding carrot, cucumber, onion, and garlic for improved quality and nutritional value. *Horticultura Brasileira* 11: 171–173.

———. 2000. New opportunities for an old crop: The origins of seed production in garlic. *Mostly Garlic* (Spring): 30–31, 38.

———. 2002. The origins and distribution of garlic: How many garlics are there? *The Garlic Press* (Spring) 40: 1–2.

Simon, P. W., R. M. Hannan, M. M. Jenderek, and R. E. Voss. 2003. Environmental and genetic effects on garlic growth, flowering, and bulb characters. *HortScience* 38: 783. (Abstract)

Simon, P. W., and M. M. Jenderek. 2003. Flowering, seed production, and the genesis of garlic breeding. *Plant Breeding Reviews* 23: 211–244.

Simon, P. W., J. M. Myers, M. E. N. Fronseca, and L. S. Boiteux. 1995. Garlic germplasm variation, isozymes, fertility, and virus infection. From the National Onion Research Conference, Madison, Wisconsin, December 6–9. *Allium Improvement Newsletter* 5: 77. (Abstract)

Sims, W. L., T. M. Little, and R. E. Voss. 1976. Growing garlic in California. Leaflet 2948, University of California Vegetable Research and Information Center.

Sivam, G. 2000. Garlic against *Helicobacter pylori* and other bacterial infections. *Mostly Garlic* (Spring): 5, 39.

Smith, R. 1999. Growing garlic in the Northwest. *Mostly Garlic* (Spring): 16–17, 39.

Sorensen, J., and G. Pelter. 1998. Garlic germplasm evaluation. Washington State University. http://benton-franklin.wsu.edu/PDFDocs/garlic_germplasm97-98.pdf. Accessed 19 February 2007.

Stapleton, C. M. A. 1997. The morphology of woody bamboos. In *The Bamboos*. Edited by G. P. Chapman. San Diego, California: Academic Press. 251–267.

Steinmetz, K. A., L. H. Kushi, R. M. Bostick, A. R. Folsom, and J. D. Potter. 1994. Vegetables, fruit, and colon cancer in the Iowa Women's Health Study. *American Journal of Epidemiology* 139: 1–15.

Stern, D. 1993. Garlic Seed Foundation's efforts at promoting garlic production in northern climates. Allium *Improvement Newsletter* 3: 47–49.

———. 1999. Go topless in the fall . . . if you can. *Mostly Garlic* (Spring): 20.

———. 2002. Current research. *The Garlic Press* (Spring) 40: 1–2.

———. 2006. The best of the press: Director's notes. *The Garlic Press* (Spring/Summer) 40: 1–2.

Stribley, D. P. 1990. Mycorrhizal associations and their significance. In *Onions and Allied Crops*, vol. 2. Edited by H. D. Rabinowitch and J. L. Brewster. Boca Raton, Florida: CRC Press. 85–101.

Sumiati, E. 1994. Response of shallot and garlic to different altitudes. *Acta Horticulturae* 358: 395–400. (Abstract)

Sumner, D. R. 1995a. Blue mold. In *Compendium of Onion and Garlic Diseases*. Edited by H. F. Schwartz and S. K. Mohan. St. Paul, Minnesota: APS Press. 28.

———. 1995b. Fusarium damping-off. In *Compendium of Onion and Garlic Diseases*. Edited by H. F. Schwartz and S. K. Mohan. St. Paul, Minnesota: APS Press. 9–10.

Swenson, J. 1999a. Confessions of a garlic collector. *Mostly Garlic* (Summer): 14–15, 45.

———. 1999b. The pungent and piquant history of the onion. *Mostly Garlic* (Spring): 30–32.

———. 2000. Garlic. *Seed Savers 2000 Yearbook.* Decorah, Iowa: Seed Savers Exchange. 159–171.

Sydlowski, T. 1999. Garlic. Southern Illinois University Herbarium, Ethnobotanical Leaflets. http://www.siu.edu/~ebl/leaflets/garlic.htm. Accessed 22 February 2007.

Takagi, H. 1979. Prevention from freezing injury in long cold storage of garlic bulbs. *Studies from the Institute of Horticulture, Kyoto University* 9: 151.

———. 1987. Effects of storage and planting temperatures on rooting and root growth in garlic bulbs after planting. *Journal of the Yamagata Agriculture and Forestry Society* 44: 51.

———. 1990. Garlic *Allium sativum* L. In *Onions and Allied Crops*, vol. 3. Edited by J. L. Brewster and H. D. Rabinowitch. Boca Raton, Florida: CRC Press. 108–146.

USDA. 1989. Chopped garlic in oil mixes. P89–9.

Van der Meer, Q. P., and P. Hanelt. 1990. Leek (*Allium ampeloprasum*). In *Onions and Allied Crops*, vol. 3. Edited by J. L. Brewster and H. D. Rabinowitch. Boca Raton, Florida: CRC Press. 179–196.

Van Deven, L. 1992. *Onions and Garlic Forever.* Carrollton, Illinois: Louis Van Deven.

Vasconcellos, E. F. C., E. J. Scalopi, and A. E. Klar. 1971. The influence of irrigation and nitrogen fertilization in garlic growing. *Solo* 63: 15.

Volk, G. M. 2002. Garlic storage research. *The Garlic Press* (Spring) 40: 17.

Volk, G. M., A. D. Henk, and C. M. Richards. 2004. Genetic diversity among U.S. garlic clones as detected using AFLP methods. *Journal of the American Society for Horticultural Science* 129: 559–569.

Volk, G. M., and C. Walters. 2003. Preservation of genetic resources in the national plant germplasm clonal collections. *Plant Breeding Reviews* 23: 291–344. (Abstract)

Vvedensky, A. 1946. The genus *Allium* in the USSR. *Herbertia* 2 (1944): 65–218. Translated by H. K. Airy Shaw.

Walkey, D. G. A. 1990. Virus diseases. In *Onions and Allied Crops*, vol. 2. Edited by H. D. Rabinowitch and J. L. Brewster. Boca Raton, Florida: CRC Press. 191–212.

Weaver, W. W. 1997. *Heirloom Vegetable Gardening: A Master Gardener's Guide to Planting, Growing, Seed Saving, and Cultural History.* New York: Henry Holt and Company.

Whealy, K. 1999. Breaking the chain of the seed. In *Seed Savers 1999 Harvest Edition*. Decorah, Iowa: Seed Savers Exchange. 5–14.

Wrench, R. 1998. Garlic: Growing on a small commercial scale. *Mostly Garlic* (Fall): 20–22.

Woodward, P. 1996. *Garlic and Friends: The History, Growth, and Use of Edible Alliums.* Flemington, Victoria, Australia: Hyland House.

Xinhua, W., and D. Wufeng. 1997. Famous garlics native to China: Its problems and strategies. International Symposium on Edible Alliaceae. *Acta Horticulturae* 433: 133–136. (Abstract)

Yoshida, T., A. Kojima, N. B. Gogichaishvili, S. V. Shuvalov, and A. P. Pimakhov. 1994. Japan-CIS joint exploration for *Allium* germplasm in Kyrgyzstan, Kazakhstan and Uzbekistan republics in 1993. Allium *Improvement Newsletter* 4: 117–119.

Zandstra, J. W., and R. C. Squire. 2000. *Culture Management of Garlic.* Report, Ridgetown College, University of Guelph Ridgetown, Ontario, Canada.

Zewdie, Y., M. J. Havey, J. P. Prince, and M. M. Jenderek. 2004. Genetic linkage map of garlic (*Allium sativum*). *HortScience* 39: 775.

# Index

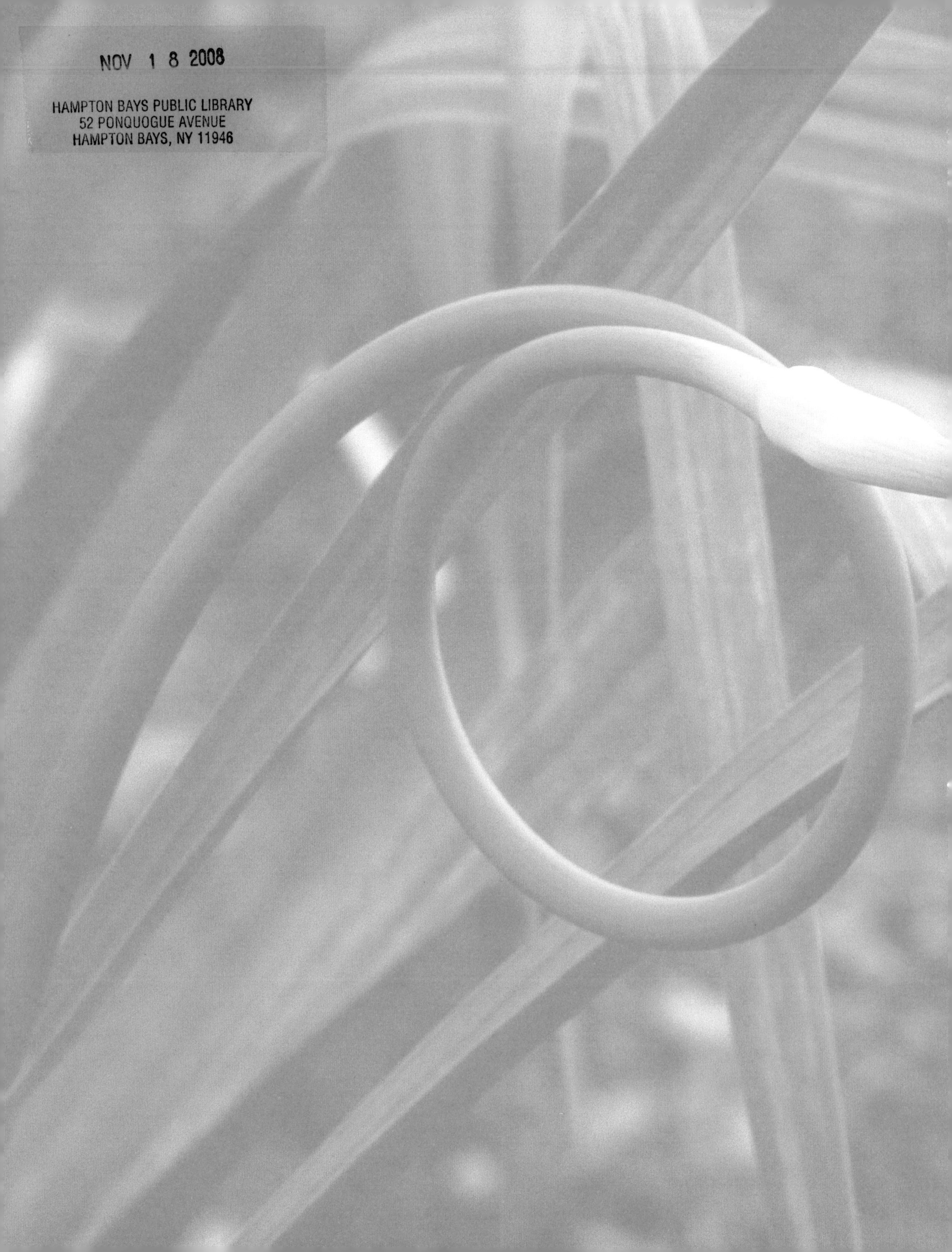